Queen Elizabeth II

by Stewart Ross

for
dummies®
A Wiley Brand

Queen Elizabeth II For Dummies®

Published by: **John Wiley & Sons, Inc.**, 111 River Street, Hoboken, NJ 07030-5774, www.wiley.com

Copyright © 2022 by John Wiley & Sons, Inc., Hoboken, New Jersey

Published simultaneously in Canada

For general information on our other products and services, please contact our Customer Care Department within the U.S. at 877-762-2974, outside the U.S. at 317-572-3993, or fax 317-572-4002. For technical support, please visit www.wiley.com/techsupport.

Wiley publishes in a variety of print and electronic formats and by print-on-demand. Some material included with standard print versions of this book may not be included in e-books or in print-on-demand. If this book refers to media such as a CD or DVD that is not included in the version you purchased, you may download this material at http://booksupport.wiley.com. For more information about Wiley products, visit www.wiley.com.

Library of Congress Control Number: 2022932770

ISBN: 978-1-119-85034-2 (pbk); ISBN: 978-1-119-85035-9 (ebk); ISBN: 978-1-119-85036-6 (ebk)

SKY10033497_030922

Table of Contents

Introduction

The subject of this book is one of the most memorable figures in recent world history, one of the very few who have become a legend in their own lifetime. This is all the more remarkable because Queen Elizabeth II did not seek power and influence, nor did she force her way onto the world stage through ambition or vanity. She inherited a job she had not asked for, and – because she sees it as her duty – she performs it with exemplary diligence, and has done so for over seventy years.

Whether or not you approve of the institution of hereditary monarchy is beside the point. Elizabeth did not have any say in the matter – she was dealt a hand and told to get on with it. So she did. It took her close to the very heart of things, meeting Winston Churchill, Jack Kennedy, Nelson Mandela . . . being there when the Berlin Wall went up and when it came down . . . witnessing the tragedies of her sister Margaret and Princess Diana. As you will discover, the story of Elizabeth's life is the story of the modern world.

About This Book

To help you make sense of Elizabeth's life, especially if you come from outside the UK, I have included a fair slice of British history and stuff about Britain's byzantine unwritten constitution. I have also done my best to be objective in coverage and judgements, though I hope not to the point of blandness. I want you to enjoy using this book as much as I have enjoyed writing it.

Throughout the book, I've used UK English – the Queen's English! Among other things, you may spot more uses of the letter "u" in words than you're used to, and "s" and "z" popping up in unusual places (if you're from the US). I feel it is important to write about Elizabeth in her own nation's version of our language.

When there are so many books, websites, blogs, podcasts, and so on, dealing with Queen Elizabeth II, what does *Queen Elizabeth II For Dummies* offer that's unique, making it stand out from the crowd? Here's an insight into my approach:

>> **A neutral read.** Unlike many authors approaching Elizabeth II, I have no axe to grind, no political point to prove. I don't believe she's a saint or a sinner, just an ordinary yet extraordinary human being. I give you the whole picture, warts and all.

>> **A non-chronological read.** What makes this book so useful, like all *For Dummies* titles, is the way it is organized for reference *and* for a pleasant read. You can dip in, check out a fact or a topic, and dip out again; or you can relax and read through a whole chapter or two.

>> **An easy-to-understand read.** To help the user, *Queen Elizabeth II For Dummies* uses handy icons, regular explanations of complex issues (I highlight these explanations with the use of *italic text*), sidebars about interesting-but-not-essential subjects, and the helpful use of bullet points.

>> **A humorous read.** Life is nothing without a smile – wherever possible, I've tried to handle the subject with wit and precision, pointing out the oddities and quirks that festoon the British monarchy.

Several places in the book have links to web addresses. If you're reading a digital version on a device connected to the internet, you can click the web address to access the site directly, like this: www.dummies.com. Alternatively, you can type the address into your browser.

To make the content of *Queen Elizabeth II For Dummies* more accessible, I have divided it into six parts:

>> **Part 1: The Road to the Throne** places Elizabeth's early life in the context of the evolution of Britain's constitutional monarchy.

>> **Part 2: The Young Queen** covers Elizabeth's coronation, her early years on the throne, and the daily life of a working royal.

>> **Part 3: The Need to Adapt** looks at how Elizabeth slowly – and at times reluctantly – adapted the centuries-old institution of monarchy to the rapidly changing post-war world.

>> **Part 4: Stormy Waters** deals with the series of painful events that beset Elizabeth in the lead up to her *Annus Horribilis* of 1992.

>> **Part 5: Steadying the Ship** brings the bitter-sweet story of Elizabeth's reign to the present day, taking in joyful jubilees, painful losses, and hopes for the future.

>> **Part 6: The Part of Tens** includes ten prime ministers Elizabeth has worked with, ten tricky situations she had to navigate, ten actors who have portrayed her on screen, and snapshots of ten of her grandchildren and great-grandchildren.

Finally, if I may, a short blast on my own trumpet. I have been teaching and writing about history at all levels, from primary school to university, for half a century. This book is a distillation of years of practice in clarifying the complex – and I hope it works like that for you.

Foolish Assumptions

As I sat writing this book, I conjured up a picture of you, the reader, in my mind. How did I imagine you?

>> You have an enquiring mind about the British Royal Family.

>> You're interested in politics, current affairs, history – and probably a bit of gossip, too!

>> English (though not necessarily British English) is probably your first language. If it's not, then you're definitely fluent. This is not a book for the English-language beginner – unless you have bags of patience and a large dictionary.

>> You may well have watched the TV series *The Crown* or the film *The Queen*, and want to know more about what was going on and how much of it is true.

Recognize yourself? I hope so, because this book is for you.

Icons Used in This Book

Throughout this book, icons in the margins highlight certain types of valuable information that call out for your attention. Here are the icons you'll encounter, with a brief description of each.

TIP

Helpful insights and tips. I use these to draw your attention to a strange or uncertain point that I think will interest you, and personal insights from me.

REMEMBER

This is the key information within the book. If you take away nothing else from these pages but the stuff flagged by these icons, you'll have Queen Elizabeth II and her reign pretty well covered. To siphon off the most important information in each chapter, just skim through to these icons.

TECHNICAL STUFF

Non-essential stuff that is interesting but not vital to getting to grips with the Queen. I use these icons to indicate background material on British politics, history, tradition, or constitutional convention.

WARNING

Watch out! I use this icon to point out where fiction, especially in *The Crown*, drifts wide of fact for the sake of a good story, or to explain incidents that you may have heard about but are unsure how true they are. Myth is fun, but it can lead to serious or hurtful misunderstanding.

Beyond the Book

Queen Elizabeth is almost 100 years old, and the British history that created the monarchy she inherited is more than 1,500 years old. That's an awful lot of information, and I couldn't possibly shoehorn all I wanted into this book. Happily, beside the abundance of information and guidance within these pages, you can get access to even more help and information online. To check out this book's online Cheat Sheet, just go to www.dummies.com and search for "Queen Elizabeth II For Dummies Cheat Sheet".

Where to Go from Here

Though the structure of this book is roughly chronological, that doesn't mean it's designed to be read from start to finish like a story book. You can start anywhere you want, depending on what you're looking for or what you're interested in.

Let's take a few examples of where you might want to start, if you don't fancy rolling up your sleeves up and getting stuck into Chapter 1:

>> If you'd like to know a bit more about the relationship of Prince Charles with Princess Diana, dip into Chapter 16.

>> There's plenty on Prince Harry, his marriage to Meghan and their decision to opt out of royal duties in Chapters 24, 25 and 29.

>> What about Elizabeth's wealth? Try Chapter 17.

>> Find out about Elizabeth's religious faith in Chapter 19, or her love of horses, dogs and other animals in Chapter 22.

The detailed Table of Contents is also a good place to begin. And if you can't find what you want there, don't forget the index. Wherever you start, welcome to the extraordinary world of Queen Elizabeth II!

1

The Road to the Throne

Queen Elizabeth II may not be as instantly recognizable as Lady Diana or Prince Harry, but without her no one would have even heard of Di or Harry. The nonagenarian monarch is the rock on whom rests every other current member of Britain's famous (and sometimes infamous) Royal Family.

That said, Queen Elizabeth does not stand alone. She is the latest in a line of kings and queens that stretches back into Britain's dim and distant past. From her ancestors she has inherited the glittering trappings of power, as well as customs, traditions and – most problematic of all – attitudes. The responsibilities these bring are enormous.

The Queen was not born into her current role. She was raised as a princess, but not as the future monarch. Only when her headstrong uncle chose love over the crown did her future suddenly change. Her father became king and she heir to his throne.

From that moment onward, it was only a matter of time.

Chapter **1**

Queen Elizabeth II: A Global Icon

Great Britain is the only country in the world without a name on its postage stamps. This is not just because Britain invented adhesive postage stamps with a 'we were here first' attitude when it comes to mail; it's also because Brits reckon an image is all that's needed for others to recognize where UK mail has come from.

The image is not a map, nor a man-made feature, nor an animal. It is a portrait of the *Head of State*, meaning Britain's reigning monarch. For almost three-quarters of a century, longer than any other person to hold the office, Great Britain's stamps have been adorned by the profile of Queen Elizabeth II.

REMEMBER

Since the time of Henry VIII (r. 1509–1547 – see the nearby sidebar to find out what 'r.' means), England's monarchs have been called 'Your Majesty'. The title had previously been used only for God. The weight of history grows heavier if we give the Queen her full title: 'Elizabeth II, by the Grace of God, of the United Kingdom of Great Britain and Northern Ireland and of her other realms and territories Queen, Head of the Commonwealth, Defender of the Faith.' That's quite a mouthful!

REIGNS AND LIVES

Dates prefaced by an 'r.' are the years of a monarch's reign. Dates given without an 'r.' are the years of a person's life or an event. A single date preceded by a 'b.' is the year a person was born.

TIP

The inheritance is as daunting as the job title. As we get to grips with what makes Elizabeth tick, bear in mind that she sees herself as a sort of athlete in a relay race. The royal baton was handed to her by her father (see Chapters 5 and 6); her job is to hand it on intact to her heir. That, above all, is what drives her.

REMEMBER

Throughout this book, you'll encounter Elizabeth's extended family, heirs, and line of succession. Check out Figure 1-1 for a diagram explaining who's who in the modern Royal Family (and flick back to this page as you're reading through the book – I honestly don't expect you to memorize this sort of thing!).

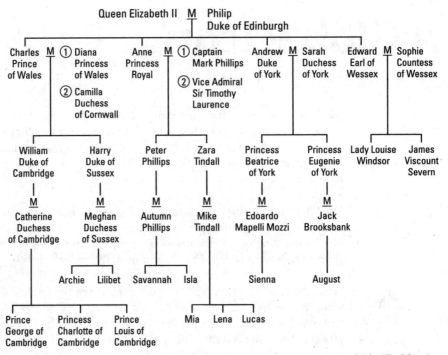

FIGURE 1-1: Queen Elizabeth II's family tree.

© John Wiley & Sons, Inc.

This chapter looks more closely at the Queen's historic inheritance and the range of work involved in trying to maintain it. It concludes with a few suggestions as to why, showing stoic toughness and blessed with not a little luck, in most people's opinion by the time of her Platinum Jubilee (2022), she had made a fair fist of it.

Carrying the Weight of History

Queen Elizabeth's paternal grandmother, Queen Mary, sometime Empress of India, was an impressive figure. She demanded that Elizabeth curtsey whenever they met, and instructed her awestruck grandchild that kings and queens never smiled in public.

Though no academic, Queen Mary was a keen historian. Her specialization was genealogy, specifically the genealogy of her family. Born in 1867, she clearly remembered Queen Victoria (r. 1837–1901) and proudly recalled how King George III (r. 1760–1820) was her great-grandfather (find out more about these monarchs in Chapter 3). From this austere figure of her impressionable childhood years, Elizabeth was left in no doubt as to the weighty significance of her royal heritage.

TECHNICAL STUFF

Perhaps appropriately, in 1913, Britain's latest armour-plated battlecruiser was named after Queen Mary. It lasted less well than its namesake, exploding and sinking during the Battle of Jutland, 1916, in World War I.

You can read more about Queen Mary in Chapter 4.

Heading up a monarchy 1,500 years in the making

Elizabeth was born in 1926. Though Britain had been severely shaken by the bloodletting and vast expenditure of World War I (1914–1918), during the years of the Princess' childhood it was still a major world power. Its industry and commerce were formidable. The sprawling British empire – the largest the world had ever seen – remained more or less intact. If self-governing Dominions (see Chapter 10) were included, it stretched from New Zealand via India and large swathes of Africa to northern Canada.

That a country less than half the size of Texas should achieve so much was a source of national pride. This was reflected in the history taught to the young Elizabeth by family members and tutors (see Chapter 4 for more on her early life). She learned that, though there had been setbacks, British history was generally a story of progress. And a number of worthy monarchs had sometimes been part of that progress.

Here are a few of the more important ones she may have been told about:

>> **Alfred the Great (r. 871–899):** The doughty King of Wessex (an Anglo-Saxon kingdom in southwest England) who resisted and then overcame an invasion by barbaric Vikings.

>> **William the Conqueror (r. 1066–1087):** The Duke of Normandy in northern France who seized the English throne, thereby paving the way for his country to become a major European power.

>> **Henry V (r. 1413–1422):** A warrior king whose victory over the French at the Battle of Agincourt (1415) inspired William Shakespeare's memorable patriotic verses.

>> **Henry VIII (r. 1509–1547):** A ruthless patriot who freed England from papal (Catholic) interference and put himself at the head of the Church of England.

>> **Elizabeth I (r. 1558–1603):** A potential role model for Elizabeth II (though she denied it!) who demonstrated how a queen could reign as competently as any king.

>> **Charles II (r. 1660–1685):** A highly intelligent king with an innate political sense who guided the monarchy through a tricky post-republican era.

>> **Victoria (r. 1837–1901):** Elizabeth's great-great-grandmother whose reign laid the foundations of Britain's modern constitutional monarchy.

As well as these stand-out characters, the young Elizabeth would probably have found out about a whole host of others. A good many were pretty average. She can't have imagined enjoying a tea party with the ineffective Henry VI (r. 1422–1461) or the oddly named Harthacnut (r. 940–942). Nor with George I, who spoke scarcely any English. And poor Edward V (r. 1485) wasn't on the throne long enough to take tea with anyone. (Not that the Brits knew what tea was back then.)

Did the Princess thrill at the martial exploits of the warrior king Edward III (r. 1327–1377)? Was she fascinated by the idea that monarchs, like her doting but grumpy grandfather George V (r. 1910–1936), were placed on the throne by God, as propounded by James I of England (r. 1603–1625; aka King James VI of Scotland)? Maybe some of the tales she heard gave her nightmares. According to Shakespeare, the source of all the best stories of medieval skullduggery, Richard II (r. 1377–1399) was slain with an axe, John (r. 1199–1216) was poisoned by a monk, and Richard III (r. 1483–1485) had two little princes murdered in the Tower of London.

The sovereigns I've mentioned are by no means a complete list and the details offered are scanty. Don't worry, we'll meet them again in greater detail in Chapters 2 and 3. They are here simply to illustrate the enormous weight of history that bore down on Elizabeth's shoulders the moment she knew she was destined to wear the Crown. Whatever she thought of the long line of kings and queens who came before her, she was their heir and could never, ever forget it.

She owed it to them, and to history, not to mess things up.

Ruling the jig-saw kingdom

Non-Brits frequently refer to Elizabeth II as Queen of England. Though this is not wrong, it is incomplete. The reason why becomes apparent when scrolling down the list of countries that springs up automatically when completing an online form. After searching in vain for 'England' or even 'Britain', down among the 'U's one finds 'United Kingdom' between 'United Arab Emirates' and 'United States'. In the British Isles, Elizabeth is Queen of the United Kingdom, a jig-saw realm.

Even Brits get confused by this one! The 'British Isles' is a geographical name for a group of 6,000+ islands off northwest Europe. The two largest are Britain (made up of the countries of England, Scotland and Wales) and Ireland. The 'United Kingdom' is the European bit of Elizabeth II's realm. It comprises England, Scotland and Wales, plus the province of Northern Ireland.

Like many countries, the United Kingdom started small and expanded over time. Between the years 43 and 410, England and Wales (but not Scotland or Ireland) were part of the Roman Empire. After the Romans left, the British Isles split up into a number of tribal units.

By the sixth century AD, some tribal chiefs were calling themselves kings, and may even have taken the title *Bretwalda* ('Britain ruler'). The title didn't mean much because England, let alone all Britain, was nowhere near a single kingdom, but it certainly made them sound more impressive.

The United Kingdom's jig-saw came together in four steps of unity:

>> In the ninth century AD, the Anglo-Saxon kingdom of Wessex fought back against Viking invaders from Scandinavia. Bit by bit, they added Viking and Anglo-Saxon territories to their realm until, by the time of King Athelstan (r. 895–939), all England lay within a single kingdom. Athelstan is Elizabeth II's thirtieth great-granduncle.

>> The *Normans* (meaning 'Northmen' from Normandy in modern-day France) conquered England in 1066 and then Ireland in the late twelfth century. With two of its four constituent parts in place, the United Kingdom was now half-way there. The English and Irish parliaments were amalgamated in 1801.

>> Wales was conquered by Edward I (r. 1277–1307) in the thirteenth century. To placate the Welsh, who had – and still have – their own ancient language, King Edward 'gave' them his infant son to be 'Prince of Wales'. The title has been given to the heir apparent ever since (see the nearby sidebar). It currently belongs to Prince Charles, Elizabeth's eldest son. With the addition of Wales, the United Kingdom was three-quarters complete.

>> Scotland took a long time to pull together its scattered and mountainous territories into a single kingdom, and finished the process only with the acquisition of the Orkney and Shetland Isles in 1472. The 1503 marriage of James IV (supposedly a distant ancestor of mine, r. 1488–1513) to a sister of England's Henry VIII, laid the foundations for the union of the two crowns. This came about when Scotland's James VI succeeded Queen Elizabeth to become James I of England. Full political union of England and Scotland followed in 1707.

But, of course, this is no more than a snapshot of the complex history of the United Kingdom! (See Chapter 2 for more details on the backstory of the British monarchy.)

WARNING

Readers with Irish ancestry may already know that the union outlined above did not last. In 1921, Southern Ireland (also known as Eire or the Republic of Ireland) left the UK after years of tension and bloodshed. As a result, Elizabeth is Queen of England, Wales, Scotland and Northern Ireland. During her reign, more Irish troubles and a Scottish independence movement further threatened the unity of her realm (see Chapters 15 and 21).

WHAT'S AN HEIR APPARENT?

The person in line to succeed a monarch on their death or abdication is their *heir*. The *heir apparent*, traditionally a first-born son, is someone whose right to succeed cannot be taken away by the birth of someone else. An *heir presumptive*, often a first-born female or a cousin of the monarch, is an heir whose right to succeed is lost on the birth of a more eligible child.

Being one of the precious few queens

REMEMBER

Britain has had dozens of queens, but Elizabeth II is only the eighth to reign in her own right. The others acquired their status through marriage. For example, Elizabeth II's mother, born Elizabeth Bowes-Lyon, became Queen Elizabeth when her husband inherited the throne as George VI in 1936. You can read more about the Queen's mum (unsurprisingly known later in life as, 'The Queen Mum', in Chapter 11).

TIP

The first monarch of a particular name is not given a number until a second person of that name takes the throne. Therefore, the first Queen Elizabeth (mentioned earlier in this chapter) was not Queen Elizabeth I until 1952, when the second Elizabeth came into her royal inheritance. Note that Miss Bowes-Lyon morphed into plain 'Queen Elizabeth', not Queen Elizabeth II. She was the King's *consort* (partner). Britain gives numbers only to monarchs who have reigned and not to their partners.

There are, therefore, two categories of queen:

>> *Queens consort,* who are married partners of kings.

>> *Queens regnant,* who are monarchs ruling by birthright.

Let's look more closely at these two queenly types.

Queens consort

All of Britain's monarchs were expected to marry, whether or not they liked the idea. It was basically in the job description. Some, such as Edward II (r. 1307–1327), did not and drew down the wrath of conservatives for openly favouring male friends. Others made multiple marriages. The best-known example is Henry VIII, whose rhyming 'divorced-beheaded-died-divorced-beheaded-survived' summary of the fate of his six wives is one of the few bits of monarchical history popular with school kids.

TIP

Royal marriage had a triple purpose:

>> **Providing a legitimate heir**. This gave the monarch pride in their dynastic prowess (because the ruling family's position had been secured) and removed the grim prospect of a disputed succession. British history is strewn with conflict between rivals for the Crown. The prime example is the so-called Wars of the Roses (1461–1487), when descendants of Edward III – the Lancastrians (using the symbol of a red rose) and the Yorkists (using the symbol of a white rose) – fought each other almost to extinction.

It is unlikely that the House of Windsor (Windsor is the Queen's family name) would have resorted to armed struggle if Queen Elizabeth, her son Prince Charles, or grandson Prince William had failed to produce an heir. Nevertheless, all three clearly took pride in their ability to fulfil their royal heir-making role.

>> **Facilitating and cementing political alliances**. Royal marriages were usually political arrangements. A good example is the marriage of Henry VIII's sister Margaret to Scotland's King James VI. The union initially failed to stop the two nations from going to war with each other, but it did eventually lead to the union of the two crowns in 1603. (See Chapter 2 for more about the tricky history of these two nations.)

>> **Providing a church-sanctioned outlet for royal sexual desires**. This was the least successful aspect of royal marriages. Adherence to a single partner is not something for which British monarchs (and their families) are renowned. Until relatively recently, royal mistresses were a lively feature of the court. The ten-year, four-child relationship between mistress Arabella Churchill and the future James II (r. 1685–1688) was the launch pad for one of Britain's most famous non-royal families (both Winston and his illustrious military ancestor John Churchill, Duke of Marlborough).

Numerous queens consort made their understandable disappointment at their husband's philandering abundantly clear, usually to no effect. Others simply accepted it as par for the course and hoped their loyalty would be rewarded in heaven. Some, showing an altogether more modern outlook, determined to make the most of their consort role. For example:

>> **Eleanor of Aquitaine**, a duchess in her own right whose lands added substantially to the empire of Henry II (r. 1154–1189), refused to play second fiddle to her ambitious, notoriously unfaithful husband, and even encouraged her sons to rebel against him.

>> **Queen Margaret of Anjou**, rather than her feeble husband Henry VI (r. 1422–1461), was the fulcrum of royal power during his troubled reign.

>> **Queen Henrietta Maria**, consort of Charles I (r. 1625–1649), wielded political and even military power during England's Civil War (1642–1645).

Readers might be shocked by the treatment of many queens consort, especially as their taking a lover was treated very differently from their husband's. While George I made no secret of his two mistresses – known behind his back as 'The Maypole' and 'The Elephant' – he divorced his wife and locked her up in a castle for the last 30 years of her life because of her alleged affair with a German count.

TIP

Was there a lesson in this for the young Queen Elizabeth II? Throughout history, the role of most queens had been to obey their husbands and produce heirs. Once the succession had been secured, many drifted into a life of respected irrelevance. That would not be Elizabeth's way. For inspiration, she needed to check out the seven female predecessors who had actually ruled – the queens regnant.

Queens regnant

The countries of Europe – as elsewhere – were traditionally unwilling to accept a female monarch. The French never did. This misogyny was endorsed by the male-dominated Roman Catholic Church. After the emergence of Protestantism in the sixteenth century, queens regnant became more common.

Here is a full list of Britain's queens regnant before Elizabeth II:

>> **Matilda (r.1135–1153):** The history of Britain's queens regnant got off to a grim start. King Henry I (r. 1100–1134) made his barons swear to accept Matilda, his only surviving legitimate heir, as queen after his death. They reneged on their word immediately after Henry died. Matilda was never crowned and her reign was marked by incessant warfare.

This was one reason why Henry VIII was prepared to turn his kingdom upside down in order to get a male heir. (See Mary I and Elizabeth I, next on this list.)

>> **Mary I (r. 1553–1558):** Another uncomfortable chapter in the history of queens regnant. The first child of Henry VIII, the king who had broken with the Pope in order to get a male heir, Mary was determined to return her country to the Catholic fold. Her harsh religious repression, marriage to an unpopular and absentee Spanish husband, and military failure ensured 'Bloody Mary' had bad press.

>> **Elizabeth I (r. 1558–1603):** Intelligent, politically adept, and served by able ministers, the 'Virgin Queen' (that's where the US state of Virginia got its name from) finally showed that a woman could be as effective a ruler as any man. Her decision not to marry meant that there was no man to challenge her authority.

>> **Mary, Queen of Scots (r. 1542–1567):** Elizabeth I's captivating but incompetent Scottish cousin reinforced male prejudice against rule by a woman. Her short, troubled reign ended in enforced abdication (see Chapter 5 for an explanation of abdication).

>> **Mary II (r. 1688–1694):** Mary was invited to replace James II, her deeply unpopular Catholic father. She accepted on condition that her Dutch husband be crowned alongside her as King William III (r. 1688–1702). Though she played little part in affairs of state, there was some resentment at his remaining king after her death.

- » **Anne (r. 1702–1714):** Anne, another of James II's daughters, was a useful example for the future Elizabeth II. Unlike her sister Mary, Anne made it quite clear that she, not her husband, was the crowned Head of State.

- » **Victoria (r. 1837–1901):** Victoria's long reign established a template for the modern constitutional monarchy. Here was a pattern and example for Elizabeth II to follow. But would a Victorian-style monarchy still be relevant in the twenty-first century?

REMEMBER

The story told briefly above is essentially a happy one. It tells how outstanding queens consort were able to make their mark in a man's world, and how that world gradually came to accept a female monarch as queen regnant. This resulted from developments in society. With the exception of Elizabeth I, queens did not shape their own positions but adapted to them. Aided by their advisors, each re-interpreted the role of queen regnant to suit their personality and the mood of the times. On ascending the throne, Elizabeth II would have to do the same.

Following in the Footsteps of Grandpa and Daddy

Elizabeth II's understanding of her role was taken from the behaviour and attitudes of four predecessors, who were her

- » great-great-grandmother Queen Victoria (r. 1837–1901)
- » uncle King Edward VIII (r. 1936–1937)
- » grandfather King George V (r. 1910–1936)
- » father King George VI (r. 1937–1952)

The example set by her outgoing, pleasure-seeking great-grandfather, Edward VII (r. 1901–1910), was so beyond her capabilities that he can be discounted. In a similar vein, the example set by her abdicating uncle taught her how *not* to do the job.

REMEMBER

Queen Victoria was a strong role model because she was a woman. If she could survive and give her name to the age in which she lived, so could Elizabeth. However, the two never met and Victoria's influence was largely passed on indirectly through Elizabeth's father and grandfather. The messages she received from each, and from their queens, were broadly similar.

George V

George V was a dull, uninspiring man. At home he was a bullying tyrant who made the lives of his children a misery. In his role as monarch, he was strictly formal and deeply conservative, accepting change only when there was no alternative. His father, Edward VII, actually said that he thought that the British monarchy would end with his son. And yet, at a time when ancient monarchies all over Europe were toppling like ninepins, George survived. Why?

Four things kept him afloat:

>> **The country George led was successful in World War I.** Had Britain lost the war, its royal family would almost certainly have gone the way of those in Germany and Russia, becoming as extinct as the dinosaurs.

>> **George was presented as being in touch with the people.** This was thanks largely to the instincts of his indomitable wife, Queen Mary (see Chapter 4). During World War I, he inspected troops, visited hospitals, and announced that the Royal Family would share people's wartime deprivations by giving up alcohol.

>> **George and Mary offered themselves as the ideal, faithful, Christian married couple – a model for others to follow.** Society at large was always swimming with scandal, but not once did tongues wag about the private lives of this king and queen. Except, perhaps, when sharp-tongued subjects thanked God that they were not married to either.

>> **Perhaps most importantly, George was saved by his very ordinariness.** It's difficult to shoot at a target without colour or distinctive features.

As a child, Elizabeth adored the man she once called 'Grandpa England', and he loved his little 'Lilibet'. She was only nine when he died, but by then she had absorbed from him an indelible image of what a monarch should be like.

George VI

Rather like his father, George VI is also credited by some as having saved the British monarchy. The threat this time was home grown. The decision of Edward VIII to prefer marriage with the American divorcee Wallis Simpson over the Crown brought the monarchy into serious disrepute. It fed republicanism and shook the foundations of the Empire that the monarch was supposed head of.

Fortunately, George lacked his brother's flair and imagination. The signal given to the fleet by Horatio Nelson before Britain's stunning naval victory at Trafalgar (1805) – 'England expects that every man will do his duty' – was engraved on

George's heart. He spoke with a stammer and was not very bright but, helped by his more outgoing wife and the loyalty of Winston Churchill, he played his part.

Such was the template Elizabeth inherited. Duty came first, above all other matters, even family. As she might have seen, however, successful monarchs rarely make successful parents. The Sword of State she would carry at her coronation was double-edged.

Wearing Many Different Hats

'Off with his head!' cries Queen Margaret in Shakespeare's *Henry VI, Part III*. It is repeated by the Queen of Hearts in *Alice in Wonderland*, and thereafter (usually jokingly) by those wanting to get rid of someone who annoys them. It is a classic example of what we ordinary mortals imagine it is like to be a king or queen. Ask – and it is done. While you lie back and sip champagne.

Sure, modern monarchs do sip champagne. They don't have to worry about the price, either. But that's one of the perks of a mightily tough job. Tough not in the sense that they have to do a load of exhausting work like a gardener does, but because they rarely get a chance to properly relax. They're multi-taskers, on show 24/7.

Ruling in theory

Check out the UK's postage stamps, coins, bills, military lists, laws, law courts . . . there she is, Elizabeth II, Head of State. The monarch is the living embodiment of every country she heads. And the very second she passes away, her heir will become monarch in her place, because without a monarch all the countries she currently presides over would be headless.

Much of the job is strictly ceremonial: inspecting troops, signing bills into law, and so forth. Even this work can be trying. Not only does the Queen have to be on her best behaviour when performing the most mundane tasks – a stifled yawn would give the game away – but she may be called upon to do some strange things (see the sidebar, "Two birthdays and riding side-saddle" for example!).

Official business as Head of State gives the monarch considerable political influence at home and abroad. The UK's democratically elected Prime Minister discusses top-level politics with the Queen every week. She has to do her homework for the occasion, too, so she's not caught out.

TWO BIRTHDAYS AND RIDING SIDE-SADDLE

The monarch's birthday has long been celebrated with outdoor parades, parties and the like. Edward VII, a jolly fellow, decided that as the weather on his actual birthday (9 November) would probably be cold and wet, he should gift himself an official fair-weather birthday in June as well. The two-birthday tradition has persisted to this day.

Therefore, the Queen's official birthday is now on the second Saturday in June. It is marked by the Queen's Birthday Parade (also known as 'Trooping the Colour') at which Her Majesty – and thousands of tourists – watches a parade of mounted and unmounted soldiers and musicians.

Initially, Elizabeth herself participated on horseback. This required that she learn to ride side-saddle, with both her legs placed to one side of the horse's back. A 'lady' should never sit astride a horse, especially in public. How vulgar and suggestive would that be!

The monarch also meets with foreign heads of state and governments. These get-togethers are essentially apolitical. Nevertheless, a formal meeting that goes well can have political repercussions by sweetening relations between the two countries. Occasionally, a monarch is known to have had a direct impact on affairs. The meeting between King George VI and President Roosevelt in June 1939, just before the outbreak of World War II in Europe, was one such encounter. It is said that as a result FDR undertook to assist the UK and its allies in the upcoming conflict with Nazi Germany.

Running the family firm

In the Windsor family, Elizabeth rules, ok? The Queen made this clear from the outset, when she insisted that her husband walk behind her on formal occasions. As top dog, she is personally responsible for the Royal Family, the large administrative machinery of the Palace, and all royal residences and estates. ('The Palace'? What's that? Check out the nearby sidebar on this very subject.)

Elizabeth has a large staff to help her, of course, and over some aspects of her brief (notably her wayward family) she has little control. Even so, in all matters royal the buck stops with Elizabeth. From security at Balmoral Castle to Prince Andrew's headline-grabbing antics, and the performance of her horses at the Epsom Derby races, she has to keep at least half an eye on everything. Multi-tasking at its most demanding.

WHAT IS 'THE PALACE'?

Literally, 'the Palace' refers to Buckingham Palace, the Queen's primary residence in London. It is her place of work, her office, while other royal residences like Windsor Castle and Balmoral Castle are more places of leisure. The term 'Palace' is also used for the Queen and her household team of advisors, secretaries, and so on. The usage is like 'The White House' in the US and 'Downing Street' in the UK, where the building is short-hand for the organisation it houses.

And Being a Mum, Too

It is tough for working women with children to strike the right balance between caring for their offspring and doing the job for which they are paid. As explained in Chapter 17, the Queen does not receive a salary.

WARNING

Even so, her position requires a great deal of work. Perhaps I should rephrase that: she demands a great deal of work *from herself*. The monarch does not actually *have* to do anything except exist and wear a crown. There's no list of duties or obligations set out in a written constitution. What they do is up to them. However, precedent from Victoria's reign made it pretty clear that if a monarch does nothing to justify their privileged position, that position soon begins to look mighty precarious. (This is explained further in Chapter 3.) So, to keep her crown, Elizabeth must do the monarchy job.

What about family matters? With few exceptions, Europe's royal families have been notoriously incompetent at child-rearing. The Windsors are no exception. In earlier times, queens handed over their babies to wetnurses rather than themselves breastfeeding. In recent years, infants were passed to nannies and nurse-maids so their parents were free to get on with their duties.

As Elizabeth's parents left their nine-month-old baby behind when they went on a royal tour in 1927, so Elizabeth and her husband Philip left the infant Prince Charles and his sister Anne when they went on protracted tours. Duty came first. They knew no different. Overt demonstrations of affection – touching, kissing, cuddling – are to some extent learned behaviours. Having not learned them from her parents, Elizabeth the mother was unable to practice them herself.

Of all the tasks laid at Elizabeth's door, mothering was the one she was least prepared for. As we shall see in later chapters, it was also the one at which she has been least successful.

The Secrets of Elizabeth's Success

A 2020 survey showed that 76 percent of Brits liked their Queen. A sizeable 58 percent thought she had done a very good job since ascending the throne; another 24 percent reckoned she'd done 'fairly well'. That's a whopping 82 percent very or reasonably happy with her performance. In contrast, Prince Charles, her heir, had a popularity rating of only 45 percent; almost a third (28 percent) of his future subjects disliked him.

While these figures suggest that Elizabeth may not have secured the long-term future of Britain's quaint monarchial system, they make it clear that she's probably managed her inheritance as well as anyone could have done. A majority of Brits never want her to abdicate. They hope she'll go on wearing the Crown to the end.

Where does this public approval come from? Let's take a look at the secrets of Elizabeth's success.

She's been queen for a long time

In 2022, Elizabeth II is approaching her Platinum Jubilee (70 years as monarch). In the UK and around the world, she has been before the eyes and in the ears of the people she serves for nigh on seven decades. Familiarity has bred affection rather than contempt.

Like Queen Victoria and Queen Elizabeth I before her, Elizabeth II's longevity has allowed her to become part of the fabric of people's lives. The great majority have never known any other monarch. Just like familiar landmarks, such as London's Big Ben, she has always been there. Whatever people think of her, they find it hard to imagine a world without her.

The passage of time may have taken away Elizabeth's youthful good looks, but it has replaced them with something more precious. It has allowed her to appear indestructible and to re-invent herself as the global grandmother.

Everyone loves granny, don't they?

Her style has evolved and adapted

Elizabeth is well aware how important tradition is for the monarchy she heads. People instinctively like tradition. It provides a sense of stability and continuity in rapidly changing and often unsettling times. Trooping the Colour, the Changing of the Guard at Buckingham Palace, the Queen's Christmas Broadcast (see Chapters 10 and 12) . . . these and similar events are like handrails, something to hold on to during a storm-tossed voyage.

Experience – sometimes bitter – has also taught Elizabeth that things cannot remain unchanged for ever. To survive, the monarchy must move with the times, or at least a few steps behind. The Queen is instinctively conservative by nature and has rarely initiated change. Instead, circumstances have forced her hand.

Elizabeth has, for example, attempted to narrow the gap between herself and her subjects by engaging in royal walkabouts (see Chapter 14) and moderating her cut-glass, upper-class accent (see Chapter 12). These small but significant adaptations have ensured that, in the eyes of many, the Queen has kept herself more or less in touch with the mood of her country.

She uses more carrot than stick

Walter Bagehot, the famous Victorian commentator on the British constitution (see Chapter 8), reckoned the monarchy had three remaining rights:

>> to be consulted

>> to encourage

>> to warn

We know that Elizabeth is consulted because she reads *state papers* (government papers) and has regular meetings with her prime ministers (see Chapter 8). What little we know about her encouragement and warning suggests that they are offered subtly.

Here's an example of this. In her 1983 Christmas message, the Queen suggested 'redressing the economic balance between nations' by a more generous sharing of technology between richer and poorer nations. The statement was both an encouragement for aid programmes and organizations like Oxfam, and an implied warning of what might happen if the gap between the haves and the have nots grew too wide.

The remark was certainly not strident. But it did give weight to a world view that was out of kilter with free market capitalism then in vogue in the US and UK. Its influence is hard to estimate, though advocates of larger aid budgets and charities such as Oxfam surely approved.

She's nothing if not discreet

Though she does not go as far as her grandmother and refuse to smile in public, Elizabeth is often accused of looking glum. Her expression is partly deliberate. We do not know whether she has read Tom Paine's *Rights of Man* (1791) – we don't know much about her reading and TV watching – but she is certainly aware of the thinking behind what Paine said about monarchy:

I compare it to something kept behind a curtain, about which there is a great deal of bustle and fuss, and a wonderful air of seeming solemnity; but when, by any accident, the curtain happens to be open — and the company see what it is, they burst into laughter.

With this in mind, Elizabeth knows how important it is to maintain at least some of that 'wonderful air of seeming solemnity'. Whatever happens, she is determined to maintain a degree of mystery about the institution she heads. If she lets in too much light, if too much is known about her thoughts and feelings, she becomes like everyone else. And if she's exactly like everyone else, then how can her privileged position be justified?

These then are her watchwords: duty and discretion. Though neither is particularly exciting, and certainly few modern celebrities would place them high on their list of priorities, over many years they have served Her Majesty Queen Elizabeth II well enough.

» **Understanding the concept of ruling by Divine Right**

» **Discovering how Britain established a constitutional monarchy**

Chapter **2**

Triumph of Compromise: Constitutional Monarchy

This chapter takes a whistle-stop tour of the history of Britain's monarchy. It explains how the institution evolved from a small-scale, purely English affair to one of global importance. It also explores how the sovereign's role changed from that of chief executive to a useful – if somewhat anachronistic – constitutional fiction.

TIP

Various technical terms come out to play in this chapter, so here are a few useful concepts that will help you to understand what's going on:

» *Monarchy.* A system of government headed by a single person, the monarch or sovereign, for the duration of their lifetime or until they abdicate. The position is customarily hereditary, though not always: Poland had an elected monarchy, for example, and England's King Harold II (r. 1066) was chosen by a meeting of elders.

Monarchy is rule by a single person, the monarch. The adjective *sovereign* means having supreme power. In a democracy the people are sovereign. As a noun, *sovereign* means the person with supreme power, so the two words are synonymous. In this book, I generally use the word 'monarch' but occasionally swap it for 'sovereign' to avoid tedious repetition!

Monarchy comes in three flavours:

- *Absolute* is when the monarch theoretically has total power, rather like a dictator. Although Henry VIII and James II may have wanted to be absolute, they never had the backing or resources to be so.

- *Limited* is when the monarch is obliged to abide by certain customs and traditions. This best explains the monarchies of England and Scotland until the middle of the seventeenth century. Wise kings took on board the mood of the court and country before acting. Those who didn't risked losing their crowns or their heads – or both.

- *Constitutional* is when the monarch remains Head of State but with powers defined and limited by the *constitution* (meaning the rules by which a country is governed; the concept is explored later in this chapter and in Chapters 1 and 8). This constitution may be written or unwritten, or a mixture of the two. The monarchy of England (and Scotland) became constitutional after the failure of the republican experiment (see later in this chapter).

» **Primogeniture.** The idea that the Crown should automatically be inherited by the monarch's eldest male child took a while to catch on. It was not generally agreed upon in Britain until the twelfth century.

» **Royal prerogative.** This means the Crown's powers that can be exercised without the legal need to refer to anyone else. Magna Carta (1215) was an early attempt to limit the prerogative in law. Further steps, such as those in the Bill of Rights (1689), curbed it still further. Nevertheless, the royal prerogative remains considerable – in theory. For example, the sovereign remains head of the executive and may appoint whomsoever they wish as prime minister. However, any king or queen who tried to do this would be forced to clear their desk pronto, and probably destroy the monarchy.

» **Succession**. The Crown's wealth and power made it the ultimate prize for the ambitious. Until the nineteenth century, the *succession* (meaning who was next in line to the throne) – was often hotly (and fatally) disputed. You'll find out more about some of these events later in this chapter.

Let's roll our sleeves up and delve back into the murky past, starting with the Roman era and following through to the eighteenth century. As a handy guide to who ruled when, I've included several sidebars (six of them in fact!) throughout this chapter listing some of the famous – and infamous – royal rulers in the British Isles up to the eighteenth century.

From Tribal Leader to King of England

The story begins over 1,500 years ago. Early details are lost in the mists of time, but historians have used archaeology and such written records as remain to piece together a credible account of what happened in those early years.

For almost 400 years, England ('Britannia') was part of the Roman Empire. When Roman control ended in 410, the country was already being settled by Germanic immigrants from Europe.

The new arrivals were Angles, Saxons and Jutes: the Anglo-Saxons (the poor Jutes got dropped from history). As well as giving the whole country a new name – Angle-land (or England) – evidence of their presence survives in several county (or 'shire') names. Sussex, for instance, was the homeland of the South Saxons. It was recently given a royal colouring when Prince Harry and his wife Meghan became Duke and Duchess of Sussex.

Who were these Anglo-Saxons? The term 'Anglo-Saxon' is shorthand for the mix of ethnic groups dominant in England from about 400 to 1066. A minority were indigenous, and the majority immigrants from the western European coastlands of the North Sea. The Angles and Saxons, creators of the Anglo-Saxon language, were the most prominent groups. Inaccurately and rather annoyingly, some continental Europeans (notably the French) still refer to English-speaking Brits and Americans as having an 'Anglo-Saxon' culture.

REMEMBER

Powerful leaders of the immigrant tribes styled themselves 'king'. One of the more prominent was King Aethelbert of Kent, in southeast England. In 597, he and Queen Bertha, his Frankish wife (from modern-day France), welcomed a Christian mission from Rome led by a monk named Augustine. England converted to Rome-style Christianity and Augustine became a saint.

Settling down with the Anglo-Saxons

The arrival of Roman Christianity had a massive impact on society and culture in the British Isles. Monarchs soon cottoned on to the power of the new faith and got the Church to incorporate it into their coronation ceremonies. To see how this relates to Queen Elizabeth II, check out 'Athelstan' in the sidebar, "Elizabeth's royal heritage part I".

ELIZABETH'S ROYAL HERITAGE PART I: THE ANGLO-SAXONS AND VIKING MONARCHS

- Egbert 827–839. Elizabeth II can trace her ancestry back to Egbert, King of Wessex. Though not crowned King of England, he claimed overlordship over the whole land.

- Aethelwulf 839–858. The 'Noble Wolf' son of Egbert is regarded as a competent warrior monarch.

- Aethelbald 858–860. Another of Egbert's sons, King of Wessex and Kent, who annoyed the Church by marrying his stepmother.

- Aethelbert 860–866. Yet another of Egbert's sons, he integrated the Kingdoms of Wessex and Kent.

- Aethelred I 866–871. Egbert's fourth son battled with the Danish (Viking) Great Heathen Army.

- Alfred the Great 871–899. Aethelwulf's son, the only monarch entitled 'Great', halted the Danish advance.

- Edward the Elder 899–924. Alfred's son, who spearheaded Wessex's fightback against the Danes.

- Athelstan 924–939. A son of Edward the Elder, he was the first widely accepted King of England. His coronation was the template for Elizabeth II's (see Chapter 7).

- Edmund 939–946. Another son of Edward the Elder, he expanded the kingdom towards Scotland.

- Eadred 'Weak-in-the-Feet' 946–955. The third son of Edward the Elder who consolidated England's expansion north.

- Eadwig 955–959. The son of Edward the Elder who fell out with the highly respected St Dunstan over sexual morality issues.

- Edgar the Peaceful 959–975. Another son of Edward the Elder, venerated by the Catholic Church.

- Edward the Martyr 975–978. The son of Edgar whose cruel death made him a rare royal saint.

- Aethelred II 'the Unready' 978–1016. Edgar's son was beset by Danish incursions ('unready' means 'no-advice').

- Edmund II 'Ironside' 1016. Aethelred II's warrior son who battled the Danes more successfully than his father.

- Cnut (aka Canute) 1016–1035. The King of Denmark who added the English and Norwegian crowns to his empire.

- Harold I 'Harefoot' 1035–1040. An illegitimate son of Cnut who grabbed the Crown while his brother was absent.

- Harthacnut 'Tough-knot' 1040–1042. A son of Cnut, also King of Denmark, who died of a stroke at a boozy wedding.

- Edward the Confessor 1042–1066. The Anglo-Saxons returned to power with this saintly, Norman-loving son of Aethelred II.

- Harold II 1066. The brother-in-law of Edward the Confessor and last Anglo-Saxon monarch. Chosen by an assembly of noblemen, he was the first monarch crowned in Westminster Abbey. Died fighting William the Conqueror at the Battle of Hastings.

TECHNICAL STUFF

St Augustine and his Christian mission arrived in Britain in 597, and with him came literacy, which had died out when the Romans left. This gave rise to *Aethelbert's Laws*, the first document written in the county's new language – Anglo-Saxon or Early English. Christianity, literacy, and common sense enabled the kingdoms of Anglo-Saxon England to flourish. Law and order were maintained, taxes paid, and systems of central and local government emerged. A reeve was the Crown's representative in a shire (county), hence 'shire-reeve' or 'sheriff'. I bet Wyatt Earp never knew that!

Over time, the Anglo-Saxon settlements consolidated into seven major English kingdoms: Northumbria in the north; Mercia in the middle of the country (the 'Midlands' in current parlance); East Anglia and Essex in the east; Kent, Sussex and Wessex in the south.

Uniting through adversity

Starting in the late seventh century AD, a fresh wave of invaders shattered the peace and prosperity of Anglo-Saxon England. These were pagan Vikings from Scandinavia who swept ashore to pillage and destroy. It didn't take them long to realize that England was not simply a good place for plunder – it was a nicer place to live than their Nordic homelands.

By 870, all the Anglo-Saxon kingdoms except Wessex had fallen to the invaders. Then, led initially by Alfred the Great (r. 872–899), the Kingdom of Wessex fought back. Under Alfred's sons and grandsons, it extended its sway north and east until all England was united into a single kingdom. This, essentially, is the English part of the realm Elizabeth II inherited in 1952.

The unified Crown of England was quite a prize. It was fought over by Anglo-Saxons and Scandinavians for a further century until, in 1066, it was seized by Duke William of Normandy. His claim to the throne was pretty flimsy. That ceased to matter when he killed the last Anglo-Saxon (Harold) king in battle and was crowned by the Archbishop of Canterbury in Westminster Abbey.

REMEMBER

The Normans introduced a host of new words and customs. Moreover, their arrival drew England more closely into the politics of continental Europe. The King of England was now a key figure on the international scene. At the time of the Norman takeover, the King of England was no longer simply a successful warlord. Increasingly elaborate coronations gave him an almost sacred status. This was confirmed by the holy, childless life of Edward the Confessor (r. 1042–1066). In 1161, Pope Alexander III declared him a saint.

There were now two powers in the land: the monarch and the Church. The king resented the Church's wealth and separate system of law courts; the Church resented any monarchial interference with its affairs.

TECHNICAL STUFF

Matters came to a head during the reign of Henry II, who wanted one law for both church and state. Following an unwise rant from the king, four knights murdered Thomas Becket, Archbishop of Canterbury, in his own cathedral. Becket was canonized and Henry allowed the cathedral monks to give him a symbolic whipping. Church 1, King 0.

Deprived of some of its glitz, the Crown was further tarnished by bitter dynastic squabbles. Some revolved around French lands held by English kings and their claim to be King of France as well as England. The result was an on-off affair known as the Hundred Years' War, actually fought for over one hundred years between 1337 and 1453.

TIP

The rivalry with France rumbled on over the following centuries: English monarchs still called themselves King or Queen of France until George III finally accepted reality and dropped the title in 1800.

At home, fighting for the 'hollow crown' (as Shakespeare described it) led to the bloody 'Wars of the Roses' (1455–1487), between the two families of Lancaster and York descended from Edward III. Remarkably, amid all the gore and mayhem, the machinery of monarchial government – court, bureaucracy, defined borders, and so on – continued to develop towards what we now call the 'nation state'.

The stage was set for monarchy's finest hour – or was it? Wars required money from taxation. To get their subjects' approval, kings had called their representatives to a parliament which voted on taxation and agreed new laws. But once Parliament had been set up, it was very difficult to get rid of it. Without realizing,

England's monarchs had called into being a rival whose claim to legitimacy was every bit as strong as their own, if not stronger (to find out how Parliament interacted with more recent monarchs, see later in this chapter and also Chapter 8).

ELIZABETH'S ROYAL HERITAGE PART II: THE MEDIEVAL MONARCHS

- William I 'the Conqueror' 1066–1087. The Duke of Normandy who said that the childless Edward the Confessor (a distant cousin) had promised him the Crown.

- William II 1087–1100. The second son of William I got England while his brother got Normandy.

- Henry I 1100–1135. The third son of William I who reunited England and Normandy.

- Matilda/Stephen 1135–1154. The throne was contested between Matilda, daughter of Henry I, and Stephen, grandson of William I. Henry I had wanted his daughter to succeed; the barons opted for Stephen. In the end, after all-out war, neither was crowned.

- Henry II 1154–1189. Matilda's son whose marriage to Eleanor of Aquitaine created a mini empire including parts of modern-day France.

- Richard I 'the Lionheart' 1189–1199. A son of Henry II, hailed as a legendary Crusader hero and friend of Robin Hood.

- John 1199–1216. To limit royal power, angry barons forced this unpopular son of Henry II to sign Magna Carta, the 'Great Charter' that is hailed as a cornerstone of UK and US rights.

- Henry III 1216–1272. John's son whose long reign saw the emergence of a two-chamber parliament.

- Edward I 1272–1307. The son of Henry III who conquered Wales and made his son Prince of Wales.

- Edward II 1307–1327. Edward I's incompetent son was horribly murdered by a faction of opponents headed by his wife Isabella and her lover Roger Mortimer.

- Edward III 1327–1377. Edward II's warrior son launched the 100 Years' War with France.

(continued)

(continued)

- Richard II 1377–1399. Edward III's grandson, who was deposed by his cousin and died in captivity.

- Henry IV 1399–1413. Another grandson of Edward III. Known as Henry of Lancaster, he seized the throne from Richard II and was crowned Henry IV.

- Henry V 1413–1422. Henry IV's son defeated the French and set up his son as King of France.

- Henry VI 1422–1461. Henry V's incompetent son whose reign saw the outbreak of the Wars of the Roses.

- Edward IV 1461–1483. A great-great-grandson of Edward III who championed the Yorkists (white rose) in the Wars of the Roses and deposed the Lancastrian (red rose) Henry VI.

- Edward V 1483. A 12-year-old king probably murdered on the orders of his uncle Richard, who then took the throne as Richard III.

- Richard III 1483–1485. The brother of Edward IV whom history has (perhaps justifiably) vilified.

- Henry VII 1485–1509. The first of the Tudor dynasty whose father was a half-brother of Henry VI. His marriage to Elizabeth of York ended the Wars of the Roses.

Ruling by Divine Right?

After the arrival of St Augustine (see earlier in this chapter), Anglo-Saxon kings liked to ally themselves with the Church. It was a mutual back-scratching arrangement. The Church got royal protection; the king got the Church's blessing. The relationship became stickier as the Church got wealthier and more powerful. We saw where this could lead with the Thomas Becket incident earlier in this chapter.

By the early sixteenth century, two trends were apparent:

>> The Church, still fabulously rich, was increasingly out of touch.

>> Fed by growing wealth and a new spirit of nationalism, the Crown's status and confidence were growing. The arts of the Renaissance added further to the sovereign's glory. Some historians talk of a *New Monarchy*, meaning greater emphasis on the monarch's power and majesty, with patronage of the arts and a more magnificent court.

Sooner or later, church and monarch were going to meet head-on. Step forward Henry VIII.

Losing my religion: Henry VIII's church reforms

Medieval Scotland never had a queen regnant, and England only one: Matilda. Her reign had been a disaster. This confirmed male prejudice: Female monarchs were not up to the job. Giving the Crown to a woman, it was argued, was a sure recipe for chaos and civil conflict.

Such was the thinking of Henry VIII, the strong-willed, self-loving Renaissance King of England in the early sixteenth century. His Spanish wife, Catherine of Aragon, had produced a daughter, Mary, but not the male heir he so craved.

Surely God was punishing him for marrying the widow of his deceased elder brother? (Even though he'd got special permission from the Pope to do so.) He was soon convinced that he should divorce Catherine and marry his latest girlfriend, Anne Boleyn.

Henry's problem . . .

Pope Clement VII was at that time a prisoner of Catherine's nephew, Charles the Holy Roman Emperor. Under those circumstances, there was no way Clement was going to grant Henry his divorce.

. . . and Henry's solution

Europe was in the throes of the *Reformation* (when the Christian Church in the west of the continent split between Catholic and Protestant sects). Several kings and princes had already severed their links with Rome and acquired a great deal of wealth by helping themselves to Church riches. Henry decided to join them.

Between 1533 and 1535, legislation was pushed through Parliament to separate England from the Roman Catholic Church and set up the Church of England, with the king at its head. That's why Queen Elizabeth II is called 'Defender of the Faith [a title the Papacy gave Henry VIII before their split] and Supreme Governor of the Church of England'.

TECHNICAL STUFF

British coins still bear the sovereign's head, name and the inscription 'FD'. This is short for 'Fidelis Defensor' (meaning 'Defender of the Faith' in Latin). In a royal context, it certainly doesn't mean 'For Dummies'!

Despite the break with Rome, Henry VIII still didn't have a male heir. Anne Boleyn had only one daughter, Elizabeth. After he'd executed Anne for treason, Henry tried again. Third time lucky: Queen Jane Seymour produced a son, Edward. Raised by Protestant tutors, the boy succeeded his father as Edward VI and his realm swung towards his version of the faith. It swung back again when he died young and his Catholic sister Mary took the throne.

ELIZABETH'S ROYAL HERITAGE PART III: SELECTED KINGS OF SCOTLAND TO 1603

- Kenneth MacAlpin 841–858. Hailed as the founder of Scotland (or 'Alba'), he united three kingdoms and was crowned on the famous Stone of Scone, as was Elizabeth II.

- Malcolm II 'Canmore' ('Big Head' or 'Great Chief') 1058–1093. Married to Margaret, an English princess and Scotland's only royal saint, he brought stability and continuity to a troubled land.

- David I 1124–1153. He modernized his kingdom with feudal practices and favoured foreigners such as the Bruces and Stewarts at his court.

- Robert I 'the Bruce' 1306–1329. Scotland's number 1 hero defeated the English and, through the marriage of his daughter, paved the way for the Stewart (aka Stuart) dynasty that eventually came to the throne in England.

- James IV 1488–1513. Scotland's Renaissance Prince and star of the Stewarts, he was killed making a disastrous foray into England. His marriage to Margaret Tudor would lead to the accession of James VI to the thrones of both England and Scotland.

ELIZABETH'S ROYAL HERITAGE PART IV: MONARCHS OF ENGLAND TO 1603

- Henry VIII 1509–1547. Despite robbing untold wealth from the Church, the infamous Tudor never had the resources to become a true tyrant.

- Edward VI 1547–1553. Henry VIII's longed-for son, an enthusiastic Protestant, he died at the age of 15.

- Mary I 1553–1558. 'Bloody Mary' was England's first female monarch for 400 years. An enthusiastic Catholic, she destroyed her reputation by executing 300 Protestant 'martyrs', many of whom were burned alive.

- Elizabeth I 1558–1603. The daughter of the executed Anne Boleyn who survived a difficult early life to become the model queen regnant.

Entering the first Elizabethan Age

Mary was succeeded by her sister, the Protestant Elizabeth. Two female monarchs in succession! Though Mary's religious persecutions made her deeply unpopular, her rule was by no means incompetent. And her sister's was positively brilliant.

TIP

Winston Churchill was thinking of Elizabeth I when, waxing sentimental at the time of Elizabeth II's accession, he said that he looked forward hopefully to a 'new Elizabethan age'.

Compared with the turmoil of the previous 50 years and the turbulence of the next 50, the reign of Elizabeth I did take on a golden hue. The Queen brought stability and good government. She re-fashioned and re-established the Church of England. Her armed forces beat off the threat of invasion. Her sailors explored the world. All this against a background of unprecedented cultural and artistic activity.

Matching the second Elizabethan age with the first would be a tought ask.

Finding Mary (Queen of Scots)

Elizabeth I, the 'Virgin Queen', had no children. Nor had her brother Edward or sister Mary. The Tudor line was at an end. Whither the Crown?

Working up the family tree, genealogists arrived at Henry VIII's sister, Margaret, who had married Scotland's King James IV. Their son, James V (r. 1513–1542), left the Crown to his young daughter, Mary Queen of Scots (r. 1542–1567).

Raised a Catholic and at one time married to the King of France, Mary's film-star personality did not appeal to the Presbyterian patriarchy dominating Scottish politics. Scandal led to rebellion and, in 1567, flight into England. Under house arrest in the realm of her Protestant cousin Elizabeth, Mary insisted that, as a Catholic, she was the true Queen of England. Elizabeth eventually responded by having Mary beheaded in 1587. One wonders whether Elizabeth II has sometimes secretly wished she could get rid of her troublesome family members in similar fashion!

The exiled Mary Queen of Scots left her only son, James Stewart, back in Scotland. He was proclaimed King James VI (r. 1567–1625) and raised as a Protestant. When the English Tudor dynasty died out in 1603, he succeeded to the throne of England as King James I. With this, Elizabeth II's four-part United Kingdom came a step closer.

- James VI of Scotland and I of England 1603–1625. Mary Queen of Scots' peace-loving son united the thrones of England and Scotland. Full political union between the two countries followed a century later.

- Charles I 1625–1649. A narrow-minded and obstinate man, with impeccable artistic taste, who challenged Parliament for control of his kingdoms – and lost. Britain's monarchy was never the same again.

Becoming a republic

James I was an academic. He also believed that God had appointed him. The state of monarchy, he told the English Parliament in 1610,

is the supremest thing upon earth; for Kings are not only God's lieutenants upon Earth and sit upon God's throne, but even by God himself they are called gods.

WARNING

Wow! You can imagine that this statement of the Divine Right of Kings did not go down well with everyone. Some even considered it blasphemy.

Happily for James, he had enough political sense not to take things too far. Not so his son, Charles I, who succeeded him.

Belief in Divine Right, contempt for Parliament (and remember that he needed Parliament for money), and a wish to steer the Church of England closer to Catholicism proved too much for many of Charles' subjects. Saying he was seriously ill-advised, they rebelled.

REMEMBER

In the complex civil wars that followed, Charles was defeated and condemned to die. On 30 January 1649, he was beheaded in front of his palace in Whitehall, London. England – but not Scotland, which had disagreed with the execution – was now a republic.

Establishing a Constitutional Monarchy

England's republic lasted for 11 years, from 1649 to 1660. The puritanical regime, dominated by the brilliant general Oliver Cromwell, governed well but austerely. Theatres were closed, Christmas was banned, and at one stage the country was subjected to military rule. Cromwell, who rejected the offer of a crown, ended up as Lord Protector. On his death, his son refused to step into his shoes, and an invitation to return was sent to Charles II (Charles I's son), the king in exile.

REMEMBER

Charles made wise promises of toleration. These were accepted, and on 29 May 1660, his birthday, he entered London amid scenes of wild rejoicing. The monarchy was back and has remained ever since. However, the clock could not be turned right back. The King still ruled, choosing ministers and so forth, but the shadow of the bloody axe could never be effaced. Parliament controlled the purse strings and had to agree to all legislation.

ELIZABETH'S ROYAL HERITAGE PART VI: BRITAIN'S FIRST CONSTITUTIONAL MONARCHS

- Charles II 1660–1685. Though in theory he retained most of the powers exercised by his father, the 'Merry Monarch' exerted his authority with tact and skill.

- James II 1685–1688. Charles II's loser brother dreamed of being an absolute monarch like his paymaster, Louis XIV of France, but ended up in humiliating exile.

- Mary II 1688–1694 and William III 1688–1702. The Dutchman and his Stuart (Stewart in Scotland) wife got England's ruling class out of a very tricky situation by replacing James II.

- Anne 1702–1714. Unspectacular but competent and reliable, 'Anna Gloria' demonstrated that a woman could handle the new constitutional arrangements as well as any man.

- George I 1714–1727. The import from Hanover, Germany, whose inability to speak English counted for much less than his Protestant faith.

- George II 1727–1760. The second Hanoverian was the last monarch to exercise his kingly right (some would say duty) to lead his troops into battle.

- George III 1760–1820. Blinkered yet well-meaning, the third Hanoverian presided (when his health allowed) over a period of revolutionary turmoil.

Charles was prepared to do whatever it took not to be exiled again. For instance, he was wise enough not to make public his Catholic sympathies. Not so his dim-witted brother, James II (and VII of Scotland), who succeeded him. Catholicism, in the British mind, meant European-style absolutism and tyranny. So when James appointed Catholic officers to an embryonic standing army and set about rigging Parliamentary elections, he had to go.

Choosing absolutism or republicanism?

TIP

We've now reached one of the major turning points in British history. Indeed, in my opinion, it's one of the major turning points in all history. This is where things stood:

>> Throughout Europe, absolute monarchy was on the rise.

>> Medieval parliaments, representing powerful groups of merchants and lawyers, were done away with or simply not called.

>> The poster boy of this royal power grab was Louis XIV, king of the strongly Catholic France. Ensconced in his grand palace at Versailles, he boasted, 'L'état, c'est moi!' (meaning: 'The state? It's me!').

What were the Brits to make of the situation? To Protestant supporters of the Church of England, the outlook was grim. Charles II and his Catholic brother had accepted French subsidies, undermining Parliament's control of government finance. But anti-absolutists couldn't rebel and cut off another king's head, could they? They had tried republicanism and it had proved a total failure.

What to do? Two things saved the day:

>> James' Protestant daughter Mary was married to William of Orange, the key figure in the Dutch government. The Dutch were bitter opponents of Louis XIV. Mary agreed to come to England as a Protestant replacement for father, on one condition: her husband should rule jointly with her.

>> When William and Mary landed in England, James II ran away.

Bringing about revolution

The events of 1688–1689 saved the country from having to choose between absolutism and republicanism. It found a third way: constitutional monarchy (flip back to the start of the current chapter for a definition of this). This system, with adjustments, persists to this day. It looks, and in many ways is, a bizarre compromise. Nevertheless, it has stood the test of time well enough.

1688–1689 was Britain's revolution. Unlike those in America, France, Russia, and elsewhere, it was a peaceful affair. Hence its name, the 'Glorious and Bloodless Revolution'. Its key features were as follows:

>> King James abdicated and the throne became vacant.

>> Queen Mary II and King William III were joint monarchs, with the executive power vested in William; all office holders in Church and State had to swear an oath of allegiance to him. The *executive* is the branch of government responsible for day-to-day administration and law enforcement.

>> A *Toleration Act* established limited religious toleration for Protestants outside the Church of England; Catholics were still beyond the pale.

>> A *Bill of Rights* (much of it later mirrored in the US Constitution) took away many of the Crown's ancient powers, such as suspending or dispensing with laws they didn't like. The Bill also outlawed raising money without Parliament's consent and keeping a standing army in peace time. Other clauses guaranteed the right to bear arms, the right to free Parliamentary elections, free speech in Parliament, and regular Parliaments.

>> A law of 1694 ensured a new Parliament would meet every three years (later changed to seven years, then five).

>> The establishment of the Bank of England, also in 1694, tied the wealthy to the new regime: if James and his supporters returned, what would happen to money stashed away in the bank?

The crisis over the succession and its impact on Crown–Parliament relations had bubbled up when it looked likely that Charles II's queen, Catherine of Braganza, would not produce an heir. That put Charles' brother, the Catholic James, Duke of York (New York was named in his honour) in line for the Crown. This divided the political classes.

The faction supporting James were known as *Tories*. Their opponents, who eventually engineered the Revolution, were called *Whigs* (see the sidebar, "What's in a name? Whigs and Tories" for more on these unusual names). Thus a party system came into being, Whig versus Tory. The significance of this was immense. It's worth nothing, however, that Whigs and Tories both came from the same wealthy, upper echelons of society.

In time, both Whigs and Tories accepted the Revolution. What each offered was not an alternative monarch, but an alternative set of ministers. Parliament divided between government supporters and the opposition. Both were loyal to the Crown.

WHAT'S IN A NAME? WHIGS AND TORIES

Whigs and Tories? These were the names of Britain's (and the world's) first political parties, and were originally terms of abuse coined by their opponents. A Whig was a radical Scottish presbyterian; a Tory was an Irish outlaw.

In politics, the Whigs were the engineers and supporters of the Revolution of 1688–1689 who rejected any thought of a Catholic monarch. The Tories, more conservative in outlook, supported James II's right to the throne, despite his Catholicism.

The Tory Party, officially renamed the Conservative and Unionist Party, is still a major force in British politics. The majority of prime ministers with whom Queen Elizabeth II has worked have been Tories. The Whigs became the Liberal Party in the nineteenth century.

Previously, to oppose the government was treason. The emergence of political parties put an end to this. For the first time ever, those opposing the Crown's ministers could be seen walking about with their heads on.

REMEMBER

The system persists to this day. After an election, Elizabeth II invites the leader of the largest party in Parliament to meet her, customarily in Buckingham Palace. There she invites them to become prime minister and to appoint ministers to Her Majesty's Government. The job of other parties in Parliament is to hold the government to account. They act as the 'loyal opposition', a phrase unimaginable to Henry VIII or Charles I. This remarkable development, now copied in many countries around the world, is why I believe the Glorious and Bloodless Revolution to have been so important.

Appointing a newcomer

Britain's fear of Catholicism ran deep. Its roots lay in Bloody Mary's burning of Protestants (see earlier in this chapter), Spain's attempt to invade England in 1588, and a 1605 plot to blow up the King and Parliament. Reports of Catholic tyranny in continental Europe fanned the flames still further.

Anti-Catholic sentiment did not evaporate with the revolutionary settlement of 1688–1689 and the coronation of William and Mary. It reappeared firstly when Queen Mary died childless and secondly when all 15 children of her successor, Queen Anne, were either stillborn or died before their unfortunate mother.

Calling himself James III, James II's Catholic son was waiting in the wings, ready to return and take up the Crown he believed to be rightfully his. As at the end of Elizabeth I's reign, genealogists scoured the Royal Family tree . . . James I's daughter (another Elizabeth) had married a Protestant German prince and produced a daughter, Sophia of Hanover. With Catholics ruled out by a law of 1701, Sophia was proclaimed heir presumptive to the British throne.

There was one more twist. Sophia died before Queen Anne and the succession passed to her son, George of Hanover. The fact that he spoke almost no English and preferred Germany to Britain didn't matter. Joining the Church of England was a small price to pay for being King of England. Problem solved.

REMEMBER

In less than 50 years, Britain had moved from the cusp of absolutism to a rent-a-king constitutional monarchy. The pageantry and symbolism remained, but a lot of the power had gone.

Learning with George: what monarchs shouldn't do

For almost half a century, the system worked well. George I and his boorish son George II (r. 1727–1760) played the game. They were kept happy with wealth, prestige and a foreign policy slanted towards the interests of their beloved Hanover, which they visited frequently. In return, they left domestic matters to ministers who commanded a majority in the House of Commons. (The division of Parliament between the House of Commons and the House of Lords is explained in Chapter 3.) The two kings' favourite minister, Robert Walpole (in power 1721–1742), is hailed as Britain's first prime minister.

The constitutional boat was violently rocked when George III, an intensely patriotic man who never set foot in Hanover, attempted to place his own stamp on domestic as well as foreign policy. He openly favoured the Tories and resented having to appoint ministers he disliked. His brazen involvement in politics made him a stand-out target for all who opposed his government's policies – most notably the citizens of the American colonies!

George's reign faded tragically into long periods of insanity. Its lessons for the monarchy were not forgotten, least of all by Elizabeth II. Stand back, keep schtum, and leave politics to the politicians.

American Republic, French Republic – Britain next?

The British monarchy took quite a hammering at the hands of American rebels. More was to come when the French Revolution (1789 onwards) overthrew the monarchy and guillotined their own King Louis XVI. Among many of the intelligentsia and *disenfranchised* (those deprived of the right to vote) middle- and working-classes, the talk was of rights, liberty and equality. Beneath the surface, another revolution bubbled.

The monarchy and its supporters had to tread very carefully indeed. Chapter 3 looks at the next generations of Royal Family, and how they dealt with an ever-modernizing world.

Chapter **3**

Victoria: The Queen Who Defined an Era

The history of Britain's royal families is at best chequered. Husbands mistreated wives (are you listening, Henry VIII?), fathers fell out with their children (Henry II's sons rebelled against him; Queen Mary II and Queen Anne both took their father's crown), and little Edward V was murdered by his own uncle. Small wonder Shakespeare declared, 'uneasy lies the head that wears the crown.' Chapter 2 gives you some idea of how things happened.

Enter Victoria, the Queen who gave her name to an era (the *Victorian* period generally refers to the years 1837–1901, the years of her reign). You can see her family and how Elizabeth II was related to her in Figure 3-1.

In this chapter, you'll discover how the British monarchy slowly adapted – not always willingly – to the world of representative democracy. The process began during Victoria's reign and continued under her successors. This enabled Britain's hereditary monarchy to survive the fate of less flexible monarchies, notably those of Germany, Russia, Austria–Hungary, and Turkey, all of which collapsed in the early years of the twentieth century.

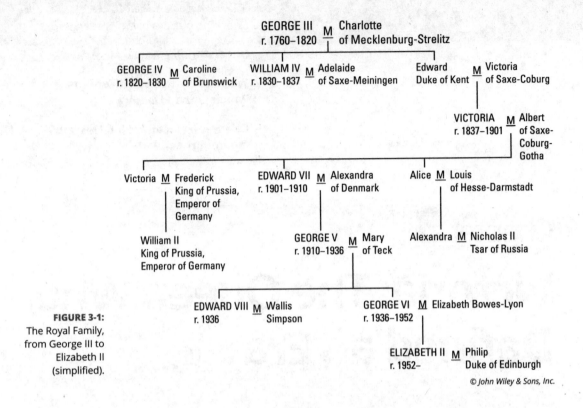

FIGURE 3-1:
The Royal Family,
from George III to
Elizabeth II
(simplified).

© John Wiley & Sons, Inc.

The Monarchs Who Came Before Victoria

Things were not going well for the Crown in the reigns preceding Victoria's. George III was succeeded by two of his sons, the philandering buffoon George IV (r.1820–1830) and William IV (r.1830–1837), the unpretentious Sailor King who hoped to abolish the coronation. These two reigns, following the insanity of George III, left the monarchy at a perilously low ebb. There didn't seem much chance of restoring its fortunes, either, for next in line was an 18-year-old princess whose mother was strongly disliked by William IV and his wife, Queen Adelaide.

TECHNICAL
STUFF

George III and Queen Charlotte had 15 children, nine of whom were male. The boys had precedence over their sisters in the succession, a situation that changed only in 2015. None of the eldest three boys – George IV, Frederick Duke of York, and William IV – produced legitimate offspring still alive in 1830. The fourth son, Edward Duke of Kent, didn't look as if he would either: he was intimately hooked up with his long-term French–Canadian mistress, Julie St. Laurent.

In 1817, George IV's daughter Charlotte died childless. Duke Edward duly ditched Julie and married the recently widowed German Princess Victoria of

Saxe-Coburg-Saalfeld. As the Princess already had two children, it was a safe bet that she'd produce another. She did, in 1819. But that was it – Edward died of pneumonia the next year. The child he left behind had been christened Princess Alexandrina Victoria. We know her as Queen Victoria.

The Young Queen

Victoria was an infuriating person. She was prone to sudden mood swings – sentimental/contemptuous, cowardly/brave, lively/melancholy – that are often the mark of a spoilt child. This was hardly surprising. Being heir presumptive from the age of 11 to the throne of the most powerful nation on earth was enough to turn most heads.

Victoria's overbearing mother and John Conroy, her private secretary, made things worse by keeping her daughter cooped up in Kensington Palace away from other children and young people. Despite her upbringing, Victoria got off to a good start. The public took to her fair-haired, blue-eyed good looks (she would insist her husband call her 'Angel'), and her naïve purity made a welcome change from the shameless licentiousness of her Hanoverian predecessors (see the nearby sidebar for more on who the Hanoverians were).

But things soon went wrong.

When her unrehearsed, chaotic coronation cost twice as much as William IV's, radicals said it was a *Tory* (pro-monarchy) propaganda exercise. She then made a fool of herself when she believed one of her unmarried ladies-in-waiting to be pregnant when in fact she was suffering from terminal liver cancer.

THE HANOVERIANS

When George I was invited to assume the British crown in 1714 (see Chapter 2), he was already ruler – his actual title was 'Elector' – of the German state of Hanover.

Hence the title 'Hanoverian' for the royal dynasty he founded.

For the next 100 years, Britain's kings were also Electors of Hanover. Hanover became a kingdom in 1814, making George III King of Hanover and Great Britain. As women were not permitted to rule in Hanover, on Victoria's accession to the British throne in 1837, the Hanoverian crown went to her uncle, Ernest Augustus.

As she was theoretically head of the executive (see Chapter 2), Victoria was intent on retaining political power. Her early pro-Whig, anti-Tory bias was blatant. Hissed in public, Victoria was in trouble. The kindly guidance of the elderly prime minister, Lord Melbourne, helped – but what really saved her was marriage.

Along Comes Albert

TIP

The form of constitutional monarchy inherited by Elizabeth II owes more to two outsiders than to any native-born king or queen. Both, I suppose, benefitted from being able to see the institution from the outside. The first was the Dutchman William III, husband of Mary II (see Chapter 2); the second was Queen Victoria's husband, Prince Albert. Another outsider, Elizabeth II's husband Philip, would hope in vain to exert a similar reforming influence (see the nearby sidebar, "The power behind the throne").

Albert (1819–1861) was prince of the small but well-connected German state of Saxe-Coburg and Gotha. He was good-looking, more stable and more intelligent than Victoria. He was also better educated than any member of the Royal Family before the later twentieth century. With wisdom and not a little forbearance, he skillfully handled the intricate British political system and his wife's mood swings. At one stage, he resorted to communicating with her by passing notes under her door.

The couple were married in St James' Palace, London, in February 1840. As she was royal and he wasn't, she had proposed to him. Though the marriage between the first cousins had been talked about for almost two decades beforehand, it was a genuine love match and – for much of the time – Victoria doted on her 'Dearest dearest dear Albert'.

REMEMBER

During Victoria's long reign, people began for the first time to discuss the Royal Family in terms other than discord and scandal. Slowly, the idea emerged that it might present a role model to the nation: mummy and daddy with a happy brood of children clustered about their knees. Ideally at Christmas. Photography, print media, and assistance from the sovereign's private secretary all helped. There was not yet a press secretary but, guided by Prince Albert, the Palace administration was modernized (see Chapter 9 for the monarch's administrative backup). Its new image accorded with the highly sentimentalized image of family life found in the pages of Charles Dickens, the greatest writer of the Victorian age (and much admired by the Queen).

THE POWER BEHIND THE THRONE

On marrying Princess Elizabeth in 1947, Philip Mountbatten must have hoped to play a role similar to that of Prince Albert. Two things stopped him:

- The monarch's power was much reduced since Victorian times. Victoria still had considerable political influence, which Albert often exercised on her behalf. He handled her political correspondence, had face-to-face discussions with government ministers on matters of policy, openly joined in political campaigns (for example, anti-slavery), and even attended the House of Lords during debates. By the time of Elizabeth II, the Crown was expected to be above politics, expressing no personal views and remaining neutral in all political matters. Her husband had no choice but to follow suit.

- Elizabeth was made of much sterner stuff than Victoria, and she was not burdened by endless pregnancies. Moreover, by the mid-twentieth century, attitudes and expectations were changing. Women had the vote and had shown in two world wars that they were perfectly capable of doing work traditionally associated with men. Victoria may have been happy to hand over responsibilities to her husband, but Elizabeth – except in some strictly domestic matters – certainly was not.

How Albert helped the British monarchy

After the turbulent times of previous monarchs, the actions of Albert added some much-needed stability to the British throne:

>> He remained faithful to his wife and posed in archetypal photographs with her and their children, helping restore the monarchy's reputation and creating a new icon: the Royal Family.

>> He acted as the Queen's personal secretary (she labelled him her 'permanent minister'), lightening the burden of everyday administration.

>> He improved management of the Palace and Crown Estates, weeding out outdated flummery.

>> Victoria suffered four assassination attempts and a violent attack. On each of these occasions, he was there to comfort her.

>> He took a personal interest in his children's education, hoping to make them better suited to their calling than his wife had been.

>> On occasion, he smoothed out Victoria's prejudiced relations with politicians. Prime ministers came to respect his judgement. After the transparent bias of George III and Victoria's early years, the Prince's more balanced approach helped distance the monarch somewhat from day-to-day politics.

>> He associated the monarchy with worthy causes and enterprises. These included the campaign to eradicate slavery worldwide, educational reform, and the outstandingly successful Great Exhibition of the Works of Industry of All Nations (1851) housed in London's glittering new, all-glass Crystal Palace.

>> His considered influence on foreign affairs, though not always successful, eased relations with other countries, especially France. Just before his death, he intervened to defuse tensions between Britain and the United States.

The royal network

REMEMBER

Elizabeth II's coronation (see Chapter 7) was attended by an extraordinarily wide-ranging gathering of princes and princesses, dukes and duchesses, marquesses and marchionesses, and other aristocrats and royalty with strange titles from all over Europe. Remarkable though it may seem, they were all the Queen's relatives. How come?

It all began with Queen Victoria. Her mother, also called Victoria, was a Princess of Saxe-Coburg-Gotha in Germany. Her father, Prince Edward, was a son of King George III. That made Victoria pretty well-connected for a start.

Queen Victoria's extended family

Victoria's uncles further strengthened her family network: Uncle Ernest was King of Hanover, Uncles George, Frederick and William married German princesses; Uncle Adolphus married Italian royalty. Victoria's aunts were also married into royalty or ruling families. Finally, the Queen's husband, Albert, was related directly or through marriage to many royal and princely families in Germany, France, Belgium, Portugal Austria, and Mexico.

Not content with an inherited galaxy of royal relatives, Victoria and Albert added to it through their children's marriages:

>> Princess Victoria (b.1840) married Frederick II, King of Prussia and Emperor of Germany. In 1837, Germany had been a patchwork of independent states; following a successful war with France, in 1870 these united to form the German Empire. Victoria and Frederick's children included Emperor William II (who took Germany into World War I) and Sophie who married the King of Greece.

>> Prince Albert Edward (b.1841, future King Edward VII) married Princess Alexandra of Denmark. Their children included George V of Great Britain and Maud, Queen of Norway.

>> Prince Alfred (b.1844) married a Russian princess and was father to a queen of Romania. Princess Helena (b.1846) married a Danish-German prince. Prince Arthur (b.1850), Prince Leopold (b.1853) and Princess Beatrice married German aristocrats. Arthur's daughter married the Crown Prince of Sweden, and Beatrice's daughter, Victoria Eugenie, became Queen of Spain.

>> The network is completed with Princess Alice (b.1843) who married a German grand duke. One of her daughters, Alexandra, married Nicholas II, the last tsar of Russia. Another daughter, Victoria, married her cousin, Louis of Battenberg. Their grandson was Prince Philip, Elizabeth II's husband!

The Victorian legacy

REMEMBER

Three things are worth bearing in mind from this extraordinary family legacy:

>> For centuries, the royal families of Europe were a very closed shop. Elizabeth II's marriage to Philip, a distant cousin, is a good example of this.

>> The Windsors clearly try to keep their heritage alive through the repeated use of the same names (such as William, Louis and Eugenie). This explains the disapproval in some circles when Harry and Meghan, Duke and Duchess of Sussex, chose to name their children Archie and Lilibet (see Figure 3-1).

>> We cannot comprehend how shocking was Edward VIII's wish to marry a divorced American commoner (see Chapter 5), nor how radical were the 'commoner' marriages of Elizabeth's children and grandchildren, unless we are aware of the heritage stretching back to the time of Queen Victoria.

From Monarch to Empress

The political world that Victoria inherited in 1837 was dominated by the same sort of aristocratic grandees who had engineered the 1688–1689 Revolution. Over the course of her reign, she appointed ten prime ministers. Seven of them were hereditary aristocrats, and she rewarded one of the other three – her favourite, Benjamin Disraeli – by making him an earl. Beneath the surface, however, things were slowly changing for the British monarchy.

Victoria Gives Way to Parliament

In the nineteenth century, step by cautious step, Britain edged towards representative democracy (see the sidebar, "The Houses of Parliament"). The electoral system was reformed and the *franchise* (right to vote) widened in 1832, 1867 and 1884. Women remained voteless (something Victoria approved of) until 1918. The balance of power in Britain's two-chamber Parliament swung firmly towards the House of Commons. Victoria's final prime minister, Lord Salisbury, was the last premier to sit in the House of Lords.

Complain though she might, Victoria was obliged to accept that the choice of prime minister was not always hers. She had to appoint a man – there were no women in Parliament – who commanded a majority in the House of Commons. That meant twice accepting Lord Palmerston, whom she hated because he took decisions on foreign policy without consulting her first. Even worse, she had to welcome the great Liberal statesman, William Gladstone, four times. She took spiteful revenge by never letting him sit in her presence.

THE HOUSES OF PARLIAMENT

Parliament is the British legislature. As in the US, it comprises two chambers: the House of Commons and the House of Lords:

- House of Commons: The Commons, which first met in 1341, comprises elected representatives of the people. Nowadays, the sovereign appoints the leader of the largest party or coalition of parties in the Commons as prime minister.

- House of Lords: Morphing from the medieval Royal Council, the modern Lords is a revising chamber, subordinate to the Commons. In it sit a few hereditary peers (lords), life peers (a position created in 1958) appointed by the prime minister, and senior clerics, mostly from the Church of England and excluding Catholics (because of the behaviour of the Catholic Stuarts, see Chapter 2).

With a nominal membership of 800+, the Lords is the world's second largest upper chamber after China's. There is almost universal agreement that it should be reformed, but no agreement on how to do so.

The monarch, still nominally head of the executive, no longer appears in Parliament except for its ceremonial opening (see Chapter 8), though theoretically they could do so if they wished.

Palmerstone and Gladstone sensed the mood of the British public better than Victoria ever did. 'We women,' she once mused, 'are not made for governing.' Not her, anyway.

Britain's New Empire

In many ways Victoria was extremely fortunate. She was born into a highly privileged position, she married a very capable and understanding husband, and she came to the throne at a time when Britain was at its wealthiest and most powerful.

REMEMBER

Victorians liked to say that the global pre-eminence enjoyed by Britain in the nineteenth century was due to some sort of innate talent or virtue. Most top nations engage in this sort of self-flattery. The truth is always more prosaic. The power of Victorian Britain stemmed from four sources.

The Industrial Revolution

For a number of complex reasons, Britain was the first state to industrialize. From being an essentially rural, agricultural nation in 1700, over the next 150 years it became an urban one. Manufacturing moved from homes and workshops to factories; railways and the telegraph transformed communications; banks flourished. In the 'workshop of the world', successful entrepreneurs and owners of natural resources made huge fortunes.

Political stability

Thanks to traditions of free speech and the compromise constitution set up in 1688–1689, the British political system was flexible enough to absorb the shocks and strains presented by the American and French Revolutions, and the angry discontent of the disenfranchised and underpaid working class. Without really realizing or even agreeing to it, the Victorian monarchy was part of this flexibility.

Lack of rivals

The countries of Europe were hampered by political unrest. Traditional monarchies were unwilling to relinquish power, and the people unable to seize it. As a consequence, rivals to British dominance – especially France and Russia – did not realize their potential.

Germany became a single entity as late as 1871. The US, riven by civil war, was only coming into its own as the century ended. India was under British control, and China was stuck in an inflexible past.

The acquisition of a large overseas empire

Most Victorians were immensely proud of their vast empire – the largest the world had ever seen – and the enormous fleet that kept open its links to the motherland.

By 1900, as well as scores of islands and enclaves, it embraced the broad land-masses of Canada, Australia and India. Large swathes of southern and eastern Africa had been added to the imperial map in the later nineteenth century.

From the lands of the empire came raw materials for British factories: sugar, cotton, tobacco, tea, coffee, wool, wood, and iron. Back the other way went British-manufactured goods, and all in British ships. Never had the old eighteenth-century song been sung with more gusto – 'Rule Britannia! Britannia rules the waves!'

Death, despair, and republicanism

1861 was, in a phrase made popular by her great-great-granddaughter Queen Elizabeth II, Victoria's *'annus horribilis'* ('horrible year'). She reacted to her mother's death in March with hysterical displays of grief. Some feared she had George III's malaise and was going mad. In November, she learned to her horror that her eldest son, Albert Edward, had been sleeping with an Irish actress. Just when she thought Hanoverian debauchery a thing of the past. . .

Then, on 14 December, the heaviest blow of all. Her beloved Albert, the rock on which she depended, passed away with his distraught wife and family at his bed-side. Victoria, never especially stable, plunged into a deep depression. She spoke of 'daily, nightly longing to die.' From then on, she dressed only in black.

Victoria withdrew from most public duties. She took herself off for months on end to the country retreats Albert had built at Balmoral in the Scottish Highlands and Osbourne House on the Isle of Wight (off the southern coast of England). This made life very difficult for ministers, who still felt obliged to consult regularly with her and get her approval on important matters, especially regarding foreign affairs.

The Queen's absences and dereliction of her duties were noticed by the nation at large. Republican Clubs sprouted up in many towns and cities, and the press crackled with anti-monarchial sentiment. When France cast off Emperor Napoleon III and became a republic in 1871, Victoria's critics called for Britain to do the same. 'The first Gate of Civilization – the Republican Gate – is ajar, and soon will be flung wide open,' wrote pamphleteer J. Morrison Davidson a few years later. 'Long live the Republic!'

That the republican gate was not flung wide was partly due to the influence of Prime Minister Benjamin Disraeli. Yet again, the monarchy was rescued by someone from outside the British Establishment. Novelist, dandy, and former independent radical, by the later 1860s the flamboyant politician was the most influential figure in the Conservative (formerly Tory) Party.

Disraeli, a Jewish bachelor outsider, won over the lonely, self-pitying Queen with an artful mix of flattery, cajolery and gossip. He offered to lighten the burdens of her office, and a genuine affection grew up between them. On occasion – contrary to the legend of her perpetual po-facedness – he even got her to smile.

REMEMBER

In 1876, and now prime minister, Disraeli pulled off his flamboyant masterpiece. His Imperial Titles Act declared Victoria to be Empress of India. At a dinner shortly afterwards, he rose to toast 'Your Imperial Majesty!'. Victoria was delighted. She was finally on a par with the Tsar of Russia, the Emperor of Germany, and the Emperor of Austria–Hungary. Her empire was bigger than theirs, too.

Celebrating Victoria's Jubilees

Fans of Queen Victoria point out that she dutifully played her role at formal occasions and during royal visits. She also exerted herself at times of crisis, being the largest single contributor to the Irish famine (1845–1852) relief fund: 5 percent of a single year's income from the state. She also supported the pioneering nurse Florence Nightingale during the Crimean War (1854–1856) and instituted the Victoria Cross for supreme gallantry. During the Anglo–Boer War (1899–1901), she sent the troops a tin of chocolate each, with a Happy New Year message.

None of this disguises the fact that she remained aloof from the great majority of her subjects. She neither understood nor cared about the needs of the working poor. She had little interest in the arts and remained suspicious of democracy. She was being booed in public even in 1887.

And yet, because she was old and dutiful and had learned not to meddle too openly in politics, Victoria gradually gained the affection of many of her subjects. In their hearts and minds, this dumpy, grumpy old woman had become the symbol of the nation of which they were so proud.

Golden Jubilee, 1887

As Victoria's fiftieth year on the throne approached, plans were made to celebrate her jubilee.

Little fuss was made at the jubilees of earlier monarchs such as Henry III (1266) and Edward III (1377). Because it fell during wartime, more was made of George III's Golden Jubilee, which was marked on 25 October 1809 with widespread festivities.

The Queen overcame initial reluctance to participate in two days of partying and pageantry. First came a dinner at Buckingham Palace for 50 kings, queens, princes and princesses, together with other dignitaries. The junketing went on the next day with processions, prayers, fireworks balls, and banquets. As would become traditional, she waved to the crowds from the balcony of Buckingham Palace.

Diamond Jubilee, 1897

By the time of her Diamond Jubilee, Victoria had been on the throne longer than any other British monarch. As previously, there were parades and parties. This time, with international tension rising, they had a distinctly jingoistic and imperialist feel to them.

Victoria was too old and frail to enjoy the celebrations very much.

The precedent had been set. People like to party, and – handled properly – royal jubilees are an excellent opportunity for them to let their hair down. Politicians like jubilees because they foster national unity, and sovereigns like them because they make people feel good about the monarchy – especially if it were to be an unprecedented Platinum Jubilee.

After Victoria

Victoria died at Osborne House, her retreat on the Isle of Wight, on 22 January 1901. There was a near-universal 'end of an era' feeling – surely the coincidence of her death and the birth of a new century was significant? Many were fearful of what the future held as her 1,100-pound, triple-layer, white-draped coffin was hauled through the silent London Streets. Among the mourners were her son, now King Edward VII, her grandson Kaiser William of Germany, and Archduke Franz Ferdinand of Austria, whose assassination 13 years later would spark World War I.

With hindsight, we understand that the air of foreboding at Victoria's state funeral was eerily prescient. At the time, others had more immediate worries. Was the new king up to the job?

Edward VII: A playboy king

Edward came with a reputation. *The Times* of London prudishly tut-tutted that he had been 'importuned by temptation in its most seductive forms.' The priggish criticism fell on deaf ears. Edward achieved in a decade (1901–1910) what had taken his mother six times as long – he gave his name to the age in which he lived: Edwardian.

The womanizing, heavy-drinking king was a snob – like most members of the upper class at that time – but his laid-back manner won the hearts of his people. Though opposed to radical causes, his interest in domestic politics was spasmodic – a useful fillip for constitutional monarchy. The 'Uncle of Europe' was related to 11 of Europe's royal families, too, and his affable manner helped foster Britain's international relations, notably with France and Russia.

George V: A dull king for a difficult time

When Edward died of a heart attack on 6 May 1910, the country – and the monarchy – was in the throes of a serious constitutional crisis. It was the sort of situation that can crop up when a country's constitution is not written down. With few rules set out in black and white, and no Supreme Court to decide the right course to follow, the British constitution had developed by evolution and adoption. The process was like that in the natural world, as expounded by Charles Darwin in his revolutionary *Origin of the Species* (1859).

As democracy expanded, the peers in the largely hereditary House of Lords wisely chose not to interfere too blatantly with laws coming from the House of Commons. Traditionally, they stayed well clear of financial legislation. Then came the Liberal government's 'People's Budget' of 1909. It imposed seven new taxes, including higher rates for the very wealthy and on 'unearned' income. Here was an arrow aimed straight at the heart of hereditary wealth and privilege – except for the monarchy, which did not pay taxes.

The Lords rejected the budget. 'Mend them or end them' roared the popular press. Edward VII had advised the Lords to give way. (One wonders whether Victoria would have been so sensible.) They refused. The government responded with a Parliament Bill limiting the Lords' powers. To ensure the Bill's passage through the Lords, Edward agreed to create as many new peers as necessary to give the Liberals a majority there. At this point, the King died of a heart attack.

George V held his father's position, the Lords backed down, and the Bill became law. Crisis over.

Britain had just witnessed the splendid irony of a monarch threatening to use his hereditary prerogative to thwart the hereditary powers of his peers. The message was clear: the monarchy would survive only if it adapted to the age of democracy.

It is easy to dismiss King George V (r. 1910–1936), Emperor of India, as a rather uninspiring, deeply conservative stamp-collector with little imagination or intellectual spark. Interestingly, his very ordinariness helped build up the idea of a non-attached constitutional monarchy rising above the turmoil of everyday troubles and strife. His relationship with the powerful Queen Mary (see Chapter 4) also offered an example of stable family life.

Four features of George's reign would be maintained by Elizabeth:

>> **Enjoying equine pursuits**, especially racing and hunting.

>> **Using the radio to speak to the nation**, first done in 1924. In 1932, George was persuaded to broadcast his first Christmas Message to the men and women of the United Kingdom and its fragile empire, ending, 'To all – to each – I wish a Happy Christmas. God Bless You!'.

>> **Making spectacular overseas tours**, the highlight being the Delhi Durbar of 1911. Following their coronation in Westminster Abbey, the King and Queen (also Emperor and Empress) sailed to India where important Indians – princes and others – paid tribute to them. A new Imperial Crown of India was made specially for the occasion. The ceremony did not win universal approval in India or back home.

>> **Realizing that the Crown carried a great weight of duty** that could not be shirked. As well as the customary round of official openings, launchings and visits, the conservative king gritted his teeth and stuck to his duty in political matters. As well as agreeing to support the Liberals in their fight with the Lords in 1910–1911, he twice reluctantly invited Ramsay Macdonald, leader of the Labour (socialist) Party to become his prime minister. Labour's ranks included many with republican sympathies.

George V was a heavy smoker, though he disapproved of women adopting the same habit. The debilitating effects of continual smoke inhalation seriously affected his health over the last ten years of his life and he frequently had to be taken around in a wheeled chair. It is believed that his death was hastened by injections of morphia and cocaine so that his passing could be announced in the morning rather than the evening newspapers. It is also thought that his last words were, 'God damn you!'.

Chapter **4**

The Birth of a Princess

This chapter looks at Elizabeth's mother and father – Elizabeth and Albert (Bertie) – their marriage and subsequent relationship, and the births of Elizabeth and her sister Margaret. You'll also find out about the princesses' early upbringing and education set against the background of Britain between the two World Wars.

Albert, Duke of York and his wife Elizabeth, Duchess of York, were the low-profile branch of the Windsor family tree. They came into the limelight only after Bertie's elder brother, Edward VIII, abdicated (see Chapter 5). Before that, the livelier echelons of high society regarded the Yorks as dreary country cousins.

The sort of people who thought like that belonged to the glittering, Gatsby-style social circle patronised by Bertie's brothers, Edward Prince of Wales (known in the family as David), Henry Duke of Gloucester, and George Duke of Kent. The favours of such people were brittle, their judgement poor.

TIP

In the long run, it was the prosaic Bertie and his loyal Elizabeth, not the charismatic Edward, who were the true servants – saviours even – of hereditary monarchy.

Bertie: The Stammering Second Son

The second son of the future George V and his wife Mary was born on 14 December 1895. As the date was the anniversary of Prince Albert's death, there could be no argument about his name, though it was soon abbreviated to 'Bertie' among family members.

TIP

In cruel modern parlance, Prince Albert Frederick Arthur George was a loser. His father could be a bully, his mother remote, his overshadowing elder brother cleverer and more charming. In contrast, poor Bertie was a dim, knock-kneed, blubbering wimp whose neuroses manifested themselves in fits of rage, a humiliating stammer, and constant gastric difficulties.

WARNING

From his teens onwards, he smoked heavily, a habit that played a significant role in his death at the age of 56. This is made clear in a gruesome episode of *The Crown*, where the King has a cancerous lung removed in a makeshift operating theatre inside Buckingham Palace.

After unsatisfactory tutoring at home, in 1907 Bertie was sent to Royal Naval College at Osborne, near the home his great-grandfather had built on the Isle of Wight. Released from the dead hand of parental authority, he covered his inadequacies by playing the fool before eventually passing out either (reports vary) 61st in a class of 67 or 68th in a class of 68.

Whatever his deficiencies as a sailor, Bertie apparently looked back on his days in the Royal Navy with affection. He served at sea during World War I and fought at Jutland, the conflict's only major naval conflict. In 1936, faced with the prospect of becoming king, he wailed 'I'm only a naval officer; it's the only thing I know.'

In 1919, Bertie went to Cambridge University to study a bit of history. After three terms, his father hoicked him out and gave him more 'useful' work attending to royal duties. While elder brother Edward, Prince of Wales, was sent to wave the royal flag overseas, Bertie, now Duke of York, was responsible for the UK.

At this point, his life suddenly took a dramatic turn for the better.

Elizabeth Bowes-Lyon: A Suitable Match

Nobody is quite sure where Lady Elizabeth Bowes-Lyon was born. Some say in her family's eighteenth-century home in Hertfordshire, others in their London residence, and others that she came into the world in a horse-drawn ambulance. The date, however, is clear: 4 August 1900. We know that because her father, Lord Glamis, with classic aristocratic disregard for bureaucratic formalities, failed to register the birth within the stipulated time. He was duly fined seven shillings and six pence.

TIP

Lady Elizabeth was undoubtedly posh. (*Posh*? How did that word originate? See the sidebar of the same name to find out.) After all, she was not just born in a castle, but one made famous by Shakespeare in *Macbeth*. Her family was also distantly related by marriage to the royal Stewarts (see Chapter 2). For all their titles and ancestry, however, the Bowes-Lyon dynasty was not super-rich.

Elizabeth spent her early years in Hertfordshire and London. Her nurse, a farmer's daughter named Clara White (whose nickname 'Allah' is, by modern standards, a masterpiece of political incorrectness), played the customary major role in her charge's upbringing. Elizabeth's education, at home and for periods in respectable schools, was unacademic, though she was well tutored in French. This has stood her in good stead. We are told that all her life she was able to read, hold conversations and give speeches in the language.

During World War I, Elizabeth worked in the makeshift hospital established in Glamis Castle, the family's ancestral home in Scotland. When her mother left, she virtually ran the place. Shortly after returning to London in 1919, where she was much sought-after by eligible young men, she met the stuttering, chain-smoking Bertie. What attracted him to the good-looking, competent young woman he met at balls and parties is not hard to guess. It is less easy to see what she saw in him, other than royalty. Perhaps her wartime experience had left her with an unconscious desire to assist damaged young men?

REMEMBER

Queen Victoria had proposed to her future husband, Prince Albert (see Chapter 3). That move made it clear from the outset who was in charge. But Bertie was frightened of proposing to Elizabeth. Wooing her was risky enough anyway – no leading member of the Royal Family had married a non-royal since James Duke of York, the future James II, married Anne Hyde in 1660. Rejection would only undermine Bertie's fragile self-confidence still further.

POSH

The British term 'posh' means belonging to (or seeming to belong to) the upper or upper-middle class. The word is supposed to come from the position of a person's cabin on the voyage to and from India. Sunlight made accommodation on the southern (right, or starboard) side of the vessel uncomfortably hot on the voyage out and equally unpleasant on the left (port) during the return voyage. The most expensive cabins, therefore, were on the **p**ort side for the journey **o**ut and the **s**tarboard side for the journey **h**ome. Accordingly, those who could afford them were labelled P-O-S-H.

In the end, Bertie screwed his courage to the sticking place and in 1921 asked Elizabeth to marry him. She wasn't surprised, but had her doubts and answered no. A second plea met with the same result. Finally, during a walk in winter woods in January 1923, she said yes. The couple were married by the Archbishop of Canterbury, Randall Davidson, in Westminster Abbey three months later.

The relationship between the ineffectual prince and his charming yet strong bride worked well. To him she remained 'the most wonderful woman in the world'. To her he remained a simple, hard-working, and devoted husband. Though his essential kindness was marred by angry outbursts ('gnashes'), marriage into the Royal Family was not without its benefits. Bertie could be amusing, too, and would always allow her one hand on the tiller.

The couple had a grand London house at 145 Piccadilly and a comfortable lodge in Windsor Great Park, the estate of the famous castle. They made well-received state visits to the Balkans in 1923, Northern Ireland in 1924, and East Africa in 1924–1925. Two years later, they boarded the battleship HMS *Renown* for a grand imperial tour that took in the Caribbean, Australia, and New Zealand.

WARNING

Before setting out, Bertie had begun treatment for his stammer from the Australian speech therapist Lionel Logue. The outcome was certainly not the triumph portrayed in the film *The King's Speech*, and newsreels continued to be binned if they revealed too much of Bertie's handicap, but his delivery (and self-confidence) did improve.

Princess Lilibet is Born

A miscarriage ended the Duchess of York's first pregnancy, and her second child was a breech birth. On 21 April 1926, after a 24-hour labour, Elizabeth Alexandra Mary Windsor was born by caesarean section at a Bowes-Lyon family home in London's Mayfair. Note the change in family name – Windsor; the sidebar, "A new name", examines the reasons for this.

TECHNICAL
STUFF

James II's high-handed, pro-Catholic policies had united the aristocracy opposition (read more about this in Chapter 2). The event that finally tipped the scales against him was the birth of a male heir in June 1688. The spectre of an endless line of tyrannical Catholic kings arose. To counter it, a rumour spread that the baby was not the Queen's, but had been introduced into her bed in a warming pan. From then until the birth of Princess Margaret in 1930, the home secretary was obliged to attend every royal birth (actually turning up a few moments after) to confirm that the new arrival was not a warming-pan imposter.

A NEW NAME

How come Edward VII's family name was Saxe–Coburg–Gotha, whereas the baby Elizabeth was a Windsor? The answer lies in a decree issued by George V on 19 June 1917. The Royal Family's strong links with Germany (see Chapters 2 and 3) looked rather embarrassing when Britain and Germany went to war in 1914. At a time when even dachshund dogs were reportedly stoned in the street for their 'Hunnish' (German) heritage, the King's Saxe–Coburg–Gotha surname was an unpatriotic liability. Never a man to move fast, George finally ordered his family to change their name to Windsor, evoking an ancient English fortress, and banned his family from using any Germanic titles or surnames.

When Princess Elizabeth was born, Bertie wrote anxiously to his father, 'there has been no one of that name in your family for a long time.' Like Queen Elizabeth I (see Chapter 2), the future Elizabeth II was born in troubled times. See the sidebar, "Britain between the wars" for why this was.

REMEMBER

Even at this moment of 'tremendous joy', Bertie remained pathetically anxious in his correspondence with his parents. Would they 'sooner have had [a] grandson'? he asked. No, they were quite happy with a granddaughter. After all, she was only third in line to the succession after her uncle Edward and her father. There was a good chance that a boy would come along to overtake her.

BRITAIN BETWEEN THE WARS

TECHNICAL STUFF

The interwar years were difficult for Britain. The country's Victorian pre-eminence had faded fast, hastened by the dispiriting and debilitating experience of World War I. The US was now the world's leading economic power. The British Empire, once a source of pride, was starting to be more of an embarrassment than a boon. If Southern Ireland, a state on Britain's very doorstep, could successfully bid for independence, what hope had the British of hanging on to places like India?

There was unease at home, too. The Labour Party, strongly allied to the trade union movement, was replacing the Liberals as the party most likely to assist the poor and underprivileged. Industrial relations, soured by class differences, were rock bottom.

Four days after the birth of the future Elizabeth II, a strike by coal miners prompted the Conservative government to declare a state of emergency. Nine days later, the country was stricken by the *General Strike* (when a significant proportion of the work force, across a range of occupations, went on strike at the same time).

Baby Betty steals the limelight

The birth of Princess Elizabeth brought a cheer to royalist hearts made heavy by the bitterness of the General Strike (see the sidebar, "Britain between the wars") and talk of a socialist revolution. Speculation about the character and antics of the attractive little girl filled the press and popular magazines in the UK and overseas. In Newfoundland, her image even appeared on a postage stamp. The Australians were particularly fascinated by the distant child they dubbed 'Betty'.

TIP

At home, Elizabeth was known by the touching soubriquet 'Lilibet', derived from her early inability to pronounce her own name. The name assumed greater formality in June 2021, when Prince Harry, Duke of Sussex, and Meghan, Duchess of Sussex, named their Californian-born daughter Lilibet Diana Mountbatten-Windsor (see Chapter 29). What the Queen thought of this appropriation of her family nickname is not (yet) known, though rumours suggest it did not meet with universal approval.

Grandma knows best

Impressions of Elizabeth's infancy vary. Some descriptions depict her early life as carefree and at times idyllic. Other more critical biographers say she led a solitary, lonely childhood. The truth may lie somewhere between the two.

TIP

Whichever line one favours, Elizabeth's childhood was certainly happier than that of Victoria and the four men who succeeded her. One obvious reason was her status as heir presumptive, not heir apparent. Neither she nor those around her were burdened by the looming certainty of an eventual coronation. A second reason was her parents' wish for their children to have as normal a childhood as possible.

In consequence, Elizabeth grew up like any other little princess. Unfortunately, that did not make her upbringing normal – at no stage is the life of any princess 'normal'.

There were three predominant influences on the young Elizabeth:

>> **Her parents.** The Duchess of York, whose own early years had been filled with fresh air and fun, was more influential than her husband. When not away on royal duties, she did her best to oversee a loving home life. She read to her daughter at bedtime and taught her to read when she was older. Her husband's heart was in the right place, but upbringing had equipped him with few of the skills and little of the understanding needed to raise a child, especially a female. His temper tantrums didn't help, either.

>> **Her nanny and nursery maids.** The Duchess's own nanny, 'Allah' Knight, was already in the Yorks' employment. As a reward for her long service, she was made an honorary 'Mrs' though she never married.

She was joined in the nursery by the under-nurse Margaret ('Bobo') MacDonald (see Chapter 8) and her sister Ruby, the nursemaid. Bobo would remain in royal service for 67 years, becoming one of the grown-up Elizabeth's closest confidantes.

The young Elizabeth saw more of this devoted trio than of her mother. It was they who dealt with the daily routine of baths, cleaning teeth, getting dressed and undressed, and the messy business of nappies and toilet training. Those chores were not the sort expected of a duchess.

>> **Her grandmother.** Queen Mary, sternness personified with her own children, melted before the little Elizabeth. She proudly displayed her at tea parties, and when the Duke and Duchess (prompted by Mary) went on their Imperial Tour, they left their baby under grandma's supervision in Buckingham Palace. Elizabeth saw her three times a day, something that did not happen with Mary's own children.

Mary's attention verged on spoiling, and apparently led to Elizabeth getting rather full of herself. We are told, for example, that once, when the Lord Chamberlain gave her a cheery 'Good morning, little lady!' she snapped back, 'I'm not a little lady. I'm Princess Elizabeth.' Queen Mary made sure she was duly chastised.

REMEMBER

From her grandparents as well as her parents, Elizabeth saw how royalty behaved. She was photographed with the king and queen, and was presented on the balcony of Buckingham Palace with them. In 1930, Queen Mary organised a propaganda film that showed the Duke and Duchess of York and their two children as the embodiment of ideal family life. From her grandmother as much as anyone, Elizabeth gained an understanding of the importance of the façade that screened hereditary monarchy from the outside world.

What sort of child was emerging beneath the bustle of nursery staff, the fawning of Queen Mary, and the sincere yet sometimes remote affection of her parents?

TIP

Elizabeth inherited a quick temper from her male ancestors, but unlike them she learned at an early age to control it. In fact, control and order soon became the watchwords of this serious-minded little girl.

She folded her clothes, she set out her toy horses and soldiers in rows, and at the age of three she helped clean her room with her own dustpan and brush. Meticulous, careful, self-disciplined – traits that would remain with her for the rest of her life. They may have been a bit strange, dull even, in a young girl. But for a future constitutional monarch, a figurehead Head of State, they were ideal.

A sister is born

Elizabeth's sister, Princess Margaret Rose Windsor, was born on 21 August 1930 (also by caesarean section). Almost from the outset it was clear that her personality was very different from that of her elder sister. The Duke adored his second daughter's sparkle and sense of fun – all so un-Windsor-ish!

Where Elizabeth was steady, Margaret was bouncy one moment, sulky the next. Margaret was an actress, Elizabeth was not. From a young age, Margaret was keen on her 'toilettes' while Elizabeth 'never cared a fig' about what she wore. When the two fought (yes, even royal kids have their spats), we are told that Elizabeth punched and Margaret bit. Such conflict was rare, and despite their contrasting temperaments, the sisters' relationship grew into one of mutual love and affection.

Educating a princess

From an academic perspective, the education given to the two princesses was woefully inadequate (see Chapter 6). *The Crown* TV series brought this out rather cruelly when the young queen admitted to having no formal qualifications at all. This was not surprising. She never went to school and met few other children. Her syllabus was dictated by Queen Mary. It was delivered by her nanny, Marion Crawford ('Crawfie'), who was given the job before she herself had finished her education.

To be fair to Elizabeth's parents and Crawfie, no one crossed Queen Mary. If she saw no point in a girl learning science, then there was no science. And when she demanded Elizabeth be taught more history, arithmetic had to make way. The nature of that history was also of the Queen's dictation. It was about fact, not research, sifting through evidence, or reaching of balanced conclusions. And 'fact' meant genealogy, specifically the reigns of the kings and queens of England. They were the pegs, Crawfie explained on behalf of her instructress, on which all English history hung.

With the history went grammar, poetry, geography, literature, and (at George V's insistence) writing. Elizabeth read widely, embracing a range of classics that included Stevenson and Dickens. A tutor gave her fluency in French, and from a children's newspaper and then *The Times*, she kept up with current affairs.

When the Duchess of York gave Crawfie the nanny job, she explained, 'we want our children to have a happy childhood which they can always look back on.' So it was. Between the lessons came hours of games and fun, starting in their parents' room first thing in the morning. Elizabeth learned to ride a horse before she learned to read.

Yes, she had a happy time. But perhaps later in life there were moments when she wished it had been something more than just happy. She might, for a start, have gone to school and learned a bit more about the people who would one day be asked to sing 'God save the Queen!'

Chapter **5**

Edward VIII: The King Who Abdicated

Hereditary monarchy is a delicate flower. One day it blooms with a beauty that is everywhere admired, the next it droops and withers, its glory quite gone.

As the nine-year old Princess Elizabeth was taking in grandma's history syllabus and playing with her sister in the garden (see Chapter 4), her future was being shaped by events elsewhere. Over these, neither she nor her parents had any control. George V died in January 1936 and the Crown passed to his eldest son. The prospect had filled the dying man with apprehension.

'After I am dead,' the king reportedly told Prime Minister Baldwin, 'the boy will ruin himself in 12 months.' A grumpy stick-in-the-mud he might have been, but George was proved correct. His solution proved correct, too: 'I pray to God . . . that nothing will come between Bertie and Lilibet and the throne.'

In this chapter, we see this borne out in the short, unfortunate reign of Elizabeth's uncle, Edward VIII.

Edward Prince of Wales

George V's eldest son was born on 23 June 1894 – Queen Victoria held him in her arms (briefly). He was christened Edward, Albert, Christian, George, Andrew, Patrick, David. The first two names were the king's father and grandfather. The third reflected the king's faith – he would criticize Lilibet's parents for not holding regular family prayers. The last four names were the patron saints of the four countries of the United Kingdom: (St George – England, St Andrew – Scotland, St Patrick – Ireland, St David – Wales). At home, the boy was known as David.

Having gone heavy on his son's names, George went light on his education. Edward was brighter than younger brother Bertie but received little training or instruction that might allow him to make use of his potential. His tutor, a former schoolmaster, offered a sporting curriculum that left his charges, in the words of one commentator, ill-read 'intellectual pygmies'.

TIP

In later life, Edward decided he had felt unloved by his parents. This convinced him not to have children of his own. King George and Queen Mary may have cherished their pretty boy David in their tight-laced manner, but they were not good at showing it. When he was 13, they packed him off to naval college. Here he was bullied (as Bertie had been) and humiliated with the nickname 'Sardine'. His father thought this would, in the popular phrase, 'toughen him up'. It didn't. The young man remained as he always had been: charming, restless, and deeply insecure. From an early age Edward felt himself to be, in his own words, 'a misfit'.

The 1909 budget debacle (see Chapter 3) had drawn unfavourable attention to the anomaly of an hereditary Head of State in a democratic country. Accordingly, the newly crowned George V looked around for something to polish up the monarchy's image. The Palace came up with a colourful PR stunt. Perhaps prompted by his wife's knowledge of royal trivia, they decided that a ceremonial investiture of Prince Edward as Prince of Wales would do the trick. It would invoke centuries of tradition on the side of the Establishment and provide a fine photo opportunity.

Just one snag: when all was ready, the central actor refused to go on stage. The pageant required Edward to dress up in a costume that would have looked silly even in a poor school production of a Shakespeare history play, and he refused. He couldn't face the teasing he'd receive from his contemporaries. In the end, the stronger personality prevailed. In July 1911, Edward submitted to his father's pressure and went ahead with the ceremony wearing a ridiculous-looking tin-pot crown. It didn't do his fragile self-esteem much good.

A Populist Prince

After a fruitless time at Magdalen College, Oxford, when war broke out in 1914 Edward was allocated to the army's prestigious Grenadier Guards. It was a token posting – his commanders couldn't possibly allow him to go to the front line in case he was killed or, worse still, captured. Instead, he spent his time doing what members of the Royal Family were expected to do – visiting, inspecting, and encouraging.

TIP

Here, at last, was something Edward was very good at. His charm and relaxed, easy manner won him friends wherever he went. He was the first top royal in modern times to make a point of shaking hands with those he met, whatever their social class. His work and his 'quasi-egalitarian' manner of going about it also brought him into contact with a far broader range of people than his immediate predecessors.

Edward's other education

During the war, Edward gained experience in other matters. In France and back in London, he developed a taste for high society. His boyish good looks and genial manner surprised and delighted those with a taste for fast cars, dancing, drinking, drugs, adultery, and (if rumours are to be believed) more.

His puritanical parents were horrified. Unable to rein in the wayward Prince, they fought to maintain the façade of normal family life – hence Queen Mary's desire to cosset young Lilibet, and make public display of their own relatively calm relationship.

The foreign press ran gossipy stories about what was going on, but the British papers, loyal to the monarchy, kept quiet. The nearest anyone dared go, in public at least, was to titivate by implication. 'I've Danced with a Man Who's Danced with a Girl Who's Danced with the Prince of Wales,' ran the lyrics of Herbert Farjeon's hit song of 1927.

REMEMBER

The dashing Prince of Wales's mix of populism and party-going continued throughout the 1920s. He visited charities and working men's clubs, showing genuine concern for the tough lives of ordinary people. The Establishment (see the nearby sidebar to find out who these people were) grew alarmed that he was getting too political: open sympathy for the poor and unemployed suggested criticism of the system that made them so.

Edward ignored these warnings. He was flattered by his experiences and the personal approval they brought, and came to believe, without thinking it through carefully or discussing the matter with the Establishment, that his mission was to introduce a new, less aloof style of monarchy.

THE ESTABLISHMENT

The British *Establishment* is a unique mix of ancient institutions and hereditary privilege, headed by the monarchy. The former includes the Church of England, a handful of leading universities, the public schools, the City of London, top civil servants, the armed forces, the law, and other sought-after professions. It maintains itself through adherence to time-honoured traditions and systems, and by carefully absorbing new talent into its ranks.

An attempt to get Edward out of the way by sending him on overseas tours served only to reinforce his fragile narcissism. The Americans adored the free-speaking Prince. The *Dominions* (self-governing colonies), always instinctively loyal, were delighted to meet a member of Britain's notoriously stuffy Royal Family who was at ease in their more relaxed societies. He even went down well in ultra-conservative Japan.

The reign of Edward VIII, he dreamed, would herald the birth of a brave new world. In fact, it did the opposite. Edward's failure succeeded only in entrenching the old ways, thereby making reform of the monarchy more difficult.

A trial run

In 1928–1929, George V fell seriously ill and was thought likely to die. This gave Edward an opportunity to practise being king. As acting Head of State, he took over many of his father's duties and saw state papers normally reserved for the eyes only of monarch and cabinet. The experience confirmed the Establishment's worst fears. The Prince did not change his hedonistic ways and paid only scant attention to official documents. Worse still, some feared that his talkativeness and poor choice of associates made him a security risk.

The Duke and Duchess of York understood what was going on and may have understood its implications, but they wisely shielded it from little Lilibet. She would decide what it all meant when she grew up.

Enter Wallis Simpson

As outlined in Chapter 1, all monarchs were expected to marry. Hereditary monarchy depended on it – without legitimate heirs, the institution collapses. Moreover, to remove uncertainty and give time to prepare the next generation for the task ahead, members of the Royal Family traditionally married young. Victoria married at the age of 20, her son Edward at 21, and his son George at 28. In 1934, when the Prince of Wales celebrated his thirtieth birthday, he was not even engaged and showed no signs of wishing to be so. Tongues started to wag.

WALLIS SIMPSON

Bessie Wallis Warfield was born in a hotel in Blue Ridge Summit, Pennsylvania, on 19 June 1896. Well-educated and bright, in 1916 she married the boozy aviator Earl Winfield Spencer Jr. She travelled abroad before divorcing in 1927.

By this time, she was in an affair with Ernest Simpson, an Anglo-American businessman and former British army officer. The couple married in Chelsea, London, in 1928.

Wallis first met Edward Prince of Wales at a party given by Lady Thelma Furness, the sister of one of Wallis's friends. At the time, Lady Thelma was herself in a relationship with the Prince.

Well might they have done. Among his friends and in the foreign press, Edward's many affairs were now well known. Some were no more than passing flings, others were deeper, longer-lasting relationships.

His most enduring was with Freda Dudley Ward, a name familiar to fans of the TV shows *Downton Abbey* and *Edward and Mrs Simpson*. The Prince was never fully faithful during the 22-year, on–off affair (1918–1934), but it finally ended when Freda was supplanted by the woman whose legendary charms torpedoed the Prince below the water line and sank him: Wallis Simpson (you can read more about her background in the sidebar, "Wallis Simpson").

The couple met in January 1931. Over the next two years, Edward came to see that she was the woman he had been searching for all his life. She was not sexy, but immensely attractive in a vivacious way. He liked her angular, almost school-ma'amly appearance that gave the impression of someone who might scold him for his all too obvious failings. Wallis's attitude to the relationship was perhaps more cerebral. Whatever went on between the youth whom gay men found attractive and the lean woman swooned over by lesbians, by 1934 they were lovers – on one occasion Edward even managed to sneak his paramour into Buckingham Palace. Queen Mary was asleep.

Accession and Abdication

George V died on 21 January 1936. So began the shortest reign of a British monarch – 327 days – since Edward V (see Chapter 3). As George's coffin was being carried into Westminster Hall to lie in state, the Maltese cross on the top of the imperial crown fell off and tumbled into the gutter. 'Christ!' the new king was heard to mutter, 'What's going to happen next?'

Precisely.

Edward VIII officially took over his father's court and Buckingham Palace secretariat and set up an alternative HQ in Fort Belvedere, a converted folly (appropriate, eh?) in Windsor Great Park. His chief confidants were Wallis and two mates (buddies): 'G' and 'Fruity'. Fruity liaised between the Fort and the Palace.

Once official mourning was done, Edward hosted semi-formal dinners. At first, the guest list included 'Mr and Mrs Simpson', then just 'Mrs Simpson'. She sparkled, she charmed – and she spat. A prime target was the York household of Bertie and his 'fat' (Wallis's word) wife. She saw their middle-class appeal as a threat to her own more flamboyant version.

On it went into the summer of 1936. Edward remained popular at public engagements, chatting, sympathizing, and shaking hands as before. Wallis was never far away, the lady literally in waiting. Out of the public eye, the king deliberately spoke German and expressed 'warm sympathy' for the land of his ancestors (see the sidebar, "Edward and the Nazis"). The widowed Queen Mary, Prime Minister Baldwin, and the King's Private Secretary were all exasperated – where was it all heading? Archbishop of Canterbury Cosmo Lang, of a strict Scottish Presbyterian background, sat frowning in the background.

In July, Wallis sued her husband for divorce, citing his adultery. During August and September, she and Edward openly holidayed together on a luxury yacht in the Mediterranean. When he returned to London, his affair was the talk of the town (but not yet the British press). Who was this woman? Was he going to marry her? Was it true she was American *and* divorced?

EDWARD AND THE NAZIS

Edward Prince of Wales was proud of his family's German heritage and showed early approval of Hitler's policies after he had come to power in 1933. When these pro-Nazi sympathies persisted, Edward became a security risk. Even as king, he was checked by MI5, Britain's domestic security service.

Suspicions rose still further when, after his abdication and against the express advice of the British government, Edward and his wife Wallis were much feted during a visit to Germany as guests of the Nazi regime.

On the outbreak of war in 1939, the couple moved to neutral Lisbon, Portugal, from where they maintained their contacts with the Nazis. Finally, in 1940, Churchill made Edward Governor of the Bahamas to get him out of harm's way.

All would soon be revealed.

REMEMBER

Why so much about Edward VIII in a book about his niece? Because his reign and abdication had a massive effect on her. It helps explain her:

>> determination never to abdicate

>> devotion to the memory of her mother and father

>> unwillingness to allow too much light into the workings of the monarchy

>> reluctance to modernise the institution she inherited

>> suspicion of divorce and divorcees

>> dislike of those who make a show of their emotions

>> steadfastness in the face of trials and tribulations

>> conviction that duty comes before everything else.

The dramatic end of Edward's reign can be seen as a play in three acts, through October to December 1936. Let's look at what happened.

Act I: October 1936

Here's the lowdown on what happened in October:

>> Edward rents a house for Wallis in Regent's Park, London. He has probably decided that they will marry.

>> Cinema audiences hiss when the national anthem – 'God Save the King!' – is played before a show.

>> On 20th October, Prime Minister (PM) Baldwin warns the king to behave more appropriately and dissuade Wallis from the divorce proceedings against her husband.

>> On 27th October, the Simpsons' divorce case is heard at Ipswich, Suffolk. A decree nisi is awarded (see the nearby sidebar for the meaning of this). The king says his friend's divorce is a 'private matter'.

DECREE NISI

A *decree nisi* is a preliminary court pronouncement in a divorce case. It states (i) all legal and procedural requirements have been met and (ii) there is no reason why the divorce should not be granted – *unless* (that's what 'nisi' means) circumstances change. A *decree absolute*, confirming the divorce, follows after a specified time.

Act II: November 1936

By November the situation was getting worse:

» On 16th November, Edward tells the PM that he intends to marry Wallis. The PM explains that for her to be queen, the marriage would have to be conducted according to the rites of the Church of England, of which the king is head. But the Church did not accept the remarriage of divorcees (such as Wallis). Moreover, the PM goes on, the press, Parliament and the Dominions would not accept Wallis as queen. Okay, replies Edward, then I will abdicate. Impasse.

» On 18th–19th November, fuel is thrown on the fire: Edward's sympathy for discontented steelworkers in south Wales is interpreted as a criticism of the government.

TIP

Throughout the crisis, evidence suggests the working class supported the king while the Establishment and middle classes found him an embarrassment. A similar situation, in reverse, would occur during the Charles–Diana tragedy (see Chapter 16).

» On 25th November, Edward tells the PM he's okay with morganatic marriage with Wallis as Duchess of Cornwall (fast-forward 69 years: the same title is given to Camilla Parker-Bowles on her marriage to Prince Charles). The PM says the morganatic idea will not wash with the Dominions or the public. (See the sidebar, "Morganatic marriage".)

Wallis accepts the morganatic marriage idea. She even agrees to being the king's official mistress – as long as he doesn't have an arranged marriage with someone else.

» On 27th November, the cabinet and the Dominions reject the idea of a morganatic marriage. Some suggest the government was using the marriage question to lever Edward off the throne because of his un-royal lifestyle and political activity.

MORGANATIC MARRIAGE

A form of marriage between a couple of different social rank. The lower-ranked party foregoes all claim to the rights and privileges of their partner. Traditionally, such marriages were between an aristocratic or royal man and a 'commoner' (in this sense, someone who was not a member of the hereditary upper class). The wives of Princes Charles, William and Harry are commoners.

Act III: December 1936

December saw the final act, and the curtain fell on Edward's reign:

>> On 2nd December, the PM presents Edward with three choices:

- finish with Wallis

- marry her, in which case the government would resign

- abdicate.

>> On 3rd December, the British press spills the story, criticising Wallis and the marriage idea. She goes to France, saying she's taking herself out of the king's life.

The cabinet blocks the king's proposed broadcast about his marriage. Churchill is shouted out of the House of Commons for urging a delay.

>> On 5th December, Edward bows to pressure and decides to abdicate.

>> On 10th December, Edward signs an official Instrument of Abdication in the presence of his brothers Albert Duke of York (the future George VI), Henry Duke of Gloucester, and George Duke of Kent.

>> On 11th December, in his last act as king, Edward signs the Act of Parliament setting out his abdication in law.

>> And finally, that evening, Edward makes his famous broadcast, which Churchill helped to write:

You must believe me when I tell you that I have found it impossible to carry the heavy burden of responsibility and to discharge my duties as King as I would wish to do without the help and support of the woman I love.

Edward VIII, before he had even been crowned, voluntarily abdicated – officially and permanently surrendering his position as king and emperor. The effects on his family were momentous. Bertie became king, calling himself George VI to provide continuity with his father's reign. His ten-year-old daughter Lilibet became heir to the throne.

Chapter **6**

Preparing for the Throne

This chapter traces the story of Elizabeth and her family from the time her father became king in December 1936 to when she succeeded him 16 years later. This time of dramatic challenge and change had a considerable impact on Elizabeth, not least in making her determined to maintain the Royal Family as a living link with a more stable past.

You'll also find out about how the Royal Family served in and survived World War II, and how twentieth-century monarchs had to find ways to work alongside the political leaders of their day.

Bertie Steps up to the Plate

TIP

The abdication of Edward VIII (see Chapter 5) struck the Royal Family hard. On realising what it meant, we are told that the Duke of York, now King George VI, 'sobbed like a child' before his mother. We do not know its immediate effect on his ten-year-old daughter Elizabeth. Though her parents continued a well-meaning policy of sheltering their children from the harsh realities of what lay ahead, certain changes could not be avoided.

For a start, the new king's daughters had to curtsey before him. Lilibet herself was also seen in a new light. To Margaret she was no longer an elder sister; she was *the* elder sister who would one day inherit all the glory. To the servants in daily attendance – Crawfie, Allah, and Bobo, introduced in Chapter 4 – she was doubly precious. To visitors at Buckingham Palace and Windsor Castle she was the future queen, a figure to be viewed with a mix of respect and fascination.

REMEMBER

Overnight, Elizabeth had become very special. The change in status might have made her conceited, obnoxious even. But her careful upbringing and strong personality ensured it was the stoic traits inherited from her father and grandfather that prevailed, not the bonhomie of her disgraced uncle.

In some ways the new king, George VI (known by his family as Bertie – see Chapter 4), was a lucky man. He was

>> everything his brother was not: methodical, dutiful, hardworking.

>> blessed with a popular and competent wife, and two attractive children, at a time when the Royal Family was being held up as a model of middle-class propriety (see Chapters 4 and 20).

>> supported by two able private secretaries (see Chapter 9), each as conservative as himself on matters domestic.

>> on the throne during a successful war, when his steadfast qualities were seen at their best.

Invariably guided by his wife and private secretary Sir Alexander Hardinge, George took up the reins of kingship with surprising speed. Hardinge, startled at his new master's ignorance, undertook to oversee the bulk of the King's public actions and pronouncements.

Interestingly, because of his lack of confidence when speaking in public, George let lapse his grandfather's tradition of making a Christmas broadcast. He took it up again in 1939 when the country was at war.

TIP

The importance of his wife Queen Elizabeth (Elizabeth II's mother) in George VI's reign is illustrated by two unusual developments:

>> At the coronation on 12 May 1937, the King's and Queen's thrones were set side by side rather than with his above hers. Elizabeth II did not give similar parity to Philip at her coronation (see Chapter 7).

>> In 1943, the Queen was made a councillor of state, empowering her to deputise for her husband if necessary. She was the first consort to be so honoured.

Queen Elizabeth's hand was also noticeable in George's relations with his brother Edward, now Duke of Windsor. Three things soured the already strained relationship:

- » The Duke did not come clean about his wealth when arrangements were made for his maintenance.

- » His demand that Wallis be given the title of Her Royal Highness was rejected. Elizabeth (the future Queen Mother) may, understandably, have had a hand in this.

- » The Duke and Duchess's over-friendly visit to Nazi Germany in 1937 was viewed with distaste in England. Elizabeth was more sensitive to the inappropriateness of her brother-in-law's behaviour than her husband.

Peeking out from behind the glass curtain

With her parents now wrapped up in affairs of state and royal duties, how was young Lilibet getting on? Three things stand out in the years 1937–1938.

Remaining isolated from the world

Nanny Crawford ('Crawfie') spoke of a 'glass curtain' drawn between the world of the Palace and the world outside. The phrase accurately describes the environment in which Princesses Elizabeth and Margaret were raised. Always the centre of public interest, they never met anyone from the public. The only people with whom they came into meaningful contact were servants and their families, and members of the upper-class invited to formal court occasions.

Elizabeth was undoubtedly sheltered from the sort of bullying that would be meted out to her son Charles when he was thrust into 'normal' teenage life (see Chapter 14). That does not necessarily mean her extreme isolation was the best preparation for the path ahead.

While bridesmaid at the wedding of her Uncle George, Duke of Kent, in 1934, had she heard rumours of his louche lifestyle, his bisexuality, and his drug-taking? Almost certainly not. Instead, she had played innocent games with her sister and nanny in the Palace grounds, and joined the Palace Guide (a specially formed group of Girl Guides made up of the princesses and the daughters of palace staff). She once went to the seaside at Eastbourne, and every summer she romped in the glens above Balmoral.

There were formal garden parties at the Palace. Occasionally, she was allowed to attend a formal ball in a frock. And that, until the outbreak of war, was that.

Idyllic, maybe. But unsettlingly so for what lay ahead.

An unchanged upbringing

King George was immensely proud of his Lilibet. In her, perhaps, he saw his own strengths without his weaknesses (now she had her temper under control). He dressed her in a special little coronet for his coronation and tried discussing serious matters with her. She may have shared his attitude towards appeasement: she cried when she heard of Chamberlain's resignation in 1940.

At the age of 13, Elizabeth was escorted by Crawfie twice a week to the study of Henry Marten, the Lower Master at nearby Eton College (Britain's leading private boarding school for boys). One of the leading history teachers of his day, he introduced the patient Elizabeth to some of the more intricate details of modern history.

WARNING

What the innocent teenage girl really made of the eccentric, crusty old bachelor we don't know, but the initial meeting between them made an amusing incident in Netflix's *The Crown*.

Elizabeth, Crawfie reckoned, 'was far more strictly disciplined than Margaret ever was.' The effect of this 'very high standard' demanded of her is hard to judge, though it probably reinforced a natural desire to do the right thing. At one stage – when she was getting out of bed several times a night to make sure that her shoes were aligned correctly – it came close to an obsession.

Becoming a very serious-minded woman

At her parents' coronation, Elizabeth kept a sharp eye on her younger sister, nudging her when she 'played with her prayer book too loudly.' The heir to the throne, 11 at the time, already displayed a strong sense of propriety. We witness something similar two years later: 'I don't think we should talk about battles and things in front of Margaret,' she told Crawfie on hearing that war had been declared. 'We don't want to upset her.' Kindness, certainly, but also the mark of someone who was already thinking like an adult.

Building up to war

TECHNICAL
STUFF

Initially, George was an enthusiastic supporter of *appeasing* the aggressive demands of Nazi Germany (see the sidebar, "Appeasing the Nazis"). In 1938, he even suggested writing a personal letter to Hitler, 'as one ex-serviceman to another'. At the insistence of Foreign Secretary Anthony Eden, the letter was never sent.

APPEASING THE NAZIS

A foreign policy of appeasement means avoiding conflict by making concessions to an aggressor. Before 1939, it was the favoured policy of Prime Minister Chamberlain and King George VI towards fascist Italy and Germany. This can be explained by:

- a determination to avoid the horrors of World War I.
- the belief that Germany had been harshly treated after World War I.
- a need to re-arm before going to war.
- the hope that Hitler's Germany would act as a buffer against communist USSR.
- a naïve trust in Hitler's and Mussolini's promises to end aggressive action.
- the knowledge that Britain could do little militarily to influence events in eastern Europe.

The failure of appeasement had a significant impact on American foreign policy in the post-war world, helping to explain US engagement in a number of wars against authoritarian regimes.

When Chamberlain returned home from meeting Hitler in Munich in September 1938, he declared that he brought 'peace in our time'. He stood with a delighted George VI on the balcony of Buckingham Palace, taking in the applause of the crowd.

Several Tory grandees, including Winston Churchill and Foreign Secretary Lord Halifax, were more sanguine. The King's desire to decorate Chamberlain was deemed premature – wisely, as it turned out. Hitler soon resumed his aggressive expansion. When Europe went to war in September 1939, Chamberlain's policy of appeasement was scorned as an embarrassing failure.

REMEMBER

We mustn't be too hard on George. In July 1938 he and Queen Elizabeth had made their first state visit. The destination was Paris, capital of France and Britain's key ally in the arm wrestle with the fascist regimes of Italy and Germany. The visit was a great success, with the Queen's white dresses by designer Norman Hartnell winning strong approval from the fashion-conscious French.

By the spring of 1939, George realized appeasement had failed. War loomed. When it came, Britain would need all the allies it could muster. The consequence was a state visit to Canada in May and June 1939. The tour was arranged by Lord Tweedsmuir, the Scottish novelist John Buchan (of *The Thirty-Nine Steps* fame), now governor-general of Canada. It was adjusted at the last minute to include a six-day detour into the United States for a person-to-person meeting with President Roosevelt and his wife.

Once again, the diplomatic charms of Queen Elizabeth (USA's Woman of the Year, 1939, no less!) helped counterbalance her husband's dullness, and both visits were deemed a success. While Canada joined World War II in September 1939, however, the USA stayed out. Nevertheless, in 1940 Roosevelt engineered destroyers-for-bases and Lend-Lease agreements to help Britain in its struggle.

Choosing a premier

The choice of prime minister is theoretically the sovereign's. In practice, the choice is made for them. They simply have to send for the leader of the party commanding the largest number of seats in the House of Commons and invite them to form a government. The buck stops with the political parties, not the monarch.

Today, Britain's political parties choose their leaders not at conventions, as in the US, but by complex and sometimes tortuous balloting. Each party does this in its own way. During the reign of George VI and into Elizabeth's, the Conservative Party had no ballot arrangement. Instead, the party leader was said to 'emerge' like Venus from the sea in a scallop shell.

As you can imagine, this antediluvian 'emerging' process risked drawing the monarch into the political fray. Since Elizabeth II would become thus entangled in 1963 (see Chapter 12), let's see how her father and grandfather (her guides and mentors) handled the problem.

George V's wartime quandary

In May 1915, during World War I, the political parties had come together to form a coalition government under the Liberal leader, Herbert Asquith. By late 1916, news from the battlefield was not good. On 5 December 1916, under fire from all sides for his handling of war, Asquith resigned. To King George this was a 'great blow' that would 'buck up the Germans'. He needed to act fast.

Not easy. In an unprecedented situation, George had no compass to steer by. Doing what he believed correct, he asked the Canadian-born Conservative Andrew Bonar Law, leader of the largest party in the House of Commons, to become prime minister. Bonar Law said he would do so if the King dissolved Parliament (see the nearby sidebar for more on this), thereby calling a general election. George refused, saying he was allowed to dissolve Parliament only if instructed to do so by the Prime Minister. As Bonar Law was not prime minister, no dissolution could take place.

DISSOLVING PARLIAMENT

Dissolving a parliament means bringing it to an end. New elections are thereby triggered to provide a new parliament.

- Traditionally this was done at the monarch's whim (for example if a parliament was annoying them); dissolution is now carried out at the prime minister's request.

- The maximum length of a parliament is stipulated by law, not in any constitutional document. In other words, Parliament itself decides how long it remains in being. This has varied widely: Charles I's three-week Short Parliament of 1640 was followed by the infamous 20-year Long Parliament, 1640–1660!

- A parliamentary year is known as a *session*. It is concluded by a prorogation called by the prime minister. In 2019, this power would involve Elizabeth II in an unpleasant constitutional squabble (see Chapter 25).

Seeking a way out, the King called leading politicians from the major parties to Buckingham Palace. Two results 'emerged':

» Bonar Law rejected the offer of the premiership.

» David Lloyd George, leader of the Liberals and most dynamic member of the coalition cabinet, became prime minister. He remained in position to the end of the war.

George VI's prime ministers

George VI's first prime ministerial appointment was easy. In 1931, during the slump that followed the 1929 Wall Street Crash, British politicians came together to form a non-partisan National Government. The majority of its MPs were Conservatives. So, when Stanley Baldwin resigned in 1937, the King had no qualms about asking Neville Chamberlain, the acknowledged Conservative leader, to take over as prime minister.

Things were much trickier when Chamberlain found the House of Commons turning against him in May 1940. After the fall of Norway to the Nazis in the spring of 1940, the House of Commons accused Chamberlain of weak and unsuccessful leadership. The damaged premier wanted to replace the Tory-dominated National Government with a coalition dedicated to winning the war. The Labour Party liked the idea but refused to work under him.

If not Chamberlain, then who? The King wanted Lord Halifax. Great-grandson of the reforming politician Earl Grey (best remembered as a blend of tea) and born in a castle, Halifax was at the heart of the Establishment. The other candidate was also a member of the Establishment, born in a palace and descended from a brilliant general and former chancellor of the exchequer. He was, however, mistrusted after a long and maverick career tarnished by serious errors of judgement in both World War I (the Dardanelles Campaign) and more recently (in World War II) in the failure to hold Norway against the Nazis. His name was Winston Churchill.

Labour agreed to work with either of the two candidates. The King thought Chamberlain had been treated 'grossly unfairly' and Halifax 'was the obvious man' to succeed him. He was wrong. When Halifax said he was not interested in the job, the King dutifully sent for Churchill . . . and the rest is history.

In May 1945, George VI was once more caught in the appointment snare. Though the war with Japan was still raging, the Labour Party was eager to press ahead with their innovative programme of reforms for the post-war world. Churchill, wishing his wartime coalition to continue for a while longer, resigned. Twice on the same day, the King – loath to risk losing his favourite prime minister – refused to accept his resignation (!) before finally acceding to Churchill's wish for Parliament to be dissolved and an election held.

To the surprise of many – not least the King – Labour won by a landslide. On Churchill's advice, George sent for Clement Atlee and invited him to form a government. Five years later, it was Atlee's turn to call for a general election. He won again but with a majority of only five seats. When the next year he sought to increase his majority by calling another election, he lost, and the dying King welcomed back Churchill. He was in post in 1952 to welcome Elizabeth in typically florid style.

Throughout this turbulent time, dutiful George kept his political views (pro-Conservative, anti-Labour) largely to himself. His daughter would do the same with regard to her own political thoughts.

The Royals at War

Britain's showman war leader, Winston Churchill (appointed prime minister after Chamberlain's resignation in 1940), understood as well as anyone of his generation the value of propaganda. In the Royal Family he recognised a priceless agency in the battle to win the hearts and minds of the people, and thereby maintain the country's morale in its 'darkest hour'.

Previous monarchs had played their part in wartime, of course – medieval sovereigns like Henry V actually led their armies into battle. After this obligation died out with George II, subsequent kings and queens did their bit in less militaristic ways. Queen Victoria sent chocolate to her troops (see Chapter 3) and George V and Queen Mary made endless visits and inspections, and even gave up alcohol (temporarily).

Yet neither Victoria nor her dutiful grandson entered into the battle on the home front anywhere near as wholeheartedly or as conspicuously as Bertie and his lodestar Elizabeth.

The war was their finest hour.

Royalty on rations

On VE Day (8 May 1945), huge crowds gathered before Buckingham Palace chanting 'We want the King! We want the Queen!' What had the most privileged couple in the country done to earn such adulation?

WARNING

Before getting too carried away in praise of the King and Queen's war work, as had the Buckingham Palace crowds, we need to remember that public perception of the Royal Family was carefully manipulated to show them in a favourable light. This was not so much flattery as a wartime necessity – the nation needed a non-political focus for its loyalty.

Selected photographs maintained the image of a loving family refusing to be shaken by the dangers and deprivations of war. Other pictures showed them inspecting defences, chatting with ordinary people, and visiting areas that had been bombed.

The reality was slightly different. It is now known, though covered up at the time, that on one visit to a shattered part of London's East End (where the poorest and most deprived lived) the royal couple were received with boos. The crowd resented what they saw as a patronising visit from smartly dressed people who spent their nights secure in concrete underground air-raid shelters.

George helped the wartime propaganda effort with only occasionally faltering broadcasts. His speech to the nation on the outbreak of war is still remembered for the uplifting lines he quoted from the poem 'God Knows' by Minnie Haskins:

I said to the man who stood at the Gate of the Year,

Give me a light that I may tread safely into the unknown.

As the war dragged on, cinema audiences took to applauding whenever the King and Queen appeared on newsreels.

Working towards victory

Visits are the modern-day royals' bread and butter. Shaking hands, asking clichéd questions, and making uncontentious observations is what they do best. During the war, George and Elizabeth acted the part splendidly. Sometimes, to the irritation of the authorities, they even set off on their own initiative.

In November 1940, for instance, they went to the city of Coventry the day after it had been *blitzed* (heavily bombed). We are told they brought sandwiches with them in order not to use precious local resources.

On a more practical level, both King and Queen carried small arms and learned to use them. In a sideswipe at European royal families who had submitted to the Nazis, Queen Elizabeth reportedly said she'd use her pistol rather than 'go down like the others.' When necessary, the King wore military uniform. The Queen, nominally commandant-in-chief of various women's forces, was always in civilian clothes to bolster her 'unflappable mum' image.

TIP

King George visited front line forces when it was safe to do so. In the latter stages of the war, he went to North Africa, Normandy, Italy, and Belgium. He did not enjoy the experience and had to be almost dragged from his tent to carry out an inspection. This was not, of course, reported until after the war. Nor was his remark that, when attending ceremonies, he sometimes wanted, 'to stand up and scream and scream.'

Every Tuesday throughout the war, the King and Churchill met over lunch. Churchill did most of the talking. George listened but took no notes. One of his few known attempts to influence the conduct of the war was when he suggested D-Day be delayed. He was overruled. Nor had it been reported how, learning of the fall of France in 1940, he'd said, 'I feel happier now that we have no allies to be polite to and pamper.'

Sharing hardship

When it was suggested early in the war that the Royal Family leave the country for the security of Canada, the Queen retorted, 'The children could not go without me. I won't leave the King, and of course the King will never leave.' Whatever His Majesty's thoughts on the matter, that was it. The Queen had spoken.

Throughout the war, George and Elizabeth slept in Windsor Castle and spent their days in Buckingham Palace. They commuted between the two in an armoured car. When, as sometimes happened, it was stuffed with her luggage, they fell back on an unarmoured Daimler car. Both residences were heavily targeted, some 300 heavy explosive bombs falling around the castle.

The Palace, which had a makeshift air-raid shelter in the housemaids' sitting room, was hit nine times. One bomb that fell close to the royal quarters failed to explode. 'I'm glad we've been bombed,' Elizabeth was overheard to say. 'We can now look the East End in the face.' No doubt she was thinking of the booing.

The princesses at war

The lives of Princesses Elizabeth and Margaret were, if anything, even more sheltered during the war than they had been before it. As soon as hostilities were declared, they decamped to Windsor Castle, their principal residence until 1945. It was by all accounts a miserable place of low-power light bulbs, blacked-out windows and draughty corridors. When the air-raid siren sounded, the girls slipped into their one-piece 'siren suits' (boiler suit) like every other citizen and headed for the shelter.

REMEMBER

It was from the castle's drawing room that, on 13 October 1940, Elizabeth made her first public broadcast. Speaking on the BBC's Children's Hour, she addressed children who had been evacuated from the cities to the safety of the countryside. 'My sister Rose [Margaret] and I feel so much for you,' she said in her piping, upper-class voice. 'We send a message of true sympathy, and at the same time we would like to thank the kind people who have welcomed you to their homes in the country.'

Reactions to the broadcast were mixed. Some found it 'sweet'; others dismissed it as patronising propaganda from someone who didn't have a clue how ordinary children lived.

After this, Elziabeth's contribution to the war effort was limited to inspecting a parade of Grenadier Guards (she had been made their honorary colonel) and being photographed working on the Windsor Castle allotment (a small parcel of land for growing vegetables and flowers). At 16, she was allowed to sign on at the local labour exchange, but nothing came of it.

Nor was much progress made with her education. She still read widely, picked up bits and pieces from Crawfie, and traipsed over to Eton for history classes with Marten. The one bright spot was the arrival of the Belgian refugee, Mme Antoinette de Bellaigue, whose inspired French teaching gave Elizabeth a sound grounding in the language.

More lively were trips to Balmoral later in the war, and the occasional formal balls to which young officers were invited. The princesses were allowed to join in, carefully chaperoned, for some of the evening. Then there was the annual show organised by Crawfie and the girls every Christmas. It graduated from a conventional nativity play to full-blown pantomimes like *Aladdin*, with Elizabeth apparently singing and dancing in the central role.

TIP

It's not difficult to imagine the lively Margaret playing like this, but Elizabeth? Even in her teens, she was a very earnest young woman. Three pieces of evidence come to mind:

>> When Eleanor Roosevelt visited Britain in 1942, she found the heir to the throne 'quite serious' with 'a great deal of character and personality'. Incidentally, the First Lady was also startled to find the Windsors had painted a black line round the inside of their bath, indicating the maximum depth of water permitted by austerity regulations!

>> Crawfie tells us that at one stage Elizabeth's craving for order became an obsession: she got out of bed several times a night to check that she had laid out her shoes in precisely the correct, neat position. This desire for routine and order would remain with her in later years (see Chapters 8 and 9).

>> The King's love for his elder daughter was augmented by a growing admiration for her stoic qualities and sense of duty. She was, he declared, just like the doughty Queen Victoria.

In spring 1945, the 18-year-old Elizabeth was finally allowed to do some semi-serious war work. Each day, a chauffeur drove 230873 Second Subaltern Elizabeth Alexandra Mary Windsor to the local training centre of the Auxiliary Territorial Service (ATS), the women's branch of the British army. Here she was taught to drive and learned the basics of vehicle maintenance. By the time she qualified, already promoted to the rank of Junior Commander, the war was over. Hugely photographed, the whole business was essentially a publicity stunt.

We are told that Queen Elizabeth once observed wistfully, 'We aren't supposed to be human.' I don't know whether Lilibet heard her mother say this, but by 1945 she was beginning to understand what was expected of a member of the Royal Family. She may or not have been a hit as Aladdin, but she was certainly learning to act the part of twentieth-century royalty.

The only recorded time when she came near to letting her hair down was on VE Day and the evening after. Elizabeth and Margaret pleaded with their parents to be allowed to go out in the streets and join in the fun. Eventually, permission was given. Carefully escorted by Crawfie and a band of a dozen or so army officers, they mingled with the crowds and stood before the gates of Buckingham Palace shouting with the others for the King and Queen.

Never such freedom again.

Countdown to the Crown

There isn't much more to say about dull, dutiful George VI. The VE Day appearances on the balcony of Buckingham Palace (eight altogether) were his finest hour. The last years of his life were plagued by illness brought on by incessant smoking. The continuing presence of Queen Elizabeth, smiling and graceful in that special detached way known only to royals, made official visits less difficult than they might otherwise have been.

REMEMBER

The King spent as much time as he could with his eldest daughter. What they talked about, we will almost certainly never know. We can be fairly sure, however, that he was reassured by her strength, her pragmatism, and her determination to continue the conservative, remote style of monarchy pioneered by Victoria and George V. She could not possibly emulate the 'hail-fellow-well-met' approach of Edward VII or the ill-judged 'man-of-the-people' efforts of Edward VIII.

Father and daughter shared their love of the outdoors, especially hunting, shooting and fishing. Under his guidance – he wearing a specially made, electrically heated waistcoat – Elizabeth caught her first salmon with rod and line, and shot her first stag. Together they visited the Royal Stud at Sandringham, established by Edward Prince of Wales (the future Edward VII) in 1886 and maintained enthusiastically by all subsequent monarchs. Elizabeth reassured her father that she would not let the tradition slip (see Chapter 22). It is unlikely that they chatted about art, literature or the theatre – such matters rarely came within the royal field of vision.

By 1948 the King was clearly unwell. Typical of men of his type and generation, he was reluctant to seek medical advice. When he did, he was diagnosed with severe *arteriosclerosis* (blocked and hardened arteries). An operation did little to improve his condition. Two years later, in September 1950, he was found to have lung cancer. His doctors euphemistically described the condition as 'structural abnormalities' of the left lung, which was removed in a makeshift operating theatre set up in Buckingham Palace – a scene graphically reconstructed in *The Crown*.

Reaching out to the Commonwealth

From the age of 18, Elizabeth increased her royal duties. She made her first public speech in 1944 and was given her own suite of rooms when the family returned to Buckingham Palace after the war. She was served by two ladies-in-waiting, a footman, a housemaid, and the ever-present Bobo. Nominally the Princess's dresser, Bobo acted as factotum-cum-confidante, and remained in Elizabeth's service until her death in 1993.

TIP

The Royal Family's visit to South Africa in early 1947 has been described as their 'Last Hurrah'. The King, Queen, 20-year-old Elizabeth and 16-year-old Margaret arrived aboard Britain's last battleship, HMS *Vanguard*. They toured by Daimler, a marque that would shortly lose its royal warrant (see the nearby sidebar), and in a 14-carriage 'palace on wheels' known as the White Train – not the wisest choice of names in South Africa. On the 4,500-mile trip that took in 400 stopovers of one kind and another, the royals are said to have spoken with (or perhaps this should read 'at'?) 25,000 people.

TECHNICAL
STUFF

ROYAL WARRANT OF APPOINTMENT

First granted 600 years ago, a *royal warrant* is issued to providers of goods and services to the Royal Family – specifically the Queen, the Prince of Wales and (until recently) the Duke of Edinburgh. Holders display a royal coat of arms and use the honour for promotional purposes.

Justerini & Brooks, the wine merchants, are the longest warrant-holders (over 250 years). Some of the quirkier ones include BT, 'the official Supplier of Communications, Broadband and Networked Services to HM The Queen', and Shield Pest Control which has been keeping the royal residences free from pests such as rodents, insects, birds and squirrels since 2008. (Appropriately, the company is based in feline-sounding Catford.)

In 2000, Prince Philip removed the royal warrant from Harrods, the department store owned by Mohammed Fayed, father of Dodi Fayed, the boyfriend with whom Princess Diana was killed in 1997.

Later that year, India and Pakistan would become independent and the King would lose his imperial title. Under these circumstances, one wonders whether the deeply divided South Africa – on the cusp of the *apartheid era* (South Africa's racially motivated social and political system enforcing strict separation between the country's white and non-white populations) – was a wise choice of destination. Whatever the political ramifications of the trip, it gave the young Elizabeth a chance to set out her stall for the future. 'I declare before you all,' she announced in a speech on 21 April, 'that my whole life . . . shall be devoted to your service and the service of our Imperial Commonwealth to which we all belong.'

Elizabeth has stuck to this pledge all her life, though she might now regret the use of the word 'imperial'. (See Chapter 10 for more on the Commonwealth.)

Courting Philip of Greece

Now in her twenties, Elizabeth was very much her own person. The picture we have is of an athletic, attractive young woman with curly brown hair, a fine complexion, and blue eyes.

WARNING

To play the middle-aged Elizabeth in *The Crown*, Olivia Colman tried to change her eye colour with blue contact lenses; it didn't work and the inaccuracy was left in.

Elizabeth's deportment was queenly even before she became queen. Estimates of her personality ranged from near saintly to serious, stubborn and even imperiously cold. She had learned to control her temper, but could still smoulder.

TIP

She showed her stubbornness in her choice of husband. She first met him in 1939, when the 13-year-old Princess and her parents visited the Royal Naval College at Dartmouth in south-west England. According to Crawfie, she 'couldn't take her eyes off' a certain young man. And that – according to the fairy tale accounts – was that.

The Princess's heart-throb was her third cousin, Prince Philip Schleswig-Holstein-Sonderburg-Glücksburg. Born on the sunny island of Corfu in 1921, the six-foot, fair-haired, blue-eyed 'Viking Prince' (Elizabeth's words!) was the son of a member of the impoverished Greek Royal Family.

As well as being hard up, Philip's family (like the Windsors) did not boast a sparkling line-up of superstars: Philip's father was a dilettante exile who had been dismissed from the Greek army for disobeying orders; Philip's congenitally deaf mother, Princess Alice, had spent time in a psychiatric sanatorium before devoting her life to religious charity.

Philip, the last of their five children, had lived a peripatetic, worldly life until taken under the wing of his uncle, Louis Mountbatten. Undaunted by her parents' disapproval, Elizabeth persevered with her obsession. She cherished photographs of Philip, avidly followed his wartime naval career, and exchanged letters with him. From time to time they met – he was in the audience for the performance of *Aladdin* (see earlier in this chapter) – and the relationship deepened.

TIP

Not everyone was so keen. The King and Queen had grave misgivings: was Philip royal enough? Could he be trusted to stay faithful? Wasn't he a bit rough and ready? Was it wise for their virginal daughter, who had probably never been kissed, to get so entangled with the first man she met? Mountbatten's unashamed pushing of the match for family reasons didn't help, and he was told to back off.

Eventually, Elizabeth's parents were won over to her choice. George decided the young naval officer thought about things 'in the right way' – whatever that might mean. In 1946, Elizabeth was told that if she felt the same about Philip when she was 21, she might get engaged to him. Her feelings did not change, though she thought it was 'horrible' when, on a visit to a factory, a worker cried out, 'Where's Philip?'

REMEMBER

In March 1947, Philip changed his family name to Mountbatten, dropped the title 'Prince', and became a British citizen. Four months later, Buckingham Palace announced the engagement of 'their dearly beloved daughter Princess Elizabeth to Lieutenant Philip Mountbatten, RN'.

Approval was by no means universal. The Establishment (see Chapter 5 for the low-down on them) disparaged Philip as the 'greasy Greek'. Others referred to him behind his back as 'the Hun'. The antipathy of Princess Elizabeth's mother (the future Queen Mother) to all things German did not help, nor did the fact that three of Philip's sisters had strong Nazi connections. Interestingly, the 30 guests attending Philip's funeral included three of his German relatives: Bernhard, Hereditary Prince of Baden; Donatus, Prince and Landgrave of Hesse; and Philipp, Prince of Hohenlohe-Langenburg.

Living the family life

Philip and Elizabeth were married in Westminster Abbey on 20 November 1947. The occasion was, in the words of Winston Churchill, 'a flash of colour on the hard road we have to travel.' Though not broadcast live on TV, it was filmed and sent out later the same day so millions throughout the world could wonder at the massed crowds, the glittering coaches, and the bejewelled array of royalty and aristocracy among the 2,000 guests. (Neither the bride's Uncle Edward nor Philip's German relations were invited.) Strikingly composed at the centre of it all was the

Princess herself in a silver-trimmed dress inspired by Botticelli's famous 'Primavera' painting. It was paid for, apparently, by clothing ration coupons.

The wedding breakfast, limited to 150 guests by wartime austerity, featured Filet de Sole Mountbatten and Bombe Glacée Princess Elizabeth. Among the presents were countless pairs of nylon stockings, then in desperately short supply. From India came a piece of cloth hand woven by Gandhi himself. Queen Mary, in her distinct German accent, gave an ugly blast from the past when she condemned it as the Mahatma's 'loin cloth'.

TIP

With marriage, it is said, nothing changed for Princess Elizabeth and everything changed for Philip Mountbatten. The aphorism contains more than a grain of truth. Her job as a royal continued as before, growing ever more all-encompassing. He gained two new titles – Duke of Edinburgh and His Royal Highness – but he was not Prince Consort as Albert had been. His career in the Royal Navy was doomed. Their children would be Windsors, not Mountbattens. To please his new wife, he had even given up smoking. From this moment onwards, he would be the man who walks behind.

After a three-week honeymoon on the Mountbatten estate in Hampshire and in snowy Scotland, the newlyweds returned to London. Here the nineteenth-century mansion of Clarence House (currently the London residence of the Prince of Wales) was refurbished for them. While Elizabeth returned to royal duties, her husband had a Royal Navy desk job in the capital.

In May 1948, Elizabeth's private secretary Jock Colville organized a successful first overseas tour. Paris in the spring could hardly have been better, and the Princess's eyes were reported to have brimmed with tears at the rapturous reception she received from the delighted Parisians. They might have cheered even louder had they known that – despite the couple having separate bedrooms back home – Elizabeth was four months pregnant.

REMEMBER

Prince Charles Philip Arthur George was born in Buckingham Palace on 14 November 1948. Elizabeth beamed with happiness, Philip's chest swelled with pride, and even Queen Mary nodded her approval. Elizabeth breastfed the baby for two months before handing him over to the care of two nurses.

Chapter 5 explains how the short, sad reign of Edward VIII scarred the minds of his royal contemporaries. This was borne out in unwise remarks Elizabeth made to a Mothers' Union meeting in 1949. Divorce, she declared, was responsible for 'some of the darkest evils in our society today'. For the first time, she had shown how out of touch she was with the lives and experiences of ordinary people – and how unprepared she was to handle the crises that would arise in her own family.

Indeed, she may have sowed the seeds of one of those crises when, in October, Philip returned to active service on the Mediterranean island of Malta and she accompanied him. Charles was left behind.

Elizabeth, pregnant again, returned from Malta in May 1950. She now had a new private secretary, Michael Charteris. Eton-educated and from an army background, he would ensure that her court remained firmly wedded to the old-fashioned, traditional Establishment.

Philip returned from Malta for the birth of Princess Anne Elizabeth Alice Louise on 15 August. He flew back to the Mediterranean two weeks later. Once more, Elizabeth breastfed her baby before handing her over to nurses.

REMEMBER

As George VI's health deteriorated through 1951, Elizabeth took on more and more of his duties. By the time she replaced him at Trooping the Colour that summer (see Chapter 1), she was really acting regent for her ailing parent. Approval for her performance in the role was near universal.

So it was, too, when she and Philip toured Canada and the USA in October. The only fly in the ointment was when people asked where the children were. They were back in London. The children were behind again in January 1952 when Elizabeth and Philip started a grand tour of Australia, New Zealand and Ceylon (Sri Lanka) with a stopover in Kenya.

George's true health condition was withheld from the patient himself, his family, and the public. It now seems fairly certain that the cancer had already spread to the right lung. Quite what killed him during the night of 6 February 1952 is unclear. Coronary thrombosis was the widely accepted answer, though complications arising from his cancer have been suggested. He was 56.

Elizabeth and Philip were still in Kenya, staying in the remote Treetops Hotel, when Charteris received a call from London:

The King is dead – Long Live Queen Elizabeth!

2

The Young Queen

Brits have long regarded the reign of the first Queen Elizabeth (1558–1603) as a golden age. The country beat off foreign invaders, sent intrepid sailors around the world, and basked in the glory of Shakespeare's unique talent. Many hoped that the accession of the second Queen Elizabeth in 1952 would herald a similar flourishing of national spirit and fortune.

In some ways, they were not disappointed. The long, dark years of the Second World War (1939–1945) were finally over, and the throne was freshly occupied by a young and attractive queen. Surely, Britain and its monarchy were on the cusp of something new and exciting?

Wartime austerity was indeed cast off and the country, in the words of Prime Minister Harold Macmillan, 'had never had it so good'. However, the Queen saw it as her duty not to lead Britain into a brave new world, but rather to preserve its roots with the past. As a result, slowly and inexorably, she found herself and her household getting more and more out of synch with her people.

Chapter **7**

Coronation: 'I Present Unto You Queen Elizabeth'

What is a Coronation? The word is commonly used to show the final achievement of something great, such as the Olympic medal ceremony being a winning athlete's 'coronation'.

A *coronation* means adorning the head with some sort of garland. For rulers – monarchs, pharaohs, tsars, emperors, and so forth – this garland is a crown. The most traditional form of crown is a circle of metal, usually gold or silver, although those of ancient Egypt were more like party hats. A crown is a purely symbolic garment with no practical purpose. Emperor Joseph of Austria once mocked it as a hat that lets the rain in.

Useless though they may be as a piece of headgear, crowns have an almost mystical importance. Wearing one makes the ruler unmistakably top dog. That's why putting the crown on for the first time – the coronation – is so significant. The ceremony has grown increasingly elaborate over time. In Britain and elsewhere, to make it extra special, the ceremony was fashioned as a religious service and took place in a church or cathedral. The message of a coronation is that God Himself has appointed this ruler; mess with them at your peril. To disobey the Lord's anointed is to flout the will of the Almighty.

REMEMBER

Strictly speaking, a coronation is not a mark of final triumph but a statement of what's to come: not a conclusion but a start. A royal coronation shows that the chosen individual is now the undisputed monarch, and that their reign can officially begin.

In this chapter, I walk through the steps of Queen Elizabeth's coronation and the special touches that made the event unique. Then I offer some insights on how the world celebrated this momentous occasion.

An Occasion of Pomp and Ceremony

Everyone agreed: the Coronation of Queen Elizabeth II had to be a truly memorable occasion. As time was needed for meticulous planning, the ceremony was booked for Tuesday, 2 June 1953. The date also gave a fair chance that it wouldn't be raining. The venue was easily sorted, too. It had to be Westminster Abbey, the church founded by King Edward the Confessor in 960 and the site of innumerable previous coronations. Other arrangements were less easy.

Should the Duke of Windsor, the former Edward VIII, be invited? Answer: no, definitely not. Should Philip, Duke of Edinburgh, be crowned with his wife? After all, in 1937, the Queen Mother (Queen Elizabeth as she was then) had been crowned alongside her husband. But this time, no. The Queen allowed Philip to chair the committee organizing the ceremony, but he would not be crowned. She was the boss and needed to show it.

What about showing the whole thing live on TV? The Queen and Prime Minister Winston Churchill were against it. When this leaked out, howls of protest forced a climbdown. Though no close-ups would be permitted, all but the sacred (and, as you will see, intimate) anointing part of the ceremony would go out live.

The following sections offer more details on this grand event.

Glamour in Westminster Abbey

The weather was the only feature of the Coronation that did not go to plan: the day was douched in a persistent drizzle. Nothing daunted, a million people braved the rain and came to witness what they hoped would be a once-in-a-lifetime event. Among them were 40,000 Americans, including Californian Governor Earl

Warren. By 9am, when the Coronation parade set out, hundreds of thousands lined the streets between Buckingham Palace and the Abbey.

What followed was based on traditions that went back to the Coronation of William (the Conqueror) in 1066. I'll set out the 1953 version as the *12 Steps of Coronation*:

>> **Step 1:** For two hours, a glittering parade of 29 bands, domestic and foreign dignitaries, soldiers, sailors and aircrew from 50 nations moved slowly through the thronged streets. As at major golf tournaments, stands had been erected along the route to give everyone a good view of what was going on.

>> **Step 2:** At 11am, the Queen, last in the procession, left her 24-foot Gold State Coach and entered the packed Abbey. Here, her six Maids of Honour (unmarried daughters of the highest nobles in the land) draped her with the 18-foot, crimson Robe of State. With an anxious 'Ready girls?', Elizabeth set off down the aisle towards the high altar. As she arrived, choirboys chanted in Latin, 'Vivat Regina Elizabetha!'

>> **Step 3:** Elizabeth said a quick prayer then stood beside the Coronation Chair for the 'Presentation'. The Archbishop of Canterbury, the senior cleric of the Church of England, announced to four groups of dukes, earls, lords and other distinguished invitees, 'I Present Unto You Queen Elizabeth.' Pretending they had not seen her before, each group in turn cried 'God Save Queen Elizabeth!'

>> **Step 4:** Now everyone knew who Elizabeth was, she took the Coronation Oath seated on the Coronation Chair. She promised, among other things, to stick to the law and uphold Protestantism. She had to do so twice, once for the Church of England and a second time for the Church of Scotland.

TECHNICAL STUFF

The Coronation Chair, aka St Edward's Chair or King Edward's Chair, was commissioned by King Edward I in 1296. Edward, 'Hammer of the Scots', had just carried off the ancient Stone of Destiny on which Scotland's kings were crowned. The chair was specially constructed to house this red sandstone lump in Westminster Abbey. Scottish nationalists stole it in 1950. Though it was recovered, it was officially returned to Scotland in 1996 in an effort to quell a rising tide of tartan discontent.

>> **Step 5:** We've reached the religious part of the three-hour ceremony. It incorporated a communion service (a mass) and the anointing of the Queen with holy oil. This last was perhaps the most bizarre episode of all. The only remaining bottle of oil – a curious mix of musk, cinnamon, orange, rose, and the digestive juices of a Sperm whale – had been smashed by a German bomb in World War II. Fortunately, an ancient chemist who had kept a few drops as a souvenir, managed to cook up a bit more. Elizabeth donned a low-cut white linen robe. The Archbishop poured some of the oil into a twelfth-century anointing spoon, dipped his fingers in and made oily signs of the cross on Her

Majesty's hands, forehead and breast. This was the bit the Queen had refused to be televised. Queen Victoria had gone further and cut out the breast-oiling altogether.

>> **Step 6:** The newly anointed Elizabeth was set up in her full Coronation robes, all 36lbs of them. This gave her a priestly appearance, something she felt appropriate. Like a priest, she had been given a holy status that would remain with her until death. Unlike her uncle, who had not been anointed (see Chapter 5), Elizabeth will never abdicate.

>> **Step 7:** The Queen was back on TV and ready to be kitted out with the royal regalia. As she was the symbol of the nation, she needed to be seen with tangible symbols of her monarchial status. These strange but precious objects – orb, sceptre a-gleam with gemstones, and others – are explained below.

>> **Step 8:** At last, all was ready: the Queen was finally to be crowned. Watched by his chaplain (my father-in-law), Archbishop Geoffrey Fisher blessed the 5lb, solid gold crown encrusted with 444 gems. He then raised it high, and lowered it slowly onto Elizabeth's head. On every side, lords and ladies did the same thing with their cut-price coronets. The congregation cried 'God save the Queen!', guns fired salutes in the Tower of London, and it was done.

>> **Step 9:** Well, not quite done. A long line of the great and the good, headed by the Archbishop and the Duke of Edinburgh, went through the medieval custom of paying 'homage' to the crowned monarch. This meant accepting her as their feudal chief by placing their hands between hers and swearing to accept her as their lord.

TECHNICAL STUFF

The feudal 'system' meant that, in theory, the whole of society was arranged in a pyramid of land-in-exchange-for-service. The monarch at the top owned all the land. They handed this out to nobles in exchange for loyalty and service. The nobles did the same to those below them on the feudal scale. And so it went on down to the landless peasants or 'serfs' at the bottom. In Britain, feudalism had virtually disappeared by the sixteenth century.

>> **Step 10:** Feeling a bit frayed, Elizabeth took a short break in a side chapel. She stepped out of her weightier garments and swapped crowns for the lighter (only 3lbs) Imperial State Crown. The Archbishop generously offered those present a quick sip from his brandy flask.

>> **Step 11:** Still clutching the orb and sceptre and dragging the 18-foot train, Elizabeth left the Abbey for a banquet lunch next door. The menu? Coronation Chicken, of course! The specially created dish comprised cold chicken in a rich, mildly spicy, curried sauce.

>> **Step 12:** The journey home. Safe in the Gold State Coach with Philip at her side, the crowned queen waved and smiled at the cheering crowds that lined the seven-mile procession route back to the Palace. The rain had not let up all day.

It was over. Looking back almost 70 years later, what are we to make of this extraordinary ceremony? Opinions differ. For many, it was a statement of hope, looking forward to a bright future based on ancient foundations. Others saw it as a sort of *Monty Python* pantomime, a sad and ridiculously expensive attempt by a once-great power to show the world that it was not yet finished. Which of these proved correct depended to some extent on how Elizabeth chose to play the game.

The glory of the Crown Jewels

Britain's Crown Jewels is the collection of precious ancient objects traditionally rolled out for a monarch's use at their Coronation and on other formal state occasions. They're not all as old as they are sometimes made out to be: a lot of the medieval bits and pieces were dismantled and melted down when Britain became a short-lived republic in 1649 (see Chapter 2).

The 142 separate items, called the royal 'regalia', include crowns, coronets (mini crowns), sceptres (rods of gold and silver), orbs (balls of precious metal surmounted by a cross, signifying God's dominance over the world), robes, rings, and swords. There's also a lot of gold and silver plate, and, strangely, a jewelled walking stick.

The royal regalia is, literally, uninsurable: its estimated value is around £5 billion. This is hardly surprising considering that they glisten with 23,578 individual gemstones. The Cullinan diamond, the world's largest, weighs in at a startling (and sparkling) 530 carats.

The regalia is currently housed in the Tower of London, the massive fortress William the Conqueror built to dominate the city shortly after his coronation in 1066.

The Crown Jewels need to be seen to be believed. Visitors to London are urged to call in on the Tower's Jewel House vault. It is open to the public and attracts around three million visitors a year.

Mixing family and politicians on the guest list

The Coronation guest list is doubly fascinating. It opens a window onto a lost world where monarchs still ruled and hereditary power was not yet an anathema. Princes and other *plenipotentiaries* (ambassadors and diplomats), for instance, represented the kings or emperors of Afghanistan, Laos, Ethiopia, Iraq, Egypt, and Vietnam.

The list also throws into sharp relief the uneasy relationship between Britain the democracy and Britain the monarchy. As well as 36 members of Elizabeth's Royal

Family (ranging from husband, sister, son and mother through to numerous cousins of one sort or another), the Abbey pews were thronged with every conceivable type of hereditary noble, including marquises, dukes and earls.

By accident of birth, many of these were entitled to wield political influence by virtue of their seats in the House of Lords. How to reconcile hereditary privilege and representative democracy was a conundrum Elizabeth could hardly avoid.

A Day to Remember

Elizabeth had been crowned Queen not just of the UK, but also of Australia, Canada, Ceylon (Sri Lanka), New Zealand, Pakistan, and South Africa. In all these domains, the event was marked with national holidays, fireworks, parties, concerts, and a variety of commemorative medals, coins and other objects (see the nearby sidebar). To cap it all, news came through that the New Zealander Edmund Hillary and his Nepalese sherpa Tensing Norgay of the British mountaineering expedition, had become the first people to ascend Mount Everest, the world's highest peak. For 24 glorious hours, it seemed, Britain was on top of the world.

In the UK, an average of 17 people per TV screen watched the Coronation in black and white. Many households had bought their first sets for the occasion. The ceremony was filmed in colour, too. Immediately it finished, reels were flown around the world for viewing on TV and in cinemas. In the US, CBS and NBC provided their own broadcast, while ABC transmitted a signal relayed from CBC in Toronto. In total, the Coronation was seen by an estimated worldwide audience of 275 million.

PARTIES AND PAGEANTS THROUGHOUT THE LAND

I am just old enough to remember the Coronation. As a young boy at primary (elementary) school, I was unaware of the street parties and fireworks taking place elsewhere; nor did I fully understand the joy shown by adults now the long years of war and rationing were over. But I do recall having a jolly time.

As with events in the Abbey, it was all very retro. We danced clumsily round a maypole and paraded as medieval knights with wooden swords and cardboard armour.

At the end of the day, we were given a Coronation mug. I accidentally broke mine a few weeks later. I'm unsure whether this had symbolic significance.

Chapter **8**

The Queen Goes to Work

What does the Queen actually *do*? There can be no definitive answer to this question because no two days are exactly the same, and the timetable varies from week to week and month to month. Moreover, the daily routine of a woman of 95 is bound to be different from one of 35.

Nevertheless, this chapter looks at the sort of pattern Elizabeth is said to have followed for most of her reign.

Some people will ask, 'Does the Queen really work hard? The short answer is: it all depends what you mean by 'work'. The Republic website (https://www.republic.org.uk/) makes no bones about its position:

. . . let's be honest the royals don't really work at all . . . When they talk about working hard they are usually referring to the number of official engagements they do in a year. A typical engagement – turning up at an event, cutting a ribbon or meeting business leaders for example . . . Quite often these engagements last no more than 20 minutes.

TIP

Fair enough. But work does not necessarily mean *doing* things. For almost 70 years, Elizabeth has been on show. Even at home, she is aware of the need to behave in an appropriate manner and to watch what she says. However close the security, however discrete her servants, tongues will wag and the justification for her unique position would be undermined by indiscretion. In public, it's worse. She cannot relax for a split second.

This may not be hard labour, but might it not be described as hard work? You can decide for yourself after you've read this chapter!

Working Daily as a Dutiful and Diligent Monarch

If she is still asleep, the Queen is woken at 7:30am when a housemaid draws back the curtains of her bedroom on the northern side, overlooking Green Park. Until her retirement around 1993, the ever-faithful Bobo then arrived with tea and biscuits, and prepared Elizabeth's clothes and jewellery for the day (see the nearby sidebar on, "Margaret 'Bobo' Macdonald"). With Bobo invariably arrived a troupe of corgis (see Chapter 22 for more about these little dogs).

The royal bath is run with water seven inches deep and measured, apparently, with an ancient, wood-backed thermometer, at precisely 70 degrees Fahrenheit. Bath over, Elizabeth dresses and has her hair done while listening to the news on the BBC.

Breakfast is taken in a private dining room in which the daily newspapers are laid out for inspection. Her first read is a sporting newspaper specializing in horse racing. We are told the Queen moves on to the news and crosswords in the conservative and strongly pro-royalist *The Daily Telegraph*. More balanced coverage comes from *The Times* before a quick – and no doubt exasperated – glance at the more sensationalist *tabloid papers* (smaller-format, cheaper newspapers which tend towards sensationalism).

Her Majesty breaks her fast with toast and marmalade, and perhaps a boiled egg. Butter comes from the royal dairy at Windsor and is stamped with the royal monogram.

MARGARET 'BOBO' MACDONALD

Born in a humble railway worker's cottage in 1904, the Scots-born hotel chambermaid entered the service of Elizabeth's parents, the Duke and Duchess of York, in 1926. Initially a nursemaid, over the years she became the queen's dresser and closest confidante outside her immediate family. She called Elizabeth 'Lilibet' to her face (a rare privilege) and was not often far from her side. She died in her private Buckingham Palace suite in 1993.

Finally, most bizarre of all, Elizabeth is regaled with 15 minutes of Scottish bagpipe music played by the Piper to the Sovereign. The tradition dates from Victoria's days at Balmoral and is no easy sinecure – the Queen objects to hearing the same tune too often, obliging the piper to memorize some 700 melodies.

Dressing the part

No figure in the history of the world has had their dress more closely scrutinized over a longer period of time than Queen Elizabeth II. The wardrobe of the 5ft-2in monarch has been praised, criticized, but never ignored.

The pressure this puts on her and her dressers is enormous. If she dresses down, she's said to be dowdy; if she jazzes it up a bit, she's said to be attired inappropriately. On the whole, she's managed successfully to steer a middle course between the two.

TIP

Certain items have now become trademark Elizabeth II:

» Kilts, usually in the Royal Stewart tartan, to go with her Scottish heritage.

» Gloves, so she does not have to touch anyone's skin when shaking hands.

» Military uniform, as when attending the Trooping the Colour (see Chapter 1).

» Hats and headscarves, the latter a favourite covering for informal outdoor activities.

» Jodhpurs and jacket, when on horseback.

» Barbour jacket, when out in the wild.

» A string of pearls and/or a priceless brooch such as the Cullinan V Brooch made by the Crown jewellers Garrard in 1911.

» A practical handbag, in black, white or cream.

Guided by designers like Norman Hartnell, Hardy Amies and, more recently, Angela Kelly, Elizabeth has favoured soft pastel greens, blues, pinks, and lemon. Her heels are never too high, her skirts never too short. She appears to like pleated skirts and is not often seen in public wearing trousers. Her generally cautious wardrobe is sometimes enlivened by bold prints, floral and otherwise, especially when on a royal tour to a country whose weather is a little more clement than that back home in the UK.

Heading to work

It's not easy to ascertain exactly what happens next. Enthusiastic royalists paint a picture of the Queen pouring over papers or moving from one formal engagement to another. Critics suggest a far more leisurely routine punctuated by long holidays and relaxing days at the races. Whichever is true, here are the sort of things Elizabeth has to do:

>> **Attending to her correspondence.** The Queen is assisted in this task by her correspondence secretaries (see later in this chapter).

>> **Meeting important people.** Such people include foreign diplomats, judges and bishops. It's rare for any individual to get more than 20 minutes of royal attention. During a conversation – which is 100 percent confidential, of course – Elizabeth does most of the listening.

>> **Bestowing honours, decorations and medals.** This is generally done around mid-morning in the Buckingham Palace ballroom. The complex British honours system is discussed in Chapter 12.

>> **Making official visits.** Travelling by car, train, helicopter or plane, the Queen attends to ceremonial duties and royal visits.

>> **Having afternoon tea.** A small but vital part of the routine, involving china cups, finely cut sandwiches and a cake or two.

>> **Attending evening functions.** Of course Elizabeth will spend evenings at home watching TV just like the rest of us, but she frequently has to be on duty at premiers, social events, and formal dinners hosted by herself or others.

TECHNICAL STUFF

In 1805, George III became so fed up with rumours about what he and other members of the Royal Family were and were not doing, that he set up the Court Circular. This detailed the royals' official activities. The tradition has been maintained ever since, with today's Court Circular available in some newspapers and online at www.royal.uk/court-circular.

As with Elizabeth's daily routine, her annual calendar varies considerably. Nevertheless, certain regular customs and traditions are well established:

>> **December and January.** The Royal Family spends Christmas at their privately owned Sandringham House on the 20,000-acre Sandringham estate in Norfolk on England's east coast (see Chapter 9).

>> **February and March.** Traditionally the time for royal tours overseas (to escape the rigours of a British winter), Elizabeth now spends these months at home. She passes the weekdays in Buckingham Palace and goes to Windsor

Castle for the weekend (see Chapter 9). She leaves touring to younger family members – see Chapter 10 for more on royal tours.

>> **April.** The only significant tradition at this time of the year is for the family to gather at Windsor Castle for Easter.

>> **May.** Spring fixtures include the five-day Royal Windsor Horse Show (rwhs.co.uk) in the private grounds of Windsor Castle, and the Royal Horticultural Society's Chelsea Flower Show (www.rhs.org.uk).

>> **June.** Let's go racing! This is the month of two of the Queen's favourite events, the famous Epsom Derby (www.epsomderby.co.uk), held each year since 1780, and the sartorially showy Royal Ascot (www.ascot.co.uk). Chapter 22 explores Elizabeth's love of horses.

>> **August and September.** As summer comes to an end, six weeks in Balmoral Castle in the Scottish Highlands are *de rigueur* for the Queen (see Chapter 9). Most of her family call in at some stage during the visit. Prime ministers and their spouses are also invited. An awkward visit by Mrs Thatcher and her husband provided *The Crown* with one of its more amusing episodes!

WARNING

In 2021, Prince Andrew took refuge in Balmoral when he was implicated in an American sex abuse scandal.

>> **October and November.** The autumn is another popular time for royal overseas tours (see Chapter 10). It also features two time-honoured traditions, the State Opening of Parliament (www.royal.uk/state-opening-parliament) and Remembrance Day (www.royal.uk/remembrance-day).

A lot of work, a lot of fun, and a lot of holiday!

Ploughing through the paperwork

Every day of the year, the sovereign receives hundreds of messages of one sort or another from people all over the world. She could not possibly handle all these herself.

TECHNICAL STUFF

As far back as 1805, George III appointed the first private secretary to the sovereign to help him with his paperwork. The position remains to this day, and has expanded far beyond correspondence to become that of close personal advisor on almost everything.

The private secretary now heads a large Private Secretary's Office that includes a deputy private secretary, an assistant private secretary, and a platoon of equally discreet individuals (see Chapter 9 for more details on these helpful people) who handle the political side of things.

Nevertheless, ordinary correspondence still matters. Every day, the secretary's office devotes many hours sifting through the endless stream of papers, letters, e-mails, tweets and other contacts that flood into the royal inboxes and post boxes. If the Queen were to do everything herself, she'd spend the better part of her day just responding to the 2.2 million followers of her Twitter account: @RoyalFamily.

We're told Elizabeth reads the more significant communications and may glance at others as her secretariat deems fit. An effort is made to reply to most correspondence, though she will not respond on political issues or those that call on her to take sides in a dispute.

Why do she and her secretaries bother to reply? It's all part of the Queen's overwhelming sense of duty. In return for the privileges she has inherited, she feels obligated to respond to her citizens – and others – when they get in touch. Can you imagine the ill-feeling that would arise if she did not?

TIP

Through the contact page on the royal website you can test the system yourself: www.royal.uk/contact. You almost certainly won't get a letter signed by the Queen herself, but it'd be fun to try!

Relaxing with some downtime

Though the Queen's schedule looks punishing, it is never pell-mell. It would never do for the sovereign to look hurried or flustered. She has trained herself to stay calm under any circumstances. Moreover, she likes her schedule to leave room for the things she really enjoys.

There must be time allocated for her dogs – where possible she cares for them herself (see Chapter 22 for more about the Queen and her dogs). At weekends she walks in the grounds of Windsor Castle or takes a horse ride in the Great Park. Life at Sandringham and Balmoral is less stressful, offering more opportunity for the outdoor life she so enjoys. She no longer shoots and fishes, but walking through the Highland heather never fails to raise the spirits.

Then there are the off-duty evenings. Her daily 2:1 mix of gin and Dubonnet, a taste inherited from her mother, is legendary. The years finally caught up with her as she neared her Platinum Jubilee. We are told that after a spell in hospital in 2021, her doctors advised her to go easy on the booze.

WARNING

When the family is together, there are parlour games that can make guests feel quite awkward – as shown in the episode of *The Crown* when Prime Minister Thatcher and her husband visited Balmoral.

Otherwise, like the rest of us, there's TV, terrestrial and digital. As well as popular talent shows, we're told she enjoys soap operas, quiz shows and, of course, the coverage of horse racing. A keen fan of *Downton Abbey*, she liked trying to spot anachronistic errors!

Acting as a Political Figure

REMEMBER

The monarch's transition from an actual Head of State to a purely formal one was a long and at times painful process (you can read more about this in Chapters 2 and 3). It led to the bizarre situation in which Elizabeth finds herself today. In theory, the government is hers; the armed forces are hers (officers must swear an oath of allegiance to her); and the law is also hers (her coat of arms adorns every court room). Yet neither the government, nor the military, nor the law courts are actually hers. They function in the name of the Crown, which she personifies.

Therein lies the paradox – in one sense Elizabeth is all powerful; in another she has the power only to influence. But as the age of social media has taught us, influencers can be very powerful!

Understanding the relationship between the Crown and Parliament

TECHNICAL STUFF

Technically speaking, Parliament comprises the House of Commons, the House of Lords and the Crown.

Today, the Crown's participation is limited to five actions:

>> **Summoning the leader of the largest party in the Commons to form 'Her Majesty's' government.** During the reigns of Elizabeth's father and grandfather this drew the monarch into the political sphere (see Chapter 6). Chapter 12 describes how Elizabeth herself was similarly drawn into a quasi-political role in 1963.

>> **Formally opening a parliament with a spectacular ceremony and reading out the government's proposed legislative programme in the 'Queen's Speech'.** This is a classic example of how monarchical rule has melded with the democratic process. As parliaments were once literally summoned and dismissed by the monarch (see Chapter 2), for tradition's sake a new parliament is still formally opened by the Queen. The ceremony is also a reminder to the government that they are not at the pinnacle of the constitutional pyramid. Similarly, the government is theoretically the Queen's, which is why she – and not the prime minister – announces its programme.

>> *Proroguing* (ending) a parliamentary session on the advice of the prime minister. In 2019, the process carried out in her name drew Elizabeth to the edge of the political fray (see Chapters 6 and 21).

>> **Dissolving a parliament on the advice of the prime minister.** A parliament was originally summoned to assist the monarch (see Chapter 2). Once it had done what was required of it, the monarch was at liberty to dismiss (dissolve) it. Ever since the time of the Civil War (see Chapter 2), Parliament has decided for itself when to dissolve. Nevertheless, the dissolution is still made in the monarch's name – just to remind the prime minister that they are not quite top dog. (See Chapter 6).

>> **Granting Royal Assent.** A *bill* (piece of legislation) becomes an *Act* (a law) only when it has been accepted by the Commons and the Lords and signed by the monarch. This signature is known as the *Royal Assent*. (The process is very similar to that set out in the US Constitution, when an Act does not become law until signed by the President.) Granting Royal Assent involves a convoluted, centuries-old process culminating in the chief officer of the House of Lords announcing assent in Norman-French! Royal Assent has not been withheld since 1708.

In short, Elizabeth still has to dress up and play her part in the pageantry of Parliament, but for 95 percent of the time she's insulated from its politics.

Meeting with the prime minister

Now we move on to more controversial ground. When she is in London, the Queen meets with her Prime Minister (PM) – there have been 14 of them so far in her reign – once a week, usually at 6.30 pm on a Wednesday evening at Buckingham Palace. Why? There are no easy answers, but we might suggest three:

>> She is a woman of habit and routine and has no wish to break with tradition. Her prime ministers have no wish to, either.

>> Most PMs have said they find the experience helpful. It enables them to clarify their own thinking and get difficult issues off their chest. No one else is present in the Audience Chamber where the couple meet. Harold Wilson (PM 1964–1970 and 1974–1976) said he could be frank with the Queen about any political matter because he knew his remarks would not be leaked.

>> With some of her PMs – for example Churchill, Wilson, and John Major (PM 1990–1997) – Elizabeth had a close relationship. With others – Margaret Thatcher (PM 1979–1990) is often cited – the relationship was more formal.

But are these weekly chats merely prime ministers talking freely to a neutral listener? Because they are wholly confidential, we will never know the answer until Elizabeth's private diaries are published (if they ever are) after her death. Nevertheless, her admission that she may, as she put it in 1992, occasionally 'put one's point of view' suggests that she is not without political influence.

There's more on Elizabeth and her prime ministers in Chapter 26.

>> As a Head of State who frequently meets with other heads of state – monarchs, presidents, prime ministers and so forth – it is important that Elizabeth knows what her government is thinking. There's no better way of finding this out than by talking to the PM.

To ensure she's up to speed, every day (apart from 25 December and Easter Day) Elizabeth is sent a red box full of *state papers* – key government letters and e-mails, policy documents, and so forth. We're told she sifts through them carefully and signs where appropriate. Each evening, when Parliament is sitting, a government whip sends the Palace a précis of the day's proceedings.

TIP

I once asked one of those responsible for doing this why Her Majesty couldn't just watch the news like everyone else. He replied that his daily letters were 'different, more complete and sometimes more gossipy' than formal communications, and he spent a long time composing them.

Hosting heads of state

Until recently, scarcely a year went by without the Queen and her husband hosting a foreign dignitary on a state visit. The impressive display of pageantry and protocol (see the sidebar of the same name) involves

>> a formal greeting, usually on London's Horse Guard Parade. Mounted soldiers, guns firing salutes, riding through the streets of the capital in a horse-drawn coach, lots of bowing, scraping, and handshaking – the visiting celeb is given the full works.

>> a grand state banquet for some 150 guests in the Buckingham Palace Ballroom. Cordial relations are sealed with carefully crafted speeches and toasts. Food is generally sourced from the Royal Estates, sparkling English wine served as an aperitif, and classic French wines poured with the meal. Most foreign visitors find the whole show pretty impressive.

PROTOCOL

Where the Royal Family is concerned, *protocol* means etiquette – what one must and must not do in the royal presence.

Some things are well known: don't ever lay a hand on the Queen (Donald Trump being a famous rule-breaker here), curtsey/bow on meeting her, address her as 'Your Majesty' at first, then as 'Ma'am' (pronounced as in 'smarm').

Other unwritten rules are less well known. For example, when eating with the Queen – you should be so lucky – finish your meal when she does, even if you're hungry and there's still stuff on your plate.

To give you a flavour of the variety of leaders the Queen meets, here are some of the recent state visits she has hosted:

>> October 2014: President Tony Tan and First Lady Mary Tan of the Republic of Singapore

>> March 2015: President Enrique Peña Nieto and First Lady Angélica Rivera of the United Mexican States

>> October 2015: President Xi Jinping and Mme Peng Liyuan of the People's Republic of China

>> November 2016: President Juan Manuel Santos and First Lady María Clemencia Rodríguez of the Republic of Colombia

>> July 2017: King Felipe VI and Queen Letizia of Spain

>> October 2018: King Willem-Alexander and Queen Máxima of the Netherlands

>> June 2019: President Donald Trump and First Lady Melania Trump of the United States of America

Carrying On with a Continuous Round of Visits and Ceremonial Duties

The Queen is expected to attend numerous formal engagements, as outlined earlier in this chapter, from state banquets to opening Parliament and investing people with honours. Besides these, she has to carry out a range of other duties.

Touring her realm: visiting, opening, and launching

As befits a lady in her 90s, Elizabeth is no longer slave to a long list of public engagements.

In the past, scarcely a day went by when she was not opening a new road or shopping centre, launching a ship, visiting a hospital, or giving her blessing to some other worthy enterprise. In Britain alone, there are hundreds of structures that bear her name, ranging from the Queen Elizabeth Bridge over the River Thames to the east of London, to the Queen Elizabeth Law Courts in Liverpool. Nearly all of these she opened in person.

Running 'The Firm': the Windsor family business

In 2020, Queen Elizabeth carried out 136 official engagements – not bad for a 94-year-old. Her eldest son, Prince Charles, carried out 146, and her daughter Princess Anne another 144. Other leaders in the royal work stakes were Prince Edward with 123 working days, and Prince William with 103. His wife, Catherine Duchess of Cambridge, was eighth in the line-up with 79 engagements – as well as spending a very un-Windsor amount of time with her three children.

TIP

The Royal Family like to call themselves 'The Firm'. The phrase was coined by George VI who supposedly observed (with typical grumpiness): 'We're not a family. We're a firm.' The remark suggests two things. First, the royals see themselves as doing a job, running a family business. Second, at times some of them appear to do so grudgingly, resenting the burdens and loss of privacy that their status brings.

The Firm never closes.

Chapter 9

Back-up: The Royal Household

This chapter looks at Elizabeth's working environment, the grand buildings, and the mix of ceremonial and paid personnel that make up the 'court'.

Excluding properties overseas, Elizabeth and co have the use of 16 residences belonging to the state. Let's face it, no one actually *needs* so many houses. The Swedish royal family has an impressive 11, the Japanese imperial family eight, and the Dutch royal family five. The President of the United States – the wealthiest nation on Earth – has to make do with just two.

It's not simply the number of Britain's royal castles and palaces that raises questions. The sheer size, age and cost of maintaining them is massive and is mostly paid for – directly or indirectly – by the British public. (See Chapter 17, where royal finances are dealt with.) The restoration of Windsor Castle after the 1992 fire (see Chapter 20) cost some £35 million. The Queen chipped in £2 million of her own money and agreed to pay some tax to help further.

WARNING

The property problem is part of the problem of the monarchy itself. When Britain has a serious shortage of housing, does the Royal Family's multi-home set-up convey the right message? Tradition and a proud heritage are needed to bind a country together . . . but at what price? Even Prince Charles, it is rumoured, would like to decommission the gargantuan Buckingham Palace.

No-one seems able to work out how many staff the Royal Family employs. It is said there are 1,100 in Buckingham Palace alone. Scattered across the many Royal Households, the staff ranges from maids on basic wages to executives on six-figure salaries. Elizabeth's own Royal Household is by far the largest. But it's not that simple – is it ever with the royals? – because 'household' includes ceremonial and symbolic positions as well as practical ones.

At Home With the Windsors

The properties occupied by the Windsors divide into three groups:

>> those owned by the Crown.

>> those owned by the Duchy of Cornwall.

>> those owned by the family themselves, privately.

Let's take a look at each of these in turn.

Crown properties

Officially known as the Occupied Royal Palaces Estate, these properties are held in trust for the nation and its sovereign. The big four used by Elizabeth are:

>> **Buckingham Palace** (`www.royal.uk/royal-residences-buckingham-palace`): The 775-room headquarters of the British monarchy was bought by George III in 1761 for £21,000 (£4,777,500 at today's prices – a bargain!).

>> **Windsor Castle** (`www.royal.uk/royal-residences-windsor-castle`): The 900-year-old fortress, set in a 13,000-acre estate, is the largest occupied castle in the world. The Queen regards it as her principal home, and the flightpath of planes using the nearby Heathrow steers neatly around the castle.

>> **Holyrood Palace** (`www.royal.uk/royal-residences-palace-holyroodhouse`): The twelfth-century former abbey in the heart of Edinburgh is the sovereign's base when on official business in Scotland

>> **Hillsborough Castle** (`www.hrp.org.uk/hillsborough-castle`): This eighteenth-century country house in County Down, Northern Ireland, is the official residence of the secretary of state for Northern Ireland and of the sovereign when on official business in the province.

TIP

Parts of all four buildings are open to the public at certain times; check the websites shown above ahead of any visit so that you're aware of what you will (and won't) be able to see.

Elizabeth's household team (see later in this chapter) is also responsible for:

>> **Clarence House (www.royal.uk/royal-residences-clarence-house):** Originally built for the future King William IV, this nineteenth-century mansion was Elizabeth's home when she was first married and then the London residence of her mother. It is now the London HQ of Charles Prince of Wales and his wife, the Duchess of Cornwall. (Open to the public at certain times.)

>> **Kensington Palace (www.royal.uk/royal-residences-kensington-palace):** The birthplace of Queen Victoria was bought by William III in 1689. It is the official London residence of the Duke and Duchess of Cambridge (William and Kate). Two of George V's grandsons, the Duke Gloucester and Prince Michael of Kent, also live there with their families. (Open to the public at certain times.)

>> **St James' Palace (www.royal.uk/royal-residences-st-jamess-palace):** A popular royal residence for centuries, the red brick Tudor palace is now the official London residence of the Princess Royal (Anne, the Queen's daughter) and three other high-ranking members of the Royal Family. (Not open to the public.)

There are six more large Crown properties occupied by other members of the Royal Family in the UK, and a further seven abroad. There is further information on the royal residences on www.hrp.org.uk and www.royal.uk/royal-art-and-residences.

The Duchy of Cornwall

The Duchy of Cornwall isn't a building – it's a huge sprawling estate that embraces property far beyond the borders of the county of Cornwall. The Duchy is managed by Prince Charles as Duke of Cornwall (that's why Camilla, his second wife, is Duchess of Cornwall). He is entitled to the income derived from the Duchy's large estate and its portfolio of investments. Its star property and Charles's favourite residence, the eighteenth-century Highgrove House, was acquired in 1980. Its gardens are open to the public: www.highgrovegardens.com.

The Duchy also provides two other royal residences: Llwynywermod Myddfai, Carmarthenshire (the official Welsh residence of Prince Charles) and Tamarisk House on the remote Isles of Scilly off the coast of Cornwall.

Private Properties

In addition to Crown properties, the Windsors own private property, too. Their personal portfolio includes:

>> **Sandringham House (www.sandringhamestate.co.uk):** A Georgian mansion set in a large estate where the Royal Family spends Christmas German style, following traditions – such as opening gifts on Christmas Eve – established by Prince Albert (see Chapter 3). (Open to the public at certain times.)

>> **Balmoral Castle (www.balmoralcastle.com):** A Disney-esque retreat in the Scottish Highlands, built by Victoria and Albert in the 1850s, is the Royal Family's late summer residence. (Open to the public at certain times.)

The Windsors also have a wide portfolio of other properties, including six distinguished manors, halls and stately homes.

Are You Being Served? Meeting the Royal Household

TIP

Formerly known as the *Royal Court* (all those paid or unpaid in regular attendance on the sovereign), the name is now out of fashion and appears only at uber-formal occasions such as coronations and in the 'Court Circular' (see Chapter 8). It has been replaced by the less snobby *Royal Household*.

The official titles of members of the Royal Household go back many centuries. They are often largely irrelevant. There's a Master of the Horse, for example, but no Master of the Motor Car; a Keeper of the Privy Purse but no Keeper of the Royal Credit Card; loads of Gentlemen Ushers but not one Lady Usher, and so on. Some of these titles relate to actual jobs, others are honorary.

Let's look at how one of these positions works: ladies-in-waiting. These are the women who *attend* – look after – a member of the Royal Family, in our case the Queen. Working servants like Bobo Macdonald (see Chapter 6) are not included. One or more of these well-bred ladies-in-waiting is in attendance on the Queen on all public occasions. They do things like hold coats and umbrellas, and handle the bouquets of flowers with which the Queen is often presented.

The names and titles of these courtiers read like characters in a children's story book. For example: Fortune FitzRoy, the late Duchess of Grafton (Mistress of the Robes); American-born Virginia Ogilvy, Countess of Airlie (Lady of the Bedchamber); and the Ladies-in-Waiting, Lady Diana Farnham, Lady Susan Hussey, and Lady Susan Elton.

WARNING

Britain is often criticised for its class system based on birth rather than ability. Whatever the merits of an hereditary monarchy, is it sensible in the twenty-first century for it to remain the pinnacle of an aristocratic pyramid?

The five key departments of the household

The Royal Family is supported by a vast team of support staff, but the five most important roles are as follows:

>> The **Private Secretary's Office**, run by the private secretary to the sovereign, is the heartbeat of the household. It has a section to itself later in this chapter.

>> Finance is dealt with by a man (always a man) known as the **Keeper of the Privy Purse** and **Treasurer to the Sovereign**. His lieutenants are the Deputy Treasurer to the Sovereign, who handles money the household receives from the state, and a Deputy Keeper of the Privy Purse (see Chapter 17) responsible for personal matters such as the finances of the Queen's racing stables.

TECHNICAL STUFF

The household's financial system changed little between 1952 and 1996. The first four keepers for Elizabeth were military men from the Establishment with no serious accountancy training. The first, Brigadier-General Charles Tryon, 2nd Baron Tryon was the grandson of a Victorian vice-admiral who was responsible for one of the Royal Navy's most embarrassing peacetime disasters. (The vice-admiral drowned when his battleship sank after colliding with another in broad daylight and on a calm sea.) The Duke of Edinburgh described the second, Major Sir Rennie Maudslay, as a 'silly little Whitehall twit.'

With the appointment of Sir Michael Peat in 1996 the job finally went to a qualified accountant. Though Eton- and Oxford-trained, like so many of the Establishment, Peat had a French MBA, years of accountancy experience, and had conducted a detailed study into the working of the royal finances in 1986. His two successors were both accountants from KPMG. The latest, Sir Michael Stevens (appointed 2018) is not even a graduate of either Oxford or Cambridge University. Slowly, like the institution they served, the office of Keeper of the Privy Purse was chivvied into the twenty-first century.

>> The day-to-day management of the household – what might be termed 'below stairs' matters – is in the hands of the **Master of the Household**. Once again, Elizabeth has chosen to work with people from the same background as Philip and herself. From Lieutenant-Colonel The Honourable Sir Piers Legh in 1952 to the appointment of Vice-Admiral Sir Tony Johnstone-Burt in 2013, her household masters have all been either admirals or high-ranking army officers. Not that that makes them unsuited to the task.

Johnstone-Burt had a distinguished career in Helicopter Command, fighting organised crime in Kabul, Afghanistan, and as Chief of Staff to NATO's Supreme Allied Command Transformation. In a 2016 interview, he praised his boss's caring side. On his handling of staff matters, she always asked, 'Master, are you being kind?' He answered yes, of course. Kind or not, I don't imagine he has much trouble sorting out squabbling Palace chefs.

>> The **Lord Chamberlain's Office**, once responsible for theatre censorship (see the nearby sidebar for more on this story), now looks after the pageantry. This means occasions such as the state opening of Parliament, royal garden parties (see Chapter 21), royal weddings, and funerals. In 2021, the position of Lord Chamberlain was filled by Andrew Parker, Baron Parker of Minsmere, a former head of MI5 (Britain's domestic security service).

As the post of Lord Chamberlain is part-time, the Queen's comptroller manages his department's everyday matters. The current incumbent, Lieutenant Colonel Michael Vernon, had his work cut out arranging the 2021 funeral of the Duke of Edinburgh during the Covid crisis.

TIP

Though no one talks about it openly, Vernon and his department have plans for the Queen's funeral tucked away in a bottom drawer. It's codenamed Operation London Bridge and will be launched by the phrase 'London Bridge is down.'

>> The **Royal Collection Department** is responsible for the world's largest private art collection (see Chapter 17). The department grabbed Elizabeth's attention in 1964 when its part-time Surveyor of the Queen's Pictures, Professor Anthony Blunt, was outed as a Soviet spy.

Extraordinarily, though he eventually confessed his treachery, Blunt kept his knighthood and remained in post until 1972. Exposing him, Elizabeth was told, would have alerted the Soviets. Others see it differently, saying Blunt was saved by his privileged public school and Cambridge University background.

Two of the three top jobs (known as the 'Great Offices') in the Royal Household are purely ceremonial. The post of Lord Steward is currently held by a Scottish landowner, and the Master of the Horse is an English hereditary peer. They dress up for special occasions but play no part in royal administration. As described earlier, the third Great Officer, the Lord Chamberlain, still has work to do.

The power behind the throne: the Private Secretary's Office

It's clear from *The Crown* that Elizabeth's Private Secretary is a figure of huge influence in British life. Supported by a large and talented staff in the Private Secretary's Office, they are at the very heart of the Establishment.

The private secretary's job is to support the sovereign in their role as Head of State. He (the post has to date always been filled by a man) acts as a pause button, a counsellor, and a buffer, protecting the sovereign from hasty or unwise decisions and shielding them from direct criticism. Like an interpreter, they speak for someone who may not speak for themselves. To do this, they:

>> Liaise between the monarch, the media, the Church, and the armed forces.

>> Act as a go-between, linking the Crown to its governments in the UK and overseas realms.

WARNING

Though not all the details are correct, *The Crown*'s depiction of the influence of private secretaries like Lascelles and Adeane over the under-educated and inexperienced Elizabeth is insightful.

As a consequence, the first secretaries, as much as Elizabeth herself, have guided the monarchy's course over the past 70 years. The holders of the post have been:

>> **Captain Sir Alan Lascelles (1952–1953):** Having resigned from the service of Edward VIII, whom he loathed, Lascelles steered the new Queen down her father's narrow, traditional road. This meant sidelining Philip, the would-be modernizer, where possible.

>> **Lieutenant-Colonel Sir Michael Adeane (1953–1972):** Secretary-cum-confidant who assured the public that there was no 'rift' in the royal marriage in 1957 (see Chapter 12). In 1963, he guided Elizabeth during confusion over Prime Minister Macmillan's successor (see Chapters 12 and 27).

- **Lieutenant-Colonel Sir Martin Charteris (1972–1977):** Bright, supple and extremely useful. Aware of the Queen's 'impeccable negative judgement' and of her mother's 'ostrich' qualities, he helped Elizabeth accept a Labour government in 1964. He wanted Blunt (see the previous section) to 'disappear' – meaning to play no further part in public life rather than something more sinister.

- **Sir Philip Moore (1977–1986):** Famous for explaining why the Queen was late for a formal appointment: she needed her 'tiara time'.

- **Sir William Heseltine (1986–1990):** An Australian who tactfully defused a supposed row between the Palace and Prime Minister Margaret Thatcher over a long-running coal miners' strike.

- **Sir Robert Fellowes (1990–1999):** An Eton-educated banker, son of the Queen's land agent at Sandringham, married to Princess Diana's sister . . . he had 'Establishment' written all over him (see Chapter 5 for more about the connotations of 'the Establishment').

- **Lieutenant Sir Robin Janvrin (1999–2007):** A public-school-educated naval officer and career diplomat.

- **Sir Christopher Geidt (2007–2017):** Played a key role in keeping the Crown out of politics when the 2010 election gave no party a parliamentary majority.

- **Sir Edward Young (2017 until the time of writing):** Entered the Royal Household in 2004 after a career in TV, with the Conservative Party, and in corporate communications.

Working for the Royal Family

Has the message finally got through? In 2021, the Royal Family website (www.royal.uk) declared that the household employed 'the very best talent, regardless of gender, race, ethnic or national origin, disability, religion, sexual orientation or age'. Fair enough. All organizations have to put out statements like that nowadays.

What follows is more interesting: 'we seek out future potential . . . recruiting from the widest available pool. Our approach to recruitment and selection is fair, open and based purely on merit.'

WARNING

If this really is the case, then Elizabeth's household – so long a bastion of the public school, Oxford and Cambridge Universities, and the armed forces establishment – really is beginning to change. She will have shaken off the heavy shroud of tradition and inflexibility previously laid upon her shoulders. In so doing, she may have ensured the long-term survival of the institution she heads, and that, in the long run, may prove her finest achievement.

Chapter **10**

The Globe-trotting Monarch

This chapter looks at Elizabeth's international role, both as ambassador for the UK and head of the Commonwealth (see "Touring the Commonwealth of Nations" below for the lowdown on what this is). Even before the age of constitutional monarchy, kings and queens understood how important it was to be seen by their people. King Henry VIII and Queen Elizabeth I, for example, were continually parading around the country with their court. And when Victoria locked herself away after the death of Prince Albert, Britain's republican movement went into overdrive (see Chapter 3).

TECHNICAL STUFF

Despite being head of a massive overseas empire, Victoria never set foot outside Europe. Even then, her foreign jaunts were largely to visit her family. Her elder son, Prince Albert, was the first royal to venture as far as Australia (1867). It was a fairly riotous visit, during which, while picnicking on a beach near Sydney, he survived an assassination attempt by an Irish nationalist. Albert's brother Edward, first as a prince then as King Edward VII, was the true pioneer of the modern state visit. His numerous trips took in the USA and Canada, India, Egypt, Russia, France, and Greece.

Georges V and VI built on the foundations laid by Edward, though neither could match the popular flamboyance of the natural crowd-pleaser. War and ill-health limited their touring, leaving the way open for Elizabeth to launch a new era in royal globe-trotting.

Let's take a look at how she handled things.

Taking Those All-important First Steps

Having been sheltered from bombs and unwanted publicity during the war (see Chapter 6), in July 1945 the 19-year-old Elizabeth joined her parents on her first official visit. The trip to Ulster (Northern Ireland) was also the first time she had flown. She appeared shy and nervous, and seemed to have taken to heart her grandmother's remark about royalty not smiling in public.

A year later, Elizabeth was back in Belfast, Ulster's capital city, on her own. Twelve months older and without her parents, she was more relaxed – even spontaneous – as she launched Britain's latest aircraft carrier, HMS *Eagle*. The launching of the warship set up Elizabeth's career as the visitor everyone everywhere most wanted to see.

In 1945, while still prime minister, Winston Churchill decided that it would be a good idea for the King and Queen to pay an official visit to the Dominion of South Africa (see the nearby sidebar for an explanation of "The Dominions"). It would be a sort of thank-you for the support the self-governing country had given Britain during World War II. There was a second, unspoken reason for the trip.

TECHNICAL STUFF

THE DOMINIONS

The Dominions were self-governing nations within the British Empire. The term was invented in 1907 as a way of formalizing the independent status of white-dominated former colonies while keeping them within the creaking British Empire.

The factor unifying all of them was loyalty to the Crown as Head of State. The first Dominions were Canada, Australia, New Zealand, Newfoundland, and South Africa. They were later briefly joined by India and Ceylon (Sri Lanka) before the term was abandoned in 1949.

South Africa, bitterly divided on racial and cultural lines, was already under fire from the emerging United Nations. The bulk of the population were black Africans who lived as second-class citizens, without a vote, poor, and outlawed from government and the professions. The minority white population was split between those of British heritage and *Afrikaners* of Dutch heritage. The former's attitude towards black Africans was one of paternalistic benevolence; the latter advocated a policy that would soon be known as apartheid or 'separate development'.

At the end of Victoria's reign, only 46 years previously, the British and the Afrikaners had fought a bitter war. Mutual hatred and suspicion remained. How to create a single nation out of this rancid casserole of bigotry and inequality? The British government's answer was to support Prime Minister Jan Smuts, a British-educated Afrikaner with moderate (by the standards of 1940s South Africa), anti-apartheid views. And the obvious way to demonstrate that support was to show him being warmly befriended by the King and his genial, smiling family.

The plan backfired. The journey around the country was a sparkling success. George VI, Queen Elizabeth, and the Princesses Elizabeth and Margaret were everywhere received by vast, cheering crowds of all colours and backgrounds. During their four-month, 5,000-mile trip (excluding a flight to Rhodesia, now Zimbabwe) they were regaled with dancing, dinners and diamonds. Smuts loaded Elizabeth with 87 diamonds (sources differ on exactly how many) on her 21st birthday.

But in the all-white election the following year, Smuts's party was defeated and the apartheid-bearing Afrikaners came to power. Why had the electorate turned against Smuts? Undoubtedly, his close association with the British Royal Family – living symbols in the Afrikaner mind of an interfering and uncomprehending alien power – counted against him. Of course this was not the fault of the King and Queen, and especially not of Princess Elizabeth.

TIP

Elizabeth carried away from her South African trip two things:

>> Duty came first. She had not wanted to be away from her beloved Philip for so long, but the call of duty was stronger than that of the heart.

>> Politics was a great deal more complicated than she had realized. Seeing that the cheers of the crowd can turn to boos overnight, the best policy was to sit tight, smile, and say nothing.

Travelling Around the World 42 Times (Without a Passport)

The South African experience seemed to give Elizabeth a taste for travel. She had never been abroad before and therefore had not experienced the exotic riches of faraway places – we're told she was astounded by the abundance of food available in South Africa compared with the rationed misery in war-torn Britain.

And she had no need of a passport. Everyone knew who she was.

Elizabeth also enjoyed royal tours because they took her away from the cloying stuffiness of the British court. In other lands they might call her 'ma'am' and attempt an awkward, unpractised bow or curtsey, but there was none of the innate deference that hung over every occasion back home. In Britain, with its aristocrats in stately homes, its House of Lords, and its acute awareness of everyone having a place on the social scale, she was always top dog. Abroad, she was more likely to be seen as a glamorous and perhaps important alien oddity. As such, the pressure was off.

REMEMBER

Excluding visits to Commonwealth countries, during her 70 years on the throne, Elizabeth has made 93 official state visits. (See sidebar "What's the point of state visits?" for more on what happens during them.) The total nears 100 if one adds unofficial visits, stopovers, and her trip to the US as Canada's Head of State. She made her last overseas visit in June 2015, when she was hosted by President Gauck of Germany.

WHAT'S THE POINT OF STATE VISITS?

The Queen needs to visit the Commonwealth countries of which she is Head of State. In her absence, she is represented by a governor-general, but her subjects like to see the real thing once in a while.

At some stage during her reign, the Queen has been Head of State in 32 independent countries. When she came to the throne, the number was seven: Australia, Canada,

Ceylon (Sri Lanka), New Zealand, Pakistan, South Africa, the UK. In 2021, the total was 16:

Antigua and Barbuda	Papua New Guinea
Australia	St Kitts and Nevis
Belize	St Lucia
Barbados	St Vincent and the Grenadines
Canada	Solomon Islands
Grenada	The Bahamas
Jamaica	Tuvalu
New Zealand	

Several countries, notably those granted independence during her reign, adopted the Queen as Head of Sate for a while before choosing to go it alone. These include Malta, Nigeria, Trinidad and Tobago, and Uganda. She was official Head of State in Fiji from its independence in 1970 to the military coup in 1987. Thereafter (until it was abolished in 2012), Fiji's Great Council of Chiefs adopted Elizabeth as their Number One Chief of Fiji ('Tui Viti') and her image remained on the country's banknotes. The Queen responded, as is her custom in difficult situations, with silence. She did not add Tui Viti to her list of titles.

A more embarrassing incident occurred in 1965, when the breakaway white-dominated government of Rhodesia (Zimbabwe) insisted that Queen Elizabeth II was still their Head of State. She rejected the role and never used the title. Understandably, when Zimbabwe became independent in 1970, it did not retain the Queen in her titular role (see Chapter 12 for more on this).

Touring the Commonwealth of Nations

Elizabeth has travelled more widely and more often than any other Head of State ever. This is partly because she is not simply head of *a* state but of many.

In her first major speech (see Chapter 6), Elizabeth dedicated herself to the Commonwealth and has steadfastly held her promise. She never forgets that her Christmas broadcasts are addressed to a global audience of whom she seems genuinely very fond. Her love affair with the Commonwealth began with the highly successful 44,000-mile 'coronation tour' of 1953–1954, when she and Philip visited the West Indies, Australasia, Asia and Africa.

Understanding the Commonwealth's role

Today's Commonwealth of Nations (usually just called 'the Commonwealth') describes itself as 'a voluntary association of 54 independent and equal countries'. Its 2.4 billion people from every background and level of wealth have a common goal 'to promote prosperity, democracy and peace, amplify the voice of small states, and protect the environment.'

TIP

Starting as the British Commonwealth of Nations in 1926, and assuming its modern form in 1949, the institution was born out of the ashes of the British Empire. Its survival into the post-colonial world, therefore, is an extraordinary achievement. Elizabeth, the organisation's symbolic head, must take much credit for this, especially as the majority of members are republics and five have their own monarchies.

REMEMBER

The Commonwealth brings together people from across the world, bound together by history and a common language to:

>> foster trade between members

>> Offer mutual support on matters of security and defence

>> share ideas and culture

>> enhance education

>> participate in sport at the four-yearly Commonwealth Games.

Member states cannot be expelled; nevertheless, they can be suspended from membership, as Zimbabwe was in 2002.

Some countries have chosen to leave: South Africa pulled out in 1961 (rejoining in 1989), Pakistan left in 1972 (rejoining in 1994). The Republic of Ireland has not participated since 1932.

Other countries were late to the party: Cameroon joined in 1995, Rwanda in 2009 – these two are the only Commonwealth countries the Queen has not visited.

Drawing the crowds and spreading joy

One third of all Elizabeth's overseas visits have been to members of the Commonwealth. In the ten years from 1960 to 1969, she went to no less than 28 of them, from Canada in the north to Australia in the south, Malta in the Mediterranean to Trinidad and Tobago in the Caribbean, Fiji in the Pacific to Pakistan in Asia.

TIP

Even her sternest critics admit that, almost without exception, these tours were immensely successful. It's difficult to put one's finger on exactly why. It was partly because, in countries where daily life was grindingly hard, she brought a little stardust, a glimpse of something almost unreal. The crowds had never seen anything like it before, a waving and usually smiling figure from a far-off land who said she was delighted to be with them.

Elizabeth's love of the Commonwealth is sincere. In her 1957 Christmas speech, she declared, 'I cannot lead you into battle, but I can do something else. I can give my heart and my devotion to these old islands and to all the peoples of our brotherhood of nations.' She did not write the speech, but she meant it.

REMEMBER

Elizabeth's non-political stance also helped. Unlike other visiting heads of state – politicians, generals, and the like – she had no axe to grind. All she wanted from a tour was to show Britain in a good light and to make friends. Her hosts could relax more with her, and she won their trust. The benefits of this were shown on a number of occasions, especially when it came to the Commonwealth's position over apartheid South Africa (see earlier in this chapter).

Bowling them over: Elizabeth and the Aussies

Yes, that is a cricket reference. So apt for a section about Anglo–Australian encounters! In England, we're always keen to mention our successes in this great sporting rivalry; we inevitably skip over those (frequent) occasions when we lost.

REMEMBER

In Australia, Elizabeth is styled 'Elizabeth the Second, by the Grace of God Queen of Australia and Her other Realms and Territories, Head of the Commonwealth'. No mention of the UK. Herein lies the Aussie problem: for how much longer will it put up with an absentee Head of State?

The Queen has done her best to make up for her non-residence by visiting Australia 16 times. However, as she admitted during her 2000 visit, it's up to the inhabitants of this rugged, honest and creative land to decide for themselves what they want. They had a chance in 1999, when 54 percent voted to retain the monarchy. The result was said to have been more against the suggested alternative of an appointed president than in favour of the status quo. By way of comparison, in recent years support for the monarchy in Britain varies from around 75 percent (2011) to 58 percent (2021).

TIP

As with many other aspects of the institution, the monarchy's reputation rests on the irreplaceable Elizabeth. When she goes, it is unlikely Australians will welcome a 'King of Australia' for long. Certainly not Charles.

The Saviour of the Commonwealth?

In 1970–1971, British Prime Minister Edward Heath wanted to sell helicopters to the South African regime. The Queen understood the fierce opposition of Africa's Commonwealth leaders and advised caution (see Chapter 15).

WARNING

In 1986, the problem flared again when Margaret Thatcher objected to sanctions against South Africa. The Queen disagreed, as shown in a strong episode of *The Crown*. At the first ever Buckingham Palace working dinner, Elizabeth calmed the anti-Thatcher fury of the seven Commonwealth heads seated with her. Had she failed, the Commonwealth might have fallen apart. Nelson Mandela would say that the Commonwealth had saved South Africa. He might have added, had he known, that Elizabeth II had saved the Commonwealth (see Chapter 18).

Acting As a Royal Ambassador

A state visit from the Queen is always said to benefit Britain. Thanks to her supreme tact, her unflappability, and her ability to appear interested and even excited by whatever is put before her, she invariably gets good press. Cheering crowds and royal waves make good news footage. The majority of the estimated four million people she has met during her state visits have come away with a favourable impression of the UK.

TIP

Favourable yes, but perhaps not always meeting the needs of post-imperial Britain. By definition, hereditary monarchy is associated with the past, with tradition, with solidity, and perhaps with eccentricity – all good for the tourist industry but not necessarily for a state that wants to be seen as dynamic and forward-looking.

THE GHANA DANCE

Much is made of Elizabeth's 1961 state visit to Ghana, especially in an episode of *The Crown*. Here is the background:

- Ghana became an independent state in 1957. Since then, its leader, President Kwame Nkrumah, had been engaged in a power grab, undermining the country's democratic constitution by taking more and more powers for himself. Anti-Nkrumah bomb attacks were detonated in the capital, Accra, shortly before the Queen was due to arrive. The presidential regime needed international support.

- A number of British politicians urged Elizabeth not to travel as her security could not be guaranteed. She rejected the plea, arguing, 'I am not a film star. I am the head of the Commonwealth — and I am paid to face any risks that may be involved.' She then added a more personal note. 'Nor do I say this lightly. Do not forget that I have three children.' She went to Ghana.

- In 1960, Ghana had removed Elizabeth from her position as Head of State and was talking of leaving the Commonwealth.

- In 1961, the Cold War was at its height (the terrifying Cuban Missile Crisis would erupt the following year). The West and the Soviet Union were competing with each other for influence in Africa. Nkrumah, who had visited Moscow and instigated a policy of 'African Socialism', was seeking funds for his showpiece Volta Dam and its attendant hydroelectricity programme.

On arrival, the Queen was greeted by ecstatic crowds. At a state dinner, eager to curry favour with his guest, Nkrumah heaped praises on Elizabeth's head. She replied courteously, and the couple sealed their concord by dancing together before the cameras. At the time, the sight of a young white queen dancing with a black African leader was unusual and attracted much comment. (To grasp its significance, think of apartheid in South Africa, segregation in the USA, and legal 'No Blacks' notices on properties for rent in the UK.)

Subsequently:

- The US funded the Volta Dam, supposedly prompted by British Prime Minister Macmillan's remark to President John F Kennedy, 'I have risked my Queen. You must risk your money'.

- Ghana remained in the Commonwealth.

- Nkrumah continued his socialist policies until ousted by a coup (probably engineered by the CIA) in 1966.

Whether or not the famous dance was a turning point in the West's relations with Ghana – and the rest of black Africa – is open to debate. What is not questioned, however, is Elizabeth's skill, bravery, and the undoubted impact of her state visit.

There's always the gaffe danger, though. In 1997, the Queen and Philip visited India to celebrate the fiftieth anniversary of the country's independence from Britain. The trip went horribly wrong. First, before she landed, British Foreign Secretary Robin Cook made contentious remarks about Kashmir, a territory disputed between India and Pakistan. Then Philip tactlessly questioned the numbers killed by the British in the 1919 Jallianwala Bagh (also known as Amritsar) massacre, where British troops fired on unarmed protestors, killing between 379 and 1500 (estimates vary wildly). None of this was Elizabeth's fault, but she has never returned to the sub-continent.

In general, because of her studied neutrality and bland tactfulness, a royal visit fosters goodwill. (For an example, see "The Ghana dance" sidebar.) When Britain agreed to hand back Hong Kong to China, Anglo–Chinese relations remained uneasy. Time for a state visit! In 1986, Elizabeth duly obliged – the first British monarch ever to visit the Chinese mainland. She could not afford to put a foot wrong, and she didn't. She was warmly greeted and her tour was deemed a great success. Even Philip couldn't spoil it, though he did his best by calling Beijing 'ghastly' and telling British students in China that they ran the risk of getting 'slitty eyes'.

Twenty-five years later, the royal couple clocked up another first – no other British monarch had visited the Republic of Ireland since it achieved independence in 1921. Elizabeth and Mary McAleese, Ireland's elected Head of State, appeared to get on well, and the visit played a notable part in sweetening Anglo–Irish relations after long years of tension and difficulty.

Forging special relationships: Elizabeth and America's presidents

During her 70-year reign, Elizabeth has met 13 out of the 14 incumbent US presidents. Only Lyndon B. Johnson missed out.

TIP

The transatlantic heads of state have got on well, with only one or two awkward moments. Richard Nixon's plan to pair off Prince Charles with his daughter Tricia was not appreciated, nor was Jimmy Carter kissing the Queen Mother on the lips! Jackie Kennedy famously muddied the water by describing the Queen as 'pretty heavy going', to which Princess Margaret retorted, 'But that's what she's there for.'

Jackie was the exception. Michelle Obama got on so well with her royal hostess that she slipped her arm round her. Unphased, Elizabeth responded in kind. (She did not repeat the gesture when Donald Trump, who had insisted on walking in front of her, did the same.) Elizabeth had a good relationship with her early presidents: Harry Truman spoke well of her, and Dwight Eisenhower says he 'got on famously' with the lady he had first met in London during World War II.

The real success stories were the Reagans and the Bushes. George W. Bush lauded the Queen as 'a great friend' who was 'very, very easy to be with'. But even he could not supplant Ronald Reagan in Elizabeth's affections. The movie-star president was given the rare honour of an invitation to stay overnight in Windsor Castle, and the next day she took him riding in Windsor Great Park. She was 'charming' he told the eager press, 'so down to earth'.

Reagan repaid the hospitality by inviting Elizabeth and Philip to Rancho del Cielo, his family ranch in California. By all reports, a good time was had by all. Six years later, the Queen gave him an honorary knighthood, the highest award the UK can grant to a foreigner. 'Sir Ronald' was delighted.

Boosting trade

The monarchy is expensive (see Chapter 17). It's not just the amount of cash the Windsors receive each year from the state, but the amount the state does *not* receive from them because of their unique tax status (see Chapter 17). Monarchists are swift to point out that the Palace team brings in more than it takes out. One way it does this, they say, is through trade deals that come on the back of royal tours.

Unfortunately, this is impossible to verify or quantify. The sort of evidence that's banded about is like that from Henry Catto, US ambassador to the Court of St James' (meaning the UK in political dialect – quaint titles, as I'm sure you now realize, are all part of the show) between 1989 and 1991. In 1976, the Queen visited the US on board the Royal Yacht *Britannia*. When she invited the heads of mega global businesses to official functions on board, Catto said they found it 'impossible' to refuse and 'corporate moguls would devise the most outlandish reasons as to why they should be invited.'

Sure, who wouldn't want to meet the grand lady for themselves and see what she is really like – I've done it myself – but I very much doubt that they came aboard with cheque books or ready-signed trade deals in their breast pockets. Besides, even if they did, a trade deal does not guarantee profit. A poorly worded one can have exactly the opposite result.

In 2017, a consultancy firm estimated that the revenue brought in from all royal visits, not just those made by the Queen, averaged about £150 million a year. A large sum? Not compared with the £543 billion brought in from all the UK's exports. And there is no way of telling whether trade deals would have been struck anyway, with or without a royal visit.

Nevertheless, the high personal esteem in which Elizabeth is held in most parts of the world – whatever their views on hereditary monarchy – can only spill over into the country's diplomatic, security and commercial spheres. Such soft power cannot be priced, but it is undeniably strong.

Passing the baton to other royals

Elizabeth stopped making overseas tours in 2015. Her family had been helping with the touring schedule for many years, so taking over the whole lot did not make too much of a difference. (Except that no one draws the crowds like the Queen herself, and none of her relations has managed to match her calm unflappability in all conditions and situations).

Charles heads the list of secondary tourists. His style is more relaxed than his mother's. In 2014, for example, he was applauded for joining in a traditional sword dance in Saudi Arabia. Earlier, he had been criticized for not looking back at his fiancée as he boarded a plane for a tour of India. Diana remained on the tarmac, weeping. On the tour he half-jokingly remarked, on a visit to the Taj Mahal, that if he were a Muslim he could have 'lots of wives'. Not exactly tactful from someone about to get married (see Chapter 16 for more about his royal wedding).

When Charles returned to India 12 years later, this time with Diana, he stayed in Delhi while she visited the Taj Mahal, the monument to undying love, by herself. In 2016, a tearful Prince William (Charles and Diana's elder son) made a point of being photographed with his wife Catherine in front of the iconic symbol where his mother had sat alone. The young couple has made official visits to 19 other countries to date, including two trips each to Canada, France, and the United States.

Using Planes, Trains and Automobiles

It's all well and good for Elizabeth to travel to so many countries, but how does she get there? And how does she move around her own country? One thing's for sure: she doesn't roll up at an airport's transportation hub or call a cab.

Let's take a quick look at all of Elizabeth's means of transport, not just those used on overseas state visits.

Royal coaches

How did Cinderella get to the ball? In a glittering horse-drawn coach, of course. That's exactly what Elizabeth and other royals use for short journeys on state occasions. They have dozens of horse-drawn wheeled vehicles and a handful of royal sleighs at their disposal.

GOLD STATE COACH

Commissioned by George II on his accession, the four-ton, gold-gilded vehicle has been used at every coronation from 1821 onwards. Though it looks amazing, the lumbering lump of sculpture is seriously impractical. It turns slower than a container ship. A team of eight Windsor Grey horses haul it along at a walking pace – any quicker and its anti-quated suspension would probably shake to pieces.

Elizabeth politely described her coronation ride in its velvet and satin interior as 'not very comfortable', and she declined to use it for her Diamond Jubilee. The baroque (some would say vulgar) figures on the outside represent England, Scotland and Ireland, and eighteenth-century Britain's maritime prowess. When on the road, the rolling symbol of monarchial pomp is manned by four, traditionally beardless men (*postilions*) guiding the horses, and accompanied by a bevy of grooms, footmen and guards.

TIP

Most of the royal carriages are housed in the Royal Mews, London, and when not in use can be seen by the public (www.rct.uk/visit/the-royal-mews-buckingham-palace).

Stand-out pieces are the Gold Coach (see the nearby sidebar about this thing of beauty), the large-windowed Glass Coach of 1881 (used at the weddings of Elizabeth and Philip, and Charles and Diana), and the Australian-built, three-ton Diamond Jubilee State Coach (built in 2012). Oddest of the lot is Britain's first charabanc, presented to Queen Victoria by France's last king, Louis Philippe, in 1844. As a fairy-tale coach needs suitably attired drivers and attendants, the Royal Mews has a full range of red and gold fancy-dress uniforms (known as *livery*) for the royal coachmen.

Royal cars

Motor vehicles for royal use are housed next to the coaches in the Royal Mews (see the previous section). The collection was started by Edward VII and has been kept up to date (more or less) ever since. Official state cars have no number plates and are painted in sombre black and claret. They bear the royal coat of arms on a small shield above the windscreen, and a potentially pedestrian-gouging emblem on the front of the bonnet that, for safety reasons, would not be permitted on a standard production car.

For everyday use, there are Daimlers (see Chapter 6), Bentleys, stately Rolls Royces, Jaguars and, of course, a number of Land Rovers and Range Rovers that reflect the Royal Family's love of the outdoors.

Philip insisted that a Land Rover should carry him to his final resting place in 2021, and personally oversaw the design of this customized, military green hearse.

The royal train

Queen Victoria was the first British monarch to travel by train. She was so impressed by the experience that she became a regular rail user, though her drivers were never to exceed 40 mph during the day and 30 mph at night. She bought her own set of royal coaches – plush palaces on wheels that featured one of the first on-board toilets (which she refused to use). The station at Ballater, Aberdeenshire, was specially built to provide rail access to Balmoral Castle. There has been a royal train ever since.

REMEMBER

Though an expensive way to travel (costing £1 million each year to maintain) compared with flying, the 35-year-old set of coaches, dining car and sleeper car offer a very secure means of transport. It also enables royals to work as they travel, and avoids disrupting Britain's overcrowded road network. To save costs, Elizabeth sometimes travels to Sandringham (see Chapter 9) on a regular train – first-class, of course!

The most recent use of the train was in 2020, when William and Kate (Duke and Duchess of Cambridge) toured the UK to thank all those who had worked so hard during the COVID-19 pandemic.

The royal yacht

Elizabeth is not renowned for expressing her emotions in public, but she could not hold back a wistful tear when decommissioning the Royal Yacht *Britannia* in 1997. Launched by the Queen in 1953, and designed as a floating palace that could double as a hospital and even a nuclear shelter in the event of war, during its lifetime the vessel carried Elizabeth and others on 696 overseas visits.

It was on the 133-foot *Britannia* that the Queen welcomed US Presidents Dwight Eisenhower, Gerald Ford, Ronald Reagan, and Bill Clinton. Prince Charles and Princess Diana honeymooned on board. The million miles it sailed included taking the Royal Family on an annual summer tour of Scotland's Western Isles. *Britannia* can now be visited in Leith Docks, Edinburgh: https://www.royalyachtbritannia. co.uk.

For 44 years, the royal yacht was a symbol of majesty and Britain's status as a maritime power. The decision not to replace it rankled with traditionalists. When Prime Minister Johnson announced in 2021 that he was planning a new £200-million yacht (suggested name: 'Prince Philip'), his proposal was greeted with delight and alarm in equal measure. Some saw it as a striking reminder that Britain was still a global power; others condemned it as folly, a costly nod to former glory.

Apparently, Princes Charles and William were not sold on the idea, and the Palace kept quiet. Maybe Elizabeth saw the implications behind the *Financial Times*' observation, 'greatness does not lie in the trappings of history'?

Royal flight

Edward VIII pioneered the concept of a King's Flight of aircraft dedicated to royal use. The concept, renamed the Queen's Flight in 1952, survived until it was merged with the Royal Air Force in 1995. Since then, Elizabeth has flown in specially chartered planes, including the supersonic Anglo-French Concorde.

TIP

The Queen's chosen airline is British Airways, with whom the mother of Kate, Duchess of Cambridge, once worked as an attendant.

The Royal Household also operates the Queen's Helicopter Flight for short-haul journeys. It is said that the Queen, aware of public criticism of her family's extravagant flight-chartering habits, has set a limit of what they may spend on non-standard air travel.

Chapter **11**

The Queen Mother

'Queen Mother' is an ancient title dating from at least the sixteenth century. When given to the widowed wife of George VI in 1952, ordinary folk found it a bit stuffy and in popular parlance it was shortened to the more affectionate 'Queen Mum'.

No one objected publicly, though Queen Mary – Elizabeth's formidable grandmother and George V's wife – cannot have approved of the un-aristocratic associations of the word 'mum'.

Despite the ancient title, the modern Queen Mum's role was very different from any royal mother who came before her, and this chapter looks at the unique precedent she set both for herself and the wider Royal Family.

Creating a New Role for the Former Empress

The former Queen and Empress of India was deeply saddened by the passing of Bertie, her 56-year-old husband. In her wretchedness she blamed Wallis Simpson for burdening him with a crown whose weight had helped crush him to death (see Chapter 5).

THE CASTLE OF MEY

Visiting friends in the north of Scotland shortly after her husband's death, the Queen Mother drove past the semi-derelict Barrogill Castle. On impulse, the story goes, she decided to buy it. She restored the fabric and the original name, the Castle of Mey, that had been changed to Barrogill in the later eighteenth century.

Some say the Queen Mother bought the castle for £1.00, others £100 (between $1.30 and $130.00 at the 2022 exchange rate). Whichever is correct, the owners were only too pleased to get the place taken off their hands. And for the bereft ex-queen, it seemed the ideal place in which to lock herself away and feel miserable. The mood soon passed. Over the next three years, she paid out of her own pocket (or overdraft) to convert Scotland's most northerly castle into a habitable dwelling – her 'country cottage'.

Never a palace and never especially comfortable, the building Princess Margaret called 'Mummy's drafty castle' was a retreat where the dowager queen could supervise her gardeners, entertain guests, and be treated – in some ways – as a member of a local community.

The castle is now held in trust and is open to the public at certain times: www.castleofmey.org.uk. Why not take a visit if you happen to be passing?

REMEMBER

No longer the power behind the throne, Elizabeth decided her glory days were over. She had retired from public life for only a few weeks before she realized – prompted by Winston Churchill – that she could carve out a new and perhaps enjoyable role for herself. She would, as she put it, 'continue the work we [George VI and herself] sought to do together.' But this time, as queen mother rather than queen, she could relax and re-fashion herself into the nation's well-loved grandmother.

She could follow the horse racing calendar uninterrupted, keep a friendly eye on her daughters and grandchildren, collect art, hold parties with whoever she wished, make the occasional formal appearance, go on a few interesting overseas tours . . . it was all going to be rather fun. And it was, too. She even purchased a new castle for herself (see the sidebar, "The Castle of Mey").

More importantly, Elizabeth the Queen Mother conveyed that sense of enjoyment to almost everyone she met.

Sharing the Queen's Duties

Elizabeth the Queen Mother was only 51 when she was widowed. Maintaining what her grandson Charles called an 'effervescent enthusiasm for life', she justified her handsome recompense from the state (see Chapter 17) by undertaking a fair number of official duties.

Popularity led to thousands of requests from all kinds of organizations for the Queen Mother to be their patron or president, and she accepted around 350 of them. They ranged from extremely formal positions, such as Colonel-in-Chief of a regiment, to patron of the Royal School of Needlework.

Flying the royal flag

The Queen Mother made 40 solo overseas visits in all, including a successful trip to the USA in 1954. At home, she is reported to have kept up a regular 100 or so official visits per annum well into her 80s.

TIP

Similar to Princess Diana – and unlike most other members of her family – she liked the camera and had a good rapport with the media. She rarely appeared wooden (unlike her over-duteous daughter, Elizabeth), or tetchy (unlike her grandson, Charles), or rude (unlike her son-in-law, Philip). Journalists appreciated this, and frequently hailed her as the country's favourite royal.

Wherever she went, her ready smile and willingness to talk to everyone won her a string of admirers. She was quick-witted, too. When in South Africa she was once accosted by an elderly Boer who said that he could never forgive the English for what they had done to 'his' country in Victoria's reign. 'I do understand that so well,' the Queen Mother replied with a nod. 'We in Scotland feel very much the same.'

On one widely reported occasion in 1968, when toilet rolls were thrown in her direction by protesting students, she picked one up, handed it to a nearby dissenter, and asked with cheeky innocence, 'Is this yours?'

TIP

I have a personal memory of this common touch from when she came to my secondary school to open a new science block. The ceremony involved an official unlocking of the front door. As she struggled to get the key in the lock, she observed with a grin, 'The bloody thing doesn't fit!' A member of the Royal Family actually swearing (albeit mildly) instantly won the hearts and minds of her schoolboy audience. (The only other time I met her she was very elderly, and shaking hands was like grasping an empty rubber glove.)

Much is made of the Queen Mother's hospitality. A keen art collector – Monet and Augustus John were among her favourites – she liked nothing better than to host a table of sparkling wits. Accompanied by sparkling wine, of course. All kinds of stories circulate about her drinking habits.

Loyal courtiers say the Queen Mother drank like any aristocrat: cocktails before meals and wine with. Those less discrete support the image of her in the British *Spitting Image* satirical TV puppet show: perpetually tipsy. I have read one suggestion that her weekly alcohol consumption was 70 units per week, 56 more than the 14 recommended by the government. If true, it doesn't say much for government guidance. 101 (the age at which she died) is a pretty good innings.

Remaining the Queen's mother (not just the Queen Mother)

Before her death in 2002, aged 101, the Queen and her mother spoke on the phone almost about every day. Much of the time, we're told, the subject of their conversations was horses: Was such-and-such a mare coming along well? What were the odds on a three-legged, blind racehorse in the 3:30 at Chepstow (I jest here, but they did discuss horseracing)?

Inevitably, on the phone and in person, they also discussed more serious matters. The Queen Mother did not approve of the influence of 'Dickie' Mountbatten, Philip's uncle and Elizabeth II's second cousin once removed (see Chapter 14). She played a major role in preventing her daughter from adopting 'Mountbatten' as her married name.

The queen dowager wept at her daughter Margaret's doomed love affair with Group Captain Peter Townsend (a commoner, not of royal blood – see Chapter 13), and comforted Prince Charles when he was subjected to a 'toughening-up' education by his insensitive father (see Chapters 12 and 16). Herself a commoner, she sympathized with Princess Diana's difficulty in adapting to life with the Windsors (see Chapter 16).

REMEMBER

Throughout it all, the Queen and her mother remained very close friends. The former queen played the game by deferring to her daughter in matters of protocol, such as standing aside to let the sovereign pass first through a doorway. In return, the Queen always made sure her mother was well cared for (see Chapter 17) and kept in funds – even paying off the £4 million overdraft that the Queen Mother had maintained in order to reduce death duties (inheritance tax).

Flipping the Coin: The Other Side of the Queen Mother

The Queen Mother was no saint. Some of her remarks, especially in private, sound today suspiciously like racism. She made no secret of her wartime-bred dislike of the Germans and Japanese, and could be pretty scathing about the French too – 'How can one trust them?'

On the other hand, she was a pioneer among the royals for her open acceptance of gay men. Indeed, she once said that if she were not allowed to employ them, she would have to resort to doing her own chores.

Like all the royals, she could be a dreadful snob, failing to understand the lives of ordinary people. When taking tea with a friend who had moved into a smaller house with an unprepossessing view from the front window, she remarked, 'Darling, you must have them close the petrol station and move that school.' I suppose, if one is allowed to run up a £4 million overdraft, that is the sort of way one thinks!

Then there is the question of her 'hidden nieces'. The public were never told that two of the Queen Mother's nieces, Katherine and Nerissa Bowes-Lyon, had been committed to a psychiatric asylum in 1941 because of their severe learning difficulties. In 1963 they were reported in *Burke's Peerage* (a listing of the British aristocracy and landed gentry) to have died. In fact, both were still alive. Katherine died in 1986 and Nerissa in 2014, her grave marked by a plastic tag bearing a serial number.

The reason for the 'hiding' of Katherine and Nerissa has never been officially explained. It may have been done out of a mix of shame, and reluctance to give the Nazis anything that might be used for anti-British wartime propaganda.

WARNING

The Bowes-Lyon family paid only a minimal annual fee to the asylum where the two 'imbeciles' lived. Apparently, neither received a visit, a birthday or Christmas card from the family. It is unclear whether the Queen Mother, who was patron of a leading charity for people with learning difficulties, knew any of this. The issue features in *The Crown*.

Sharing Royal Duties Around the Family

Until 2000 and beyond, the Queen bore the brunt of important royal duties, the opening and launching, meeting and greeting. Her mother helped until she became too frail, and the rest of the immediate Royal Family have always helped out with more than 2,000 official functions each year.

REMEMBER

Having survived two bouts of cancer, the Queen Mother suffered a number of falls in 2000–2002 and died in her sleep on 30 March 2002. Huge queues formed to view her coffin as she lay in state (see Chapter 21), and an estimated crowd of one million admirers turned out for her state funeral.

Over the years, a visit from the Queen Mother – more relaxed and often more amusing than one by her daughter – had been one of the highlights of the social calendar for millions. The example she set was a hard act to follow. She had taken on fewer duties as her years advanced, however, and by the later decades of the twentieth century, more junior members of the family were stepping up to the plate.

Out and about with Charles and Anne

Since they came of age, Prince Charles and Princess Anne have been among the most committed of their mother's assistants. Neither had an easy start – Charles was the 'loony prince' and Anne the 'difficult teenager' – but over time each carved out a distinctive niche for themself (see Chapters 14 and 16).

At the beginning of Charles's first state visit, the President of Finland walked right past without recognizing him. Things could only get better, and they did. He found the crowds of ordinary people easier to handle than the media, with whom he never got on well, and by the end of the century he was undertaking 600 engagements each year. By the time he reached his 70s, he was still clocking hundreds of engagements a year.

Princess Anne's style is very different from that of her brother. The *Princess Royal* (a title bestowed on her by her mother in 1987), is down to earth and practical like her father. She is extremely hard-working, too, often coming top of the royal engagements league table. (These unofficial tables, gleaned from the Court Circular – see Chapter 8 – appear in many British newspapers). Anne's most notable work has been as president of Save the Children and with The Princess Royal Trust for Carers, a charity she established in 1991. Sports fans note that, as patron of the Scottish Rugby Union, she almost never misses a Scotland rugby international.

Remaining a working family

As well as Elizabeth, Philip, Charles and Anne, other members of The Firm have played their part in tape-cutting and hand-shaking. These include the Queen's cousins and their wives, and the families of her other two children, Princes Andrew and Edward.

At the time of writing, Edward's wife, Sophie Countess of Wessex, is very much the flavour of the month on the Windsor PR website, Royal Family (www.royal.uk).

TECHNICAL STUFF

In 2018, Prince William is said to have attended 220 official events, Prince Harry 193, and Kate and Meghan 174 between them. In the same year, Charles logged 507, and his 92-year-old mother 283 – the Queen Mother would have been proud of her.

3

The Need to Adapt

The style of monarchy inherited by Queen Elizabeth II was based on that established by George V and Queen Mary. After Edward VIII's brief and turbulent reign, the institution withdrew into the past, emphasising tradition, stability, and duty. Those qualities had served well during a time of war but looked increasingly out of place in the years that followed.

Elizabeth was guided by old men, such as Churchill and Lascelles, with roots in the pre-war era. Conservative by nature and upbringing, she was also weighed down by her sense of duty. As a consequence, she struggled to come to terms with post-war culture. She and the hereditary monarchy she had sworn to uphold, began to look like a museum piece.

In response, one cautious step at a time, the Queen learned to adapt. As the chapters in this part explain, it was a difficult and at times painful process. Nevertheless, she managed it. Her reward was a Silver Jubilee awash with affection and growing respect.

Chapter **12**

Times They Are a-Changing

Today's Britain was born in the 25 years following the end of World War II. It was a quarter century of painful readjustment in almost every area of national life, not least in its time-honoured monarchy. As the British Empire crumbled, so too did the attitudes and values that had held it together.

Deference and duty, the twin pillars of the Establishment, were mocked by a younger generation that refused to respect something simply because it was old or traditional. This put the monarchy – the very epitome of age and tradition – under the sort of strain not felt since the abdication crisis of 1936.

How did Elizabeth handle this changing world? Read on!

Witnessing Britain's Waning Influence in the World

It had always been strange that a small group of damp islands off the northwest coast of Europe should have acquired a global empire. Indeed, some claimed that it had been done 'in a fit of absence of mind' rather than as part of a deliberate policy. Certainly, it was always more of a commercial agglomeration than a military one.

Britain's brief period of global dominance rested on three pillars:

>> political stability.

>> the wealth created by the world's first industrial revolution (roughly 1750–1850).

>> the sea power that enabled the acquisition of an empire and secured overseas trade.

By the time of Elizabeth's accession in 1952, political stability remained but the other two were in sharp decline.

REMEMBER

In 1945, after six years of world war, Britain was bankrupt. A $3.75 billion loan from the USA tided things over for a short period but could not hide the country's underlying economic flaws:

>> low productivity and investment

>> outdated practices and plant

>> over-reliance on trade with a shrinking empire

>> huge costs of an expanding welfare state and large-scale nationalisation

By 1970, rival economies of countries such as West Germany and Japan were leaving Britain in their wake. The USA had already overtaken Britain at the start of the century. Against this background, the glittering wealth of the Royal Family was more conspicuous than ever.

Elizabeth's problem was that the institution she inherited, with all its majestic imperial trimmings, had been designed to head a world-wide empire. By 1952, that gilded majesty was starting to look pretentious – shabby even – now the empire was dissolving like snow in the springtime.

No longer ruling an empire

The Empire had grown in fits and starts, first with colonies in North America that were soon lost, then with a gradual acquisition of other territories around the globe. The bulk of it was put together in a short period of time, roughly 1750–1900, and dismantled over an even shorter period.

It began with the granting of self-government to the Dominions (see Chapter 10). Ireland broke away immediately after World War I, followed by India, Pakistan and Ceylon (modern-day Sri Lanka) following World War II. Barbados joined their ranks as recently as 2021.

The quitting by the Indian subcontinent nations heralded an avalanche of independence, much of it during the reign of Elizabeth II. Before long, in the words of the ground-breaking 1960s satirical TV show *That Was the Week That Was*, Britain was left with 'sweet Rockall'. (Rockall is an uninhabited rocky outcrop in the North Atlantic.)

No longer ruling the waves

Before World War I, Britain built 60 percent of the world's ships. On D–Day, 1944, a fleet of 900 British warships escorted the Allied forces across the Channel to the beaches of Normandy, France. The fleet that retook the Falkland Islands after an Argentinian invasion (see Chapter 18) numbered 115 vessels. By 2016, Britain could muster a total of 37 frontline warships, half of which were under repair or maintenance.

Within a few years, the pomp and circumstance of the 1953 coronation had begun to look more like a yearning for what had been than the launchpad for a glorious future (see the nearby sidebar on the 1956 Suez crisis). During a period of decline, is it best to hold to the past or steer ahead into uncertain waters? Elizabeth had to decide.

No longer ruling the Middle East

Looking at the places Elizabeth has visited during her long reign (Chapter 10 travels the world with her), perhaps you are wondering why so many countries *wanted* to see her? It was partly out of curiosity and partly because of their strong historical and cultural links with Britain.

BRITAIN AND SUEZ, 1956

In 1956, after the West had refused to fund his Aswan Dam project on the River Nile, Egyptian President Gamal Abd al-Nasser seized the Suez Canal. Britain and France, in league with Israel, sent in troops to occupy the globally important canal zone. The US objected strongly, even threatening to ruin the British economy, and the invaders pulled out. This humiliation is said to mark the end of Britain as a global power. Elizabeth had been kept abreast of events; unlike many of her subjects, she had not made public her opposition to the operation.

This short timeline shows some of the states east of the Suez Canal that Britain withdrew from during the Queen's lifetime. That they welcomed a visit from Elizabeth after independence suggested there were no hard feelings – Britain (perhaps learning from the American experience of 1775–1783) managed its twentieth-century colonial withdrawal with far less rancour and bloodshed than Europe's other imperial powers:

1932 Iraq

1946 Jordan

1947 India, Pakistan

1948 Ceylon (now Sri Lanka), Burma (Myanmar), Palestine

1951 Oman

1954 Egypt ceases to be a client state

1957 Federation of Malaya (Malaysia, Singapore, Sarawak, North Borneo/Brunei)

1961 Kuwait

1971 Bahrain, Qatar, United Arab Emirates

1997 Hong Kong

No longer ruling Africa

In the second half of the nineteenth century, much of the African continent was colonized by European powers. By the time Elizabeth came to the throne, the existence of vast swathes of Africa under the rule of a tiny foreign minority had become an anathema. For moral as well as financial reasons, Britain had to ditch its African colonies.

Elizabeth went along with the move. She knew colonialism was doomed, and she saw in its replacement – the Commonwealth – an opportunity for her to maintain her status as a global monarch. Moreover, she had seen from events in South Africa the nightmare that might arise if a white minority refused to accept a black majority into the government (see Chapter 10 for more details).

REMEMBER

As Britain handled the decolonization process in a relatively peaceful manner (compared with France and Portugal), many African countries – as with those in Asia – welcomed a visit from their former queen. In 1979, to take just one example, she was warmly received on a state visit to Botswana.

Here's a timeline of British withdrawal from Africa during Elizabeth's lifetime:

1931 South Africa largely independent

1956 Sudan

1957 Ghana (previously Gold Coast)

1960 Nigeria, Somaliland

1961 Tanzania (Tanganyika), Sierra Leone, South Cameroon

1962 Uganda

1963 Kenya

1964 Malawi (Nyasaland), Zambia (Northern Rhodesia)

1965 Zimbabwe (Southern Rhodesia), Gambia

1966 Botswana (Bechuanaland), Lesotho (Basutoland)

1968 Eswatini (Swaziland), Mauritius

1976 Seychelles

Joining the European Economic Community

Following World War II, Winston Churchill spoke of the possibility of a 'United States of Europe'. Though no USE emerged to balance the power of the USA and the USSR, first steps were taken with the creation of the European Economic Community (EEC) in 1957.

Whether or not to belong to this continental club (latterly the European Union or EU – see the nearby sidebar of the same name) has remained a major issue in British politics ever since.

TECHNICAL STUFF

Britain's application to join was twice vetoed by France's President de Gaulle (1962 and 1967). The UK finally became a signed-up member of the EEC in 1973. Membership was opposed by those on the left and right of British politics. It particularly rankled with hard-right members of the Conservative Party, who finally engineered Britain's withdrawal from the Union in 2020 after a referendum in 2016 (see Chapter 25).

TIP

Elizabeth's attitude to the EEC when Britain joined was hard to fathom: as always, she avoided making public reference to current politics. In 1962, she cancelled her sister's visit to France when it rejected Britain's application to join the Community; ten years later, she helped Britain's successful application by making a state visit to the same country.

The nearest Elizabeth came to commenting on what she called 'one of the most significant decisions of my reign' was in her 1972 Christmas broadcast. 'New links with Europe will not replace those with the Commonwealth,' she declared. 'They cannot alter our historical and personal attachments with kinsmen and friends overseas.' The words may well have echoed her own sentiments as well as those of the government, with the former probably predominant. To emphasise the point, she went on, 'Britain will take her Commonwealth links into Europe with her.' She would do so, anyway.

THE EUROPEAN UNION

In 1949, ten west European states set up the Council of Europe for greater political cooperation. Two years later, Belgium, France, West Germany, Italy, Luxembourg and the Netherlands established the European Coal and Steel Community (ECSC) to increase economic integration.

This morphed into the European Economic Community in 1957, and then into the European Union in 1993.

It aimed to foster political and economic union between its 27 members. The EU is controlled by an appointed commission and an elected parliament; 19 of its members use the same currency, the euro.

However it was dressed up, Britain's joining the EEC from a position of weakness was another mark of waning power. The UK could not afford to go it alone, with or without the Commonwealth.

Surviving Gossip, Constitutional Complications, and Political Scandal

The glittering coronation, the talk of a new Elizabethan age, and reaping the harvest of peace . . . We can now see that Britain was deceiving itself, hiding from a gloomier reality.

The shield behind which it hid was its lovely new queen. It was all too good to last – and it didn't.

Philip's solo world tour

'It is quite untrue that there is any rift between the Queen and the Duke of Edinburgh' – Buckingham Palace's sudden and unprecedented announcement on 22 February 1957 shocked the world. What on earth was going on?

Well might we ask. Welcome to the world of nod and wink, rumour and denial. Essentially, there are two schools of thought:

>> The foreign press and several books clearly state that during his long marriage to Elizabeth, Philip had several affairs.

>> The deniers accept at face value refutations by the Palace (as in the opening sentence of this section) and Philip himself that any royal dalliances took place.

WARNING

The Crown hinted at Philip's indiscretions but left it to the viewer to decide. For the time being, that's probably the wisest line to take. (I have been warned: in a previous book about the Royal Family, the publisher's lawyer told me to stay away from stories of Philip's philandering!). After all, when the Queen is no longer with us, it is likely that further evidence – if there is any – may come to light.

Does any of this really matter? In one sense, no. What the husband of the monarch got up to in his spare time is his own business. On the other hand, if the rumours are to be believed, then we have been lied to. That's not a good example for the Head of State to set.

Weathering the storm

The rumours began in 1956–1957 when Philip left his wife and family back home and boarded the royal yacht Britannia for an extensive Commonwealth tour. As well as performing a number of official duties, such as opening the Olympic Games in Melbourne, Australia, he also had a good time. He was on board a ship again and free to relive the pranks of his days in the Royal Navy. Blind eyes, it is alleged, were dutifully turned.

This all might have been brushed under the carpet had not Eileen Parker, the wife of Philip's private secretary and close friend Mike Parker, sued for divorce during *Britannia*'s voyage home. She cited her husband's adultery. When he resigned and the air was thick with scandal, the Palace issued the extraordinary denial quoted at the start of this section.

The following year, the Parkers divorced, Philip was made a Prince of the United Kingdom, and he and Elizabeth toured Canada together. One ship had sunk; the other had weathered the storm.

Listening to dinner-table gossip

Some argue that Philip's alleged misdemeanours arose from a double frustration. As a macho man of action, he was humiliated by his role as number two. His plans to streamline the monarchy were thwarted by his wife and the Establishment, he was never allowed to see state papers (unlike Victoria's Albert), and he was bored by the formalities of official visits. More than once he was heard to mutter, 'Let's go!'.

Philip managed some reform in the running of the royal palaces. Too often, though, he was reduced to making small and largely irrelevant changes, such as no longer requiring footmen to powder their hair (!) and stopping a bottle of whiskey being placed beside the Queen's bed every evening. (The custom began when Queen Victoria's doctor prescribed a bedtime tot for her cold, and had persisted ever since.)

'I'm just a bloody amoeba!' the despairing Philip is supposed to have cried.

Philip's other frustration, some say, was sexual. The coronation changed Elizabeth, instilling her with an iron belief that God had given her His blessing to rule. Her primary marriage was now to the divinely ordained monarchy; her marriage with Philip thus became secondary. As Princess Diana would famously say many years later (see Chapter 16), there were three in the marriage. Elizabeth and Philip had always had separate bedrooms. For several years after the coronation, it is whispered that she kept the door between the two firmly closed.

All this might help to explain why:

>> Eileen Parker said Philip and Mike Parker used the pseudonyms Murgatroyd and Winterbottom to slip out of the Palace at night to have fun on the town.

>> Courtiers hinted that the moment the Queen left Buckingham Palace, Princess Alexandra, her beautiful cousin, regularly turned up to go 'swimming' with Philip.

>> Stories circulated of affairs and demi-royal offspring in cities around the world.

>> When it was announced in 2021 that Philip's will would remain secret for 90 years, scandalmongers alleged this was to hide payments to those the Palace wished to remain silent.

What Elizabeth knew or believed of any of this gossip we may never know. In private, she was undoubtedly angry and upset. The pristine monarchy burnished so dutifully by her father and grandfather now had dirty fingermarks on it.

Was she surprised? Probably not.

TECHNICAL STUFF

Elizabeth knew of Philip's dashing bachelor days, and she knew, as the loyal Bobo had said reassuringly, 'boys will be boys'. Georges V and VI apart, the Royal Family had never been hot on Biblical virtue. Elizabeth's uncles, including Edward VIII, were well-known libertines, and her great-grandfather, Edward VII, had even presented his mistress Lillie Langtry to Queen Victoria!

If Philip did err from the straight and narrow, he would have found the path well worn.

The princess and the politician

When the Philip scandal broke, Elizabeth was only just recovering from the trauma of her sister's shattered love affair (see Chapter 13). By 1952, the lively, capricious Margaret was sleeping with Group Captain Peter Townsend. The dashing war ace had been a trusted and well-liked courtier for several years. In many ways it was the perfect relationship: the pretty, modern-minded young royal with an honorable and respected friend of the family.

Just one snag: Townsend was divorced. Divorced! The word sent shivers down the royal spines as images of Wallis Simpson floated before their eyes. It didn't matter that Townsend had been the 'innocent' party in the separation; what did matter was that the Church of England, of which the Queen was head, did not at the time recognize divorce. If Margaret and her paramour were to marry, it would have to be a civil service.

With a grinding of teeth and a flapping of ermine, the Establishment closed ranks to prevent the union.

>> The Archbishop of Canterbury and several Tory peers were opposed.

>> Lascelles (who Margaret said she would curse to the grave) and the household were set against it.

>> Prime Minister Eden said he faced resignations if it went ahead.

>> Even Prince Philip, supposedly a reformer, refused to back Townsend. Some say he was jealous of the man's popularity.

Against such an array of angry negativity, the Queen, Margaret and her lover, and almost certainly the majority of the British people, were powerless. Feeling 'mute and numb', in October 1955 Margaret made a public announcement stating that because of 'the Church's teaching that Christian marriage is indissoluble' she would not be marrying Group Captain Townsend.

REMEMBER

Many believed Margaret never fully recovered from the disappointment (see Chapter 13 for the full story and its aftermath).

Political shenanigans

Whatever the gossip emanating from the Royal Family during the first ten years of Elizabeth's reign, it was nothing compared with the scandal bomb that burst over the heads of the Conservative government in 1963.

The Profumo Affair

TIP

Though it did not concern the Crown directly, this scandal gave sensationalist newspapers another chance to speculate on Philip's misbehaviour. The fallout also brought Elizabeth embarrassingly close to the edge of the political sphere.

Details of what became known as the Profumo Affair are not our direct concern, but they did affect the way the Establishment – and thus the monarchy – was viewed:

>> A well-connected osteopath-cum-artist named Stephen Ward organized high-society parties. Some took place at Cliveden, the estate of Conservative bigwig Lord Astor. Guests included John Profumo, (Secretary of State for War),

the Soviet naval attaché Ivanov, and two attractive young women, Christine Keeler and Mandy Rice-Davies.

>> At one stage, Keeler was having an affair with both Profumo and Ivanov. As rumours mounted, Profumo made a statement to the House of Commons saying he had met Ivanov just twice, and there was 'no impropriety whatsoever in my acquaintanceship with Miss Keeler.' Later that day, he was seen chatting with the Queen Mother at a race meeting.

>> When the truth (or some of it) came out, Profumo resigned, Ward (whose commissions included drawings of Prince Philip and Princess Margaret) committed suicide, and Harold Macmillan decided to step down as prime minister. The choice of successor was not clear-cut.

>> Though none of the Royal Family were known to have been involved in the scandal, its leading figures were certainly part of a social circle headed by the Royals.

>> Gossip spawned in the fetid atmosphere: around my school meal table we felt sure that the waiter serving guests at Ward parties, wearing only a mask, was none other than His Royal Highness Prince Philip!

Two tricky choices

In the first decade of her reign, Elizabeth made a pair of tricky political decisions. In both instances she may have acted unwisely – even incorrectly.

The Suez Crisis of 1956 (see the sidebar, "Britain and Suez, 1956", earlier in this chapter) had drawn the inexperienced Elizabeth into politics:

>> At the time of the invasion, Philip's uncle, Louis Mountbatten, 1st Earl Mountbatten of Burma, was Britain's first Sea Lord and chief of the naval staff. He believed the Israeli–Anglo–French operation against Egypt to be unwise, but was overruled by the politicians who had dreamed it up. Elizabeth, too, opposed the attack but did not make her views public.

We don't know what the Queen said to Prime Minister Anthony Eden in private, though he got the impression she did not support war with Egypt. Private Secretary Charteris believed she thought the premier 'mad'! Britain's subsequent humiliation inevitably had a negative impact on its Head of State.

>> The failure of the Suez operation led to Eden's resignation and his replacement as prime minister by Harold Macmillan. The choice surprised many, who expected Elizabeth to send for the talented R. A. Butler, the politician who had, more than anyone else, helped move the Conservative Party forward in the post-Churchill years.

Sticking to constitutional propriety, Elizabeth had not acted on her own when appointing Macmillan as prime minister. She took the advice of a handful of elderly Conservative grandees, including Winston Churchill – a move that was not universally popular. Again, the image of the bright new monarchy had been tarnished.

The second tricky decision Elizabeth was faced with came in the autumn of 1963, when Prime Minister Macmillan was taken ill with a prostate problem. Early in the morning of 18 October, the Queen received a letter from him announcing his resignation. A few hours later, she went to see him in hospital.

She was understandably shaken. It is said there were tears in her eyes as she asked Macmillan what to do. He handed her a manuscript in which he proposed Alec Douglas-Home (14th Earl of Home) as his successor. Home was, Macmillan told her, the choice of the cabinet. Elizabeth duly asked Home to come to Buckingham Palace.

Meanwhile, three other leading contenders for the job of PM had met with the chairman of the Conservative Party and agreed that one of them, R. A. Butler (again), should be the man. Too late.

Macmillan had acted improperly – even unconstitutionally – by nominating a successor when he was no longer prime minister. The Queen acted improperly – even unconstitutionally – by accepting the advice of a person who was, at the time, simply an ordinary member of Parliament.

Home accepted Elizabeth's invitation to form a government. Having done so, he resigned his peerage so he could sit in the House of Commons. He was in office for less than a year, but during that time he did the Queen, who was a personal friend, one great service: he arranged that henceforward the Conservative Party would elect its leader and not wait for them to emerge out of the political mist.

Saying farewell to Winston

Margaret's heartbreak, the Suez debacle, stories of Philip's philandering, the Profumo scandal, the Douglas-Home embarrassment . . . Elizabeth's ten-year introduction to her job had not been easy. Moreover, by the early 1960s, it was clear that the old ways in which she was steeped would not serve forever – nor would the old men on whom she had relied for advice.

Winston Churchill died of a stroke on Sunday 24 January 1965. Elizabeth herself made the decision to give him a state funeral, the first commoner to be so honoured since the Duke of Wellington in 1852.

Attended by the leaders of 110 countries and watched by a crowd of many hundreds of thousands, it was an awe-inspiring ceremony. The coffin, resting on the gun carriage used for Queen Victoria's funeral, was hauled through the streets by 120 naval cadets as muffled drums beat out their solemn steps. The chilly air reverberated to the boom of a 90-gun salute.

No eulogy punctuated the half-hour service – Winston's achievements and impact had spoken for themselves. Breaking with customary protocol, the Queen and her party entered St Paul's Cathedral before the coffin and left after Churchill's family had followed it out.

REMEMBER

More than any other single event, Churchill's funeral marked the end of an era. Elizabeth now had to find a new way ahead across increasingly unfamiliar terrain.

Ruling Through the Swinging Sixties

There is almost as much mythology about the 1960s as there is about the British monarchy. That said, the decade undoubtedly saw dramatic and far-reaching changes in almost every aspect of British life, from satire to sexual mores, from what people wore to where they went on holiday.

TIP

The challenge for the monarchy, and Elizabeth in particular, was to make itself relevant in the new climate. I offer one example from personal experience of the way the mood in the country had changed: In the mid-1950s, when I first went to the cinema, the national anthem ('God Save the Queen') was played at the end of every screening. The moment the anthem's opening drumroll began, the audience rose to their feet in silence. By the early 1960s, the drumroll meant time to leave the building, and playing the anthem was discontinued.

God and the monarchy were losing their grip. Elizabeth had to get it back.

Satire and the Establishment

Throughout their history, the British have always had an equivocal attitude towards those in authority, especially hereditary authority. They tugged forelocks to the faces of lords and ladies, then laughed behind their backs. With the advance of democracy and the rise of the Labour Party in the twentieth century, the laughter was less often concealed.

During World War II, traditional deference was propped up by the need for unity in the face of a common danger. The King and Queen received a rough reception when visiting bombed housing, but this was kept quiet (see Chapter 6). From the 1950s onwards, with peace, rising prosperity, and widespread access to radio and television, the attack on the old class barriers was renewed:

>> The charge against class was led by the well-loved BBC radio comedy, *The Goon Show*. Its eccentric, surreal humour satirized the foibles of the Establishment. Class structure, politics, the armed forces, and the police were all ridiculed. This anarchic satire, exemplified by the corrupt, cowardly Major Bloodnok, inspired generations of British comedy, from *Monty Python* to *Blackadder* and *Mr. Bean*.

>> *The Goon Show* stayed clear of the monarchy . . . perhaps one reason Prince Charles liked it so much? The 1960 revue *Beyond the Fringe* also avoided the monarchy, though it openly and rudely mocked Prime Minister Macmillan when he turned up in the audience. The fearless BBC TV review *That Was The Week That Was* (1962–1963) showed less restraint and caused considerable resentment. *Private Eye* magazine (founded 1961 and still going) also targeted anything – royal or not – it considered corrupt or ridiculous.

>> The Royal Family was now fair game. The popular anti-Elizabeth single 'God Save the Queen' by the Sex Pistols punk rock band gatecrashed the 1977 Silver Jubilee celebrations (see Chapter 15 for more on this). In the next decade, the Royal Family were ridiculed in the *Spitting Image* satirical puppet show (see Chapter 21): the penny-pinching Queen took clothes from rubbish bins, Philip was a naval buffoon, and the Queen Mother and Margaret were always at the gin.

REMEMBER

In coronation year, none of this would have been imaginable. The Crown, the aristocracy, and the Establishment had sat secure on their gilded perches. From the 1960s onwards, these perches began to wobble.

Elvis and four boys from Liverpool

The advent of 'pop' music exemplified the new atmosphere. It was all about youth, freedom, open sexuality – the very antithesis of Establishment values. The older generation regarded Elvis Presley's swaying hips as 'disgusting'.

Race and class meant nothing in music which had its roots in the culture of the deprived and abused black people of America's southern states. And The Beatles' meteoric rise from ordinary Liverpool lads to global superstars ran clean contrary to the hereditary principle.

On the advice of Labour Prime Minister Harold Wilson (see Chapters 14 & 26 for more about him), the Queen decided she should show how 'with it' the monarchy was by honouring the Fab Four for their contribution to culture and the arts. The decision to award them MBEs (making them Members of the Most Honourable Order of the British Empire) caused an outcry from the Establishment. How could pop stars be given equal status with war heroes? Some traditionalists returned their gongs in protest. Find out more about these awards in the nearby sidebar, "The British honours system".

Interestingly, at the time the Beatles did not appear to object to being made members of the empire, a racist institution that no longer existed. Silver-tongued Paul McCartney went so far as describing the Queen as 'lovely' and 'like a mum'.

However, the band did later admit to having thumbed their noses at the Establishment by smoking a joint in a Buckingham Palace bathroom. John Lennon, always the most anti-Establishment of the quartet, returned his MBE in 1969 in protest at the Vietnam War.

TECHNICAL STUFF

THE BRITISH HONOURS SYSTEM

The British honours system is of Byzantine complexity. Elizabeth is probably one of the very few people who fully understand it. The awards are purely honorary and carry no obligations or responsibilities.

Technically speaking, all honours are 'orders of chivalry' or 'orders of merit' and are awarded by the monarch in person (though Charles and other top royals sometimes deputize at the award ceremony). In most cases, recipients are nominated by carefully selected committees.

The chivalric stuff includes the very rare Order of the Garter, dating back to Edward III (1327–1377). Its motto *Honi soit qui mal y pense* ('Shame upon him who thinks evil of it') is seen on the royal coat of arms. Recipients become a Knight (Lord) or Lady.

Most honours belong to the orders of merit, with convoluted and out-of-date titles such as Knight or Dame Commander of the Most Honourable Order of the British Empire (KBE/DBE), Commander of the Most Honourable Order of the British Empire (CBE), Officer of the Most Honourable Order of the British Empire (OBE), and, bottom of the lot, plain Member of the Most Honourable Order of the British Empire (MBE). The continued reference to the empire has led a number of those recommended for an award to reject it, including the poet Benjamin Zephaniah. The singer David Bowie twice rejected an honour (a CBE and a knighthood), saying 'I don't know what it's for.'

Changing social attitudes

TIP

By 1970, so much that Elizabeth and the monarchy stood for was in sharp contrast to the most prominent public values of the day. Here are some examples, with the monarchy-headed Establishment ones first, followed by popular opinion of the day.

>> **Deference:** 'Sir' and 'madam' (and Ma'am') *versus* 'yeah' and 'ok, mate'.

>> **Social class:** A fair and reasonable way to hold society together *versus* an outdated and immoral way of perpetuating unjustifiable privilege.

>> **The armed forces:** Respected and admired *versus* the enemy of peace and love, man.

>> **Chastity:** An admirable Christian virtue *versus* an old-fashioned restriction on natural instincts.

>> **Divorce:** An un-Christian mark of weakness *versus* a necessary release for relationships that were no longer working.

>> **Homosexuality:** An illegal sin *versus* a normal aspect of human behaviour.

>> **Hair:** Men – short and clean-shaven; women – neat and tidy *versus* men – long, moustaches and sideburns; women – anything goes.

>> **Dress:** Sober suits, tweeds, ties, and frocks *versus* jeans, T-shirts, and psyche-delic designs.

>> **Drugs**: Dangerous and illegal *versus* cool.

Being Stuck in a Time Warp?

Even before the bongs of Big Ben had announced the arrival of the Swinging Sixties, certain intrepid intellectuals were daring to suggest that Elizabeth's style of monarchy was out of synch with the times. These were not communist mutterings in a pub or student rants. They were the thoughtful reflections of sensible citizens who wanted the best for their country.

Malcolm Muggeridge

A former communist turned patriotic wartime spy and devout Christian, Muggeridge commented on the state of the British monarchy in two well-known articles, one in 1955 and the other in 1957: the court was a ludicrous soap opera set in a male-dominated, all-white past.

Muggeridge lampooned the Queen as a 'generator of snobbishness and a focus of sycophancy' who went about her duties like a sleepwalker. He asked why couldn't the Royals live 'simply and unaffectedly' like their counterparts in continental Europe?

John Grigg

Radical Tory John Grigg, 2nd Baron Altrincham, came from the classic Establishment background: Eton, Oxford University, Grenadier Guards. When he set out his views on the Queen and the monarchy in 1957, people listened.

He condemned the court as a 'tight little enclave' of 'tweedy' aristocrats. The Queen, who had received a 'woefully inadequate training', showed no public personality, and in her dull speeches sounded like a 'priggish schoolgirl'. It was not her fault, he explained, but that of the hidebound system she represented.

John Osbourne

This radical playwright followed Muggeridge's thinking but scorned the monarchy in even harsher words. The institution was not just futile in itself: it was a symbol of a deeper national malaise. Echoes of faded imperial glory spiced his slamming of a 'splendid triviality': the 'last circus of a civilization which has lost faith in itself.'

And the monarchy? Simply 'a gold filling in a mouth full of decay'. Wow!

Reactions from the monarchists

The Establishment, from the Archbishop of Canterbury to the proprietors of daily newspapers, roared their condemnation. Such vulgar attacks on the 'accumulated experience of centuries' were unpatriotic and wholly unacceptable. Griggs's comments, howled the *Daily Mail*, were outpourings of an 'infinitely tiny and temporary' mind.

Fired up by press outrage, conservative monarchists elsewhere took revenge. Grigg was assaulted in a London street. Muggeridge had packages containing excrement and razor blades shoved through his letterbox. He was ostracized by the BBC (see the nearby sidebar for more background on the UK's national broadcaster). Such violent reaction was partly defensive: even the Queen's most fervent supporters must have recognized the truth in some of what the critics were saying.

THE BBC

The British Broadcasting Corporation is the UK's national broadcaster, and the world's oldest and largest national broadcaster. Founded in 1927, it now broadcasts worldwide on radio and TV, and has an extensive online presence. Funded by a license fee that all UK citizens who use its services must pay, it is theoretically independent of the government. However, a government minister sets the license fee, and in 2027 the government will review the charter that establishes the BBC's remit. Over the years, the broadcaster has prided itself on remaining politically neutral, though both left and right have accused it of bias.

Because it is a national broadcaster, the BBC is obliged to provide careful coverage of Elizabeth and the Royal Family. It has a dedicated royal correspondent, specializes in formal royal occasions such as weddings, Trooping the Colour (see Chapter 1), and the State Opening of Parliament (see Chapters 1 and 8), and for years it was the only broadcaster to carry the Queen's Christmas message (see Chapter 19).

More recently, it was criticized for the way it persuaded Princess Diana to give a controversial interview in 1995 (see Chapter 16), and over-compensated – perhaps seeking to regain the approval of the Establishment – by devoting a huge number of hours to the death and funeral of Philip, Duke of Edinburgh (see Chapter 25). Balancing the interests of the people, the government and the Head of State is not easy.

Behind the scenes, reaction in the Palace was more considered. The Queen herself appeared not to understand, but Philip – himself a thwarted reformer –reckoned Grigg spoke a lot of sense. He was not alone. Statistics are hard to come by, but journalists on mass-circulation newspapers found the criticisms chimed with the thoughts of many ordinary working people.

When all around was changing fast, the Crown and the Establishment were trapped in a time warp.

Chapter **13**

Margaret: Elizabeth's Troubled Sister

This chapter traces the eyebrow-raising life of Elizabeth's younger sister, Margaret Rose. Sparks flew whenever she was around – sparks that brightened and delighted, but also burned. The story of sparkle and caprice is tinged with deep sadness, even tragedy. Hereditary monarchy is a merciless taskmaster.

It was a script straight out of Hollywood. Two sisters, one earnest, sober and dutiful, the other spirited and self-orientated. Of course, things are never that simple. Elizabeth, especially before she became heir presumptive (see Chapters 5 and 6), could be lively and amusing, and Margaret was not the all-out hedonistic good-time girl she was sometimes made out to be.

Nevertheless, from a very early age, it was clear the two children of King George VI and Queen Elizabeth (the future Queen Mother) could hardly have been more different.

Looking at the Early Life of the Lively One

Margaret was born by caesarean section on 21 August 1930. The place: Glamis Castle, the Scottish seat of her mother's family, the Bowes-Lyons. She was the first royal to be born in Scotland for 300 years. Looking back, the venue was ominously appropriate. Fate had drawn a cruel line down the centuries, linking Shakespeare's tragedy of *Macbeth*, Thane of Glamis, to the twentieth-century figure of Margaret, Babe of Glamis.

REMEMBER

Queen Mary decided early on that Margaret was 'a more complicated and difficult character' than her elder sister Elizabeth. And grandmother was correct. Even as a child, Margaret was sprightly but unreliable. Where Elizabeth was respectful, Margaret was naughty. At children's parties, governess Crawfie (see Chapter 4) observed that Margaret was always the centre of attention, laughing and making jokes.

King George VI made things worse by spoiling her. This was partly out of sympathy for her status as Number 2, the also-ran, the one who – in affairs of state – didn't really matter. Whatever his motives, Margaret was seen as his pet, his plaything. He rarely chastised her, allowing her to stay up for formal dinner parties as soon as she reached her teens. 'Lilibet is my pride,' he supposedly said. 'Margaret my joy.'

TIP

To her great credit, Elizabeth never showed jealousy towards her more attractive sibling. If anything, she sympathized with her, treating her almost as would a mother. To make Margaret feel less left out, her parents dressed her and her sister in identical clothes, a move that continued into Elizabeth's teens when short, little-girl dresses looked rather silly.

Margaret was even less well educated than Elizabeth. She did not, for example, accompany her sister on visits to Henry Marten at Eton College (see Chapter 6). In later life, she resented her poor schooling and blamed her mother. She made up for it with a quick wit, a fine singing voice, skill on the keyboard, natural theatrical flair and – by the age of 16 – unmistakable sex-appeal. Even when she scorned them or cut them dead, men found her magnetically attractive.

Becoming the All-singing, All-dancing Playgirl

In her 1950 memoir of life in the Royal Household, *The Little Princesses* (Cassell & Co), governess-tutor Marion Crawford ('Crawfie') contemplated Margaret's many talents. Old men were frightened of her, she reckoned, because 'she had too witty a tongue and too sharp a way with her.' Had Margaret not been royal, she speculated, she might have used her skills to make a name for herself 'as an artist, a singer, a dancer.'

These were wise words. Unfortunately for Crawfie, the Palace did not think so: the family ostracized her completely on publication of the book. She became depressed at the end of her life and attempted suicide. When she died in 1988, neither her charges (Elizabeth and Margaret) nor their mother (the Queen Mother) sent a wreath to her funeral.

According to the standards of her day and status, Margaret grew up into a precocious young woman. By the age of 18 she was the belle of the occasional ball that her parents gave at Buckingham Palace or Windsor Castle. It was at one of these, the story goes, that her childhood naughtiness took on a more grown-up form.

TIP

After a formal ball at Windsor Castle, dutiful parent George VI decided to check that his children were safely tucked up in bed. Imagine his royal astonishment when, on entering a drawing room, he found a partly dressed Margaret on a sofa with a youthful army officer. His Majesty was decidedly not amused. Margaret was sent straight to her room, and her paramour challenged for his name and rank before being shown the door. Two days later, the young lothario was posted overseas.

Details of Margaret's other teenage adventures remain happily hidden. Aged 20, she was being hailed as 'the world's most eligible bachelor-girl', and the press called her aristocratic and well-born companions the 'Margaret Set'. Though a diminutive five feet one inch tall, her clear blue eyes, hourglass figure, and 18-inch waist were the epitome of 1950s loveliness.

REMEMBER

Newspapers could not get enough of her: pictures and stories of the partying princess brightened the gloom of post-war, bomb-damaged Britain. Without making the differences too openly, the press contrasted the two sisters. Once they had set up Elizabeth as the sober one, the goody-goody, they livened up the story by presenting Margaret as the opposite. As she herself put it, in the eyes of the press, she had to be 'wicked as hell'.

There were suitors aplenty, including the son of the American ambassador to the Court of St James' (as ambassadors to the UK are known). All were monied, many were titled, and some were handsome. With each of them, Margaret drank, danced, smoked, and flirted. But no young man captured her heart. That was already secretly pledged elsewhere.

Falling in Love . . .

Margaret was a disaster waiting to happen. Spoilt, attractive, capricious, cloistered until her late teens . . . what followed was sadly predictable.

Everything might have been okay, or at least acceptable, had Margaret fallen for a different man, or even lived at a different time. But in post-war Britain, especially in a family rocked to the core 20 years earlier by the relationship between Edward VIII and Wallis Simpson (see Chapter 5), Margaret's choice of partner was a catastrophe (see Chapter 12 for more on this incident).

Introducing Group Captain Peter Townsend

From a colonial background in Burma (now Myanmar), where he was born in 1914, public-school-educated Group Captain Peter Wooldridge Townsend was – in the language of the day – a jolly good chap. He was handsome, and had a chest-full of medals testifying to a distinguished record as an RAF fighter pilot in World War II.

TECHNICAL STUFF

At the beginning of World War II, Townsend had married Rosemary Pawle, a socialite from a landed gentry background. Hasty wartime marriages often foundered, and theirs was no exception. He was away from home for long periods and she entered into an affair with another man. They divorced on the grounds of her adultery early in 1952.

REMEMBER

Long before this, Townsend had moved into royal circles as an *equerry* (a male attendant on a member of the Royal Family) to George VI. 'Bad luck, he's married,' Elizabeth is reported to have told her sister when they first caught sight of the dashing airman. Later, he escorted the two princesses on their clandestine VE Day jaunt onto the streets of London (see Chapter 6). He also went with the Royal Family on their visit to South Africa in 1947.

It was on the South African tour, when he was 33 and she 17, that Townsend said he fell for the 'pretty and highly personable young princess'. (See the sidebar "Townsend's Swoon" for his description of her.) Apparently, the feeling was mutual, though for another four years neither spoke about it. At least, that's what they said afterwards. It's difficult to imagine the impetuous Margaret being quite so restrained.

After returning from South Africa, the younger princess decided she would no longer be 'Margaret Rose' but just plain 'Margaret'. It was a sort of coming-of-age statement. She was now her own person. Her new-found freedom was reinforced when Elizabeth married and gave birth to Prince Charles and Princess Anne. Margaret slipped from second to fourth in line to the throne.

TOWNSEND'S SWOON

Writing many years later, Peter Townsend retained a gloriously romantic memory of Margaret at this time:

'She was a girl of unusual, intense beauty, confined as it was in her short, slender figure and centred about large, purple-blue eyes, generous lips and a complexion as smooth as a peach . . . She was coquettish, sophisticated. But ultimately what made Princess Margaret so attractive and loveable was that behind the dazzling façade . . . you could find . . . a rare softness and sincerity.'

WARNING

Though the arrival of Elizabeth's children liberated Margaret, it also fuelled her jealousy. As brought out in *The Crown*, she felt that it was she, the fun one, who should have been queen, not the stodgy Elizabeth. Now that she had been shoved further down the ladder of succession, her dream of coronation was no more than a shimmering mirage.

Between her partying and dancing, Margaret found time to fulfil her royal duties. But the top jobs went to her mother and father and Elizabeth, leaving Margaret to open small-town bazaars and congratulate girl guides. She found it rather dull and humiliating. On top of it all came the death of her father, King George VI, in January 1952. His passing upset her deeply. Some have claimed that it was he, rather than Peter Townsend, who was the real love of her life.

When she ascended the throne, Elizabeth and her family moved into Buckingham Palace. Margaret was given a private apartment in Clarence House, her mother's palatial residence. Mysteriously, Peter Townsend, recently elevated to Assistant Master of the Queen Mother's household, also had an apartment in Clarence House. Here, in April 1953, Townsend asked Margaret to marry him. She accepted and told her sister.

TECHNICAL STUFF

Elizabeth and the Queen Mother had few objections to Margaret marrying the man she loved. Ancient legislation, however, decreed that the union would need the monarch's consent if it took place before the Princess reached the age of 25. Given the hoo-ha over Edward VIII marrying a divorcee (see Chapter 5), and the Queen's position as Supreme Governor of the Church of England (see Chapter 19), Elizabeth could not give formal consent. Margaret was told to wait until after the coronation before making things public. On her 25th birthday – so long as Parliament agreed – she could marry whomsoever she wished.

REMEMBER

It was easier said than done for Margaret to marry Peter Townsend. Not least because to marry a divorcee was against the laws of the Church of England. But a number of other crucial questions were thrown forward too:

>> Would Margaret be obliged to surrender her portion of the Civil List (see Chapter 17)? If so, would she be happy to live on an RAF officer's moderate salary?

>> Would Margaret – and any children she had – still be in line for the throne? If not, wouldn't adjusting the line of succession twice in 20 years further damage the principle of hereditary monarchy?

>> Would a Tory-controlled Parliament agree to the marriage?

>> Would the Commonwealth accept the marriage?

>> Could Margaret, a deeply religious woman who attended church twice a day after her father's death, square the marriage with her Anglican (episcopalian) faith? (She was told she would not be permitted to receive Holy Communion if she married Townsend.)

TIP

At the coronation of Elizabeth, Margaret was seen picking a piece of fluff from the shoulder of Townsend's uniform. With that kindly, loving gesture, the secret was out. The press went into overdrive with speculation. Tory political grandee R.A. Butler called the relationship 'scandalous'. In general, the Conservative-supporting newspapers and the Establishment agreed with him. The popular press, reflecting the views of most ordinary people, held Margaret's marriage to be her own business.

REMEMBER

To let things cool off before she reached 25, Margaret went off with her sister and brother-in-law on a royal tour of Southern Rhodesia (now Zimbabwe). Townsend was moved first to the Queen's household, then made an air attaché in Brussels, Belgium. The couple were apart for almost two years. During that time their ardour cooled.

Calling it off

There is some confusion over what happened next. This appears to have been the situation:

>> Traditionalists (including *The Times* newspaper), the Church of England, and Commonwealth heads were still opposed to the marriage because of Townsend's status as a divorcee.

>> The Queen and Prime Minister Eden (himself a divorcee) were prepared to accept the marriage so long as Margaret and her children were removed from the line of succession. They were even okay with Margaret keeping her royal title and allowance.

>> A clear majority of the population were in favour of the love match. Opposition to it, declared the *Daily Mirror* newspaper, was from 'a dusty world and a forgotten age'.

It was now up to Margaret and her lover to decide what to do.

REMEMBER

On 1 November 1955, the BBC interrupted its Home Service radio broadcast for an announcement from Her Royal Highness Princess Margaret:

I have been aware that, subject to my renouncing my rights of succession, it might have been possible for me to contract a civil marriage. But, mindful of the Church's teachings that Christian marriage is indissoluble, and conscious of my duty to the Commonwealth, I have resolved to put these considerations before others.

And that was that.

WARNING

Do we take Margaret's statement at face value or was she thwarted by the Establishment and dark memories of her uncle's abdication? Recent revelations suggest that her faith played a greater part in the decision than had previously been thought. In which case, she had fallen on her sword of her own volition. She had never been known for gestures of unselfish sacrifice, and she never would be again.

Margaret finally got married in 1960 (see the next section of this chapter). The year before, Townsend had married a 20-year-old Belgian beauty and heiress, Marie-Luce Jamagne. He clearly liked younger women.

. . . And (Eventually) Getting Married

Margaret's decision not to marry Peter Townsend divided the nation as sharply as had their relationship beforehand. The antis, especially the clergy, were delighted that the lost sheep had returned to the fold. For the younger generation and the more enlightened greyhairs, it was a national embarrassment. Over time, a relaxed, liberal view of divorce prevailed in time for a spate of royal divorces (see Chapter 20).

How was Margaret now going to fill her days? Days weren't too much of a problem – she didn't care to put in an appearance before noon – leaving just the evenings and nights to fill. She didn't find it too difficult.

TIP

As before, she partied, she sang (delightfully, apparently), she danced, she drank freely, and she smoked 60 cigarettes a day, placing each in the long cigarette holder that became her signature accessory. The press loved her because she was unpredictably fascinating – an endless source of gossipy stories and flash photographs. She continued to flirt, of course, and the year after her break-up with Townsend she came close to marrying an old friend, Billy Wallace. But when he jetted off to the Caribbean for a final bachelor fling, she promptly dumped him.

Tolerant she was not.

REMEMBER

Despite her unhappiness, her wild social life, and her personal over-indulgences, for the time being Margaret still retained her sense of dignity and duty. She knew – and her sister reminded her – that to justify her privileges, she had to play the part of a princess. She had put on an impressive performance when touring the Caribbean before her separation from Townsend, and the next year her open manner was wowing people in East Africa and the islands of Mauritius and Zanzibar. The Sultan of Zanzibar was so taken with her that he personally awarded her the Order of the Brilliant Star of Zanzibar (First Class) for meritorious services to the Sultan and his family.

At home, too, Margaret fulfilled a reasonable number of routine official engagements – openings, launchings, and so forth – and supported worthy organizations with her patronage. The arts were her principal interest. The Northern Ballet Theatre, the Birmingham Royal Ballet, the Scottish Ballet, and The Royal Ballet all benefitted from her support. She was personal friends with two of the finest dancers of her generation, Dame Margot Fonteyn and Rudolf Nureyev.

Being the odd one out

Margaret's love of the arts (she was a great fan of the work of the philosopher-novelist Iris Murdoch) set her apart from the rest of her family. While they were never happier than striding through damp Scottish glens or thundering across the turf on horseback, she preferred to put on a piece of jazz or classical music, pour herself a stiff drink, light a cigarette, and curl up with a good book. Prince Charles was the only other royal who shared some of these interests but he, poor chap, is not as bright as her.

A quick wit and love of the creative and off-beat probably saved Margaret from being even more heavily criticized for her rudeness and snobbery. Two universities awarded her honorary PhDs. The world of writers, dancers and musicians recognized her as one of their own. They knew that clever, creative people were often difficult. That's what made them interesting – and Margaret was always interesting.

TIP

Being interesting is not a good idea for a member of a highly privileged family whose status depends on accident of birth. Successful royals – and none is more successful than Elizabeth – rarely say or do anything interesting. It is their job just to exist. Therein lay Margaret's misfortune. Gore Vidal hit the nail on the head when he observed that she was 'far too bright' for the job she was expected to do.

Finally . . . a marriage

When she did marry, Margaret was not going to choose one of those chinless tweedy aristocrats her parents had lined up for her. She was going to marry a commoner. And not just any old commoner, but a dashingly talented and creative one with a wit as sharp as her own. His name was Anthony Armstrong-Jones.

TECHNICAL STUFF

From a wealthy upper-middle-class family, Anthony was an archetypal child of the age. He ditched his posh-sounding 'Anthony' for the more class-neutral 'Tony' (Prime Minister Anthony Blair would do the same 20 years later). Tony dropped out of architecture at Cambridge and into photography. Thanks to an instinctive talent and useful connections, he rose rapidly to become one of the most successful photographers of his generation, specializing in portraits. His subjects included both the Queen and the Duke of Edinburgh.

Margaret and Tony met at a dinner party in 1958. The attraction, they say, was immediate: sexual, intellectual, aesthetic. That explained both their mutual affection, and the seeds of their future troubles. They were peas from the same pod: clever, spirited, artistic, charismatic, and self-seeking. (See the sidebar "Tony's love child" for more on Tony's lifestyle.)

In the autumn of 1959, Tony was invited to Balmoral, ostensibly as a photographer. The Queen and her mother were smitten by his charm and good looks, and Margaret accepted his proposal of marriage shortly afterwards. They say she did so immediately after hearing that Peter Townsend was re-marrying. Tony presented his fiancée with a ring he designed himself. Inspired by her middle name, it featured a ruby encrusted with diamonds.

REMEMBER

The couple were married the following spring. Monarchy, especially the British one, thrives on ceremony. As there hadn't been a full-scale public show since the coronation, the wedding of Margaret and Tony was an opportunity for a relaunch. Out came the glass coach (see Chapter 10), on went the tiaras, up went the flags. Crowds cheered and waved, in the 1000-year-old Westminster Abbey the organ thundered, and the choir sang sweetly.

WARNING

TONY'S LOVE CHILD

The rejection of Jeremy Fry as Tony's best man was not the only problem haunting the groom as an estimated 250 million TV viewers watched him walk up the aisle.

Jeremy's wife, Camilla, was pregnant. Surely this wasn't anything to do with Tony, was it?

Yes, it was. After years of denial, DNA tests in 2004 proved that the father of Camilla's daughter Polly, born during Margaret and Tony's honeymoon, was Anthony Armstrong-Jones.

Everyone who was anyone was there. The 2,000 guests packed into the pews included the Queen and Prince Philip, the Queen of Denmark, the Prime Minister, dukes, duchesses, lords, ladies, friends and family. Just one man was missing. Jeremy Fry, one of Tony's hedonistic friends, had been chalked in as best man. Before an announcement had been made, he was found guilty of 'importuning for immoral purposes' (allegedly approaching a man for sex, which was illegal in Britain at that time) and swapped for a more wholesome alternative.

Heading Downhill: Sex, Drink, and Cigarettes

At first, all appeared to be going fine in the marriage. Margaret and Tony had a fantastic Caribbean honeymoon on the Royal Yacht *Britannia*. Afterwards, he played the royal game by walking a couple of steps behind Her Royal Highness and letting her speak first when they were addressed. Having initially rejected the idea, in 1961 he even accepted a title – Earl of Snowdon – so their children, David (b. 1961) and Sarah (b. 1964), would not be mere commoners.

Divorce and depression

Those who knew Tony predicted that he would never be satisfied with one woman (see the "Tony's love child" sidebar). They were right. He was discreet, but not long after getting married the lure of friends and photographic models got the better of him. His studio was a handy meeting place for his trysts, and trips abroad to shoot on location gave him further opportunities to fish in other waters. It seems likely, too, that he was happy to philander with either sex.

SISTERLY CARE?

REMEMBER

Margaret was not amused. Their marriage had always been fiery, fuelled with drugs and alcohol; now it was assuming a darker hue. Unused to neglect, she did not have the experience or personality to cope. (For Elizabeth's attitude, see the "Sisterly care?" sidebar.) She drank more and sank into bouts of depression. To her great credit, in the midst of all this she succeeded in raising two happy and well-balanced children.

TECHNICAL STUFF

Margaret's many affairs, which seem to have begun in 1966, were painfully public. At least some of them were. A list of those actually or allegedly involved with her at some stage or another would fill a whole page. Robin Douglas-Home (nephew of a prime minister), actors Peter Sellers and Warren Beatty, musician Mick Jagger . . . there is no need to go on.

The final, cover-blowing exposé came in February 1976. A British newspaper printed a picture of Margaret and her latest flame, landscape gardener Roddy Llewellyn – 17 years her junior – in swimming attire at her property on the Caribbean island of Mustique. By this time they had been close friends for two years. Now that the breakdown of Margaret and Tony's marriage was out in the open, they had no option but to acknowledge it. Left-leaning newspapers and MPs blamed it all on Margaret, the 'royal parasite'.

The decree for the divorce was granted in May 1978. Days later, Margaret was hospitalized with alcoholic hepatitis. Earlier, she had said that her relationship with Llewellyn had given her 'a renewal of spirit' – for an alcoholic, the wording was unfortunate – and after one of their separations, she had taken an overdose of sleeping pills. 'Uneasy lies the head that wears the crown' – and those next to it.

(Just about) Remaining a dutiful royal

Against continual press complaints that she was not pulling her weight, Margaret carried on with some royal duties at home and abroad. Her care of children was reflected in the charities she supported: she was president of the National Society for the Prevention of Cruelty to Children in both England and Scotland, and gave lifelong support to the Girl Guides.

WARNING

Margaret had stood in for her sister at Jamaica's 1962 independence ceremonies. She was still with Tony when she made her most famous visit of all, to the USA in November 1965. Though not quite as wild as depicted in *The Crown*, Margaret and President Lyndon B. Johnson certainly hit it off. The friendship did not play a part in America approving Britain's loan of £500 million (£4.5 billion in today's prices), as intimated in *The Crown*. Indeed, Britain may have wished for even more when the bill for Margaret's trip came through: it cost the taxpayer an eye-watering £30,000 (£5 million at today's prices!). She was not allowed on an official overseas tour for a long time afterwards.

An Australian trip (by herself) in 1975 was more or less alright until she got home and said she had hated it. Her 1979 US visit was worse. Upset by the Provisional Irish Republican Army's murder of Louis Mountbatten (see Chapter 18), she was reported to have called the Irish 'pigs' at a formal dinner. Her security was doubled and she left under a dark cloud.

In the end, when making a nine-day official visit to China in 1987, her children – Viscount Linley and Lady Sarah Armstrong-Jones – went along to keep an eye on her.

Margaret's final years

Margaret's final years, dogged by ill-health, make sad reading. She was treated for clinical depression, had a section of cancerous lung removed, and badly scalded her feet in an accident after learning her Mustique house had been sold. In the end, she suffered a number of strokes and died on 9 February 2002. Following a private funeral service in St George's Chapel, Windsor Castle, her ashes were placed in the tomb of her parents. She was 71.

TIP

It is hard to argue that someone blessed with every conceivable material comfort had a hard life. Nevertheless, doesn't Margaret merit some sympathy? She was ill-educated and under-prepared for a role imposed on her, not chosen. And unlike her indomitable elder sister, she did not possess the qualities to make a go of it.

That, surely, is tragedy.

Chapter **14**

The Royal Response to Criticism

REMEMBER

Two stand-out features of Queen Elizabeth II are abundantly clear. First, she is, and always has been, a deeply conservative woman. Second, she is wedded to the concept of duty before all else. These qualities have been both her strength and her weakness.

Over time, the Queen's conservatism has allowed her to morph into a sort of ageless phenomenon, like London's Big Ben clock tower or the ancient circle of megaliths at Stonehenge, Wiltshire. She has become a fixed point, an unchanging landmark in the whirling kaleidoscope of modern life. However, as explained in Chapter 12, a reluctance to change at any faster pace has led critics to suggest that she and the expensive institution she represents are no longer relevant.

This chapter further examines the Queen's conservatism, and looks at the steps she took to bring the monarchy more into line with the times.

The second theme of this chapter – indeed, of her whole reign – is though Elizabeth's iron fixation on her duty may have been good for the monarchy, and perhaps the country, too, it left in its wake a trail of family unhappiness. This would eventually force her to adopt changes, notably the acceptance of royal divorce, against which she had set her heart.

This is one of the ironies of her long reign.

The Raising of Charles and Anne

It's now time to step back a few years and see how Elizabeth's first two children – Charles (born 14 December 1948) and Anne (born 15 August 1950) – were getting on in the rarefied atmosphere of the Palace. Their material needs were amply catered for, but with a workaholic mother and an overbearing father, life for the young prince and princess was not easy.

Prince Charles at school and beyond

REMEMBER

Psychologists amateur and professional have written reams on Charles' upbringing and early life. It was certainly, by modern standards, odd: a strict regime of meals, play, bath, and bed. Affection came from nursemaids and short stints with 'mummy' when she was not engaged in royal business. It is said that Charles never recalls his mother telling him that she loved him. Philip was not interested in babies.

TIP

It's probably safe to say, therefore, that Charles grew up with more titles – Duke of Cornwall, Duke of Rothesay, Earl of Carrick, Baron of Renfrew, Lord of the Isles, Prince and Great Steward of Scotland – than overt parental affection. His mother was always the Queen, a somewhat distant, remote figure. His father, perhaps jealous of Charles's status as heir apparent, was determined to fashion his son in his own mould.

After private tuition in the Palace, Charles was sent to a day preparatory school in London and then as a boarder to Cheam, Philip's old school. He was the first heir apparent ever to go to school. The regime was harsh (nothing new for Charles, who was, allegedly, accustomed to being beaten by his father) but the academic tuition sound. The introverted, retiring young man with few friends was good at English and artistic subjects but hopeless at mathematics.

Charles's loneliness was not solely the result of his parents' remoteness. Though they asked that he be treated as any other boy, that proved impossible. The press were always snooping around in search of a photo or a story. His fellow students remained aloof, knowing that HRH was different, someone special. This was made clear when, considering it unfitting for Charles to bathe in public baths, he and his classmates were ferried to the Buckingham Palace pool for their swimming lessons.

GORDONSTOUN

Founded in 1934 by Kurt Hahn, a Jewish refugee from Nazi Germany, Gordonstoun was an all-boys boarding school in a remote part of north-east Scotland. (It is now co-educational and much changed.) It sought to produce future leaders of society through an education programme focusing on physical activity, self-discovery, and subjugation of the individual to the needs of the group. Its tough regime – frequently caricatured as nothing but cross-country runs and cold showers – had suited Prince Philip but was not the sort of place for the more aesthetic Charles.

REMEMBER

Charles may have been bullied by a father who spouted old-school axioms about 'making a man of you' and 'standing on your own two feet', but the young Prince still desperately wanted to be like him. Sadly, or perhaps thankfully, he never would be. In consequence, he developed a superficial 'Philipness', engaging in macho activities, and becoming a stickler for the snobbish detail of country gentleman attire. This made him a difficult figure for the public to admire. Smartly polished brogues and tweed jackets do not look right on a schoolboy or an undergraduate.

After a few months at the pomposity-free Timbertop campus of Geelong Grammar School in Victoria, Australia (an experience Charles thoroughly enjoyed), he returned to finish his secondary education at Gordonstoun. 'Colditz in kilts' is how he famously described the place (Colditz was a German prisoner of war camp in World War II); find out more about this school in the sidebar of the same name.

Sporting fair exam grades, in 1967 Charles moved on to Trinity College, Cambridge University. Here he studied archaeology, anthropology and history, and became the first heir apparent to earn (rather than simply be awarded) a university degree. He'd enjoyed his studies, though the perpetual presence of a detective and a ban on joining groups such as Amnesty International ensured that this unsure young man could never forget who he was – and what he was destined to become.

Princess Anne grabs the headlines

Majesty, and its attendant pressures and responsibilities, affects those burdened with it in different ways. It turned Elizabeth into a duty-bound automaton; Charles, a less resilient personality, retreated into a curious mix of introversion and old-fashioned rigidity; Anne, inheriting her father's no-nonsense attitude to life, just got on with it.

BENENDEN SCHOOL

TECHNICAL STUFF

Founded in 1923, Benenden School for Girls (or, more accurately, 'young ladies') was a secluded boarding school in the county of Kent for the daughters of the rich and, sometimes, the famous. Though the academic education was sound, the school emphasized happiness and all-round talents. For Anne this meant horse riding, sport, and drama.

REMEMBER

Anne was helped by her declining position in the line of succession. At the coronation of her mother, she was in silver medal position: second in line to the throne. After the birth of Charles' children, she has steadily fallen to her current position of 17th (January 2022), an also-ran. Unlike Charles, whose position becomes weightier with each passing day, Anne has been able to enjoy a life that has become more normal.

However, Anne's life did not start normally. Like her mother, she was home-educated by a governess. Catherine Peebles ('Mipsy' – the Royal Family like to give everyone a nickname), who was also responsible for Charles' early education, guided Anne to the age of 13.

Keeping Anne away from school until her teens was old-fashioned even for those far-off times. It may explain the difficulty she had in adjusting when she was finally launched into the world beyond the Palace walls.

TIP

Anne was 13 when she entered Benenden School (see the "Benenden School" sidebar). Her intake included three other royals from different parts of the world. Unlike Charles, for whom boarding school was something to be endured, Anne loved almost every minute. She was not an easy pupil, however, and was liable to rude outbursts of stroppy behaviour. Rather like her dad.

University? No way. After school, Anne wanted to get on with life. This included undertaking a few royal duties – and a vigorous social life that for a time made her a regular feature of newspaper headlines. Unlike her mother and elder brother, she did not respond to the media's questions with bland platitudes but with waspish retorts that implied 'mind your own stupid business.' Again, like her dad.

REMEMBER

Anne's 'bad girl' image did not last long. By the time she was out of her teens, she was acquiring a reputation as a more than competent horsewoman. She went on to represent Great Britain in the 1976 Montreal Olympic Games.

Poor Charles. As more than one commentator reflected at the time, what a pity that he and his sister could not swap places.

Heading Towards the 1960s

By the early 1960s, it was clear that pomp and majesty papered over not simply a few cracks in Britain's global status, but fissures of historic proportions:

>> The country was undergoing a significant economic and industrial decline.

>> The Empire was melting away; its replacement, the Commonwealth, had yet to take root.

>> Britain's military power, especially its navy, was shrivelling.

Alongside all this (see Chapter 12), the Crown and the Establishment were rocked by:

WARNING

>> Personal scandals involving Prince Philip as well as Princess Margaret. In 1966, Elizabeth was herself criticised for waiting eight days before visiting the Welsh mining village of Aberfan that had been overwhelmed by a landslide from a colliery waste tip. One hundred and forty-four people had died, 116 of them children. There were echoes of the incident, made into an episode of *The Crown*, when in 1997 Elizabeth was slow to react to the death of Princess Diana (see Chapters 21 and 27).

>> Political scandals centring around the Profumo affair and the appointment of the aristocratic Lord Home as prime minister.

>> Open attacks on the institution of hereditary monarchy by politicians and satirists. Labour minister Tony Benn proposed (unsuccessfully) to have the Queen's head removed from postage stamps. The TV show *That Was The Week That Was* portrayed the monarchy as a sinking barge.

REMEMBER

To the disappointment of a republican minority, the Elizabethan barge did not go under. I suggest why in greater detail in Chapter 15. For the time being, here are three broad reasons why it remained afloat during the stormy 1960s (and early 1970s):

>> The more turbulent the social and political scene, the more people held fast to the monarchy as an unsinkable object in a tempestuous sea. In other words, Elizabeth's conservatism changed from being a weakness to a strength.

>> The Queen's emphasis on her role as head of the Commonwealth gave the impression, through glowing images and reports of popular royal tours, that Britain remained a global power.

>> Gradually, and usually reluctantly, Buckingham Palace started to adapt to the new mood. In the eyes of many, the changes were too few and too slow, but at least they were made. By 1970, thanks largely to a more modern approach to handling the media, especially TV, the monarchy was beginning to look less like an Edwardian relic brought out from the back of the cupboard of history.

Welcoming Two New Boys to the Family

REMEMBER

There was one obvious way for Elizabeth and Philip to scotch the rumours of marital discord (as detailed in Chapter 12). The 33-year-old Queen gave birth to Prince Andrew, the future Duke of York (1986), on 19 February 1960. Four years later, her fourth child, Prince Edward, the future Earl of Wessex (1999), was born. The births took place in Buckingham Palace, and the boys were each baptised into the Church of England (see Chapter 19).

Prince Andrew

TECHNICAL STUFF

Andrew was named after the patron saint of Scotland and his paternal grandfather, Prince Andrew of Greece. It was appropriate that he should be linked to Philip's side of the family because, of the three boys, he most resembled his father in personality and proclivities.

At Philip's insistence, after attending a private prep school, Andrew followed Charles to Gordonstoun, the tough, all-boys school in the north-east of Scotland (see earlier in this chapter). While Charles had hated the place, Andrew's oafish personality thrived in the macho atmosphere.

As a teenager, Andrew was already showing characteristics that would mark him in later life: bullying self-confidence, lack of academic intelligence, and poor judgement of character. In 1977, during a six-month stay at the élite Lakefield College School, Canada, he became close friends with the school Anglican chaplain, Father Keith Gleed. It later proved to be an unfortunate friendship. Though Andrew knew nothing about Gleed's activities at the time, a few years after the priest's death in 2001, former pupils revealed that he was a paedophile who had preyed on vulnerable young pupils.

TIP

Andrew's temperament and abilities were better suited to a life of action rather than one of contemplation, and he was sent to join the Royal Navy. Service life appealed to him, and he deserves credit for refusing to shirk active service. He proved an able helicopter pilot and successfully completed a course with the distinguished Royal Marines Commandos. That said, he was not always popular with his comrades (see the sidebar, "Being beaten up on the way to war").

BEING BEATEN UP ON THE WAY TO WAR

Andrew's blunt and brutish manner won him few friends. When sailing to the Falkland Islands on HMS *Invincible* in 1982 (see Chapter 18), his fellow junior officers grew so tired of his bragging, bullying manner that they beat him up. The Palace was told of the incident but no disciplinary action was taken against the perpetrators.

The pummelling at sea may have caused Andrew to moderate his behaviour, and he is said to have served most creditably in the Falklands. Unfortunately, the credit was short term. Far worse was to follow (see Chapter 25).

Prince Edward

TIP

During their infancy, Andrew and Edward benefitted from closer attention from their mother than had Charles and Elizabeth. Nevertheless, they were raised mainly by nursemaids and nannies. And when it came to schooling, once again Philip had his way: the boys needed toughening up by the Gordonstoun regime. Its no-nonsense approach, he thought, would make a man of them both.

This treatment may have worked for Andrew – who would probably have benefitted from softening down rather than toughening up – but it had not suited Charles, and Elizabeth realized it would not suit the shy, sensitive Edward either. Her plea that he attend a more normal school was overruled.

The retiring Edward disliked Gordonstoun as much as Charles had done. Unlike Charles, he responded by developing a disagreeable arrogance. On leaving with very average results, he took a 'gap' year in Collegiate School, New Zealand, one of the country's leading private schools.

WARNING

At Wanganui and at Jesus College, Cambridge, where he went next, Edward maintained his unfortunate combination of arrogance and incompetence. This was brought out in an episode of *The Crown* in which he comes across as both rude to his mother and unpleasantly haughty. How had he turned out like this?

TIP

A strain of very average intelligence runs through the Windsor family (think of Georges V and VI as described in Chapters 3 and 6), and Edward was unlucky to have inherited it. His condescending haughtiness was probably an attempt to cover up his failings by copying his father's intolerant bombast.

Edward's cover was blown when, on leaving Cambridge, he dropped out of a Royal Marines training course after only a few months. Philip's furious reaction left the young man in floods of humiliating tears. Chucking in the military, Edward turned to a career in entertainment and film-making – without notable success (see Chapter 24).

Living With Unsavory Rumours

TIP

Because we always see them in public, surrounded by crowds and courtiers, it is easy to forget that the position of a monarch can be very lonely. This must have been especially the case for Elizabeth in less equality-minded times than our own. Whom could she trust? To whom could she turn for advice and to talk over things that were on her mind?

The Queen is blessed with extraordinary resilience. She has a special ability to compartmentalize experiences so that the good and the bad do not intrude on each other. She is not renowned for a powerful imagination. Even so, like all of us, she does need people to confide in. Philip was often away and had other interests. His advice, if called for (and even when not) was sometimes brusque and unsubtle. Besides, she could not discuss matters of state with him.

REMEMBER

Apart from her mother, with whom she spoke on the phone every day, and the ever loyal and discreet Bobo McDonald (see Chapter 8), Elizabeth is reported to have had three special friends:

>> **'Uncle Dickie':** Louis Mountbatten (Earl Mountbatten of Burma), Philip's uncle, great-grandson of Queen Victoria, Supreme Allied Commander South-East Asia in World War II, last Viceroy of India, and latterly First Sea Lord. Wickedly manipulative and over-confident of his own abilities, Mountbatten was nevertheless a man of the world whom Elizabeth relied on for advice about things she knew little about, such as the rumours of her husband's philandering and the mood on the street.

>> **'Porchy':** Henry Herbert, the distinguished-looking 7th Earl of Carnarvon, formerly Lord Porchester, the Queen's racing manager who in private called her 'Lilibet' and with whom she shared her passion for all things equine. Until his death in 2001, they saw a great deal of each other, travelling abroad in each other's company on horse business. At one time he was rumoured (falsely) to be the father of Prince Andrew.

>> **'Master of the Revels':** Elizabeth's favourite equerry, the ineffably smooth, capable, charming Patrick Plunket, 7th Baron Plunket. He and the Queen would walk together, talk endlessly together, and even sneak out to dinner together in secret. Their relationship was certainly non-sexual. Nevertheless, she seems to have truly loved him and was heartbroken when he died of cancer in 1975, aged 52.

Living with the Labour Party

To most people's surprise, the aristocratic Lord Home (see Chapter 12) did better than expected in the 1964 general election. He still lost. The Labour Party, headed by the 46-year-old former academic Harold Wilson, won a tiny majority of seats in the House of Commons and Elizabeth invited Wilson to form the government.

Fireworks were expected at the Palace. After all, Wilson's party was unashamedly democratic socialist and many leading party members were enthusiastic republicans. One of Labour's election pledges had been to reform the House of Lords, which was dominated by hereditary peers.

WARNING

If the hereditary principle were to be removed from parliament, then the next target would be the last bastion of hereditary privilege, the monarchy itself. It did not happen. Hereditary peers were allowed to remain in the Lords, though no more were appointed, and the monarchy was never seriously challenged. Indeed, as made clear in *The Crown*, Elizabeth and Harold got on remarkably well. Elizabeth finally had a prime minister near her own age, and he, an instinctive royalist, found someone he could chat with easily.

The pair also needed each other. He found that having the Crown on his side eased people's fears that Labour would usher in some sort of revolution; she, by working well with a socialist leader, emphasised her credentials as a non-partisan figure (see Chapter 26).

TECHNICAL STUFF

Whether the Queen liked them or not, the Labour government introduced a copious portfolio of radical reforms:

1964 Hanging for murder suspended; abolished 1969.

1967 Sexual Offences Act legitimized homosexual activity in private between males over the age of 21. Abortion made legal.

1968 Theatre censorship abolished.

1969 Voting age reduced to 18.

The Divorce Reform Act allowed couples whose marriage had 'irretrievably broken down' to divorce without either party needing to prove 'fault'. Elizabeth reluctantly granted royal assent in 1971.

Following Philip's admission on American TV that the Royal Family was about to go into the red, the House of Commons set up a committee to examine royal finances (see Chapter 17 for more on this incident). Two years later, the Queen and her family were granted an extra four percent each year, allowed to keep their private fortune secret, and remained exempt from paying tax (see Chapter 20). Game, set and match to the monarchy.

Opening Up to the World (A Little)

REMEMBER

In 1965, the Palace made one of its more astute appointments. William Heseltine, an Australian with a First-class Honours degree in History and experience in politics and handling the media, was appointed as the Queen's assistant press secretary. Three years later, he was full press secretary. Eventually, in 1986, he became Elizabeth's private secretary (see Chapter 9).

'Bill' Heseltine, unhampered by the traditional Eton-and-Guards background, saw that the monarchy, like a politician or movie star, needed to cultivate a favourable public image. His relaxed yet impeccably polite approach enabled him to steer through a revolution in Palace PR. Rather than keep the shutters closed and firefight when things went wrong, the Palace would now open up a bit.

Henceforward, its output would be proactive rather than purely reactive and defensive.

TECHNICAL STUFF

In 1967, Elizabeth was persuaded, against her instincts, to allow her Christmas message to be broadcast in colour. To persevere with black and white at a time when the world was switching to colour, she was told, would only perpetuate the perception of her as fuddy-duddy and out of date. In the same year, she knighted the round-the-world yachtsman Francis Chichester – not in a stiff ceremony in Buckingham Palace but on the quay beside his boat, the cameras, and approving crowds.

WALKABOUTS

Before 1970, the public knew the royals – especially the monarch and her immediate family – only as remote figures waving from a passing car, carriage, or distant balcony. In 1970, in one of the Queen's most visible attempts at modernization, all this changed. Starting in New Zealand, Elizabeth introduced 'royal walkabouts'. At long last, the Queen left her vehicle to exchange a few words with members of the crowd thronging to greet her. To a lucky few, she even extended a gloved hand for a gentle shake. Other members of the family soon followed their leader's example.

The *Royal Family* documentary

The year before the first walkabout brought the Queen into physical contact with her people (see the sidebar on "Walkabouts"), they were allowed unprecedented visual contact via a documentary film. The groundbreaking project was extremely carefully directed, shot and edited 1968–1969.

Elizabeth was filmed in 172 locations, embracing the formal and informal life of the royal enigma: on a state visit to Brazil, chatting onboard the royal yacht *Britannia*, meeting foreign dignitaries, sitting on a sofa with her kids, and cooking a barbeque in the grounds of Balmoral. Forty-three hours of film were skillfully cut to a 110-minute, black-and-white BBC documentary.

Charles and Anne were there, as was Philip doing his best not to appear bored. And the dogs, of course, enabling one critic to dub the show 'Corgi and Bess'.

REMEMBER

Did it work? On the whole, yes. The reception in the UK and around the world was extremely favourable. There was mockery of the posh accents and stuffy clothes, but on the plus side were glimpses of the Queen as something other than a head on a postage stamp. The central character, who had initially been opposed to the idea, and was no natural before the cameras, managed in some sequences to come across as a real human being.

The Investiture of Charles

If the *Royal Family* documentary was more about Elizabeth than her family, Charles's moment came a few weeks later when he was invested as Prince of Wales. The designed-for-TV show was intended to echo the investiture of the first English Prince of Wales in 1301. It had followed the conquest of Wales by his father, King Edward I (see Chapter 2).

TIP

The 1969 investiture was stage-managed by Lord Snowdon (Princess Margaret's husband, Anthony Armstrong-Jones). Charles learned some Welsh and, wearing a film-set crown, paid homage (see Chapter 7) to his mother while kneeling on the carpeted grass inside the medieval walls of Caernarvon Castle. Trumpets blared, the 6,000 invited guests clapped and cheered, and around the world an estimated audience of 500 million wondered how Disney had managed to knuckle in on the British monarchy.

The general feeling – except among Welsh nationalists (see the sidebar, "Welsh nationalism", to find out more about this movement) – was favourable. After the *Royal Family* documentary had brought the Queen and her family down to earth by showing them as a working household, the investiture had raised them up once more into the realms of fantasy.

WELSH NATIONALISM

Wales was conquered by England in medieval times. Since then a distinct Welsh culture, marked by its ancient Celtic language (*Cymraeg*) and its own sporting teams (especially rugby and football), flourished under the umbrella of the UK.

Though the majority of the Welsh were consistently against full independence, the call from the Party of Wales (*Plaid Cymru*, founded 1925) for greater self-rule led to the establishment in 1999 of the Welsh National Assembly (*Senedd*).

The continued need for a little mystery

The *Royal Family* documentary was a gamble. Britain's hereditary monarchy is an expensive, quirky luxury that survives in part because of the mystery that surrounds it. If too much light is let in, the magic is dispelled. On the other hand, if no light is admitted, it runs the risk of being an irrelevant museum piece. Charles's investiture was a gamble, too. Pomp and ceremony can deteriorate into a tacky show or costly showing off.

Happily for Elizabeth and The Firm (see Chapter 8), the film and the investiture got the balance just about right. The task now was to maintain it.

Chapter **15**

Celebrating 25 Years: The Silver Jubilee

This chapter begins with a look at the troubles besetting the UK during the 1970s. It goes on to examine how, remarkably, respect and admiration for the monarchy grew in inverse proportion to these troubles. Appreciation of Elizabeth herself and what she stood for culminated in the *Silver Jubilee* of 1977 (the 25th anniversary of her accession to the throne).

TIP

In the 1950s, the people of the UK had seen Queen Elizabeth as something new and slightly exotic. By the 1960s, the glamour was fading and she and her advisors had to work hard to maintain her relevance in a changing world. As a result of their efforts and the passage of time, by 1977 the Queen had become a well-loved national and international institution.

Britain's Difficult Decade: The 1970s

The 1970s were not unlike the 1930s – the decade when the post-war boom came to a crashing halt. Neither the Conservative government of Edward ('Ted') Heath (prime minister 1970–1974) nor the Labour governments of Harold Wilson (prime minister 1974–1976) and James Callaghan (prime minister 1976–1979) were able to revive the optimistic spirit of the previous decade's 'Swinging Sixties'.

TECHNICAL STUFF

Fortunately for Elizabeth, the two main political parties now chose their leader by ballot. This meant that after the election of 1970 and the two of 1974, she had a clear constitutional duty to send for the elected head of the party with the greatest number of seats in the House of Commons. This applied even in the second 1974 election, when Wilson had a majority of just three seats.

REMEMBER

One point of constitutional friction is worth noting. Early in his premiership, Prime Minister Edward Heath fell out with the Commonwealth over selling military equipment to South Africa (see Chapter 10). Heath was a blunt bachelor who had only one woman (Margaret Thatcher – see Chapter 18) in his cabinet. Despite his devotion to the monarchy, he and Elizabeth had little in common. He lacked aristocratic polish and did not do small talk. Their weekly chats at the Palace were tough going, and she was certainly put out when he banned her from attending the 1971 Commonwealth Conference (officially known as the Commonwealth Heads of Government Meeting) in Singapore because of the arms to South Africa row.

Three other constitutional matters exercised the Queen during this period:

>> Britain joining the European Community in 1973 inevitably weakened the UK's relationship with the Queen's beloved Commonwealth (see Chapter 12).

>> The growth of independence movements in Scotland and Wales threatened Elizabeth's crowned status as Queen of the *United* Kingdom. The Scottish National Party (SNP) and its Welsh equivalent Plaid Cymru said they wished to retain the monarchy after independence. The Queen made no public statement as to whether she would be happy to go along with that. See the sidebar "Scottish nationalism" for more about this.

>> Far more serious was the escalation of violence in Northern Ireland (Ulster) between the Protestant majority (Unionists) and the discontented Catholic minority. The latter wanted to be part of a united Ireland outside the UK. Inevitably, this drew the Queen into the conflict. See the sidebar "Northern Ireland" for more details of Ireland's troubled history.

This conflict touched Elizabeth personally when her cousin Louis Mountbatten ('Uncle Dickie') and several members of his family were killed by an IRA bomb in 1979 (see Chapters 14 and 18). The episode features in a dramatic episode of *The Crown*.

WARNING

The Queen was embarrassed by the extreme loyalism of the Union-Jack-waving Unionists (see the sidebar "The Union Jack"), and further distressed when, in 1972, British peace-keeping troops shot dead 13 members of an illegal protest (see Chapter 18). Her determination to visit the province as part of her Silver Jubilee celebrations can be seen either as an attempt to promote unity or as a challenge to extremist Catholic republicanism.

SCOTTISH NATIONALISM

For centuries, Scotland was an independent nation with its own monarch and parliament. Relations with its larger, wealthier and more powerful southern neighbour were strained. This eased with the union of the two crowns in 1603 and the two governments in 1707 (see Chapter 2). Nevertheless, a distinct Scottish identity – accent, tartan, bagpipes – remained.

In the twentieth century, Scottish nationalism revived. The Scottish National Party (SNP, founded 1934) demanded full independence from England. Its cause was greatly helped by the discovery of North Sea oil reserves off the coast of Scotland in 1974, making Scotland a net donor to the overall UK budget rather than a receiver (no longer the case with the move away from oil towards green energy.)

The UK government responded to the nationalist surge by setting up a Scottish Parliament (1999) and holding a Scottish referendum on independence in 2014. Though the country voted to remain in the UK, the issue revived in 2016 when Scottish voters opted to stay in the European Union when the majority of the UK voted leave (still part of the UK, Scotland reluctantly left the EU along with the rest of the nation).

Elizabeth, with a highland home in Balmoral Castle (see Chapter 9), has always professed a strong affection for Scotland. She clearly dislikes the idea of breaking up the UK into separate countries (see Chapter 25).

NORTHERN IRELAND

In the seventeenth century, the north of Ireland was settled (some say colonized) by Protestant immigrants from mainland Britain. They remained at odds with the southern Irish and fiercely loyal to their British heritage. When Ireland became independent in 1922, the country was partitioned north–south. The north, with its Protestant majority, was still under the Crown and cemented its dominance with discriminatory measures against the Catholic minority.

At the end of the 1960s, the situation flared into three decades of violence (known as *The Troubles*). Marches, riots, bombings, and tit-for-tat killings became endemic until the 1998 Good Friday Agreement finally brought the conflict to an end. The rest of the UK became involved when British troops, sent in to restore law and order in 1969, were targeted by the Catholic Irish Republican Army (IRA). In 1971, the bombings spread to mainland Britain, where they continued until 1996.

Dealing with trouble and strife

Looking back, the 1970s was not a particularly good decade for any Western country. An oil crisis caused massive disruption and sent stock markets reeling. The US was knocked back by defeat in Vietnam (a conflict lasting 1955–1975, with US ground troops involved 1965–1973), the Watergate scandal (1972–1974), and the humiliating Iran hostage situation (1979–1981).

Britain's sickness was largely caused by the flare-up of long-term illnesses that had never been properly treated:

>> **Out-of-date business practices**. In 1971, the Conservative (Tory) government reluctantly agreed to nationalize the world-famous Rolls Royce company to stop it going bankrupt. The move was an embarrassment for both the free-market government and for the nation as a whole. It appeared to encapsulate the British problem: an adherence to traditional practices and systems when the rest of the world was rapidly moving on. Was admiration for the monarchy – another institution similarly rooted in the past – a help or a hindrance?

>> **The UK's unemployment rate.** This remained between four and five percent throughout the 1970s, with two million registering as unemployed in 1977. More alarming, the country's *GDP* (Gross Domestic Product – a measure of a country's wealth, usually arrived at by computing the total value of all goods and services) fluctuated wildly, often registering negative growth. The balance between imports and exports was often negative, too.

>> **Dire industrial relations.** These often reflected class-based animosity, and European commentators dubbed the never-ending strikes that culminated in the 1979 'Winter of Discontent' as the 'British disease'.

>> **Oil crises.** On top of high unemployment came the oil crises of 1973 and 1979. The first occurred when Arab oil-producing nations quadrupled the price of oil and cut production in retaliation for Western support of Israel in the 1973 October War (or Yom Kippur War). Prime Minister Heath ordered Britain to adopt a three-day working week. Oil prices soared again following the Iranian Revolution of 1979, which brought a fundamentalist Shia Muslim regime to power.

>> **Inflation.** Rising prices and the falling value of the pound sterling fed double-digit inflation. In 1975, it stood at a savings-eroding 25 percent. This in turn led to high wage demands (the coal miners got 35 percent). If demands were not met, further strikes were called. The cycle seemed never-ending. In 1974, future Prime Minister James Callaghan confessed, 'If I were a young man, I should emigrate.'

» **Unease over immigration.** Hundreds of thousands did indeed emigrate, choosing life in the US and the Dominions. At the same time, many thousands – mainly from the West Indies and the Indian sub-continent – were settling in Britain. Large-scale immigration caused social difficulties, especially when the new arrivals formed distinctive, close-knit communities in cities.

In his often misquoted 'Rivers of Blood' speech (1968), Tory MP Enoch Powell had warned against unrestricted immigration. His prophesy did not come true, partly because the 1968 Race Relations Act had started the long fight-back against racism. Even so, in several parts of the country the arrival of immigrants led to unsavoury incidents.

Finding reasons to be cheerful

It would be wrong to paint the 1970s as a decade of unalloyed conflict and gloom. Despite many signs to the contrary, living standards continued to rise. Far more people owned cars and an array of household gadgets in 1980 than 1970.

REMEMBER

Undaunted by the heel-dragging of Ted Heath, the women's movement continued to chip away at male prejudice and condescension. In 1975, a Sex Discrimination Act came into force, offering the prospect of equality for women in the workplace. Interestingly, however, males still took precedence in lines of hereditary succession, including the Crown.

A powerful signal of the way things were going came when the Conservative Party, a bastion of tradition, elected Margaret Thatcher as its leader in 1975. From that moment onwards, the country faced the unprecedented possibility of two women at the top: one as Head of State and another as prime minister (see Chapter 18).

REMEMBER

In the early 1970s, the Queen's place at the centre of the royal stage was temporarily taken by her daughter Anne. She had sloughed off her stroppy teenager phase and become something of a royal hero. First came her success as an Olympic horsewoman (see Chapter 14), then her glamorous wedding to Captain Mark Phillips in November 1973. For a short time, the deprivations and blackouts were forgotten. Out came the glass coach (see Chapter 10) and the crowds. The world-wide TV audience was larger than ever and, after the obligatory balcony appearance, the royal couple sailed away on the *Britannia* (see Chapter 10) for a honeymoon that took them to the other side of the world.

Not long after her return, Anne was brought down to earth (not that she was ever prone to flights of fancy) by a kidnap attack (see the sidebar, "Not bloody likely!"). She coped as she did her challenges in the saddle, with jaw-dropping sangfroid.

In 1987, Elizabeth bestowed a personal mark of approval on her plain-speaking daughter. She became the Princess Royal, only the seventh eldest daughter of a reigning monarch to be awarded the title since it was instigated in the reign of Charles I (1625–1649).

TIP

Keeping Calm and Carrying On

By 1975, a whole generation of Britons had grown up knowing no-one but Elizabeth II as their Head of State. Whatever else was going on – Philip's naughtiness, Margaret's turmoils, Anne's stroppiness, the protests, strikes, riots and terrorist bombings – the Queen was still there, doing her duty.

Elizabeth had come to embody the famous slogan from the days of the German bombings of World War II: Keep Calm and Carry On. Ordinary people liked that because it reflected their own behaviour during difficult times. Also, like them, the Queen carried on working.

TIP

At the start of the 1970s, Parliament voted the Queen a considerable pay rise (see Chapter 14; the royal finances are explained in Chapter 17). The increase was a tacit thank you for Elizabeth's unflagging adherence to her royal duties.

Now let's put some flesh on the bones. Here is a very small sample, taken from December 1970 to June 1971, that illustrates the sort of tasks (and not the number of tasks, which was 50 times greater) the Queen undertook year in, year out:

December 1970 Opens joint headquarters of the Cancer Research Campaign and the Royal College of Pathologists, London.

February 1971 Visits Family Welfare Association Area Casework Office for Kensington, Chelsea and Westminster, London.

March 1971 Visits Royal Air Force base at Brize Norton, Oxfordshire.

April 1971 Attends London film premiere of *Tales of Beatrix Potter*.

Official civic visit to city of Birmingham.

May 1971 Attends Royal Horticultural Society's Chelsea Flower Show, London.

June 1971 Visits baby care unit at St Mary's Hospital, Manchester.

On horseback at Horse Guards' Parade, London, for the ceremonial Beating the Retreat parade.

Chapter 8 discusses that a major part of Elizabeth's role is to act as a global ambassador for the UK. With very few exceptions, her work in this sphere has been spectacularly successful – not because she sings along with presidents like her sister Margaret (see Chapter 13), but because she is impeccably polite and rarely puts a foot wrong.

To give some idea of the work involved during the 1970s, take a look at these three lists:

>> **Countries from which the Queen received a state visit:** Japan, Afghanistan, Netherlands, Luxemburg, West Germany, Mexico, Nigeria, Zaire, Denmark, Malaysia, Sweden, Tanzania, Brazil, France, Romania, Portugal, Kenya, Indonesia.

>> **Commonwealth countries to which the Queen made a state visit, often more than once:** Canada (6 times, excluding refuelling stopovers), Fiji, Tonga, New Zealand, Australia, Singapore, Malaysia, Brunei, Seychelles, Mauritius, Kenya, Cook Islands, Norfolk Island, New Hebrides, Solomon Islands, Papua New Guinea, Bermuda, Barbados, Bahamas, Jamaica, Hong King, Western Samoa, Tonga, British Virgin Islands, Antigua and Barbuda, Tanzania, Malawi, Botswana, Zambia.

>> **Other countries to which the Queen made a state visit:** Turkey, Thailand, Maldives, France, Yugoslavia, Indonesia, Mexico, Japan, Finland, United States, Luxemburg, American Samoa, West Germany (including West Berlin), Kuwait, Bahrain, Saudi Arabia, Qatar, United Arab Emirates, Oman, Denmark.

Almost without exception, each visit was marked by cheering crowds, prominent display of the UK flag, and a general feeling of goodwill towards Great Britain. That, surely, is what the role of a Head of State is all about?

Planning Elizabeth's Jubilee

Holding large-scale celebrations for Queen Elizabeth II's Silver Jubilee was a bit of a gamble.

As outlined earlier in this chapter, 1970s Britain was having a tough time. Unemployment was high and strikes common. Class and racial tensions were never far beneath the surface, and the country had to borrow billions from the International Monetary Fund (IMF) to stay afloat. Against this background, would the people accept spending millions on a pageant to honour a fabulously wealthy woman who owed her position to an accident of birth?

The answer, which took a while to emerge, surprised the most fervent royalists. From the people of Britain and the Commonwealth came a clear and resounding YES! Even the Queen herself was taken aback by her popularity.

TIP

The idea of a Silver Jubilee was relatively new. Victoria didn't have one. Only in 1935 did George V become the first monarch to participate in public celebrations marking the 25th year of his reign. Part of the pageant involved the Princesses Elizabeth and Margaret parading around London in a coach with their grandparents. Memories of 1935 inspired the festivities of 1977.

REMEMBER

The lead-up had not been particularly auspicious. Besides the difficulties in the country, the Royal Family had had their own ups and downs. In 1972, the Queen celebrated her silver wedding anniversary quietly, perhaps hinting in that year's Christmas message at how life with Philip was not all champagne and roses: 'No marriage can hope to succeed without a deliberate effort to be tolerant and understanding.'

Perhaps the words were levelled at her sister Margaret, whose marriage was clearly falling apart? Or were these words of advice to her daughter Anne, whose marriage to Mark Phillips would take place the next year?

Behind it all was the shadow of another royal marriage. Earlier that year, the Queen made a trip to Paris to visit her uncle Edward, Duke of Windsor, and his wife Wallis (see Chapter 5). The former Edward VIII was extremely ill and Elizabeth spoke with him for only a few minutes. He died ten days later.

Against this gloomy background, Elizabeth's 1975 Christmas message sounded rather like a sermon. 'Kindness, sympathy, resolution, and courteous behaviour are infectious,' she declared. 'Acts of courage and self-sacrifice, like those of the people who refuse to be terrorized by kidnappers or hijackers, or who diffuse bombs, are an inspiration to others.' Weighty stuff. And it was followed by a call for unity, the central theme of the upcoming jubilee.

THE UNION JACK

The United Kingdom's Union Flag, commonly known as the *Union Jack*, has its origins in the union of the crowns of Scotland and England in 1603 (see Chapter 2). In 1606, a royal decree stated that the kingdom's official flag would comprise the English flag (the red cross of St George against a white background) combined with the Scottish flag or *saltire* (St Andrew's white cross on a blue background). The Irish red cross (*saltire*) of St Patrick was added in 1801.

The result, widely considered one of the most attractive and distinctive of all national flags, is incorporated into the flags of several Commonwealth countries, including Canada, Australia, New Zealand, and Bermuda.

Remarks like this seemed to strike a chord. Hereditary monarchy might be outdated and some members of the Royal Family not worthy of their privileges, but the Queen herself was something different. Disapproval of the monarchy, never getting above 20 percent in the opinion polls, dwindled. 'Stuff the jubilee' badges lay unsold. In their place, shops stocked up on jubilee mugs, scarves and other patriotic paraphernalia. Union Jack underpants made their first appearance!

Entering Jubilee Year

Jubilee year opened with some half-hearted and unofficial attempts to mark the 25th anniversary of the Queen's accession on the precise day – 6 February 1977. Winter is not a good time of year for celebrations, and 1977 was no exception. The cold, rain, and darkness ensured that in the UK the date passed largely unnoticed by the bulk of the population.

Meanwhile, in the background the royal PR machine had swung into operation with the publication of an official 37-page jubilee calendar of events. First up was a February trip to the Commonwealth Pacific islands of American Samoa, Western Samoa, Tonga, and Fiji. The Queen was warmly received in all of them.

From Fiji, it was on to a two-week, 11-stop stay in New Zealand. Modelled on the rapturous 1953–1954 tour noted in Chapter 10, it was also deemed a great success. Serious talk of *Aotearoa* (the Māori name for the islands, usually translated as the 'Land of the Long White Cloud') becoming a republic was some way off. Australia, however, was a trickier prospect.

GOVERNOR-GENERAL OF AUSTRALIA

The Queen is represented in Australia by the country's governor-general. The position is in theory a Crown appointment, though in practice the choice is made by the Australian government.

The governor-general's non-political role mirrors very closely that of the monarch in the UK – commander-in-chief of the military, appointing ministers, bestowing honours, giving assent to legislation, taking part in ceremonies, and so on. Should Australia become a republic, which is a distinct possibility within the next decade (2022–2032), the governor-generalship would be abolished.

REMEMBER

Between 1971 and 1976, Prince Charles served in the Royal Navy (see Chapter 14). What should he do next? He suggested he might become Governor-General of Australia as he liked the country and wanted to buy a house there (see the sidebar "Governor-General of Australia"). Palace advisors were sceptical. Charles would need to be married to do the job properly, and buying yet another house at a time when Britain was facing an acute housing shortage might be seen as tactless.

Charles's Australian dream was quashed by the Dismissal Crisis of 1975. When Australia's Labour Prime Minister Gough Whitlam failed to get his budget through Parliament, Governor-General Sir John Kerr promptly dismissed him. Liberal leader Malcolm Fraser accepted Kerr's invitation to take over as PM, and remained in power until 1983.

TIP

Kerr had acted precipitously. His action highlighted the Crown's awkward position in Australia (see Chapter 20). Making Charles governor-general, even if Australians wanted him, would risk involving him in constitutional issues that could further damage the monarchy. Interestingly, in Australia's 1999 referendum on whether to retain the monarchy (see Chapter 20), Whitlam and Fraser both campaigned to make their country a republic.

Happily for Elizabeth, by the time of her jubilee visit in 1977, the furore over the Dismissal had died down and she was warmly welcomed. Just not by Gough Whitlam.

The Queen was back in the UK by the spring. In May, she began a 7,000-mile, six-tour peregrination around Britain; it started with the launching of a new air-craft carrier, HMS *Invincible*, in the north-western shipbuilding town of Barrow-in-Furness.

The rest of May was taken up with visits, receptions and other formal occasions. These included a loyal address from the two Houses of Parliament, a gala performance at London's Royal Opera House, and an all-stars football (soccer) match in Glasgow.

REMEMBER

Responding to Parliament's address, the Queen came close to overstepping the bounds of constitutional propriety. She reminded her audience that she was 'Queen of the United Kingdom of Great Britain and Northern Ireland,' and wondered whether the Jubilee was a good time to remember 'the benefits which union has conferred, at home and in our international dealings, on the inhabitants of all parts of this United Kingdom.'

The challenge to Irish republicans and Scottish and Welsh nationalists was unmistakable.

Celebrating in June 1977

Jubilee Day, 6 June, was declared a *bank holiday* (a national holiday) so everyone was free to join in the festivities.

TIP

The day began with the Queen lighting a huge bonfire in Windsor Great Park. The blaze sparked a chain of 100 beacons across the land. Many were on the same sites as those used in 1588 to warn of the approach of the Spanish invasion armada during the reign of Elizabeth I (see Chapter 2). In London, the thousands who had slept beside the road in order to get a good view of the day's events crawled out of their sleeping bags and went to look for breakfast.

In mid-morning, a crowd estimated to be around one million thronged the route from Buckingham Palace to St Paul's Cathedral where a service of thanksgiving was to be held. Hundreds of millions more watched on TV around the world.

The Queen rode in the newly gilded (but still remarkably uncomfortable) Golden State Coach (see Chapter 10). Prince Charles accompanied her on horseback, and other members of the family smiled and waved from the Glass Coach, the Irish State Coach, and Queen Alexandra's State Coach. Troops of soldiers, including the Household Cavalry in red jackets and plumed golden helmets, provided a dashing ceremonial guard.

REMEMBER

The service, whose large congregation included all living prime ministers, was followed by a walkabout. As the Queen made her way on foot from the cathedral to a banquet at the Mansion House, she spoke to a smiling child at the roadside. 'We're here because we love you,' the girl explained. Genuinely moved, Elizabeth replied, 'I can feel it, and it means so much to me.'

Away from the centre of London, parties were in full swing on streets and village greens. 'Liz rules OK' grinned down-to-earth lapel badges. To the surprise of many observers, the jubilee spirit was entered into by men and woman of all ages and from all socio-economic backgrounds. Truly, the unity Jubilee had worked its magic.

REMEMBER

6 June was not the end of it. Jubilee stamps and coins continued to be produced and circulated. Jubilee ale was downed by the barrelful. The Queen opened a Jubilee Line extension to the London Underground's railway line and attended a Jubilee cricket match and several Jubilee military tattoos. To Wales, Scotland, Northern Ireland, England north, south, east and west she went, even cutting short her two-month Balmoral holiday.

In the autumn, Elizabeth was abroad again, this time visiting Canada, the Bahamas, and other Caribbean islands. Finally, in her Christmas message she thanked all who had helped to make the year such a successful and enjoyable one. 'Last Christmas, I said that my wish for 1977 was that it should be a year of reconciliation,' she reminded listeners. 'You have shown by the way in which you have celebrated the Jubilee that this was not an impossible dream. Thank you all for your response.'

Only time would tell how long the reconciliation would last.

4

Stormy Waters

This part follows Elizabeth's story from her 1977 Silver Jubilee to the nadir of her reign, the 'Annus Horribilis' of 1992. Along the way, we step aside to examine two aspects of the Elizabethan monarchy in more detail: the Queen's wealth and her strong religious faith.

Three women take pride of place in the narrative section: Elizabeth herself, Britain's first female prime minister, Margaret Thatcher, and Prince Charles's extraordinarily charismatic wife, Princess Diana. We also see how the woman who had once described divorce as undermining the moral fibre of the nation, was forced by circumstances to accept its presence within her own family. It wasn't just the marriage of her eldest son that collapsed, but that of her daughter and second son, too.

Finally, symbolic of the fall of the House of Windsor, fire devastated Elizabeth's priceless and beloved Windsor Castle. The conflagration could have been a scene from a Gothic horror movie. Remarkably, like a boxer who refuses to go down under a rain of blows, Elizabeth battled on – as dignified and duty-bound as ever.

Chapter **16**

The Tragedy of Charles and Diana

This chapter covers the biggest royal relationship story since the abdication of Edward VIII in 1937 (see Chapter 5). It begins with Charles's love life before marriage and ends with the death of his former wife, the flawed superstar Diana.

REMEMBER

Why is Charles's love life so important? Because the succession (see Chapters 1 and 2) requires Charles – as heir to the throne – to marry and produce an heir of his own.

In former times, it was so easy. Monarchs – straight, gay, or indifferent – knew it was their duty to produce a legitimate heir, preferably male, who would take over the Crown after their death. Marriages were arranged and children duly appeared. When they didn't, it spelt trouble. That's why Henry VIII was prepared to turn the country upside down in order to get a son (see Chapter 2).

In the twentieth century, the pressures were still there, though less intense. However, they were complicated by the relatively modern belief that a royal marriage should be a happy amalgam of two elements:

» Dynastic duty

» Romantic love

Victoria managed it. Edward VII didn't, though he seems to have had a solid enough friendship with the uber-tolerant Queen Alexandra. There wasn't much romance in George V's marriage to his deceased brother's ex, Queen Mary (see Chapter 3). His eldest son, Edward VIII, went for romance over duty (see Chapter 5).

The stars happily realigned for George VI and his Queen Elizabeth (Bowes-Lyon), who rediscovered the elusive Victorian recipe of love and duty. For Prince Charles, they swung out of kilter once more, with tragic results.

Stepping Out With Charles

TIP

By the 1970s, Charles Prince of Wales, heir to the Crown of the United Kingdom, Northern Ireland, Canada, etc. etc., was probably the world's most eligible bachelor. Who wouldn't want to become a queen? Quite a few women, actually. The glamour and money were okay, but not being endlessly on display like a mannequin in a shop window. And the potential in-laws – weren't they a bit stuffy?

Despite not getting the Governor-General of Australia job (see Chapter 15), Charles was kept busy by his naval career, his royal duties and his pet project, The Prince's Trust (detailed in the nearby sidebar of the same name). Nevertheless, he did have time for other things, notably playing polo, fishing, and dating young ladies of suitable birth and breeding. The press called them 'Charlie's Angels' after the American TV drama.

Charles's first girlfriends

Because Charles was destined to succeed to the throne after his mother's demise, and his children would continue the Windsor line after him, Charles's love life attracted continual interest from the media across the world. Who was his latest flame? Would he marry her?

THE PRINCE'S TRUST

Founded by Prince Charles in 1976, The Prince's Trust is one of the leading charities dedicated to helping young people at risk of going off the rails.

Each year, it assists around 60,000 youngsters who are unemployed or in trouble at school or with the police. The practical help takes the form of training, financial support and confidence-building.

Since its inception, the Trust is believed to have helped almost one million people, and its network now extends right around to globe to cover countries as far apart as New Zealand and Canada, Australia and the United States. It is an undoubted success story in which Charles continues to take an active interest.

There was no shortage of candidates linked to the man the press dubbed 'the world's most eligible bachelor':

>> **Lucia Santa Cruz.** Charles met the daughter of the former Chilean ambassador to London in 1967, when they were both studying at Cambridge. Of unknown age, though supposedly five years older than the Prince, she was his first proper girlfriend. We don't know why they broke up. She and Charles remain friends – indeed, it was Lucia who introduced him to the lively Camilla Shand (who we shall be introduced to later in this chapter).

>> **Caroline Longman.** An aristocratic date from the 1970s, whose friendship with the Prince was short-lived.

>> **Susan George.** A horse dealer and uninhibited actress, linked to Charles from time to time in the 1970s. Her topless appearance in the film *Straw Dogs* ruled out any possibility of her being a candidate for queen.

>> **Lady Jane Wellesley.** In the mid-1970s, there was serious gossip about Charles and Lady Jane marrying. As the daughter of the Duke of Wellington (whose ancestor had defeated Napoleon at Waterloo – one of Britain's most famous military victories – and gone on to be prime minister), the press considered her eminently suitable. She herself did not, retorting sharply when questioned, 'Do you honestly believe I want to be queen?'

>> **Davina Sheffield.** The prospects for Davina, a cousin of former Prime Minister David Cameron's wife Samantha, sank to zero when the press learned of her previous sexual experience. Finding someone who had not been 'compromised' (as a Tory peer once tactfully put it) was not going to be easy.

- » **Lady Sarah Spencer.** The aristocratic elder sister of Lady Di briefly went out with Charles in 1977. They had fun but it was not a love match. Nevertheless, she did introduce Charles to her younger sibling.

- » **Sabrina Guinness.** The lively heiress to the Guinness brewing fortune met Charles in 1979. All was going well until Elizabeth raised questions about Sabrina's uninhibited past. The quest for an upper-class virgin went on.

- » **Lady Amanda Knatchbull.** Lady Amanda, granddaughter of Louis Mountbatten (see Chapter 15) and an eminently suitable partner, knew all about being in the spotlight. So when Charles proposed to her in 1980, she allegedly replied with a polite but firm 'no way'.

- » **Anna Wallace.** Another rejection for the Prince. Anna 'Whiplash' Wallace, fiery daughter of a wealthy Scottish landowner, turned down Charles twice before finally dumping him in 1980 when she found him two-timing with the now-married Camilla (see the next section).

Charles's number one: Camilla Shand

In one sense, Camilla Shand came from a good pedigree. Though no aristocrat, her great-grandmother, Alice Keppel, had been the lifelong mistress and confidante of Prince Charles's great-great grandfather, Edward VII. Camilla was fun, too, with the same sense of humour as the Prince. He was attracted by her affectionate and straightforward manner: the fact that Charles was Prince of Wales didn't alter her approach to him one jot.

REMEMBER

The couple met after Charles had graduated from Cambridge. His university paramour, Lucia Santa Cruz, reckoned Camilla would be 'just the girl' for him. She was right, and Charles was smitten straight away. Here was mother and lover in one jolly package. She, it seems, was less head-over-heels for him, and therein lay the problem. Charles did not propose, and a few months later, while he was away on duty in the Royal Navy, she agreed to marry another man.

That, in most stories, would have been it. But not in this case. Camilla's husband, Andrew Parker-Bowles, was a friend of the Royal Family. When he visited them at Balmoral and elsewhere, his wife came with him. She and Charles became best friends, and then a bit more. This is when his then-girlfriend, Anna Wallace, dumped him.

WARNING

Rumours of Charles's affair with Mrs Parker-Bowles leaked. Alarmed, the Palace warned Charles of the damage his behaviour might do to his own and his family's reputation. In 1978 he had turned thirty, the age by which he had declared he ought to be married. But Camilla already had a husband. Of course, she could divorce him . . . Once again, that dreaded word echoed down the carpeted corridors of castle and palace. Divorce.

Charles would have to marry someone else.

Introducing Lady Diana

TIP

With hindsight, one might see the relationship between Prince Charles and Lady Diana Spencer as doomed from the start. Possibly. Their needs and wishes were so different and yet in some ways so similar that it's hard to speculate. They both tried to make a go of it – and failed. The reverberations of that spectacular failure persist to this day.

In the end, one figure came out of the entire royal soap opera with their dignity more or less intact. Queen Elizabeth II.

The early life of Lady Diana

TECHNICAL STUFF

A number of commentators have sought to explain Diana Spencer's wretched married life by her childhood experiences. The similarities between the early married life of Diana's mother, Lady Frances Spencer, and that of her younger daughter are curious.

Frances married Johnny Spencer, 8th Earl Spencer and a former Queen's Equerry, at the age of 18. She produced four children (Diana was born in 1961), then left the rural blandness of the family estate in Norfolk for the bright lights of London. Playwright Noel Coward's description of Norfolk as 'very flat' was not just geographically accurate. The dull landowner Earl got custody of the children in an acrimonious divorce in which he was accused of mental cruelty. We're told the divorce turned the six-year-old Diana from a bouncy little girl into a shy and introverted one. The situation was not helped by the Earl's choice of second wife, Raine, Countess of Dartmouth. The children knew her as 'Acid Raine'.

As was customary with aristocratic families, Diana was sent to boarding school before the age of ten. She proved a well-liked if unremarkable pupil, who showed some musical talent but failed all her exams at first and second attempts. Aged sixteen, she was packed off again, this time to a finishing school for young ladies in Switzerland, where she picked up a smattering of French.

By 1978, Diana was living with friends in a small flat in London. She took a series of low-paid jobs, including working as an assistant in a nursery school. It was while she was there that a 31-year-old man named Charles came looking for a wife.

TIP

Was Diana the sort of woman who would make a suitable wife for Prince Charles? Here is a sort of 'for and against' list that an outside observer might have drawn up, with the benefit of hindsight:

» Reasons for being a suitable wife:

- In love with Charles.

- Immensely attractive and photogenic.

- Sexually inexperienced (avoiding the future possibility of 'My Steamy Nights with the Queen' revelations in the popular media).

- Aristocratic background – her family of earls and dukes, with links to the Churchills (Prime Minister Winston was actually Winston *Spencer* Churchill) – had its roots in the Middle Ages and was a great deal more English than the German–Greek Windsors.

- Pleasantly naïve, so could be moulded into a modern royal.

- Popular with ordinary people because she had done menial jobs, had no formal qualifications, and did not speak with a haughty upper-class accent.

- Naturally maternal.

- Tougher than she looked, and quicker to learn than her exam results suggested.

» Reasons against being a suitable wife:

- Unaware of what marrying into the Royal Family meant.

- Sought in marriage the cherishing stability that Charles was not able to give. His heart was with Camilla.

- Emotional insecurity, which some labelled 'borderline personality disorder'. It manifested itself in bouts of bulimia (an eating disorder often associated with binge eating followed by fasting or purging, often taking the form of self-induced vomiting).

- Few shared interests or friends.

- Could be manipulative, duplicitous and spiteful when feeling threatened or pressured.
- Not good at public speaking or making small talk.

Eight in favour, six against – the marriage should have worked, shouldn't it? If only life were as straightforward as mathematics!

Charles and Diana get engaged

WARNING

There's a rather touching scene in *The Crown* that shows Charles and Diana's first meeting when he came courting her elder sister, Sarah. The Prince was 29 at the time and Diana was 16. Their second meeting of any significance took place a couple of years later at the house of one of Diana's friends. They sat outside on hay bales and chatted.

REMEMBER

Diana remembered thinking Charles 'pretty amazing'. When she told him how sad he had looked at Mountbatten's funeral, he was touched by her sympathetic kindness. Though she had never had a proper boyfriend, she instinctively knew how to reel a man in. Charles, she would recall with deliberate exaggeration, 'leapt on me, practically.' A dozen meetings later, including a visit to Balmoral, in February 1981 Charles proposed and she accepted.

She had no idea what she had let herself in for. But there had been a number of warning signs:

>> It is said that all along Charles knew in his heart that marriage to Diana was unwise, but it was too late to pull out. He felt, we are told, 'permanently between the devil and the deep blue sea'. He was duty bound, he insisted, 'to do the right thing' for country and family and hoped to grow to love his beautiful bride.

REMEMBER

>> Someone more experienced than Diana and less in love might also have read the runes. Asked by a TV reporter at the time of their engagement whether they were in love, Diana replied instantly, 'Of course'. Her fiancé nodded before adding a phrase that has now become infamous: 'Whatever "in love" means'. Hardly the most romantic of responses.

WARNING

>> Diana received an even clearer warning when she came across a bracelet engraved 'GF' in one of Charles's offices (an incident featured in *The Crown*). 'Girl Friday' was, apparently, one of Charles's nicknames for Camilla and the bracelet was a farewell gift for her on the occasion of his marriage.

>> Diana sensed the invisible presence of her husband's mistress at every turn. For his part, did he not pick up the warning signs of an eating disorder when his bride-to-be lost so much weight that her wedding dress had to be taken in several times?

>> Diana is reported to have secretly spent several nights before her marriage with Charles in Buckingham Palace. They were apart for the night before the ceremony itself, she in Clarence House with the Queen Mother, he in the Palace. It is rumoured that Camilla came to see him there one last time; others say he lay alone, weeping bitter tears at what lay ahead.

The Marriage of Charles and Diana

Looking back, the marriage the Archbishop of Canterbury described as a 'fairy tale event' was in fact a sham, a massive PR exercise for the monarchy. And when the wedding collapsed, as we now understand was just about inevitable, the public took their revenge by blaming Charles for hoodwinking them.

Charles and Diana were married on 29 July 1981. A few weeks before, on 13 June, a deranged young man who later explained that he 'wanted to be a somebody' fired six starting pistol blanks at the Queen as she rode by on her way to a Trooping the Colour ceremony (see Chapter 1). The Queen's horse was startled. Though she was riding the traditional side-saddle, she brought the animal under control and continued calmly on her way to Horse Guards Parade. The shooter was apprehended and sentenced to five years in jail.

TIP

The Queen's courage, and the wave of pro-Royal Family feeling already sweeping the nation in the run-up to the Prince of Wales's wedding, lifted public approval of hereditary monarchy to 86 percent.

Building up to the big day

On 3 September 1660, James Duke of York, heir to the throne of his brother Charles II, married Anne Hyde in a private house at about midnight. The next time the heir to the throne married an English bride – in 1981 – could not have been more different:

>> In the two days before the wedding, the Queen arranged a series of social events, including a dinner for 150 visiting foreign dignitaries.

>> The service was held in St Paul's Cathedral, the first time Christopher Wren's seventeenth-century masterpiece had hosted a royal wedding. 3,500 guests were in attendance, and an estimated 750 million watched on TV.

Elizabeth in June 1940, aged 14:
a carefully curated image of studious
innocence. (Chapter 4)

Eyes fixed firmly on the task ahead, Elizabeth
displays her uncertain-looking trophy
fiancé Philip, August 1947. (Chapter 6)

It's tempting to read too much into this photo of Elizabeth, Philip, Charles, and baby Anne from August 1951.
Does the Duke look a bit fed up with child-minding? And is Charles already an anxious boy? (Chapters 12 & 14)

A fairy tale made real: Elizabeth rolls home in the Gold State Coach (arguably the
uncomfortable vehicle ever built) after her coronation, 2 June 1953. (Chapter 7

Coronation moment, 1953: Flanked by the
Bishops of Durham and Bath and Wells,
holding the Sceptre with the Cross and the
Rod with the Dove, and wearing
Edward's Crown, Elizabeth is greeted with
shouts of 'God Save the Queen!' (Chapter 7)

Started in 1703 as a town hous
Duke of Buckingham, the vast,
Buckingham Palace has be
symbol of the British monar
since Queen Victoria took up
there in 1837. (Chapter

The Queen Down Under: Elizabeth and Philip in Bathurst, New South Wales, Aus[tralia] during their 44,000-mile Commonwealth tour, 1953–1954. (Chapter 10)

[R]ight: Philip, Edward, Elizabeth, Andrew, Anne, and Charles, in the garden of [W]indsor Estate, 1968. Note the formal attire even for an afternoon stroll. (Cha[pter ...])

...atting with young fans during the Silver Jubilee, June 1977. On public occasions, Elizabeth has always been more at ease with children than adults. (Chapter 15)

Elizabeth and Philip stand amid the mountain of flowers that appeared outside Buckingham Palace following the death of Princess Diana in 1997. (Chapters 16, 21 & 27)

In all her jewelled finery – including Queen Alexandra's Kokoshnik Tiara, the Greville Chandelier Earrings, George VI Festoon Necklace, and the Order of the Garter – Elizabeth puts on a show for President Gerald Ford and First Lady Betty Ford at a State Banquet as part of the 1976 Bicentennial celebrations. (Chapter 10)

The cowboy and the queen: President Ronald Reagan and Elizabeth setting out on horseback in the grounds of Windsor Castle during his highly successful 1982 state visit to the UK. (Chapter 10)

Prime Minister Margaret Thatcher greets Elizabeth on the steps of 10 Downing Street, the prime minister's official residence. The two women did not get on very well, and the Royal Family found Mrs Thatcher's ultra-deep curtseys rather amusing. (Chapter 18)

A devout Christian, Elizabeth bows her head in prayer during the 2008 Remembrance Day service, an annual tribute to the wartime dead from the United Kingdom and Commonwealth. (Chapter 19)

Windsor Castle ablaze, 20 November 1992. Public outcry at the government's willingness to meet the cost repairs obliged Elizabeth to bring forward her long-planned decision to pay income tax. (Chapter 20)

The beginning of the Windsor's most compelling soap opera: Charles and Diana on the balcony of Buckingham Palace on the day of their wedding, 29 July 1981. (Chapters 16 & 21)

Elizabeth and Charles on the Buckingham Palace balcony beside Kate and William. Meghan and Harry stand in the background. (Chapters 24 & 29)

On 4 June 2002, Elizabeth and Philip wave to adoring crowds thronging The Mall, London, during the Golden Jubilee celebrations. (Chapter 23)

Elizabeth riding side-saddle during the Trooping the Colour ceremony in 1981.
The Queen remained firmly in control of her mount, Burmese, when a wayward
young man fired six blank shots at her. (Chapters 16 & 22)

Elizabeth and Philip on their way home after opening Parliament, 2009.
While conservatives revel in such old-world traditions, reformers argue

- Over one million spectators (estimates vary) used the national holiday to line Diana's route from Clarence House to the cathedral. Diana arrived with her father in the famous Glass Coach (see Chapter 10).

- Diana looked stunning in a swirling dress of silk taffeta designed by David and Elizabeth Emanuel. It was decorated with 10,000 pearls and sported a spectacular but awkward 25-foot train.

- Three orchestras played, and the celebrated Kiwi (New Zealander) soprano Kiri Te Kanawa sang a Handel aria.

- Afterwards, 120 family guests attended a scrumptious wedding breakfast in Buckingham Palace. Non-family members ate with Prime Minister Margaret Thatcher.

- Later in the day, Charles and Diana waved to crowds from the balcony of Buckingham Palace and – another royal first – indulged in a very full and public kiss. Straight from a child's book of fairy tales.

Worrying moments of the wedding

Fairy tales are fiction: reality is always messier. And so it was with the wedding of Charles and Diana. It looked great on TV, but behind the scenes, and even in the service itself, there were some awkward hiccups:

- All the reigning monarchs of Europe were present, apart from the King and Queen of Spain. Their government told them not to attend because the newlyweds planned a honeymoon stopover in Gibraltar. (The British territory on the southern tip of the Spanish mainland, at the mouth of the Mediterranean Sea, had long been a source of disagreement between Britain and Spain: Spain wants it returned; the Gibraltarians wish to remain with Britain.)

- Diana's wedding dress train got so tangled up in the Glass Coach that it took two struggling bridesmaids to sort it out.

- As Diana walked down the aisle, she said later that she had eyes for just one figure in the congregation: Camilla Parker-Bowles. The bride said she felt like 'a lamb to the slaughter'.

- At the altar, Diana was so nervous that she muddled up Charles's initial two names. She called him Philip Charles Arthur George instead of Charles Philip Arthur George.

- Diana vetoed the presence of the Parker-Bowles family at the wedding breakfast.

Going Steady: The First Few Years of Marriage

To begin with, things seemed to be going alright. Charles and Diana both knew they had to compromise to make their marriage work: he had to accept her naivety, lack of education, and liking for urban pop culture; she had to learn to enjoy polo, fly fishing and walks in the countryside. It was a tough ask.

WARNING

No one ever knows exactly what goes on inside a marriage, the smiles and slights, the passion and pain. The truth about the marriage between Charles and Diana is even harder to get at for two reasons:

>> It was conducted under the continuous glare of global media attention; Diana learned to handle this much better than her husband and used it to turn opinion in her favour when things went wrong.

>> Both parties gave the world their own version of events in books; Diana in Andrew Morton's *Diana – Her True Story In Her Own Words* (Michael O'Mara Books, 1992) and Charles in Jonathan Dimbleby's *The Prince of Wales: A Biography* (Little, Brown, 1994). The Princess's account is far less balanced than the Prince's. However, as the two books were written when the wounds were raw, they need to be treated with care. The truth, if there is such a thing, may lie somewhere between the two.

Heading off on honeymoon

The newlyweds started their protracted honeymoon with a 14-day cruise around the Mediterranean on board the Royal Yacht *Britannia*, before returning to Balmoral Castle in Scotland for a quieter time together. The Princess was still besotted with Charles, and we mustn't take her later remarks at face value. Nevertheless, it was clear from the outset that all was not well.

The royal yacht was hardly a secluded honeymoon hideaway. The 200-strong crew did their best to be discreet, but they could not make themselves invisible. And a candlelit dinner for two was not exactly private when a Royal Marines band was playing romantic music in the background.

Charles didn't mind – he had done all this romantic stuff before. But for Diana, the openness and her husband's acceptance of it caused her anxiety. With anxiety came bulimia (explained earlier in this chapter). She wanted to talk sweet nothings; he wanted to read, paint, and discuss philosophy. At one stage, we're told, she wrecked his painting equipment in a fit of frustration.

REMEMBER

Over everything loomed the persistent shadow of Camilla. Gradually, day by day, she became an obsession for Diana, who was insecure at the best of times. Now, with Charles unable to give her the 100 percent attention and adoration she craved, she became fixated on his former mistress. Did a photo of Camilla fall out of her husband's diary? Did the two Cs engraved on his cufflinks stand for Charles and Camilla? Fantasy and fact blur together in recollection.

Sex? Well, it worked well enough, apparently, but not as either party wanted. Diana sought romantic seduction into the art of love; Charles needed to be led and mothered. 'Nothing special', he is alleged to have said of the first night of their marriage.

TIP

It was all very different from the honeymoon of Elizabeth and Philip 33 years earlier. They too were to have their difficulties, but always had happy memories to fall back on. Charles and Diana had no such foundation.

Protecting Diana from the press

Tensions between the Prince and Princess remained between themselves and their closest friends for several years. If the media knew about it, they kept quiet. The British media did, anyway, as their obsession with Diana grew.

In 1981, concerned by the continual, intrusive attention her daughter-in-law was receiving, the Queen took a highly unusual step: she summoned the editors of 21 newspapers and magazines to Buckingham Palace and politely asked them to go easy on Diana.

WARNING

A journalist from the Murdoch-owned sensationalist *News of the World* asked, quite rightly, why, if the Princess really did want less media attention, did she go out shopping for sweets rather than send a lackey? In a rare moment of indiscretion, the Queen lost her cool. The precise wording of her reply to the hapless journalist varies according to who one reads, but it was undoubtedly rude. The man had touched a raw nerve and Elizabeth, consciously or not, knew this.

Diana had discovered her power and was using it to elevate herself into a global superstar. Beside her blinding light, the rest of the Royal Family, especially Charles, appeared drab and dull. No wonder the Queen was cross. She could not compete. Her son had brought a cuckoo into the nest.

The birth of Prince William

Conceived during their honeymoon, Prince William Arthur Philip Louis Mountbatten-Windsor was born at St Mary's Hospital, London on 21 June 1982.

He was the first direct heir to the Crown not to be born in a royal residence since George III in 1738. Six weeks later, he was baptized by the Archbishop of Canterbury in Buckingham Palace. The occasion was also the 82nd birthday of the Queen Mother.

At that stage, the former queen was the one member of the Royal Family with whom Diana felt at ease. They shared the same experience of marrying into 'The Firm' (see Chapter 8), even if George VI had been a kinder partner to his wife than Charles was being to his.

REMEMBER

Charles had seen little of his parents as a child (see Chapters 6 and 14) and Diana had been traumatized by her parents' separation. But having worked in a nursery school, she knew a bit about raising children. Learning from their experiences, Charles and Diana were keen to give their own as normal an upbringing as was possible for royal princes. They took nine-month-old William (known as 'Wills') with them when they toured Australia and New Zealand. When he was a bit older, they sent him to Jane Mynor's nursery school in London along with other 'normal' children.

The Birth of Prince Harry

Diana Princess of Wales gave birth to Henry Charles Albert David Mountbatten-Windsor on 15 September 1984. Like his elder brother, he came into the world in St Mary's Hospital, London, and was baptized by the Archbishop of Canterbury. In a long English tradition stretching back at least to the time of the hero King Henry V (see Chapter 2), the child was always known as 'Harry'.

WARNING

A quick word here about the gossip concerning Harry's father. Some suggest that, because of the lack of physical resemblance, Charles is not Harry's father. This has been strongly denied. Though Diana is known to have had a number of affairs after her marriage failed, there is no evidence that she was romantically linked to the most likely candidate, cavalry officer James Hewitt (see later in this chapter for more about him), before Harry's birth.

Harry followed his brother to Jane Mynor's nursery school before moving to Wetherby School to prepare him for admission to prep school (see Chapter 24). Looking back much later, Harry described his early life in the media spotlight as if living in a cross between a zoo and *The Truman Show*.

Fulfilling Royal Duties Together

REMEMBER

Charles and Diana held it together until about 1985. The previous year, the Queen had moved to quash rumours by saying how delighted she was with her daughter-in-law. Her prepared statement said she could not be more pleased with Diana's 'activities around the world and at home'. That remained her attitude throughout the ensuing crisis – stay calm and carry on regardless.

As if to bear out the Queen's words, in 1985 the couple gave a TV interview in which Diana said that her role was to support her husband and 'be a good mother and wife'. The press swallowed it whole.

At the end of the year, the royal couple made a successful visit to the US. Successful for Diana, anyway. When entertained by the Reagans at The White House, she danced with John Travolta and flirted with Clint Eastwood, both of whom were captivated by her. She made less of an effort with her host and hostess, finding Ronnie an old bore and Nancy an attention-seeker. As was now getting almost routine, Charles felt humiliated and overshadowed by his glamorous wife.

TECHNICAL STUFF

Back home, Charles continued to work with The Prince's Trust (see Chapter 15 for more about this organization) and the many charitable organizations of which he was a patron. Not to be outdone, Diana was collecting dozens of her own charities. These came to include arts organizations such as the Royal Academy of Music, the London Symphony Orchestra, and a host of charities that helped children, the poor and the disadvantaged.

Examples of Diana's charities include the British Deaf Association, the Wales Pre-School Playgroups Association, the British Red Cross Society, the London-based Institute for the Study of Drug Dependence, and the Royal New Zealand Foundation of the Blind. Her celebrated support for the HALO anti-landmine trust is covered later in the chapter.

Diana made one of her most famous charitable moves in 1987 when she shook hands with a man suffering from HIV-AIDS. She was not wearing gloves. The brave gesture of warmth and sympathy had an enormous impact, helping dispel rumours that the illness could be spread by everyday contact.

Troubling times beneath the surface

Which of the royal couple was first to break their marriage vows is irrelevant. According to gossip, by 1984 they were no longer sharing a bed.

Around 1985 or 1986, Diana began seeing other men and Charles resumed his relationship with Camilla. His wife would insist that it had never really ended. He said his wife's impossible behaviour drove him back into the arms of his old flame. By the end of 1986, the gulf between the royal couple was probably unbridgeable.

REMEMBER

Could tragedy have been averted? Possibly, but not in such a uniquely weird family. They just didn't do 'human'. They had all been brought up in the 'grit your teeth and get on with it' school of dealing with problems. Not having encountered someone like Diana before, they had no idea how to handle her.

The Princess's temperament and upbringing had left her insecure and vulnerable. To be able to cope with the almost unbelievable pressure of her new role, she needed long, careful and compassionate care. When she didn't get it, she retaliated by cultivating the love of the wider world. It was a form of revenge.

TIP

Archbishop Runcie of Canterbury said that Diana was 'terrified' of Elizabeth. He may have been right. That rigid reserve could be pretty scary.

REMEMBER

Elizabeth, unable or unwilling to see what was happening, explained her daughter-in-law's behaviour as 'nerves' resulting from her new-found prominence. The Queen disliked Diana's relationship with the media, which she considered demeaning. She also took umbrage at the Princess's flouting of etiquette. She sat at meals with her headphones on, left the table when she felt like it, not waiting for the Queen to make the first move.

It is said that one reason Charles had bought (through the Duchy of Cornwall, see Chapter 17) Highgrove, his country house in Gloucestershire, was because it was near the Parker-Bowles's mansion of Middlewick House. True or not, by 1986 its location was proving remarkably convenient.

GOLD AND SILVER STICKS

The quaint titles of 'Gold Stick' and 'Silver Stick' date from Tudor times and refer to the metal head of the staff carried by a security officer.

Originally the monarch's body guards, the Sticks are now just honorary positions held by army officers who parade on formal state occasions. The real guarding of the monarch is done by detectives and police.

When Andrew Parker-Bowles was away, Charles would slip over to Middlewick while Diana and the boys were in London. From 1987, it became easier for Charles to see Camilla as Andrew Parker-Bowles had been made a Silver Stick (see the sidebar, "Gold and Silver Sticks"). When not able to meet in person, the lovers corresponded voluminously and spent hours on the telephone.

Nonetheless, for a long time they managed to keep their relationship relatively well hidden.

Diana's affairs

While Charles had found the love of his life, Diana was still looking for hers. In a sense she was making up for lost time, living the sort of relationship quest she had missed out on earlier in her life.

These, in roughly chronological order, are the names of the young men to whom, it is rumoured, she became romantically attached:

» **Barry Mannakee**, Diana's hunky bodyguard. He was moved from his role when people started to gossip and died in a motorcycle accident in 1987. Diana said she would have been very happy to run off with him and get married.

» **Bryan Adams**, the pop singer who made the single 'Diana' in 1985. He visited Diana in Kensington Palace, Charles and Diana's London residence.

» **James Hewitt**, a handsome tank commander with whom Diana confessed she was in love. The relationship lasted several years.

» **James Gilbey**, a wealthy young man from a family that had made its fortune from gin. He is believed to have been the caller on the other end of the 'Squidgygate' line (see later in this chapter for more on this unusual pet name).

» **Oliver Hoare**, an art dealer who refused to leave his wife and children for Diana.

» **Will Carling**, the England rugby captain who has always denied any relationship with Diana.

» **John Kennedy Junior**, a most unlikely relationship, widely denied, that supposedly followed their meeting in New York in 1995.

» **Hasnat Khan**, a British–Pakistani surgeon whose loving, two-year relationship with Diana ended shortly before her death.

The whispers get louder

WARNING

In 1989, we are told, Diana met Camilla at a party. The gloves finally came off. The Princess told the mistress that she knew all about her affair, pointing out, 'I wasn't born yesterday.' Camilla retorted that Diana had everything, including two lovely children. What more could she possibly want?

Diana's reply was short, though its truth questionable: 'I want my husband.' The Princess was adept at manipulating the facts to suit her case.

REMEMBER

By 1990, royal watchers could no longer keep quiet about what had become common knowledge: Charles and Diana were leading separate lives. The press knew who to blame, too. The following year, when Prince William was badly injured by an accident with a golf club and Diana remained at his hospital bedside for two days, the press castigated Charles for going off to the opera. His opinion poll ratings were sinking fast.

Heading Towards the End of The Marriage

REMEMBER

Andrew Morton's book, *Diana – Her True Story In Her Own Words* (Michael O'Mara Books, 1992), was the publishing sensation of the decade. At first, most people did not believe it. Morton was branded a liar and one Member of Parliament suggested he be sent to the Tower of London for treason. The public did not want their fairy tale exposed as a fraud.

But it was true. We now know that Diana recorded answers to questions about her life – embellishing, exaggerating, censoring – on tapes that were passed to Morton by the Princess's friend Dr James Colthurst. In other words, the biography of Diana was to all intents and purposes an autobiography. It gave a highly one-sided version of her marriage.

Yes, she suffered from bulimia and depression and received psychiatric help. Yes, in her wretchedness she had attempted suicide. Yes, she had thrown herself downstairs in despair when pregnant with William. And yes, there was a woman called Camilla Parker-Bowles with whom Charles had been carrying on for years. But Morton made no mention of James Hewitt or any other lover.

TIP

To those reading the book and taking it as unalloyed truth, Diana had been cruelly, even brutally treated. Charles's popularity rating sank to a feeble 9 percent. After the initial shock, Diana's soared. She was now the 'People's Princess'.

Over the next twelve months, the public became increasingly intrigued when the contents of two illicitly recorded tapes were published:

>> **'Squidgygate'.** Taking a name derived from the American Watergate Scandal (1972–1974), *The Sun* newspaper published transcripts of pillow talk between Diana and an unknown man whose pet name for the Princess was 'Squidgy'. The conversation took place before 1990, thus calling into question some of the innocence pleaded by Diana in Morton's book.

>> **'Camillagate'.** In 1989, someone managed to record a night-time conversation between Charles and Camilla. These were transcribed and published by the *Sunday People* newspaper in January 1993. It is hard to imagine a more damaging revelation for the heir to the throne.

The conversation revealed him to be still deeply in love with Camilla. Fair enough. The people could handle that, just about. After all, they now knew what his wife had been up to. What really did for Charles's reputation was the banality of the lovey-dovey banter between himself and his mistress, alongside some far more saucy content.

From then onwards, Charles – and to a lesser extent Camilla – faced the massive task of restoring their butchered reputations. Seizing her opportunity, Diana called the recording 'sick'.

In December 1993, Prime Minister John Major had told the House of Commons that Charles and Diana were going to separate. Prince Philip wrote to Diana urging reconciliation. Nothing doing. She announced that she was retiring from public life for a while and gave up the bulk of her charitable patronages.

REMEMBER

Diana had one last arrow in her quiver. Influenced by forged documents produced by the BBC (see Chapter 12), she agreed to give an interview to the national broadcaster. She answered interviewer Martin Bashir's questions with well-rehearsed, artfully presented responses. As in the Morton book, she made it clear that she had been the injured party all along. When asked what had gone wrong with her marriage, she explained, 'there were three of us in the marriage, so it got pretty crowded.'

WARNING

Twenty-three million viewers looked at each other and nodded. 'There we are,' they told themselves, 'It was Charles's fault all along. Poor girl!' It was a half-truth brilliantly told. Charles may have yearned for Camilla, but – as far as we know – he had been true to his wife for five years.

Elizabeth, who had kept aloof during the whole sorry story, now finally accepted the inevitable. 'In the best interests of the country,' she declared, her eldest son and his wife should seek a divorce. She was right, of course. Her children had dragged the institution she held so dear through so much mire (see Chapter 20 for more on what occurred) that she must have wondered whether she'd ever be able to wash it clean. Even the despicable notion of divorce was better than a continuation of the current humiliation.

TIP

The terms of the divorce, finalized in 1996, gave Diana £15 million, joint custody of the children, and accommodation in Kensington Palace. She voluntarily gave up the title 'Her Royal Highness', though afterwards she tried to say that the Queen had forced her to do this. Ever the manipulator.

Remembering Diana's Final Year

REMEMBER

Diana was a living paradox to the end. In January 1997, she gave support to the campaign to outlaw landmines by putting on protective clothing and walking across a minefield in Huambo, Angola. Those she met remember her as considerate and genuinely interested in the cause she was backing. In early August, she was back in a minefield once more, this time in Bosnia. Her brave action is remembered with admiration to this day.

Yet, in the same month, Diana was freeloading off Mohammed Fayed, the controversial owner of London's top-notch Harrods department store. As she and her children enjoyed a luxury Mediterranean holiday aboard the entrepreneur's yacht, they were joined by his son, Dodi. Towards the end of August, she returned to the yacht without her children and began a jet-set romance with Dodi.

This romance continued until the last day of the month. That night, the couple left the Ritz Hotel in Paris and were driven away at high speed to escape the pursuing *paparazzi* (news journalists). Their driver, Henri Paul, was three times over the legal alcohol limit. In the Pont de l'Alma tunnel beside the River Seine, he lost control of the Mercedes and crashed into a concrete pillar. Dodi was killed instantly. Diana died a few hours later in a Paris hospital.

Chapter **17**

The Queen's Wealth and the Cost of the Monarchy

How rich is the Queen? The oft-asked question rarely receives a satisfactory answer. The responses – and to questions such as 'does an hereditary monarch give good value for money?' – are always qualified with words like 'estimated' and 'approximately'.

This chapter seeks to throw a little light on the subject, and suggest a few answers to your questions. And there's no need to keep your calculator at hand; I'll go easy on the mathematics!

Understanding Royal Finances Over the Centuries

TECHNICAL STUFF

Just as we can't really understand how the British monarchy works unless we see it in its historical context, so we need to view royal finances in the context of their evolution over the past 700 years or so:

>> The monarch was once expected to 'live of his own': the income from his (and very occasionally her) lands, profits of justice, and so on, which should be sufficient to meet the needs of the government and household. It seldom was, especially in wartime.

>> To plug the gap, the monarch needed Parliament to vote on taxes. The elected representatives sought something in return – a say in government policy and personnel. These, the monarch insisted, were part of the inviolable royal prerogative. Impasse!

>> Tax versus representation led to the seventeenth-century Civil Wars, and King Charles I's execution. The restored monarchy was given a hopelessly inadequate £1.2 million per year to run the country, leading to further squabbles before Parliament took more or less complete control after the revolution of 1688–1689 (see Chapter 2 for more on the troubled seventeenth century).

>> King William II and Queen Mary II received only £700,000 per year to run the Royal Household, and help pay for the civil service and the salaries of certain crown servants, like judges. Parliament kept control of military spending.

Introducing the Civil List

The financial arrangement reached during the reign of William III was unsatisfactory on two counts:

>> It left the monarch to manage (pay for, at least) the domestic machinery of government. The monarchs of the House of Hanover (1714 onward; see Chapter 2) were neither competent nor particularly willing to do this.

>> The sum allocated to the task, the Civil List, included revenues from customs and excise. As the wealth of the country grew, so did this source of royal income. This gave the sovereign increased power and influence. Parliament did not approve.

THE CROWN ESTATE

The *Crown Estate* is an inalienable portfolio of assets, built up over the centuries, that belongs to the Crown. Today, the Estate (estimated value between £7.3 and £14.1 billion) is managed by an independent organization, and its profits are paid to the UK Treasury. Only a proportion of the Estate is revenue-yielding. In the financial year 2019–2020, it brought in £345 million.

The present arrangement is strange. Technically, the Crown Estate belongs to the monarch for the duration of their reign; and each year, a percentage of its earnings go to the Crown as part of its Sovereign Grant. Yet the Crown doesn't manage the Estate and may not sell any part of it. Should the UK ever become a republic, lawyers will have a field-day deciding who really owns this juicy portfolio!

The term *Civil List* dates from the reign of William III. It referred to the money required by the state for all *civil* (non-military) purposes. Civil List funds were managed by the monarch until the time of George III (discussed later in this section). After that point, government and the Royal Household expenses were gradually separated. Nevertheless, the phrase 'Civil List' continued well into the reign of Elizabeth II.

By the eighteenth century, the monarch's wealth derived from three sources:

>> Family fortune, comprising land, investments, jewelry, and so on.

>> Income from the inherited assets of the Crown – the Crown Estate, the Duchy of Lancaster and the Duchy of Cornwall. Each of these features in its own sidebar in this chapter.

>> The Civil List, granted by Parliament.

From the time of William III, the position was clarified to give the monarch a regular income and distance them from further from civil administration:

>> In 1760 the Crown lost:

- Revenue from the Crown Estate.

- Revenue from *customs* (tax collected on goods passing in and out of a country) and *excise* (tax collected on goods exchanged or manufactured within a country).

- Responsibility for meeting the cost of civil government.

THE DUCHY OF LANCASTER

The Duchy is a portfolio of lands, properties and other assets that originated in the estates owned by the medieval Dukes of Lancaster. In 1399, the House of Lancaster seized the throne, amalgamating – but not merging – the Duchy with the rest of the Crown Estate. Successive monarchs have enjoyed its revenues ever since. In 2020, it earned the Queen £23 million.

» Also in 1760, the Crown gained or retained:

- A regular fixed parliamentary income (still confusingly called the Civil List) of £800,000 per year. George III soon overspent and Parliament had to step in and make good the deficit.

- Revenues from the Duchy of Lancaster.

- An obligation to meet some civil payments, such as certain pensions. The Prince of Wales kept the revenues of the Duchy of Cornwall.

» In 1830, the Civil List was reduced from George IV's £845,727 to £510,000 for the newly crowned William IV. In return, William no longer had to meet any government expenses. The cash was for him and his household alone.

» In 1837, on her accession, Queen Victoria was granted a Civil List of £385,000. £60,000 of this was earmarked for her *privy purse* (her personal expenditure on clothes and suchlike).

REMEMBER

The Victorian system (though not the amounts) was inherited by Elizabeth II. Her Civil List of £475,000 was to pay for her household and enable her to fulfil her tasks as Head of State and of the Commonwealth. The household's accounts were not audited by any outside body.

Mixing family and state funding

REMEMBER

For the first four decades of her reign, Elizabeth's money came from four sources: the Crown Estate, the Duchy of Lancaster, the Civil List, and her private fortune.

However, as always with things royal, the situation was never quite as simple as that. Her family was also in receipt of certain extras:

» One of the many titles belonging to the Queen's eldest son, Charles, is Duke of Cornwall. This gives him the revenue of the Duchy of Cornwall.

DUCHY OF CORNWALL

The Duchy comprises a 135,000-acre estate and other assets that have belonged to the male heir to the throne, the Duke of Cornwall, since the time of the Edward, the Black Prince, in the fourteenth century. The Duke enjoys revenues from the Duchy but may not dispense with any of its assets.

In 2017–2018, the Duchy brought in £21.7 million. Its financial affairs are supervised by the Treasury and Parliament. As Crown property, it is exempt from paying tax, although Charles has made some voluntary donations.

» Government departments coughed up various Grants-in-Aid to help with the cost of maintaining official residences, communications, and travel.

» On top of everything else, by the twenty-first century Parliament was handing out £1.5 million in *annuities* (regular payments) to eight other 'working' (meaning they carry out royal duties) members of the Royal Family (for example, £359,000 per year to Philip, Duke of Edinburgh). After 1993, Elizabeth agreed to pay back these annuities to the treasury. What a muddle! The system needed an overhaul.

Reforming the System

In 2010, the outgoing Chief Secretary to the Treasury left a note for his successor. Succinct to the point of bluntness, it read simply, 'Dear Chief Secretary, I'm afraid there is no money. Kind regards – and good luck!' Even more alarming, it was true.

The global financial crisis of 2008–2009 had led to a £40 billion fall in government receipts. Sharp cuts in expenditure were urgently required.

In 2010, the Civil List, fixed at £7.9 million since the time of Margaret Thatcher, was up for renewal. Between 1990 and 2000, the Palace had kept expenditure below income, squirrelling away the surplus in a reserve fund that totals £35.6 million. By 2010, this had fallen to £15.2 million. It was estimated to shrink to zero by the end of 2012.

What's more – shock horror! – Elizabeth was spending over a million of her 'own' money (from the Duchy of Lancaster) in payments to her family for their royal work. Add in the £9 million per year that Charles was getting from the Duchy of Cornwall, and the estimated £50 million per year spent on royal security, and it was clear the whole business had to be sorted out.

Introducing the Sovereign Grant

In 2012, the old Civil List system was done away with. In its place came the *Sovereign Support Grant*, usually called just the Sovereign Grant. The idea was to establish a single annual payment to the Crown sufficient for all the needs of the Head of State.

The Sovereign Grant is permanent, in perpetuity – meaning that it will not need renewing when one monarch succeeds another. As it is paid to the monarch as Head of State, it could probably be switched to fund a president should Britain ever become a republic.

The Sovereign Grant is funded from a percentage (initially 15 percent) of the Crown Estate's revenue. Accounts are kept by the Keeper of the Privy Purse (see Chapter 9 for more on this role). These are audited and scrutinized by the National Audit Office and Parliament's Public Accounts Committee.

The *Royal Trustees*, a high-powered triumvirate comprising the Prime Minister, the Chancellor of the Exchequer and the Keeper of the Privy Purse, review the grant every five years.

The grant is for the official duties carried out by the Queen and some of her family. These include such things as:

>> Travelling to official engagements in the UK and overseas, including funding for Philip when he travelled with Elizabeth or acted on her behalf.

>> Running the Palace communications and information system.

>> Staffing, running, and maintaining the Royal Palaces (see Chapter 9 for more on these places). This includes formal entertaining (state visits), ceremonial events, and paying the household's 1,000+ staff.

The growing grant

Parts of Windsor Castle date from the eleventh century, St James' Palace from the seventeenth century, and Kensington Palace and Buckingham Palace from the eighteenth century. Buildings of this age are neither easy nor cheap to maintain.

In 2009, Elizabeth got an extra £4 million to spruce up Buckingham Palace. Her request for more the following year was rejected. Three years later, the sum needed to repair and update the Royal Palaces was put at £50 million. At £31 million, the Sovereign Grant was £20 million short. The monarchy's show-cases continued to leak and creak.

By 2016, the situation had become embarrassing. The Head of State and her family were housed in buildings that – literally – had bits falling off. In response, the percentage of the Crown Estate's revenue paid to the Royal Household rose from 15 percent to 25 percent for ten years. This hiked the Sovereign Grant to £76.1 million (2017–2018), £30.4 million of which was to refurbish Buckingham Palace.

By 2019–2020, the Grant stood at £82.4 million. A lot was tucked away in a reserve account for spending on the Palaces.

Giving the family some extras

The Sovereign Grant does not cover all royal expenses:

>> Philip received a parliamentary annuity of £359,000 per year.

>> The Queen keeps the revenues of the Duchy of Lancaster. They pay for family members who undertake royal duties. The current list includes Anne (the Princess Royal) and Edward, Earl of Wessex, and his wife Sophie, Countess of Wessex.

>> Income from the Duchy of Cornwall still goes to Prince Charles. He has shared some of it with his sons, William and Harry (see Chapter 25). The boys also got millions from their mother and from their great-grandmother, the Queen Mother.

Totalling Up the Windsors' Wealth

WARNING

Her Majesty Queen Elizabeth II is not among the world's ultra-rich. However, we do not know the extent of her private wealth, and her claim to certain other assets is obscure. The problem is threefold:

>> Her personal, family wealth is private and the Crown has no obligation to pay tax. Therefore, because she does not send in a tax return (tackled below), her income remains secret.

>> Putting a price on private assets such as Balmoral Castle is impossible. Their worth will not be known until they are put up for sale.

>> To what extent are portfolios like the Crown Estate, the Duchy of Lancaster, and the Duchy of Cornwall actually the Royal Family's? All we can say is that if Elizabeth and Charles were to claim them for their private use, the monarchy wouldn't last long.

These figures from Britain's *The Sunday Times* newspaper's Rich List illustrate the difficulty:

>> In 1989, the first year the list was published, the Queen was ranked at number one, with a wealth of about £5.2 billion (well over £10 billion today). As this estimate included the Crown Estate and other inalienable assets, it is now seen as flawed.

>> By 2015, the Queen (valued at around £340 million) was no longer in the top 300.

>> In 2020, the royal fortune had risen to about £365 million.

TIP

In 2021, Elon Musk, the world's richest man, was worth an estimated $229.6 billion (£166.85 billion). In the same year, *The Sunday Times* Rich List (UK only) was topped by Sir Leonard Blavatnik at £23 billion. Compared with billionaires such as these, Elizabeth's fortune, counted in mere millions, appears pretty paltry. But don't forget – on top of her private wealth and income from hereditary assets – in 2020–2021 Elizabeth's 'salary' (the Sovereign Grant) was £85.9 million. So she's not quite as hard-up as one might think.

Paying tax (on a voluntary basis)

Welcome to another murky area of royal finance!

Queen Victoria and Edward VII paid income tax on the Civil List. In return for meeting the cost of various royal functions, the government exempted George V from income tax. His son paid none, nor did Elizabeth before 1993. She was also exempt from other levies.

Technically speaking, this was all perfectly legal: the Crown's tax-free status was set out in legislation. Charles claimed the same tax-free status – subsequently challenged – for his income from the Duchy of Cornwall. The Royal Family always paid VAT (sales tax) and made voluntary contributions to rates (local property taxes).

Bowing to pressure

By 1992, the Royal Family's reputation had taken a battering (see Chapter 20), and a dramatic gesture was sought to pacify public annoyance at royal shenanigans. The result was a carefully worded 'Memorandum of Understanding on Royal Taxation'. Updated in 1996, 2009 and 2013, it said the Queen and Prince Charles would pay:

>> Capital Gains Tax.

>> Income tax on their personal incomes.

>> Inheritance tax on their private estates.

The memorandum was hedged about with exceptions and caveats:

>> All payments are voluntary: Elizabeth and Charles kept their tax-exempt status.

>> The Queen's personal finances – income and expenditure – remain secret.

>> No tax is paid on money used for official purposes, including the entire Sovereign Grant. As the royal books are closed, no-one knows what is deemed official business.

>> Capital Gains Tax is paid only on assets acquired and sold since 1992.

>> No inheritance tax is payable on property passed from one monarch to another, nor on property passed from the consort of a former monarch (the Queen Mother) to a current monarch.

>> Over the years, the Crown has successfully lobbied for exemption from various other levies (see Chapter 25 for more on this).

Estimating Royal Value For Money

WARNING

The UK's hereditary monarchy appears to be a ridiculously expensive and inefficient way to manage the Head of State's role. But it's not that simple. The Royal Family offer both good and poor value for the nation.

Here's a list of how the royals offer good value for money:

>> Overseas tours and state visits to the UK boost the country's international profile and reputation. This has a knock-on effect on exports – such as selling Scottish whisky embossed with the royal warrant. In 2017, this trade boost was valued at £150 million per year.

>> The profile of UK regions, like central London, Windsor, and the Scottish Highlands, is raised by their royal association.

>> Royal-inspired pre-pandemic tourism was said to be worth £1.5 billion per year.

>> Free media coverage of things royal is valued at around £300 million per year. And without the real Crown, we wouldn't have TV's *The Crown*!

>> The Royal Family underpins the UK's political stability, making it an attractive place for inward investment.

In summary, in return for a Sovereign Grant of £86.3 million (2021–2022), the monarchy was reckoned (pre-pandemic levels) to bring in about 18 times that amount for the UK economy. Surely that's good value for money?

Unfortunately, it's not all good news – in other ways the Royal Family offers poor value for money:

>> Though the Royal Family provides an annual summary of official expenditure and a report on its public finances, much is still missing. Security costs, for example, are not factored in.

>> Festivities like weddings and jubilees (especially those involving public holidays) disrupt everyday economic life.

>> The Royal Family's suggested boost to trade and tourism are counterfactual. Would fewer visitors come to the Great British Republic than do currently to the United Kingdom? And would fewer tourists visit Buckingham Palace if it no longer housed a queen? The French palace of Versailles has lost none of its attraction now that a monarch no longer lives there.

>> The £1.5 billion guesstimate of the royal benefit to the tourist industry should be seen in the light of the £22.5 billion (in 2016) earned from tourism in total. The supposed value of royal help for trade is an even smaller proportion of total earnings.

>> When one of the richest families in the land keeps its books closed and its wealth hidden, what sort of message does that send out to everyone else?

>> Stable republics such as the USA, France and Germany also attract inward investment. One might argue that the UK's old-fashioned, stuck-in-the-past image is a disincentive to investors.

WARNING

So is the Royal Family worth what is spent on it? In the end, it's a matter of opinion. At present, the British people accept the cost of the monarchy because they respect Queen Elizabeth. Who would begrudge a few *quid* (pounds) for a woman who has worked on into her nineties?

In due course, we will see whether the same tolerance is shown to her successors.

Chapter **18**

One Country, Two Women: The Age of Margaret Thatcher

TIP

Imagine a backdrop of war, terrorism, strikes, and dramatic economic upheaval. Add the spice of domestic turmoil. Now place on stage two of the most influential British figures of the post-war era – and the scene is set for a riveting historical drama the like of which had never been seen before: the Elizabeth and Margaret show. Or, as the latter would have it, the Margaret and Elizabeth show.

However, if you're expecting a comedy, I'm afraid you're in the wrong theatre.

For those acquainted with the politics of the 1980s, a few words about Margaret Thatcher (1925–2013). Nicknamed the 'Iron Lady', Thatcher was Britain's first female prime minister. She served from 1979 to 1990. A staunch Conservative and fierce advocate of the free market, the daughter of a small-town shopkeeper introduced a series of controversial reforms to limit the power of the trade unions, denationalize key industries, and free up individual enterprise. Although her tough policies earned her many enemies, she also won many admirers, including US President Ronald Reagan. (There's more on this later in the chapter.)

Comparing Elizabeth and Margaret

REMEMBER

In some ways the two women were quite similar. They were roughly the same age: Margaret Thatcher was 54 when elected Conservative prime minister in May 1979; Queen Elizabeth was 53. Each had dutiful husbands and children in their twenties. The need to do what was best for their country, above all else, had been drubbed into them from birth. Neither cared much for the arts, and both were very, very tough.

And there, abruptly, is where the similarities end. In background, upbringing, and approach to life the two women were not exactly chalk and cheese, more like oil and water. The two do not mix, and oil always rises above the water. But which was the oil and which the water?

The pragmatic Queen and her principled prime minister

On the whole, Elizabeth liked her prime ministers, and most of them said they valued what she said in their weekly meetings (see Chapter 26 for more on this). But never had she talked at length to anyone like Margaret Thatcher.

She had, of course, met dozens of powerful women; she had engaged them in polite conversation, but not once had she discussed politics or top-level policy. If she had chatted about the great issues of the day with any woman, it was either with Bobo (see Chapter 8) or with someone well versed in conventional upper-class etiquette. Thatcher was not interested in such niceties. She endorsed change with enthusiasm. The Queen mistrusted change and was wary of enthusiasm – except in horse racing.

TECHNICAL STUFF

Raised in a lower-middle class family, Thatcher had climbed her way to the top of the greasy pole thanks to intelligence, a quick wit, unstinting diligence, and a driving ambition for herself and her country. Her mission was to free individual enterprise by reforming old-fashioned, inefficient and unproductive institutions and practices.

REMEMBER

The Prime Minister's prime target was the trade unions. She believed that the restrictive practices endorsed by these traditional-minded workers' organisations held back the country's progress in key areas, such as transport, manufacturing and mining. To clip their wings, her government made it difficult for union bosses to call strikes without the support of a majority of union members.

In theory, Thatcher might also have targeted another conservative institution, the monarchy. However, when reforming zeal encountered deeply entrenched, 'finest hour' patriotism, there could be no contest. Thatcher was, after all, a true-blue Conservative (blue is the colour of the Conservative Party). 'A hereditary monarchy', she wrote, 'is above politics', a 'symbol of patriotism' that gives the country 'stability and assurance'.

The mother and the schoolmarm working together . . . for a while

We are led to believe that the first meetings between Thatcher and the Queen were tense and a little embarrassing for them both. The Prime Minister, for all her power, was in awe of the Queen. A grocer's daughter did not call in for a private chat with the reigning monarch every day.

TIP

Thatcher generally arrived early for her Tuesday evening meetings and expected to be shown straight in. Elizabeth, a stickler for punctuality, kept her waiting until the appointed time. The Prime Minister was not amused. When she was shown into the royal presence, she bowed too low and curtsied as if she had been shot. Apparently, her gaucheness became one of the Windsor's snobbish family jokes.

When it came to discussion, Thatcher had a tendency to lecture. A key part of her success was her conviction that she was right, and she was not going to take advice from someone she had not appointed, and one who generally favoured compromise and conciliation – qualities scorned by Thatcher as weak and flabby.

A snub . . .

Things got off to a bad start when it became known that the guilt of Anthony Blunt, former Surveyor of the Queen's Pictures and spy for the Soviets, had been kept secret for 25 years (see Chapter 9). Thatcher was incandescent with rage, seeing the whole episode as a disgraceful example of an Establishment cover-up. As the Queen had known of Blunt's traitorous activities since 1964, and maintained him in the royal employ until 1973, she was an implicit target of the Prime Minister's wrath.

REMEMBER

Thatcher irritated the Queen by rushing to the scene of a disaster in advance of a member of the Royal Family, to commiserate with the bereaved. Elizabeth seems to have been annoyed (as always, her true feelings are hard to fathom) at this undermining of her royal role. Thatcher's queen-like behaviour was most marked in 1987, when the cross-Channel ferry *The Herald of Free Enterprise* sank in Zeebrugge Harbour, Belgium, with the loss of 200 lives.

. . . and a counter-snub

Elizabeth was quite capable of getting her own back, especially when she considered Thatcher was getting too big for her boots. The Prime Minister once wrote suggesting that, before an event at which she and the Queen would be present, their dressers should consult to ensure their bosses were not wearing the same outfit. The Palace's tart reply? 'The Queen does not notice what others wear.'

On another occasion, after the national anthem had been played when Thatcher stepped from a plane onto foreign soil, the Palace made it known that anthem-playing was a privilege afforded to the monarch only, not the prime minister. Thatcher's wannabe-regal wings were duly clipped.

The African Queen

REMEMBER

In July 1986, the differences of opinion between Thatcher, the confrontational driver of change, and the conciliatory Queen erupted in a true mini scandal rather than a matter of idle speculation. *The Sunday Times* newspaper worked up indiscreet remarks from Michael Shea, the Palace press spokesman, into a full-blown article entitled 'African Queen'. It suggested that Elizabeth strongly disapproved of Thatcher's uncaring attitude towards the poor and her insensitive dismissal of sanctions against South Africa (detailed later in this chapter).

There may have been some truth in the allegations, but both women were shocked and upset by the article. The Palace said, quite rightly, that the Queen never, ever passed judgement on any political matter. Downing Street (the prime minister's office) expressed bitter disappointment at the suggestion that there could be any disagreement between their boss and the Head of State. After a few months, Shea found another job.

TECHNICAL STUFF

As explained in Chapter 19, Elizabeth is both the official head (or 'Supreme Governor') of the Church of England and a woman of strong personal faith. She takes a close interest in church affairs and has always influenced major church appointments, notably those of bishops. This was another area on which the Queen and Thatcher did not always see eye to eye. The Prime Minister had her way, as she had to in a democracy, but Elizabeth was not pleased to find her constitutional right to advise overlooked.

Navigating Difficulties and Dangers

During the 1980s, the Queen was in greater physical danger than at any time before or since. The main threat was from the Irish Republican Army (IRA). She also faced two potentially perilous situations of a more bizarre nature. The first occurred in 1981, when a young man fired blanks at her as she was riding towards Horse Guards Parade (see Chapter 16).

The other was altogether more strange.

REMEMBER

In June 1982, a young, disaffected and unemployed man named Michael Fagan climbed into Buckingham Palace looking for a place to relieve himself after a bout of drinking. He proved a somewhat unreliable narrator, but by his own account he mooched around, drank some of Charles's wine, urinated into the corgi food, and walked back onto the streets of London.

A month later, on 9 July, Fagan repeated his break-in. Full of whisky, he shinned up the drainpipe that he had used for his first visit, and snooped about until, shortly after 7am, he found himself in Elizabeth's bedroom. Pulling back the curtains, he sat on the bed. He was, he said, terrified.

So was the Queen. 'What are you doing here?' she piped. Fagan wasn't quite sure. After pressing her alarm bell and telephoning in vain for help, the barefoot monarch pitter-pattered from the room. The intruder, apprehended a short time afterwards, became something of a celebrity.

WARNING

With left-leaning dramatic license, *The Crown* turned the incident into a revelatory meeting between a socially isolated monarch and a representative of the working class suffering under free-market Thatcherism. It made a good episode, but the really important lesson the Queen learned from the incident was that the Palace security system was hopelessly inadequate. Heads rolled, and the whole security apparatus was modernized with the help of the SAS (Special Air Service, Britain's top-secret special forces unit).

The assassination of Louis Mountbatten

The 1972 shooting incident in the Northern Irish town of Derry – quickly christened 'Bloody Sunday' – escalated Protestant–Catholic violence in the troubled province (see Chapter 15). In 1973, the IRA and its more militant Provisional wing extended their bombing campaign into mainland Britain.

They took their tactics from Vietnamese and Palestinian insurgents, their money from sympathizers (including misguided Irish Americans), and their weapons from rogue states such as Libya. The campaign began in February 1972 with the bombing of the 16th Parachute Brigade HQ and ended on 26 March 1997 with a double attack on a mainline railway. Hundreds of lives were lost, and thousands maimed in dozens of bombings and shootings. The financial cost ran into billions.

Elizabeth's personal involvement in the IRA campaign of terror is clear from the group's name – Irish *Republican* Army – and from many of the terrorists' targets: the *Royal* Marines, for example, and the *Royal* Courts of Justice. Far closer to home was the murder (the IRA called it an 'execution') of her second cousin, Louis Mountbatten (Philip's uncle).

Former Admiral of the Fleet and last Viceroy of India, the 79-year-old Lord Mountbatten of Burma was a controversial figure. He was extremely high profile, too. From his holiday home near the Village of Cliffony, County Sligo in the Republic of Ireland, he had taken his family on a trip in his 29-foot fishing boat, *Shadow V*. Fifteen minutes from the shore, under a clear blue sky, a pre-planted 50lb packet of gelignite was detonated by remote control. The boat was blown to smithereens.

Mountbatten and two others were killed instantly. The elderly mother of his son-in-law passed away the next day, and three survivors of the attack suffered serious injury. The IRA immediately claimed responsibility for the attack, saying it had been carried out to draw the world's attention to British occupation of part of their homeland (Northern Ireland). It may have achieved this, but it also reinforced British determination not to give in to violence.

The Queen was deeply shocked by the assassination. Prince Charles, to whom Mountbatten had been a beloved mentor, was devastated. At royal insistence, Mountbatten was given a ceremonial funeral in Westminster Abbey. Elsewhere in London, a young Diana Spencer watched the service on TV. When she met Charles not long afterwards, she told him how sorry she felt for him as he had looked so miserable. The unhappy Prince was moved to consider this sympathetic young girl in a new light (see Chapter 16).

Following the IRA bombings, the assassination of Mountbatten, and the blank cartridges attack of 1981 (see Chapter 16), Elizabeth came under considerable pressure to increase security for her public appearances. A visibly armed escort was suggested for formal state events, and a bomb-proof car in place of a fragile horse-drawn carriage. She would have none of it. 'If my people cannot see their monarch on such occasions,' she is reported to have said, 'then there is no point in having a monarchy. The debate is at an end.'

Rhodesia becomes Zimbabwe

The morphing of the British Empire into the Commonwealth of Nations is one of the more extraordinary developments of twentieth-century statecraft (see Chapters 6, 10 and 12). Elizabeth, Head of the Commonwealth and monarch of several of its constituent nations, played a key role in its birth, and has subsequently done more than anyone to hold it together.

The Smith regime

As the 'winds of change' swept through black Africa in the 1960s, bringing independence to most of the former colonies, the white population of Southern Rhodesia had serious misgivings about what was going on:

>> They were worried that black majority rule would mark the end of their privileged economic position.

>> They feared that a new breed of autocratically inclined, Marxist-inspired African rulers would govern neither fairly nor competently.

Headed by Prime Minister Ian Smith, in 1964–1965 Southern Rhodesia declared itself the independent state of Rhodesia. (Northern Rhodesia had become Zambia in 1964.) Led by Britain, the UN (United Nations) condemned the UDI (Unilateral Declaration of Independence) and imposed sanctions on the regime. At the same time, Zambia-based guerrillas began a military campaign against it. In 1970, Rhodesia declared itself a republic.

Eight years later, worn down by sanctions and the continual struggle with communist-backed insurgents, Smith held talks with the moderate black Rhodesian leader, Abel ('Bishop') Muzorewa. This resulted in:

>> Muzorewa becoming prime minister of the new state of Zimbabwe-Rhodesia.

>> 'Power-sharing', which left whites in control of key areas of the state, such as the armed forces and the judiciary.

Elizabeth the diplomat

Coming to power in 1979, Thatcher thought the Muzorewa–Smith power-sharing agreement a useful compromise. Its main attraction for her was that it kept the Marxist guerrillas, led by fiery Robert Mugabe, out of power. Other Commonwealth countries, especially the African ones, condemned power-sharing as a device to preserve white supremacy.

Things came to a head at the Fifth Commonwealth Heads of Government Meeting (CHOGM), held in the Zambian capital of Lusaka during the first week of August 1979. Thatcher neither cared much for the Commonwealth nor took time to get to know it properly. (It is said that in private she and her ministers said CHOGM stood for 'Compulsory Hand-outs for Greedy Mendicants'.) In contrast, Elizabeth regarded the quirky collection of nations bound by history and language as her pride and joy. Accordingly, she set out early for the conference in Lusaka.

Before arriving in Zambia, in July the Queen made formal visits to Tanzania, Malawi and Botswana. She talked to the countries' leaders, gathering information and sounding out opinion. The outlook did not look good. If Thatcher was not careful, the African countries and others would leave the Commonwealth and the whole thing would fall apart.

In Lusaka, Elizabeth used her position as Head of the Commonwealth to meet with its leaders individually. Compromise, she urged, was the wise way forward. All this, of course, was done behind the scenes with subtle suggestions and innuendo, and the Queen left Lusaka while the meeting was still in progress. But she had done enough. The CHOGM agreed to hold further talks later in the year at Lancaster House, London.

Who was right?

The talks hammered out a solution acceptable to all parties. In return for an end to the guerrilla war and sanctions:

>> Southern Rhodesia's colonial status would be temporarily restored.

>> Britain would then grant the colony independence as Zimbabwe.

>> The country would implement a new constitution and hold one person, one vote elections.

WARNING

Zimbabwe's elections took place in February 1980. Mugabe and his Marxist ZANU-PF party won a landslide victory. One-party rule, massacres and economic collapse followed, proving Thatcher's fears to have been correct. Elizabeth may have saved the Commonwealth, but at a tragic price for Zimbabweans.

South African apartheid

TECHNICAL STUFF

Margaret Thatcher once again clashed with the Commonwealth five years after the Zimbabwe elections, this time over sanctions against the apartheid regime in South Africa (see Chapter 6). On one side stood the British and American governments, backed by their respective business interests. Sanctions, they argued, would disproportionately harm the country's poor, black majority. On the other side was a broad coalition of anti-apartheid groups, churches, academic institutions, and sporting organizations. The United Nations had called for sanctions back in 1962.

The issue came to a head at the October 1985 CHOGM in Nassau, Bahamas. It was clear that Thatcher, representing the United Kingdom, was in a minority of one.

The other 48 Commonwealth members supported full economic sanctions until the South African regime agreed to:

>> dismantle apartheid

>> introduce majority rule in South Africa

>> withdraw its forces from neighbouring Namibia

REMEMBER

Fortunately, Elizabeth, Head of the Commonwealth, was also present at Nassau. Staying aboard the Royal Yacht *Britannia*, she invited the heads of member states to come and meet her. As with the Rhodesia–Zimbabwe problem (see earlier in this chapter), she advocated compromise and conciliation. Operating with tact and suggestion rather than outright advocacy, she calmed tempers sufficiently for the sanctions issue to be handed over to the oddly named Commonwealth Eminent Persons Group (EPG).

The sanctions question was still red hot. In July 1986, 32 nations boycotted the Commonwealth Games, and there was renewed talk of the Commonwealth falling apart. After visiting South Africa twice, in August, the EPG reported back to a special CHOGM in London. As outlined in Chapter 10, Elizabeth's unique blend of dignity and gentle cajolery saved the day. And all of this from a woman who is supposed to be above politics!

The invasion of Grenada

Over one Commonwealth issue, the Queen and Thatcher were in complete agreement. At dawn on 25 October 1983, US forces stormed ashore on the Caribbean island of Grenada. Within a few days, they had taken over the whole island, removed the ultra-Marxist government, and set up an interim administration in its place. Democratic elections followed the next year.

What really annoyed Elizabeth and Margaret was that President Ronald Reagan, their friend, had ordered the operation without consulting with, or even informing them. Grenada was a Commonwealth country and the Queen was Head of the Commonwealth. What's more, she was Grenada's Head of State. Reagan's move was, at best, bad manners. Of course, the Queen did not make public her disgruntlement.

Thatcher, too, kept her annoyance to herself, and in public backed the US action. Behind the scenes, she continued to grumble: Britain had been the USA's principal ally in World War II and was currently her number one supporter in the long-running Cold War with the USSR. Ronnie could at least have picked up the phone and had a chat with her, couldn't he?

Anglo–American animosity over Grenada was short-lived. It had never much concerned the President: he'd done more than enough for Thatcher when he backed her over the Falklands conflict the previous year.

Prince Andrew goes to war: The Falklands

TECHNICAL STUFF

By spring 1982, the military junta that had seized power in Argentina six years earlier was in trouble. The economy was struggling and anti-regime protests were growing. The ruling generals needed a patriotic gesture to divert attention from the domestic situation. Retaking Las Malvinas – the Falkland Islands (see "The Falkland Islands" sidebar) from the 'colonial occupier', Britain, would suit the junta's purposes perfectly.

The Argentinian invasion of the Falkland Islands on 2 April 1982 presented Prime Minister Thatcher with a tricky decision. She was not averse to settling ownership of the disputed archipelago by diplomacy – discussions had been dragging on since the 1960s – but the attack on British territory demanded more than just talk. Was it militarily feasible to retake the islands by force? she asked her military. Probably – but operating on the far side of the world in foul weather, against an entrenched enemy only 300 miles from their homeland, would be extremely difficult and very risky.

That was enough for the Iron Lady (as Thatcher was nicknamed). She formed a war cabinet and ordered a task force to assemble and sail for the South Atlantic as soon as possible. The United Nations gave Britain its backing, as did Reagan's US and several Commonwealth countries. France and one or two other states declared themselves neutral or pro-Britain, while secretly assisting Argentina. The temptation to sell arms and military technology was too great.

THE FALKLAND ISLANDS

A chilly archipelago of rocky Atlantic islands some 300 miles off the east coast of South America, the Falkland Islands (known as Las Malvinas in Argentina) have been in British hands since 1833.

The Queen is Head of State; 3,400 self-governing islanders regard themselves as British. In the past, the islands were controlled at various times by the Spanish, the French and the Argentinians. The latter still claim Las Malvinas as theirs.

The undeclared war lasted 74 days. Britain lost 255 military personnel, several ships and aircraft, and a great deal of equipment – but retook the Falklands. Thatcher's standing soared. She organized a thanksgiving service in St Paul's Cathedral, London, on 26 July 1982 and a victory parade through the streets of London on 12 October. It was, she declared, a time to rejoice and be proud of British technology, determination, bravery, and guts.

REMEMBER

Throughout the conflict, in stark contrast to her and her father's unstinting patriotism during World War II, Elizabeth kept a low profile. She did, however, reject any suggestion that Prince Andrew, a naval helicopter pilot, should not sail with the task force. The Royal Family had to be seen to do its bit and not shelter behind hereditary privilege.

Andrew served as a co-pilot of a Sea King helicopter operating from the aircraft carrier HMS *Invincible*. His missions were anything but routine. They included dangerous action against enemy submarines and surface vessels, acting as a decoy to deflect Argentinian anti-ship missiles, and undertaking numerous transport and rescue sorties.

The Queen was very aware that the conflict was Thatcher's war. A significant proportion of the population, backed by some newspapers, opposed it. Many news outlets, headed by the BBC, maintained a fairly neutral stance throughout, and the Queen did not attend the thanksgiving service.

TIP

In his address at the service, Archbishop of Canterbury Robert Runcie infuriated Thatcher by asking the congregation to remember Argentinian death and suffering as well as British. Did Elizabeth, ever one for conciliation, share his sentiments? If so, it was a far cry from the young woman who had eagerly joined the jingoistic crowds outside Buckingham Palace on VE Day, 1945 (see Chapter 6).

Coalminers divide the nation . . . and its rulers

TECHNICAL STUFF

Two years after the Falklands conflict, Margaret Thatcher was off on another war. This time the enemy was at home – the trade unions. She regarded them not as defenders of the working class but as Marxist-inspired preservers of outdated, inefficient practices. Instead of helping the country, she said they held it back. In some ways she was right, for the more left-wing union leaders made no secret of wanting to bring down the whole structure of modern capitalism.

For years, Britain's nationalized coal industry had been kept afloat by government subsidies. Thatcher's government cut these back and pits were closed. On 12 March 1984, the National Union of Mineworkers (NUM) called a strike. As the leadership had not balloted its members, the strike was declared illegal. Nonetheless, it lasted for 12 bitter, often violent months which saw the loss of 26 million working days.

In the end, Thatcher won. The strike collapsed, the coal industry was privatized, and 30 years later Britain did not have a single working coal mine. Swathes of the country descended into poverty, and the bitterness engendered by the dispute lingers to this day.

WARNING

We do not know what passed between Elizabeth and her prime minister over the course of those turbulent months. But we can guess. Nowadays, many accept that, however harsh, Thatcher's policies were an unpleasant necessity. But at the time, there was widespread concern at the anger and division they caused. Elizabeth surely shared this anxiety and passed it on to her prime minister during their private talks.

She hinted at the ongoing dispute in her 1984 Christmas broadcast, reminding viewers that Christmas marked the 'birth of the Prince of Peace'. She spoke of a 'readiness to forgive', of 'standards of behaviour and tolerance', and of a need to 'heal old wounds and to abandon prejudice and suspicion.' One wonders what Thatcher made of it.

More Bombings, a Wedding and a 60th Birthday

The IRA's continued campaign of terror bombing on the British mainland added to the tension of these difficult years. Almost every month saw fresh slaughter. The most brazen attack was an attempt to kill Margaret Thatcher herself when she was attending the Conservative Party's annual conference in Brighton. She survived. Five others did not, and dozens were injured.

REMEMBER

Amid the mayhem, Elizabeth found consolation – in the short term – in her family. Charles's marriage to Diana and the birth of Princes William and Harry (see Chapter 16) brought her great joy. Andrew's marriage to Sarah Ferguson in 1986 (see Chapter 20) was a further occasion for domestic as well as national celebration, especially when it was followed by the births of Princesses Beatrice (1988) and Eugenie (1990).

The Queen turned 60 on 21 April 1986, a year of mixed fortunes. On the downside were:

>> the acrimonious CHOGM meeting in Nassau and the partial boycott of the Commonwealth Games

>> the 'African Queen' scandal

>> stories of the failing marriage of Charles and Diana (see Chapter 16)

>> the ongoing sectarian bloodshed in Northern Ireland

These grim events were counterbalanced by Prince Andrew's marriage, Elizabeth's good health, and her joyous 60th birthday celebrations. They began with her Piper (see Chapter 8 for more on this musical master) playing 'Happy Birthday', followed by a 21-gun salute, a service in St George's Chapel, Windsor, and a carriage ride through the streets of the town. In the afternoon, she met 6,000 children, who sang her a special song. In the evening, she attended a gala show at the Royal Opera House, Covent Garden, London.

Elsewhere, the Commonwealth celebrated with its own parties and commemorative postage stamps. At the end of the year, Elizabeth and Philip made the first ever state visit to China. Her mother and father would have been immensely proud of her. Yet again, she had done her duty.

>> **Exploring the unshakeable faith of the Queen**

>> **Looking at the chapels and churches of royal buildings**

Chapter **19**

Defender of the Faith

This chapter examines the position of monarch of the United Kingdom in relation to the Church of England (also as known as the *Anglican Church*), the nation's official or 'established' church. The chapter then looks at Elizabeth's deep religious faith and how it has influenced her over the years.

The *Anglican Church* is the country's established church. It is a moderate Protestant institution, established at the time of Henry VIII, and is formally part of the state. The monarch is required by statute to be both Protestant and an Anglican. State occasions – such as coronations, Remembrance Sunday (see the nearby sidebar), services of thanksgiving (as at the end of the Falklands War, see Chapter 18), and royal funerals – are performed using Anglican rituals in Anglican churches and cathedrals.

Elizabeth has a two-way relationship with the Church of England. As its governor, at her Coronation (see Chapter 7) she swore an oath to 'maintain and preserve inviolably the settlement of the Church of England, and the doctrine worship, discipline, and government thereof, as by law established in England.' In return, the Church prays regularly for her wellbeing.

WARNING

It is often said that Queen Elizabeth is head of the Church of England. Strictly speaking, this is not true. She is the Church's governor. To understand why, we need to take a quick look the long history of Christianity in the British Isles, in particular at the dramatic events of the sixteenth century.

REMEMBRANCE SUNDAY

World War I – originally known as the Great War – ended with an armistice at 11am on 11th November 1918. The following year, to mark the auspicious occasion and honour the fallen, George V inaugurated Armistice Day.

Nowadays, the occasion has been replaced by 'Remembrance Sunday' – an opportunity to remember those who have died or been wounded in all military conflict. The poppy, the blood-red flower that grew so readily on the muddy battlefields of World War I, has been adopted as the symbol of remembrance.

Remembrance Sunday is the Sunday closest to 11th November. In London, it involves dignified parades and prayer at the Cenotaph in Whitehall. The Queen regards attendance as one of her most sacred duties. Only in 2021, when told by her doctors to take it easy, did the 95-year-old monarch miss this sombre yet deeply moving ceremony.

So this chapter does three things. One, it looks at the role and history of the Church of England; two, it looks at Elizabeth's own faith; three, it takes a whistle-stop tour of the places of worship in the Queen's royal residences.

Once again, we begin with a journey back in time. . .

Understanding the Long Relationship Between Crown and Church

TECHNICAL STUFF

During the second half of the fifteenth century, England was scarred by a long and bloody conflict known as the Wars of the Roses (see Chapter 2). It was a largely aristocratic feud in which the families of the Dukes of York and Lancaster fought for possession of the Crown. Although the accession of the Tudor dynasty in 1485 heralded the end of the struggle, this shadow civil war still hung over the land. If there was no clear line of succession, the Royal Family feared, dynastic squabbles might once again tear the kingdom apart.

Stirring things up: The radical Tudors

In the macho mind of Henry VIII, a clear line of succession meant passing his crown to a male heir. The prospect of leaving the throne to a woman filled him with horror – the last time that had been tried, according to the historical source

Anglo-Saxon Chronicle, 'Christ and his angels slept' (see Chapter 2 for more on this). But by the twentieth year of Henry's reign, he still had no legitimate male heir. Henry's wife, the Spanish princess Catherine of Aragon, had produced only a daughter, Mary.

TECHNICAL STUFF

As outlined in Chapter 2, Henry took a radical option. He was desperate for a divorce so he could marry his no-sex-before-marriage paramour, Anne Boleyn, and beget a male heir. Accordingly, he broke with the Roman Catholic Church and set up an independent Church of England (often known as the C of E) with himself as its Supreme Head. The Archbishop of Canterbury then declared Henry's marriage to Catherine null and void. Henry married Anne and became fabulously wealthy from looted church lands and treasures.

The King's disappointment turned to anger when Anne gave birth not to a son but to another daughter, Elizabeth. When this Protestant-educated daughter eventually inherited the Crown as Elizabeth I in 1558 (find out more about her in Chapter 2), she restored her father's idea of a Church of England.

REMEMBER

Elizabeth I could not, however, follow in her father's footsteps as the Church's 'Supreme Head'. Using a biological analogy, it was pointed out that a head was part of the body. But the body of the Church excluded women, who could not be ordained into the priesthood. Elizabeth duly compromised, calling herself 'Supreme Governor'.

And that, more or less, is the situation inherited by Elizabeth II 400 years later.

Calming things down: The Anglican compromise

Elizabeth I was keen to avoid religious conflict. She had no wish, she said, 'to make a window into men's souls.' Since her time, and especially from the eighteenth century onwards, Anglicanism has remained a 'broad' church. That is to say, it embraces a wide spectrum of practices and theological positions.

Therefore, the Church of England, like constitutional monarchy, is a typical product of pragmatic English compromise:

>> The Church of England retains Catholic elements, such as bishops and archbishops, images and stained glass, vestments and railed-off altars. These were the elements that enthusiastic Protestants wished to purify the Church of – hence their name: 'puritans'.

- >> Anglican theology and many of its practices are essentially Protestant. Priests may marry (more recently, women have been admitted into the priesthood), and the Church has always employed the vernacular (everyday language) – the Catholic church stopped using Latin only in the 1960s.

- >> At the *high church* end of the faith are the 'bells and smells' Anglo-Catholics, who use incense in ornate, formal services and have priests hearing private confession.

- >> At the *low church* end are the 'happy clappy' evangelicals, with minimal formality and an emphasis on religious enthusiasm.

Elizabeth I retained bishops because they were an arm of her government. In the sixteenth and seventeenth centuries, the pulpit was the principal way for the sovereign to communicate with the people, and bishops kept a strict eye on what was said there. The Queen and her immediate successors appointed all key church positions, from the archbishops of Canterbury and York to cathedral deans and canons.

The Church of England is divided into two provinces, Canterbury – the senior – and York, each headed by an archbishop. A cathedral (one per diocese) is managed by a dean assisted by ordained and secular canons.

A couple of other points are also worth noting:

- >> The Church of England is a member of a group of similar churches in 165 countries, known as the Anglican Communion. But Elizabeth is theoretical governor only of the English version.

- >> Although England has a national church, the UK is extremely tolerant in matters of religion. Depending on the question asked, a high proportion of the population regard themselves as having no religious belief. A 2016 survey by British Social Attitudes found 53 percent of those questioned said they had 'no religion', 41 percent said they were Christian, and 6 percent belonged to other religions such as Judaism, Islam and Hinduism.

In keeping with the national mood, the Queen does not make a big thing of her faith, though it does feature strongly in her Christmas broadcast (see below). In theory, she still appoints all important Church posts. In practice, after wide consultation, the appointments are made by the prime minister.

Nevertheless, Elizabeth takes a keen interest in the matter – and this led to one of her alleged disagreements with Margaret Thatcher (for more on the relationship between these two powerful women, see Chapter 18).

In 1990, Robert Runcie announced that he was stepping down as Archbishop of Canterbury. The shortlist to replace him supposedly boiled down to two men:

» The conservative old Etonian, John Habgood, Archbishop of York, a respected scholar.

» The self-made George Carey, evangelical Bishop of Bath and Wells, who was open-minded about divorce and remarriage in church.

It is not difficult to guess which of the two Elizabeth would have preferred. Thatcher chose George Carey. The Queen behaved impeccably and said nothing, but Carey was not a great success as leader of the Anglican Church.

Figuring out Elizabeth's Faith

Elizabeth is very much a traditional Anglican. She likes to 'acknowledge and bewail' her 'manifold sins and wickedness' in private. She shows her faith by attending a service every Sunday, wherever in the world she happens to be. In England this is in an Anglican church; when holidaying in Scotland, where she is not the Supreme Governor, she goes to a morning service presided over by a minister of the Church of Scotland.

TECHNICAL STUFF

Traditional Anglicans, true to the pragmatic origins of their church, mistrust enthusiasm. Their religion is a private matter, partly spiritual, partly aesthetic. It is associated with ancient cathedrals, medieval parish churches, and the reassuring cadences of the 1611 translation of the Bible (the King James version) and 1662 Prayer Book.

It is suggested that the Queen's faith was moulded by her mother and her first Archbishop of Canterbury, Geoffrey Fisher. The former – subsequently the Queen Mother – taught her the comforting importance of kneeling each night beside her bed to say her prayers. We are led to believe that Elizabeth has continued the practice ever since. She instilled the same quaint but rather touching discipline in her son, Charles.

WARNING

From Archbishop Fisher, Elizabeth learned the sacramental – almost sacrificial – responsibilities of an anointed monarch (see Chapter 7). He prepared her for the coronation and was one of the elderly men, along with Winston Churchill, who advised her during the early years of her reign. Some say that the burden of religious and constitutional responsibility, emphasized with great seriousness by Fisher, has crushed the flashes of instinctive spontaneity that some noted in her youth.

In keeping with her sincerely held yet measured faith, the Queen does not take Holy Communion every Sunday. Instead, she is content to kneel at the altar rail to receive the bread and wine about four times a year, including Christmas, Easter and Whitsun. In her own words, she favours 'moderation in all things'.

Delivering the Christmas message

REMEMBER

Elizabeth has maintained the tradition started by George V in 1932, broadcasting to her people each Christmas. (1969, the year of the Royal Family film, was the sole exception – see Chapter 14 for more on this.) Many households in Britain and the Commonwealth regard the message, usually going out at 3pm, as an essential component of their Christmas Day. At first, Elizabeth read her short speech live on the radio. In 1957, it was televised, and two years later she pre-recorded it. The message first used additional footage in 1970.

Often reflecting on the events of the past year, the Queen's Christmas message is carefully scripted over many weeks. In a way, it is like a sermon (see the nearby sidebar on the earnest but inspiring tone of these talks). Elizabeth does not dodge the world's evils and disasters, but seeks to put them in a broader, usually Christian perspective.

In her millennium address (Christmas 2000), for example, Elizabeth drew her audience's attention to the 'impact of Christ's life . . . all around us' in numerous beneficial ways. Ten years later, she sang the praises of the King James Bible, and its 'beautiful descriptions of the birth of Jesus Christ'. In 2021, as well as reflecting on the Covid pandemic and, in a very personal way, on the death of her husband, she spoke of the hope brought by the birth of a child and how the teachings of Jesus 'have been handed down from generation to generation, and have been the bedrock of my faith.'

CARRYING THE MESSAGE IN HER WORDS, NOT HER DELIVERY

If the monarchy were elective, Elizabeth's performance at the hustings would garner very few votes. Sadly, she is no orator. Despite hours of coaxing and cajoling, her tone remains flat, her face expressionless. Though she has toned down her cut-glass upper-class accent in response to criticism, she still sounds very different from the great majority of her listeners. Yet familiarity has bred a certain affection. Her speeches attract less mockery nowadays and are more likely to be received with remarks such as, 'Grand old lady – still doing her best!'

Talking religion

On Maundy Thursday (the Thursday before Easter), medieval monarchs once symbolically washed the feet of selected poor. The gesture mirrored Jesus' act before the Last Supper. Things are now done differently. Since 1932, the sovereign has attended a church or cathedral on Maundy Thursday before distributing specially minted silver Maundy Money.

TIP

The collectable Maundy coins are given to deserving citizens noted for their service to church or community. Lucky children get the special pocket money, too. How do I know? In 1965, the Queen attended the Maundy Thursday service in Canterbury Cathedral, and afterwards gave a set of Maundy Money coins to the Dean's eight-year-old daughter. Thirteen years later, she and I were married.

Elizabeth likes talking to the clergy. As Buckingham Palace and Windsor Castle have private chapels (see later in this chapter), there is often a chaplain on call. The minister of Crathie Kirk, the church on the Balmoral estate where the Royal Family worship when in the Highlands, is a welcome guest at the castle. Back in England, the Dean of Windsor is another of the Queen's spiritual advisors.

TIP

Elizabeth met the American evangelist Billy Graham when his 'mission' brought him to the UK. Their discussions were considered controversial, for Graham's enthusiastic fundamentalist (and anti-LGBT stance) was not in keeping with the Anglican tradition of broad church tolerance. Though invited, the Queen did not attend any Billy Graham rally.

Checking out Royal Chapels and Churches

Chapter 9 checks out the various royal residences scattered around the country. As worship is such a vital part of Elizabeth's routine, it is essential that each one of them is linked to a convenient place of worship.

The two residences in which she spends most of her time, Buckingham Palace and Windsor Castle, have their own private chapels. When staying at Sandringham and Balmoral, which do not have a chapel of their own, the Queen and her family frequent a local church every Sunday.

Let's take a brief tour . . . and don't forget to bring an umbrella!

Balmoral

When in residence at Balmoral during the summer, the Royal Family worships at the small pine-and-granite Crathie Kirk. The site's Christian associations go back over 1,000 years, though the present church was constructed at the behest of Queen Victoria at the end of the nineteenth century. Its design is a curious neo-Gothic mix of tower and spire, church and castle.

Princess Anne's 1992 divorce from Mark Philips (see Chapter 20) barred her from remarriage in an Anglican church. The Church of Scotland had no such qualms. A few months after her divorce came through, Anne married Commander Timothy Laurence in Crathie Kirk. The ceremony was attended by her parents, her grandmother, her children – and happily wailing bagpipers!

Buckingham Palace

Together with the private indoor swimming pool and cinema, the private chapel is one of the many palace rooms not open to the public. The original chapel, created by Victoria and Albert in 1844, was damaged during the London Blitz in World War II and subsequently incorporated into an existing gallery.

Sandringham

Each Christmas, Elizabeth and her family decamp to their private house on the Sandringham Estate (see Chapter 9). It is where the Queen often records her Christmas message (see earlier in this chapter), and from where they go to the local church, St Mary Magdalene, for a Christmas Day service.

Sandringham parish church was built in the sixteenth century and heavily restored in Victorian times. The result is a somewhat over-ornate, bling-bursting building of little architectural merit (listed only as of Grade II importance). It is interesting, nonetheless, because of its royal associations, happy and sad.

In 1896, the future King George VI was baptized in St Mary Magdalene. More recently, it witnessed the baptisms of the infant Lady Diana Spencer (the future Princess Diana), Princess Eugenie of York, and Princess Charlotte of Cambridge. The christenings did not use either of the church's serviceable fonts (one of Italian marble, the other of ancient Greek stone). Instead, a silver font was brought down from the Tower of London. This may – like so many practices followed by the family – be simply tradition. Or perhaps they're worried that using a local font might make it a target for souvenir hunters?

WARNING

In the graveyard of St Mary Magdalene, lies the simple grave of Prince John, the 13-year-old son of George V and the notably un-maternal Queen Mary. Discovering that the unfortunate boy suffered from learning difficulties and epilepsy, his embarrassed parents shut him away and made no further public mention of him. He was eventually packed off to a farm on the Sandringham estate where he died in 1919.

Windsor Castle

When in residence at Windsor, the Royal Family has a choice of two places of worship. The smaller is a private chapel within the castle itself. After it was damaged beyond repair by the devastating 1992 fire (see Chapter 20), a smaller, 30-seat replacement was opened in 1997. The private chapel was used for the christenings of the future George V, Prince Edward and Archie Mountbatten-Windsor, and the confirmations of Prince Charles and Princess Anne. It was also where Prince Philip's coffin lay at rest before his funeral.

For major religious occasions in Windsor, the royals use St George's Chapel. This grand building, begun in 1348 and altered and restored over the centuries, retains its late medieval 'perpendicular' design. It is a cornucopia of stained glass, sculptures, banners and memorials. Most famous are the Queen's Beasts – heraldic ceiling representations of animals associated with the royals. They include the lion of England, the dragon of Wales, and the unicorn of Edward III.

St George's, boasting its own dean, chapter of canons, verger, and outstanding choir of men and boys' voices, is also the chapel of the ancient order of chivalry known as the Order of the Garter (see Chapter 12). Unsurprisingly, it almost literally drips with royalty. Here you will find the interred remains of numerous monarchs and their spouses, including:

>> Henry VI

>> Edward IV and Elizabeth Woodville

>> Henry VIII and Jane Seymour

>> Charles I

>> George III and Charlotte of Mecklenburg-Strelitz

>> George IV

>> William IV and Adelaide of Saxe-Meiningen

- >> Edward VII and Alexandra of Denmark
- >> George V and Mary of Teck
- >> George VI and Elizabeth Bowes-Lyon.

Nearby lie the tombs of the Queen's sister, Princess Margaret, and of her husband, Prince Philip. It is thought that Elizabeth has chosen St George's Chapel as her final resting place, too.

On a more cheerful note, the chapel has witnessed numerous royal weddings, including those of:

- >> the future Edward VII and Queen Alexandra
- >> Princess Margaret of Connaught and Gustaf Adolf, the future King of Sweden
- >> Prince Edward and Sophie Rhys-Jones
- >> Prince Harry and Meghan Markle.

St George's Chapel was where, in 2005, the Archbishop of Canterbury blessed the union of Prince Charles and Camilla Parker–Bowles after their civil marriage in Windsor Guildhall.

Chapter **20**

Annus Horribilis

Speaking in London's grand fifteenth-century Guildhall on 24 November 1992, the Queen declared:

1992 is not a year on which I shall look back with undiluted pleasure. In the words of one of my more sympathetic correspondents, it has turned out to be an 'Annus Horribilis'.

Annus Horribilis translates from Latin as: 'a horrible year'.

The Queen wasn't wrong. This chronology of sad events, which continued after her November speech into December, outlines why 1992 was such a grim time for Elizabeth and her family:

13 March: Prince Andrew and Sarah Ferguson separate.

23 April: Princess Anne and Mark Phillips divorce.

7 June: Publication of *Diana, Princess of Wales – Her True Story*.

20 August: Pictures published of Sarah Ferguson, Duchess of York, sunbathing topless with a friend.

24 August: Publication of Diana's private phone chat with a lover.

20 November: Windsor Castle ravaged by fire.

26 November: To quell public outcry, the Queen agrees to pay tax.

9 December: Prince Charles and Princess Diana separate.

23 December: The Queen's Christmas message is leaked two days early.

Chapters 16 and 17 cover most of these events in more detail. This chapter focusses on the troubled lives of her three elder children, and the public outcry that forced the Royal Family to reconsider their relationship with the British taxpayer.

Staying Married is Hard to Do

Windsor-watchers have long wondered why the marriages of three of Elizabeth's four children have floundered. Was it bad luck or coincidence, or did their upbringing have something to do with it? Everyone has their own theory, but the answer probably lies in a combination of all three.

What is a royal marriage?

A royal marriage is like no other. Most parents hope their offspring will marry someone whom they and the rest of the family consider suitable. Throughout history, kings and queens didn't just hope their children would marry suitably, they demanded it.

TECHNICAL STUFF

The marriages of royal princes and princesses were much more than personal or even family matters; they had deep political ramifications for the whole nation. Here are three examples:

>> When the future Henry VIII's elder brother Arthur died not long after his marriage to the Spanish princess Catherine of Aragon, the poor girl was passed on to Henry (see Chapters 2 and 19). The boys' father went to great lengths to get the second marriage sanctioned by the Church because he needed to preserve the link with Spain. Why? Because Spain was a useful counterbalance to the power of France, Britain's number one foe down the centuries.

>> Henry VIII's marriage (his fourth) to Anne of Cleves in 1540 was also for political reasons. Following his break with Rome, the King needed alliances with Europe's Protestants. Anne of Cleve's brother was a key figure among the German Protestants.

>> Henry VIII's fervently Catholic elder daughter, Queen Mary I (see Chapter 2), married the King of Spain (Europe's dominant Catholic power at the time).

Domestic marriages were equally significant. In the previous century, Edward IV's marriage to Elizabeth Woodville caused angry resentment among barons who felt their family should have taken precedence over the Woodvilles. Issues like this were a major reason why Elizabeth I chose not to marry at all – in doing so, she avoided making enemies as well as friends.

TIP

Yes, I hear you, say, but this was all way back. Surely it didn't still apply in the twentieth century? Well, in some ways it did. The main difference was that the political purpose of a royal marriage was gradually replaced by a new idea: from Victoria onwards, royals became a sort of show family, a model institution for others to emulate. Royal marriages were now expected to include an element of romantic love, giving the phrase 'royal family' greater significance. Its values came not from the wayward and often hedonistic aristocracy, but from the determinedly respectable, expanding middle-class.

The Windsor's complicated history of marriage

It's important to remember that Elizabeth was born almost a century ago. Her great-great-grandmother Victoria (d. 1901) used her children's marriages to cement friendships and alliances of political significance across Europe (see Chapter 3). A combination of Victorian sentimentality and lack of real choice served to give these relationships an air of romantic love, though it was a million miles from the flashing eyes on a Facetime screen associated with modern relationships.

Under Edward VII, royal marriage *à la* middle class took a step backwards into the past. Elizabeth's libertine great-grandfather did as duty dictated, and broke off his affair with the actress Nellie Clifden to marry Alexandra of Denmark, whom he did not know well. He told Alexandra's father that he loved her. She went on to do as expected, bearing Edward's children and turning a blind eye to his many and very obvious affairs. Did this behaviour suggest an instructive template for Elizabeth II?

The marriage of George V, Elizabeth's grandfather, followed a similar pattern to that of Princes Arthur and Henry 400 years earlier. In 1891, Victoria's eldest son, Prince Albert Victor, was steered towards the suitably royal Princess Mary of Teck, and the couple were duly engaged. Albert then died of flu.

The following year, Albert's younger brother George moved in on Mary and she accepted his proposal of marriage. Love, they say, came later, but it was hardly a flare of Tinder flame. And it was this Mary, Elizabeth's grandmother, who had a powerful influence on the growing girl. Duty first, Elizabeth. Duty first.

We now come to Elizabeth's parents, George VI and Queen Elizabeth (the future Queen Mother). Certainly there was affection on George's part as he pursued the girl of his dreams, though she was much less sure. A stammering, rather weedy second-in-line to the throne was not necessarily a great catch (see Chapters 4 and 6). However, as they said of his parents' marriage, love of some sort eventually popped its rose-garlanded head round the corner.

For a number of years, George's marriage didn't matter much. What really counted was that of his elder brother, Edward VIII. It was here that the royal tradition of duty before love really came unstuck when the young king prioritized the latter over the former (see Chapter 5). And he did not even fall for a fellow noble, as Edward IV and Henry VIII had done. No, Edward went for a commoner. And not just any commoner, but a foreigner and divorcee to boot. Really, grumbled the upholders of tradition, there are limits!

Elizabeth's mixed messages

TIP

Which brings us to Elizabeth herself. What image of royal marriage did she inherit? The messages, part modern, part traditional, were mixed:

>> From Edward VIII's abdication debacle she learned that it had to be with a suitable partner.

>> From her parents she knew that, in the eyes of the public at least, it was a working partnership.

>> The primary function of marriage was to produce children, thereby securing the succession.

>> Marriage was for life, which might mean accepting a partner's infidelity but never making a public issue of it.

>> It was the Royal Family's duty to set an example to the rest of the nation of what marriage and family life were all about.

>> Romantic love might or might not be present at the time of betrothal; with luck, over time a marriage might lead to a deep and lasting affection.

The formula worked for Elizabeth, who combined Alexandra's forbearance with her grandmother Mary's conservatism and her father's dogged devotion to duty. She was helped by being besotted with Philip at an early age and raised in the cloistered atmosphere of the court, far removed from the ideas and temptations of the wider world.

REMEMBER

Throughout her reign, the Queen has been an outsider, looking in on a reality. She understands things intellectually, theoretically, but has not experienced them. She knows what a school is and how it works, for instance, but not having attended one she can't conceive what school life is like. This enables her to give splendidly detached observations to her prime ministers, but leaves her at a loss when fostering life skills in her children. She rarely even tries. In domestic as well as political matters, she appears to float on a cloud of serene detachment.

Mucking-up marriages

The marriage formula that worked for Elizabeth had failed for her sister Margaret. Nor did it serve for Charles, Anne or Andrew. Of course personal factors played a part – probably the predominant part – in all four cases. But as well as upbringing, postwar societal changes were also influential:

» A greater emphasis on individualism, fed by flourishing capitalism, gave people a stronger sense of entitlement in all things – 'I want it now!'

» Divorce was gradually destigmatized (see Chapter 12).

» The invention of the birth control pill in the early 1960s coincided with an increasingly liberal attitude towards sex.

» The women's liberation movement made women less tolerant of male peccadilloes and more inclined to follow their own extra-marital desires.

» In Western society (but not in all areas of the world) romantic love was trumpeted as the sole basis for a marriage – going together, as the song says, 'like a horse and carriage'.

Following the Family's Progress

It soon became obvious to the Queen's children that a huge gulf lay between the bow-and-curtsey life of the Palace – little altered since the time of their mother's childhood – and the rapidly changing world outside.

Their inability to bridge this gulf and manage their romances and marriages in a manner acceptable to the court certainly contributed to the Queen's woes.

Charles: The tortured one

Charles, dominated by his father and in awe of his mother, struggled to reconcile the link between love and marriage. His first marriage reflected that tension (see Chapter 16). The attempt to place a modern building on ancient foundations led to tragic collapse.

The failed marriage of Charles, Prince of Wales, and the tragic death of Princess Diana is covered in Chapter 16. There is little further to add here other than to consider how, in the authorized biography by David Dimbleby (*The Prince Of Wales: An Intimate Portrait*, Little, Brown 1994), the Prince admitted bitterly how he felt his parents had denied him the 'affection and appreciation' he sought, and which he finally found from Camilla.

Meanwhile, his was not the only royal marriage to be unravelling in the later 1980s.

Anne: The gamechanger

Anne, made of much tougher stuff then her brother Charles, ditched the old-style royal marriage early on. Nothing was going to tie her to the pre-war world.

REMEMBER

It was Anne, not Charles, who finally forced Elizabeth to abandon her template for a royal marriage. By the early 1970s, the feisty Princess had carved out a name for herself as an excellent horsewoman. She had won the European Eventing Championships and been voted BBC Sports Personality of the Year (1971). Later, she went on to represent her country at eventing in the 1976 Montreal Olympics.

It was through horse riding that, in 1968, Anne met the shy, quietly spoken Mark Phillips, a captain in the Dragoon Guards. He was not her first boyfriend and people were surprised when they announced their engagement in May 1973. Gossips had been expecting her to choose someone more lively and extrovert, and guessed that she would be the one calling the shots. They weren't far off the target.

After a spectacular royal Westminster Abbey wedding before 100 million TV viewers, the couple settled down in Gatcombe Park, the mansion the Queen had given them as a wedding present. Even at this early stage, there were signs that the relationship was not all it might have been. Prince Philip had no time for Mark, who is believed to have been cruelly (and unjustly) nicknamed 'Fog' because he was so dense. The poor man also upset Elizabeth by turning down a title. Children born to the marriage would be commoners.

REMEMBER

After the birth of Peter Phillips in 1978, Anne entered into a relationship with her bodyguard, the handsome, blue-eyed and fair-haired Detective Sergeant Peter Cross. In time, Mark became suspicious. He confessed his concerns to the Queen and, during one of Anne's absences, Cross was moved from Gatcombe Park duty. Livid, Anne turned on Mark and told her mother that her marriage was over.

Anne's relationship with Cross (we are told that for their clandestine meetings she went under the assumed name 'Mrs Wallis'!) ended when he fell for someone else. The 'Mrs Wallis' soubriquet made the Princess's position quite clear – she wanted a divorce. Her mother did not. Surely, for the sake of the children and the image of the Royal Family, Anne could do what kings and queens had been doing for centuries: carry on with a mistress or lover while in public maintaining the pretence of a steady marriage?

No, Anne had never been one for pretence. Whether they liked it or not, she would drag the Royal Family, kicking and screaming, into the twentieth century. Her divorce in the spring of the *Annus Horribilis* was the first of a royal close to the throne since Henry VIII divorced Anne of Cleves in 1540.

Andrew: 'Randy Andy'

Andrew, the not-too-bright bully, behaved just like many younger sons had done down the ages – the only difference being that he married his mistress before ditching her.

REMEMBER

Arrogant and aggressive, Andrew Duke of York had consistently been the least popular of the Queen's children. In the Navy, he never let anyone forget who he was. One of his unattractive characteristics was to assume that he was irresistible to women. The young and naïve, flattered by royal attention, submitted to his attentions and helped build his press nickname of 'Randy Andy'. The press soaked up tales of him visiting a club where the clientele was caned by scantily clad ladies.

Andrew's more serious relationships, with the actress Koo Stark and the model Katie Rabett, were quashed by the Palace when it learned that less than chaste images of both girls were in the public domain. It was with some relief, therefore, that Elizabeth and Philip learned of their second son's engagement to Sarah Ferguson.

The bouncy, red-headed Sloane Ranger (a Sloane what? Head to the nearby sidebar of the same name to find out more about this group) ticked many of the right boxes: with ancestry traceable back to Charles II, she had known the Royal Family all her life, her cavalry regiment daddy played polo with Philip, and she knew the etiquette.

SLOANE RANGERS

Dating from the mid-1970s, the term *Sloane Ranger* was coined for a distinctive slice of young and not-so-young upper and upper-middle class English society. The name combined the US TV show *The Lone Ranger* and the expensive area of west London around Sloane Square.

Sloane Rangers (or just 'Sloanes') were identified by drawling posh accents (exemplified in the expression 'Okay, yah'), inherited wealth, private education at one of a handful of expensive schools, languid sophistication, unrepentant snobbishness, a penchant for country pursuits (fox hunting, game shooting and fly fishing), and distinctive dress (such as gilet jackets, silk headscarves for women and bright corduroy trousers for men).

They were widely mocked for being dim-witted.

Diana Spencer (the future Princess Diana) and Sarah Ferguson (the future Duchess of York) were considered archetypal Sloanes.

Unfortunately, 'Fergie' (a school nickname adopted by the media) also ticked several of the wrong boxes. Her taste was, by royal standards, vulgar. She had flexible moral standards, saw the royal connection as a resource to be exploited, and did not understand the 'duty comes first' Windsor mantra.

Following the customary Westminster Abbey carriages, crowds and cameras wedding in 1986, and the birth of two children (Princess Beatrice, 1988) and Princess Eugenie, 1990), the marriage fell apart very quickly. In 1990, Fergie fell in love with Texas oilman Steve Wyatt and was warned by the Palace to back off. She refused.

Two years later, she became entangled with her financial advisor, Johnny Bryan. Andrew, never the smartest cookie in the box, seemed unaware of what was going on until, in January 1992, pictures of Bryan sucking Fergie's toes appeared in the press.

REMEMBER

Andrew twigged, the couple rowed furiously, and the Palace poured vitriol on Fergie's head. In March 1992, the separation of Andrew, Duke of York, and Sarah, Duchess of York, was made public. The media was now talking of upper-class decadence, and the standing of the monarchy was falling fast. The *Annus Horribilis* was well and truly launched.

Despite the Palace's efforts to deflect criticism away from the Royal Family and onto wayward outsiders such as Fergie, the public wanted an explanation why the marriages of three of the Queen's four children had hit the rocks. *The Sun* newspaper gave its own answer: 'Blame the way you bought 'em up, Ma'am.' A fair number of the British public were inclined to agree.

Edward: The lost boy

Amid all the turmoil surrounding his older siblings, Prince Edward remained in the shadows. He made a fool of himself with his petulant behaviour towards the press over *It's A Royal Knockout* (see later in this chapter), and the media remained pretty dismissive of him.

At least he didn't add to the woes of the *Annus Horribilis* by making an unsuitable marriage. Inevitably, however, his single status and boyish looks gave rise to unnecessary and tasteless speculation in some media over his sexuality.

Edward, however, trod the modern path. He married a partner who – after early false steps – learned the walk to narrow path between the old and the new, and their marriage held fast (see Chapter 24).

Watching a Royal Game Show

REMEMBER

Elizabeth's *Annus Horribilis* was not a bolt from the blue. The younger generation had provided her with plenty of warning signs of the rapids further downstream: the Charles-and-Diana soap opera, the Anne-and-Mark estrangement, and – most vulgar of all – the 1987 'It's a Royal Knockout'. This slapstick TV game show illustrated with painful clarity how Elizabeth's successors rejected her old-world stuffiness, but had no idea what to replace it with.

TIP

Actually, that's not quite true. They did have an idea – a massive fund-raising farce that would show them to be just as capable of idiotic behaviour as everyone else. They wanted to be seen as genuine, normal human beings. What they failed to realize, causing immense damage to the principle of hereditary monarchy, is that they were *not* normal human beings. Like it or not, history had singled them out be different – and rewarded them handsomely to act the part.

Elizabeth understood this and hated the idea of the TV show from the outset. To his credit, Charles refused to take part and forbade Diana from doing so. The Queen, floating above everything on her cloud of royal detachment, did not follow her instincts and put a stop to it. She may have been subconsciously aware of her failings as a mother (see Chapters 8 and 14), and thus unwilling to spoil her children's fun.

What was the show all about?

» It was dreamed up by 23-year-old Prince Edward, the perceived runt of the Windsor litter, who was hoping to launch a spectacular TV career.

» Four teams of celebrities, led by Edward, Anne, Andrew and his wife Sarah, were given daft, clownish things to do in the grounds of Alton Towers stately home, Staffordshire.

» BBC TV cameras followed every embarrassing movement, with well-known presenters offering a running commentary, while a costumed crowd howled with delight or disbelief.

» The star-studded teams included internationally known celebrities such as John Cleese, Dame Kiri Te Kanawa, George Lazenby, Jane Seymour, Christopher Reeve, and John Travolta.

» Contestants wore ungainly mock-medieval costumes in vivid colours.

» Charging around on the grass or on a specially constructed gothic set, the contestants did things such as firing fake cannons, gathering giant flowers, and sliding along a revolving pole over a pool of water while being bombarded with plastic hams.

» The purpose of the good-humoured nonsense was to raise funds for charity. In that it was a success, drawing in some £1 million (around £3 million at today's prices).

» The team led by Princess Anne, by then an Olympic athlete, triumphed.

Young and naïve, Prince Edward capped his cringe–worthy show with three dreadful mistakes:

» He did not allow the press onto the set to see the event live and talk to the contestants. Instead, journalists were corralled in a tent without refreshment and obliged to watch on TV. They were not impressed.

» When he visited the press tent after the show and found the reception lukewarm, he lost his temper and stormed out. How to win friends and influence people – not!

» He failed to see how the show would expose the royal contestants, especially Andrew's wife Sarah, Duchess of York, as Sloane Rangers (see the sidebar earlier in this chapter), unworthy of royal privilege.

As *The Crown* makes clear, the Royal Family is constantly battling to demonstrate to the nation and the Commonwealth that it deserves exalted status. By almost never presenting a distinctive target, the Queen manages the task extremely well. The team leaders in 'It's a Royal Knockout' did not.

Smouldering Tension: Fire in Windsor Castle

The Sovereign's Private Chapel, Windsor Castle, 11:00am on Friday, 20 November 1992. A curtain has been moved too close to a powerful spotlight. The material smoulders for a while then bursts into flames. Within a few minutes, the chapel is ablaze and the flames are spreading rapidly through the State Apartments.

Windsor Castle to the west of London is a huge, much-modernised fortress dating from the eleventh-century. Surrounded by a large estate, this home to 38 previous monarchs is where Elizabeth likes to spend most of her weekends (see Chapter 9).

The response was quick, though perhaps not as rapid as one might have expected for such a splendid building and the unrivalled collection of artistic treasures it housed. The Castle's own fire brigade, based two miles away, arrived at 11:41am and the county fire service three minutes later. In the meantime, servants, court-iers and volunteers were hurriedly rescuing as many of the pictures and smaller *objets d'art* as they could carry. Prince Andrew was on the scene, and it is reported that he used his military training to direct the salvage operation.

Vaults and false ceilings enabled the conflagration to spread with alarming speed and ferocity. By early afternoon, 39 fire appliances and over 200 fire-fighters were on the scene. Fire breaks were created. One-and-a-half million gallons of water, some drawn from the nearby River Thames, were pumped into the fire and onto adjacent sections of the Castle to stop the blaze engulfing the whole building. By evening, it was under control, and the last pockets of flame were finally extinguished during the night.

The fire had hollowed out the entire western wing of the Castle, leaving it a skeleton of burned and blackened walls. Several of the finest chambers, including the private chapel, the State Dining Room and the Grand Reception Room, had been mercilessly gutted. In total, over 100 rooms had been damaged or destroyed. The sterling efforts of staff and volunteers had saved the great majority of the valuable contents, and only a handful of major pictures and large pieces of furniture were lost. There was no insurance claim – the priceless Windsor collection was, literally, uninsurable.

And Elizabeth? Those who saw the Queen on the fateful day recall a small woman in wellington boots, raincoat, and waterproof headscarf standing alone, staring incredulously as her favourite home, the place where she had spent so much of her youth, was devoured by flame. It was a truly apocalyptic scene. Some say that, as she turned away, her face was lined with tears.

REMEMBER

Following the fire, the Heritage Secretary, Peter Brooke, announced that the government would foot the multi-million-pound bill to restore the castle – as far as was possible – to its former glory. The decision provoked a furious outcry. Had Brooke forgotten the crass royal TV show, Fergie's cavalier exploitation of her position, and the family's apparently heartless treatment of Diana, the People's Princess? Respect for the Queen remained intact, but the institution she represented had been damaged as badly as her castle. The taxpayers had had their fill of funding the raucous, self-obsessed lifestyle of pampered royals. The monarchy was less popular than at any time since Queen Victoria had locked herself away in the 1860s (see Chapter 3).

REMEMBER

The Queen admitted there had been 'scrutiny' (not criticism) of the monarchy, and this was 'an effective agent of change'. And change duly followed:

>> Much of the cost of restoring Windsor Castle (eventually £36.5 million) would be met by a £2 million donation from the Queen, and by opening parts of the castle and Buckingham Palace to the public on payment of an entry fee.

>> The Palace brought forward its decision that the Queen and Prince Charles would start paying tax on their private incomes (see Chapter 17).

>> Government finance would henceforward be available only for the Queen, her husband, mother and sister, and her three younger children. Charles would manage on his income from the Duchy of Cornwall (see Chapter 17 for more on royal finances).

5

Steadying The Ship

This part follows Elizabeth from the *Annus Horribilis* of 1992 to her Platinum Jubilee in 2022. The broadly chronological narrative is interspersed with a chapter on the Queen's relationship with animals, especially horses and dogs.

If there is a theme running through these sunset years, it is how the monarchy continued gradually to develop from the institution Elizabeth inherited in 1952. The transformation was largely forced by external pressures bubbling up from a society that was itself evolving at an unprecedented rate. Divorce, which the Queen had once thought unimaginable for a top royal, became almost commonplace within the family. Traditional deference for hereditary institutions melted away; the ethnic and sociological make-up of the United Kingdom was transformed; technology revolutionized communications.

The Queen and her close advisors did their best to roll with these changes, though not always willingly. True to form, the Queen never instigated movement, but – like her dutiful husband – followed three paces behind. Nevertheless, despite waves of personal troubles – the sudden death of Princess Diana, the passing of Princess Margaret, the Queen Mother, and Prince Philip, the fretful bowing out of Harry and Meghan – Elizabeth somehow managed to preserve her own dignity and the magic of monarchy.

Whatever one thinks of the institution the Queen embodies, she has set an unparalleled example of service and dedication to duty. The world may rock on, but throughout it all the true rock has remained reassuringly steadfast.

» Dealing with the death of Diana

» Adapting to political and social change

» Celebrating and grieving family events

» Continuing to work as the nation's monarch

Chapter **21**

'Long to Reign Over Us': No Sign of Flagging

This chapter examines how Elizabeth's difficult 1980s merged into the equally difficult 1990s. The strains and stresses she faced were national and international as well as personal. Remarkably, clinging to her 'duty first' mantra and stubbornly insisting on the unique mystery of monarchy, she batted off fortune's slings and arrows. By the time of her 2002 Golden Jubilee (see Chapter 23), her legendary status was assured.

TIP

As Big Ben struck midnight on 31 December 1992, Elizabeth – if she was awake – must have let out a huge sigh of relief that her *Annus Horribilis* (see Chapter 20) was finally over. She had seen too much of life, however, to believe that the simple moving of a clock hand would wipe away the trials and tribulations that beset her. And so it proved.

REMEMBER

The years 1993–2002 saw the final collapse of the marriage of Charles and Diana, followed by the Princess's death, Prince Andrew's divorce from Sarah Ferguson, and the deaths of Princess Margaret and the Queen Mother in 2002. The removal of most hereditary peers from the House of Lords in 1998 called into question the rightfulness of the hereditary principle as exemplified by the monarchy.

Northern Ireland's terrible sectarian violence continued up to the peace settlement in 1998. The establishment of a Scottish parliament and a Welsh national assembly also put strain on Elizabeth's role as monarch of a united realm (see later in this chapter and also Chapters 2 and 25).

Further afield, Mozambique joining the Commonwealth in 1995 was a welcome boost for the organization the Queen headed. Nevertheless, the handing over of Hong Kong to China two years later came as a sharp reminder that the British Empire was no more. And in 1999, Australia remained a monarchy only because its citizens could not decide how best to choose a president.

It was a hard time for the British monarchy. This chapter delves into how Elizabeth dealt with the many challenges she faced in the 1990s and early 2000s.

Negotiating the 1990s

REMEMBER

The Royal Family's marital difficulties (see Chapter 20) rumbled on throughout the 1990s. Rumbled is perhaps too mild a word. In January 1993, they burst into flames with the publication of Charles's night-time, lovey-dovey telephone chats with Camilla. 'Camillagate' the more polite papers called it. Total humiliation, whatever you call it.

The patching up of the family's reputation effected by the BBC's favourable 1992 documentary *Elizabeth R* was undone in a stroke. 1994 witnessed further collapse of the older order when the Duchess of Kent, married to the Queen's cousin, converted to Roman Catholicism and gradually withdrew from public life. Far worse lay ahead. In a 1995 BBC interview with Martin Bashir, Diana came out with two of her most memorable statements:

>> Speaking of her relationship with Charles, she said, 'There were three of us in this marriage.' The implication was that Camilla had been there from the start (not true in a physical sense), and Charles had never really cared for his superstar bride.

>> Diana wished to be seen as the 'queen of people's hearts'. Wow! The criticism of Elizabeth may only have been implicit, but it was no less deadly. Diana was claiming to usurp the throne of public affection.

The Duke and Duchess of York (Andrew and Fergie) divorced on 30 May 1996; Charles and Diana followed suit on 28 August. Diana retained her Princess of Wales title and her apartment in Kensington Palace, but was no longer 'Her Royal Highness'. Her financial settlement (a huge lump sum and considerable annual income for office expenses, all provided from the Royal Family's own purse) was extremely generous.

At last, the whole messy, painful, embarrassing business seemed to be over.

It wasn't.

Dwindling public deference

TIP

Deference to the monarch cannot be taken for granted. In 1832, William IV was hissed at, and mud slung at his carriage, when he appeared to oppose parliamentary reform. Victoria was vilified during the republican wave of the 1860s and 1870s (see Chapter 3).

However, with the exception of the booing of George VI and his queen in 1940 (see Chapter 6) and some ugly muttering during the abdication crisis (see Chapter 5), during the first half of the twentieth century, the British were surprisingly sycophantic towards their hereditary monarchs.

Pride in the Empire and the need for unity during two world wars certainly helped. Nevertheless, by historical standards, this uncritical tolerance – even adulation – of the royals was the exception. So, when deference went into decline in the later twentieth century, the country was in fact returning to its normal position: healthy scepticism of anyone appearing to give themselves airs and graces . . . royals included.

Other indications of a less class-based, deferential society were also emerging:

» The BBC's espousal of presenters whose accents were not RP (*Received Pronunciation*, the formal accent favoured by the Establishment and the stereotypical 'English toff' accent). Prime Minister Blair adopted elements of *Estuary English*, the modern dialect of London and its south-eastern environs, which gradually spread further afield. These changes made the Queen's distinctly upper-class accent sound increasingly awkward and out of touch.

» The relaxation of dress codes: prime ministers appearing in jeans, ties frequently discarded, trainers worn everywhere. This made Prince Charles's tweedy jackets and formal blazers even more passé.

» The Camillagate (outlined earlier in this chapter) phone-hacking incident. It suggested that the Royal Family were now fair game for scandal-hunters, a marked decline in the deference that had shielded Prince Philip and Princess Margaret (see Chapters 12 and 13). The publication of Charles's pillow talk will make it all the harder for him to command deferential respect when he is eventually crowned king.

>> Increasing dissatisfaction with the make-up of the part-nominated, part-hereditary House of Lords. The Labour government's 1999 House of Lords Act left only 92 of the country's 800 hereditary peers entitled to a seat in the upper house. At the time of writing, there is growing pressure for the hereditaries to be outlawed from the Lords altogether. The ban would have implications for the hereditary monarchy, too, as it would call the hereditary principle further into question.

WARNING

>> The significance of popular TV costume dramas such as *Downton Abbey*, *Bridgerton* and *The Crown* (yes, *The Crown* is a costume drama!) is harder to assess. Such programmes may reflect a desire for escapism from a troubled world. On the other hand, shows in which the high-born are depicted with the same strengths and weaknesses as everyone else may appeal to society's growing intolerance of an 'us' and 'them' world.

TIP

Personal and subjective questioning suggests that *The Crown* has boosted understanding of and respect for Elizabeth Windsor as a human being, but not for hereditary monarchy and its attendant sidekicks, servants and hangers-on.

Surviving the songs and satire

By the 1960s, the Queen's hoity-toity accent was standard fare for comedians (see Chapter 12). They only had to utter the catchphrase 'my husband and I' with a posh voice to get their audience going. Pop dances in the 1960s were said to mimic the Duke of Edinburgh's stiff, nodding manner. A decade later, verbal and cartoon attacks on the monarchy were increasingly common and acerbic.

The anti-Establishment Silver Jubilee single 'God Save the Queen' (see Chapter 15) by the punk band the Sex Pistols was banned by the BBC and the Independent Broadcasting Authority. This probably helped it rise to number one in some music charts!

Popular left-wing MPs, notably Willie Hamilton and Tony Benn, were continually sniping at the Royal Family in Parliament. Their views were echoed in republican-leaning newspapers, such as *The Guardian*, *The Observer*, the *Independent*, and *The New Statesman*.

WARNING

The satirical magazine *Private Eye* (published 1961 onwards), continually at war with pretence, hypocrisy, sleaze, and corruption, has often had the Royal Family in its sights. For a time it ran a cartoon strip – 'Liz' – that parodied the royals. After the *Royal Family* documentary (see Chapter 14) tried to show the Royal Family leading normal lives, *Private Eye* has referred to them by commonplace names. The Duke of Edinburgh, for instance, was 'Keith', and Diana was 'Cheryl'.

The satirical TV puppet show *Spitting Image*, which ran between 1984 and 1996, contained some of the sharpest mockery of the monarchy since the scurrilous cartoons of the late Hanoverian era (see Chapters 2 and 3). A show of this nature would have been inconceivable in any previous decade of the twentieth century. It was revived in 2020 but suffered from self-imposed censorship for fear of offending woke viewers (crusaders against social injustice).

TECHNICAL STUFF

Elizabeth's wish to appear normal was parodied in *Spitting Image* by her sporting a Campaign for Nuclear Disarmament badge and constantly looking for second-hand clothes. Her mother's drinking habits were suggested by the bottle of gin she carried about with her at all times, and Margaret was perpetually tipsy. Diana was portrayed as a publicity-seeking Sloane Ranger (see Chapter 20), Charles an ineffectual wannabe hippie, and his father a confrontation-seeking Greek in the uniform of the Royal Navy.

The depiction of a sex-obsessed Prince Andrew plays into the hands of those seeking to prosecute him for alleged involvement in Jeffrey Epstein's illegal activities (see Chapter 25).

The Death of Diana

REMEMBER

Chapter 16 told the story of Charles and Diana to the moment of her death in a car accident. What followed was one of the rare moments when Elizabeth completely misjudged the public mood and found herself seriously at odds with the people she claimed to serve.

The scenario is explained one day at a time, unfurling events as they happened, in the following sections.

Sunday, 31 August

Diana, her boyfriend Dodi Fayed, and their intoxicated driver Henri Paul die at 12:20am when their speeding Mercedes, chased by paparazzi, hits a concrete pillar in the Pont d'Alma tunnel, Paris. Later that morning, the news is passed to the Queen, who is at Balmoral with most of her family, including Diana's two sons, William (15) and Harry (12).

At about 7.15am, Charles tells the boys of their mother's death. Harry is reported to be very upset, William more stoic. Later that morning, after the news of the tragedy sinks in and stories spread about how the press and paparazzi had hounded the Queen of Hearts to her death, the Queen issues a message of deep regret.

As on any normal Sunday, the Royal Family attend Crathie Kirk (see Chapter 19). No prayers are said for Diana. The press, keen to divert attention away from the flak coming their way because of the paparazzi pack that had pursued Diana, interpret this as cold-heartedness. The truth is more complex.

REMEMBER

Charles and his mother, eager to protect William and Harry, stick to their normal routine. The boys' cousin, Peter Phillips, helps prevent the boys from dwelling on what has happened by engaging them in outdoor activities on the Balmoral estate. Elizabeth does not want to overreact to the death of one who had, in her eyes, brought the monarchy into disrepute. On a personal level, she may have seen Diana's wish to be the queen of people's hearts as a cruel slur to which she was unable to respond.

WARNING

On the same day, the young Prime Minister Tony Blair (see later in this chapter) makes a hastily prepared speech in which he calls Diana the 'People's Princess'. This appears to reinforce the idea of a Queen versus Diana popularity poll in which the elderly and out-of-touch sovereign is the loser.

Monday 1 September

After much discussion, it is agreed that Diana's funeral should be a modern version of the traditional state funeral. At the time of her death she was no longer a member of the Royal Family. The service is to be held in Westminster Abbey on Saturday morning. By now, Charles has returned from Paris with his ex-wife's body and the coffin lies in peace in St James' Palace.

Tuesday 2 September

The Queen and her family remain in Balmoral where William and Harry are out on the hills all day, stalking deer, fishing, and careering around on quad bikes. Further south, a wave of intense grief is sweeping across the nation. The books of condolence at Kensington Palace and St James' Palace have been rapidly filled and fresh ones ordered. Piles of flowers and soft toys are mounting outside Buckingham and Kensington Palaces. Some contain messages critical of the Queen and the Establishment.

Wednesday 3 September

Crowds are now pouring into London at an estimated rate of 6,000 an hour. Mile-long queues have formed of those waiting to write in the books of condolence or add to the mountain of flowers swelling at the Palace gates.

The weeping masses are unhappy at the Palace's reaction to the tragedy. Where is the Queen? Why is she still relaxing on holiday at this moment of national despair? And why is there no flag flying at half-mast over Buckingham Palace?

WARNING

It matters not that protocol dictates that no flag is ever flown at half-mast over Buckingham Palace. There is either the royal standard (flag), indicating the sovereign is present, or nothing. However, this is not a time for age-old formalities. The people demand that their Head of State empathize with the mood of the nation. Anxious phone calls – more or less as depicted in the 2006 film *The Queen* – fly back and forth between London and Balmoral.

Thursday 4 September

REMEMBER

The mood is turning ugly. Support for the monarchy is dropping – a quarter of the population want it done away with altogether. 'Show us you care!' screams the *Daily Express*. *The Sun*, owned by the Australian republican Rupert Murdoch, asks, 'Where is the Queen when the country needs her?' Prime Minister Blair and his government are rattled; so is the Palace. The Queen is loath to give way to the posthumous demands of one who had undermined her.

Protocol is all very well, but there comes a time . . . Elizabeth backs down. She does not do so because she thinks it the correct thing to do, but because she will do anything to protect the institution she represents. It is announced that the Queen and her family are bringing forward their return to London. They will fly south on Friday afternoon, and Her Majesty will address the nation from Buckingham Palace that evening.

The vast heaps of flowers, many now composting, and the sorrowing throng in The Mall before the Palace are larger than ever. How will they receive their sovereign? Plain-clothes police and security guards mingle with the crowds in case of disturbance.

In a gesture of solidarity with the people, Princes Andrew and Edward walk among the crowd in The Mall. Of course their family cares, they insist. Especially their mother.

Friday 5 September

The Queen's plane touches down at 2pm and she is driven straight to Buckingham Palace. Her car does not sweep through the gates as usual, but stops outside. Elizabeth steps out and, with her husband, looks at the mounds of flowers and reads some of the cards. The crowd, silent at first, breaks into gentle, respectful clapping. A small girl hands Elizabeth a posy of roses, not for Diana but for herself. The Queen has returned to her people and they are glad.

At 6pm that evening, the sovereign gives a live television broadcast from Buckingham Palace. It is the first time she has spoken live on TV since an address she gave on the outbreak of the Gulf War in 1991.

TIP

The hum of the crowd outside floats in through an open window. The speech has been very carefully crafted to avoid Elizabeth having to say things she does not believe true. She speaks of her sorrow as a grandmother and praises Diana as an 'exceptional and gifted human being' who will never be forgotten. She concludes by thanking God for 'someone who made many, many people happy' – but not her, she might have added.

The delivery is, as always, flat and even rather boring. Elizabeth is no actor and certainly no rhetorician, but she had done her duty. It is sufficient.

Saturday 6 September

Diana's coffin, draped with a flower-strewn royal standard, is carried to Westminster Abbey on a horse-drawn gun carriage. Attired in black, Prince Philip, Prince Charles, Diana's brother Charles (Earl Spencer), and – controversially because of their ages – Princes William and Harry walk behind. They are followed by 500 workers from Diana's charities.

Millions line the route; billions watch on television. Elizabeth does not watch from the palace balcony but stands at street level, bowing her head as Diana moves by.

REMEMBER

The funeral service of Diana is memorable for a host of reasons:

>> Apart from a few reserved seats for the Royal Family and VIPs, there is no seating plan. Movie stars sit next to landmine clearance experts.

>> Prime Minister Tony Blair's Bible reading is over-rehearsed and over-blown.

>> Elton John's masterly reworking of his song 'Candle in the Wind' as 'Goodbye English Rose' has millions reaching for their handkerchiefs.

>> Earl Spencer, Diana's media-savvy brother, delivers a furious address about the death of someone who was the 'very essence of compassion, of duty, of style, of beauty'. He castigates the media for their merciless hounding of his sister: 'a girl given the name of the ancient goddess of hunting was, in the end, the most hunted person of the modern age.'

He also swipes at the Royal Family by saying that the young princes' 'blood family' will ensure that they are raised the way Diana would have wished, and 'their souls are not simply immersed by duty and tradition.'

>> After the Earl has finished, crowds watching on giant screens burst into spontaneous applause. The clapping spreads, like ripples on a pond, down the streets and into the great cathedral itself. William and Harry join in, but not the Queen or her husband.

Afterwards, as Diana's coffin is driven from the Abbey to its final resting place in the grounds of Althorp House in Northamptonshire (the Spencer's family seat), a Union Jack (see Chapter 15) is flown at half-mast over Buckingham Palace. Crowds bedeck Diana's hearse with flowers as it crawls through the London streets.

The aftermath of Diana's death

In due course, the high emotion of the first week of September 1997 passed away. Four features of the ongoing Diana story are worth noting:

>> The People's Princess has never been forgotten. She still features in concerts, charitable funds, memorials and statues, and a string of TV dramas and films. Among the most notable are *The Queen* (2006), *The Crown* (2016 onwards), and *Spencer* (2021). Diana has become a figure of legend.

>> Allegations by Mohammed Fayed, Dodi's father, proclaimed that Diana and Dodi's car-crash death had been plotted by the Duke of Edinburgh and the MI6 secret service. These were found to be groundless.

>> The Union Jack is still flown at half-mast over Buckingham Palace at times of national mourning.

REMEMBER

>> Observers have noted a change in Elizabeth. She allows herself to be more relaxed in public, more willing to talk with people during her visits and other engagements. Has she learned from the People's Princess? Now that the rival 'queen of people's hearts' was no more, the role was Elizabeth's for the taking.

Ancient Monarchy meets New Labour

Following Prime Minister Margaret Thatcher's resignation in 1990, her Conservative Party won a surprise victory in the 1992 general election. John Major, the new prime minister, got on well with Elizabeth (see Chapters 8 and 26), but his 21-seat majority in the House of Commons was soon shrinking as his government ran into a series of difficulties.

A number of factors came into play. After four consecutive election victories, the Tories were looking tired and devoid of new ideas. They were riven with internal squabbles about the UK's relationship with the European Union (a situation eventually leading to Brexit, see Chapter 25), and mired in accusations of sleaze as its MPs were found to have taken bribes to ask questions in the House of Commons.

In 1994, the Labour Party chose Tony Blair as its new leader. A charismatic figure with fresh, middle-of-the-road ideas, he soon had the Party soaring up the polls. Three years later, Blair's New Labour Party ('new' to distinguish it from the previous, overtly socialist organisation) swept into power with a whopping 197-seat majority.

Elizabeth had known where she was with John Major. She had spoken to the nation when his government decided to back the US invasion of Iraq in 1991, and he helped her as best he could during the Palace's troubles with Diana. Their weekly chats were said to be relaxed. Tony Blair, the first prime minister to be born since her accession (May 1953) was something different.

Elizabeth was predisposed to be suspicious of Blair for many reasons:

>> Philip didn't like him – he was probably jealous of the Prime Minister's easy manner and popularity.

>> The Queen Mother didn't trust him, calling him 'all teeth and no bite'.

>> Blair's wife, the high-powered, sharp-tongued lawyer Cherie, was a known republican.

>> Blair's Labour Party contained several other avid republicans.

>> Blair was against maintaining hereditary peers in the House of Lords – might he carry the same principle on to the monarchy?

>> Blair had called Diana the 'People's Princess' and this irked Elizabeth. She also disliked the way he had befriended the Princess before the 1997 general election, using her popularity to boost his own.

>> Elizabeth was suspicious of Blair's vainglorious projects. His year 2000 'Millennium Dome', costing £789 million, was initially regarded as an expensive failure, and Elizabeth froze with cold when she attended its opening. Later, hearing Blair talk of 'The Golden Jubilee', the Queen corrected him with a swift, '*My* Golden Jubilee'.

>> Elizabeth feared that Blair's policy of devolving powers to an elected Scottish Parliament and a Welsh Assembly (both in 1999) would weaken her United Kingdom, and perhaps prove to be a step on the road to its break-up.

>> Blair was a townie, Elizabeth a country woman. An enthusiastic supporter of field sports, she objected strongly to Labour's ban on fox hunting (2004) and lobbied unsuccessfully against it.

Like Margaret Thatcher, Blair won three general elections. He remained in power until 2007, and during that time his relations with the Queen warmed considerably. Initially nervous when he met her, he learned to relax in her presence – but never too much. No one gets 'matey' with the Queen, he observed! By the end of his premiership, even Cherie had developed a sneaking admiration for the woman her husband called 'the Best of British'.

TIP

Celebrations and Bereavements

Time waits for no man, not even a crowned Head of State. As the clock ticked towards Elizabeth's Golden Jubilee (see Chapter 23), other events reminded her of the passage of time. The first two were happy occasions:

>> In 1999, Edward, the Queen's youngest son, married the PR executive Sophie Rhys-Jones (see Chapters 24 & 29) in St George's Chapel, Windsor. Perhaps the Palace felt that a Westminster Abbey or St Paul's Cathedral venue would be tempting fate. Besides, the public were probably not ready for another royal spectacular so soon after Diana's funeral.

>> In June 2000, the Queen hosted an 800-guest ball to celebrate her mother's 100th birthday, Margaret's 70th, Anne's 50th and Andrew's 40th. It was, by all accounts, a joyous affair.

TIP

In retrospect it has a somewhat unsavoury feel about it. Among the guests were a certain Mr Jeffrey Epstein and Miss Ghislain Maxwell (see Chapter 25). One wonders who had invited them? Certainly not Elizabeth.

Elizabeth and Philip's Golden Wedding

In the autumn of the year in which Diana had died, Elizabeth and Philip celebrated their 50th wedding anniversary. It was, understandably, a personal celebration with no carriage rides or cheering crowds. Two details of the celebration of 20 November 1997 are worth noting:

>> The speech Elizabeth delivered at a luncheon in London's Guildhall. She thanked Philip for being her 'strength and stay all these years'. More interestingly, she came close to apologizing for the cack-handed way she and her family had reacted to Diana's death.

REMEMBER

The Queen thanked Blair for his 'invaluable' advice, admitting that it was sometimes hard for a sovereign to read the public mood, 'obscured as it can be by deference, rhetoric or the conflicting currents of public opinion.' And, one might add, by personal antipathy.

>> The glittering galaxy of royalty attending a private ball that evening. The guest list read like a gathering of doomed species published by a conservationist organization: the King and Queen of Romania, the King and Queen of Norway, the King and Queen of Sweden, the Queen of Denmark, Princess Sophie and Prince George of Hanover . . . At last, after all the painful trials of the past weeks, Elizabeth could relax. She was safe among her own kind, men and women who understood and sympathized as only fellow royals could.

The death and funeral of Princess Margaret

REMEMBER

Princess Margaret, Elizabeth's talented but troubled younger sister, is the subject of Chapter 13. She died following a number of strokes on the morning of 9 February 2002, aged just 71. Formal expressions of condolence came from around the world, and Charles delivered a tribute on TV. Margaret's coffin lay in state, as Diana's had done, in St James' Palace. On 15 February it was taken to St George's Chapel, Windsor, for a private funeral.

Unusually for a member of the Royal Family, her body was cremated. Her ashes were given a final resting place beside the tombs of her mother and father in the King George VI Memorial Chapel, within St George's.

TIP

The Queen's private thoughts on the death of her sister will never be known. At the funeral, Elizabeth was reported to have looked sadder than at any other moment in her life. Perhaps she considered, as she recalled her father's funeral on the same February date, and the death of Diana five years earlier, how merciless Britain's constitutional monarchy can be. It can destroy all but the very toughest.

The passing of the Queen Mother

REMEMBER

Elizabeth's resilience was soon to be tested again. Her 101-year-old mother was also tough, but even she could not hold off the inevitable. At the start of 2002, she managed to attend Margaret's funeral before her own health began to fail. She died in the Royal Lodge, Windsor Great Park, early in the afternoon of 30 March with Elizabeth at her bedside. The Queen Mother had lived longer than any other member of the Royal Family, ever.

In striking contrast to Margaret's funeral arrangements, the Queen Mother's coffin lay in state in Westminster Hall in London, the magnificent eleventh-century building adjacent to the chambers of the Houses of the Lords and Commons. Members of the armed forces – at one stage briefly replaced by Princes Charles, Andrew and Edward, and Margaret's son, Viscount Linley – stood guard while thousands filed past to pay their respects. Elizabeth and Charles delivered TV tributes to a gracious life that had brought a smile to many faces.

The Queen Mother's Westminster Abbey funeral was attended by a congregation of 2,200 representing all sections of society. Considerable numbers watched on TV, and perhaps a million mourners lined the route as the coffin was taken on its final journey to lie beside that of her husband in St George's Chapel, Windsor Castle.

TIP

Elizabeth had wept at the moment of her mother's death. But throughout the formalities of the funeral she remained as sombrely self-controlled as ever. She had to keep her emotions in check, didn't she? This was, after all, the year of her Golden Jubilee. As always, duty came first.

A Queen's Work is Never Done. . .

Amid the funerals and weddings, balls and galas, it is easy to forget that the Queen's bread-and-butter work never stops. She reads her official papers, meets with prime ministers, opens buildings, and attends parades. Between 1993 and 2002, she visited some 30 countries, ranging from lands recently liberated from communism (Hungary, Poland, the Czech Republic) to old friends in France and India. When she sat beside her dying mother in 2002, she had just returned from a popular Commonwealth tour to Jamaica, Australia and New Zealand (where, in 1986, republicans had pelted her with eggs!).

Reacting to 9/11

REMEMBER

As well as keeping to her standard routine, the Queen has faced a few special moments requiring protocol to be set aside. Such a time came following the Twin Towers attack of 11 September 2001.

On hearing the news, Elizabeth – having learned from the Diana experience – immediately flew back to London from Balmoral. A message to President George Bush spoke of her 'total shock' and the Union Jack was flown at half-mast over Buckingham Palace. Two minutes' silence were held during the Changing of the Guard ceremony outside, and the band played the American as well as the British national anthem. A few days later, the Queen attended a special memorial service in St Paul's Cathedral.

Elizabeth has always been a keen fan of the United States (see Chapter 10). The destruction of the Twin Towers upset her almost as deeply as if London itself had been the target – as it would be four years later (see Chapter 24).

TIP

Heading over to Eire

No British monarch had visited Eire (the Republic of Ireland) since 1911.

The 'Troubles' in Northern Ireland had been one of the most painful issues besetting the early decades of Elizabeth's reign. Indeed, the 'Irish problem' had plagued British governments since the middle of the nineteenth century. At its simplest, it boiled down to the fact that the largely Catholic southern half of the island wished to be an independent state, while the largely Protestant northern part (Ulster) wished to remain within the United Kingdom.

TECHNICAL
STUFF

The dilemma was solved in two stages:

>> First, southern Ireland (Eire) became self-governing in 1922 and a fully independent republic in 1937.

>> Second, John Major and, especially, Tony Blair worked tirelessly during the later 1990s to produce what was called the Good Friday Agreement. The accord of 10 April 1998 set up a power-sharing executive in Northern Ireland that was acceptable to both Protestants and Catholics. Bombings and murders ceased.

In the Good Friday Agreement, the government of Eire gave up its claim to Northern Ireland. The way was now open for the Irish president, Mary McAleese, to invite Elizabeth to undertake the first royal visit to southern Ireland since George V in 1911. The Queen duly accepted and flew to Dublin in May 2011. The four-day tour, under tight security, was a great success.

REMEMBER

Elizabeth wowed her hosts at a state banquet in Dublin Castle by beginning her speech in the notoriously tricky Irish language. 'With the benefit of historical hindsight,' she said (in English) later in the speech, 'we can all see things we would wish had been done differently, or not at all.' Though the Queen's speeches are the work of many hands, she has the final say and will never utter words with which she does not agree. The sentiments she expressed that auspicious day in Dublin Castle were very much her own.

TIP

Going online

In her Golden Wedding Anniversary Guildhall speech in 1997, the Queen reflected on the enormous changes she had witnessed since her accession. She noted how 'during these last fifty years, the mass-media culture has transformed our lives in any number of ways.'

She went on, 'Think what we would have missed if we had never . . . surfed the Net.' At this point, deadpan as always, she offered a little joke at her own expense: 'Or, to be honest, listened to other people talking about surfing the Net.'

Whether or not Elizabeth herself uses the internet doesn't matter much. Certainly those around her do, and the Palace runs a most impressive social media operation. Its website www.royal.uk is slick, sober and unfailingly positive. Everyone on the website smiles – a visitor from another planet couldn't imagine that such a happy family ever exchanged a cross word!

The other social media accounts are equally positive:

» Twitter: @RoyalFamily

» Facebook: www.facebook.com/TheBritishMonarchy

» YouTube has two channels: Royal Family and Royal Fashion

These are very interesting developments in the history of the British monarchy, because:

» They show the institution has grasped how essential it is in the twenty-first century for any business (and the Windsors are said to call themselves 'The Firm', see Chapter 8) to present itself in an upbeat light online. If one wonders about this, imagine what the world would think if the Royal Family did *not* have an online presence. People under the age of 40 would hardly know they existed!

» Certain members of the family – notably Charles and his father – long railed against the press, saying how intrusive they were and how unfair their reporting. The advent of social media enables the royals for the first time to present their side of the story, subtly suggesting that unfavourable reports and tittle-tattle are not always correct.

Perhaps the Royal Family is more cool, more up to date than its indomitable matriarch realizes!

Chapter **22**

The Queen's Animal Friends

This chapter is a little more light-hearted than some others in the book. It looks at the animals in Elizabeth's life, both the cherished and the targeted.

Like most British aristocrats, the Queen considers herself a country woman. Also, like others of her kind, she has a somewhat equivocal attitude towards the animal kingdom. She is very fond of her dogs and horses, yet is happy for others – and herself on occasion – to shoot wild animals and hunt them on horseback for sport.

Let's start by looking at her primary animal passion – horses – before moving on to consider her pets, official gifts, and her views on *bloodsports* (traditionally meaning any sport that involves killing a quarry: for example, fox hunting and deer stalking).

Horsing Around: The Princess and Her Ponies

Elizabeth loves horses and has done so since she was a little girl. Many commentators say she is rarely happier than when in the saddle or more animated than when at the races as a spectator. This passion for equestrianism is part of a tradition that stretches back into the mists of time: not for nothing is hunting on horseback known as 'the sport of kings'.

Following royal equine tradition

TECHNICAL STUFF

For much of human history, a horse was a status symbol. While the poor went on foot, the wealthy rode on horseback. This applied in peace and war – the mounted knight in armour, for instance, was the ultimate medieval war machine. The distinction between the 'poor bloody infantry' and mounted soldiers persisted until World War I (1914–1918), and vestiges of it linger on to this day. Regiments bearing the anachronistic title 'cavalry' (such as Britain's Household Cavalry) still regard themselves as a cut above the others.

Monarchs travelled on horseback until the advent of the carriage in the Renaissance era, though they didn't then abandon the saddle entirely. In 1743, for example, George II was in the saddle when he became the last monarch to lead his troops into combat (nominally at least) at the Battle of Dettingen in Germany (leading an allied army against the French). His successors liked to gallop when engaged in 'the sport of kings' (above) or when simply taking exercise. Latterly, the royals and their upper-class pals adopted the Indian sport of polo (a game once avidly played by Prince Charles and now enjoyed by Princes William and Harry).

TIP

From the time of Henry VIII (see Chapter 2), monarchs have been among the keenest fans of horse racing. James I and Charles I were notable aficionados of the sport, though a special mention must go to Queen Anne for instigating Britain's most famous horseracing venue. Anne owned dozens of horses and followed them to courses in different parts of the country. In 1711, while riding in her carriage near the small Berkshire town of Ascot, she spied what looked like an interesting spot for a horserace. Courtiers followed their sovereign's wishes and arranged a race over the undulating turf. (Anne awarded the winner a silver platter – and the race, known as Her Majesty's Plate, is still run today.) In this manner the celebrated Ascot racecourse came into being. Today it hosts the glamorous Royal Ascot meeting in June, a not-to-be-missed event on Elizabeth's sporting calendar (see later in this chapter).

As noted in Chapter 20, the Queen's daughter Anne is an Olympic horsewoman. She passed her love of equestrianism on to her daughter Zara, who has won eventing medals at both the Olympics and the European Championships (see Chapter 29). The men in the family also share the Queen's delight in horses, though not for racing. Philip played polo and was keen on carriage driving. Like their father Charles, Princes William and Harry have had a go at polo, too.

Learning to ride

In days gone by, all children of well-to-do families were expected to learn to ride. Elizabeth was no exception, and she had twice-weekly riding lessons from the age of three. A year later, on her fourth birthday, her grandfather, George V, gave her a mount of her own – a Shetland pony named Peggy. From that moment on, there was no looking back.

During World War II, when she and her sister Margaret were largely confined to Windsor Castle, they rode out regularly in the Great Park to get a breath of fresh air and let off steam. The experience kept Elizabeth fit and made her into an excellent horsewoman. It also cemented her love of horses, not just riding them but learning about their personalities and characteristics.

TIP

No doubt you have seen a picture of the Queen on horseback. Did you notice anything strange? Yes, she is not wearing a safety helmet. She never does! The reason, we are told, is because it enables her to have her hair ready for a formal occasion at a moment's notice. If her locks were squashed under a hat, she'd need a session with the hairdresser before making a public appearance. It would not do for the monarch to appear dishevelled!

In place of a hard hat, the Queen invariably keeps her hair tidy beneath a custom-made Hermès scarf. Why that particular brand? Because the firm was originally a manufacturer of equestrian gear.

Being in the saddle

When her father acceded to the throne following the abdication of Uncle Edward in 1936 (see Chapter 5), Elizabeth became heir apparent. This required her to learn all kinds of quaint and tricky skills, such as wearing a crown, waving graciously – and riding side-saddle.

At the time of Elizabeth's accession in 1952, riding side-saddle was seen as distinctly odd. The practice had originated in medieval times to allow women to ride wearing long dresses and avoid the undignified necessity of sitting with their legs apart. By the 1950s, when women commonly wore trousers and bikinis were coming into fashion, people were no longer concerned what women did with their legs on a horse. The tradition lingered on only in esoteric horse shows – and, the Establishment decided, in the Trooping the Colour ceremony (see Chapter 1).

Elizabeth took her first side-saddle lessons in 1938, and by the time she acceded to the throne, she was an expert. For Trooping the Colour, she donned a distinctly military-looking costume comprising a black tricorn hat, a red military tunic and a very long, navy blue riding skirt. On anyone else the garb would have looked like something from a revue show, but not on Elizabeth. Her dignity quells mockery at 50 paces.

The Queen's two favourite ceremonial mounts were Tommy and Burmese. She was riding the latter, a black mare gifted by the Royal Canadian Mounted Police in 1969, when she was shot at in 1981 (see Chapter 16). She had such admiration for the mare that, on its retirement in 1986, Elizabeth chose to ride in a light carriage rather than take another horse.

In older age, Elizabeth went back to where she had started, swapping full-size horses for smaller, more easily controlled ponies. She was still in the saddle in her early 90s, and regularly attends the Royal Windsor Show and the rigorous Badminton Horse Trials. At these events, she appears more attentive and animated than at the many formal state occasions she is obliged to attend. This is not altogether surprising – she knows where she is with horses and she doesn't have to listen to their small talk.

As a mark of respect for the Queen's support of all matters equestrian over many decades, in 2014 the FEI (Fédération Equestre Internationale / International Federation for Equestrian Sports) awarded Elizabeth its first ever Lifetime Achievement Award. As the FEI's president at the time was Princess Haya, daughter of King Hussein of Jordan, the awards looked a bit like royals engaging in a bit of mutual back-patting. Nevertheless, Haya's remark about the 'truly extraordinary bond' between the Queen and horses was more than just flattery.

Breeding Equine Success

In addition to her role as a queen, Elizabeth is one of the country's leading breeders of horses of many types, including thoroughbreds and rare breeds. As an owner of many fine racehorses – she is said to have some 30 in training at any one time – she takes a keen interest in race meetings in Britain and overseas.

The Queen's liking for racing and breeding is partly a family matter: she inherited the Royal Stud (the Royal Family's own stud farm where horses are bred) from her father. There is perhaps a second, less obvious, reason. Horses are, she says, 'the greatest levellers in the world'. In other words, while to other human beings she is always a queen and therefore treated differently, to a horse she is just another person. That, for a monarch, must be quite a relief.

Elizabeth is patron of The Thoroughbred Breeders' Association. The Royal Stud at Sandringham, which belongs to her personally and not to the Crown, is said to be the world's oldest thoroughbred breeding enterprise. Housed in delightful Norfolk stone buildings beside lush green paddocks, it comprises stables, yards for covering (insemination), foaling (giving birth), and a nursery. Elizabeth visits regularly and takes a sharp interest in everything that goes on. Those who do not know her well are surprised, even a little embarrassed, by her deep knowledge of the breeding process. She is not in the slightest bit phased by any of it. She knows the animals by name, and can quote the bloodstock line and history of each one.

This interest is much more than a hobby for Elizabeth. The Queen takes horse breeding extremely seriously, doing her best to produce winners and animals capable of producing further winners when sent to stud. Her *yearlings* (year old horses) are moved from Sandringham to Polhampton Lodge Stud Farm near Basingstoke, Hampshire. When ready, they progress to a selected trainer who prepares them ready for racing. On retirement, they are either sold or kept for breeding. The whole process is managed by the Queen's racing manager. For many years, the post was held by Elizabeth's close aristocrat friend, Henry Herbert, Earl of Carnarvon (1924–2001), who went by the courtesy title of Lord Porchester ('Porchie'). He and the Queen spoke on the phone almost every day, and frequently travelled together on business related to horse breeding and racing.

Almost inevitably, Elizabeth's close friendship with Porchie led to rumours of a deeper relationship. One gossip monger even surmised that Porchie was the father of Prince Andrew! Though *The Crown* hints at an affair between the monarch and her racing manager, it is generally thought that their mutual love was of horses and not each other.

As well as racehorses, the Queen breeds Shetland, Fell and Highland ponies. Without royal patronage it is possible that these rare native breeds would go into sharp decline. The Shetland and Highland ponies are managed on the Balmoral estate, keeping alive the traditional bloodlines of these sturdy little workhorses. The Fell ponies, originally from northwest England, are cared for at Hampton Court, the former palace of Henry VIII.

Elizabeth is also patron of the Cleveland Bay Horse Society. This rare breed, once the favourite carriage horse of English aristocrats, was threatened with extinction with the arrival of the motor car. It is said that Elizabeth's personal intervention rescued the Cleveland Bay bloodline when she bought Mulgrave Supreme, a stallion bound for export, and offered him to purebred Cleveland Bay mares for breeding. To this day, royal coaches and carriages are pulled by the Queen's Cleveland Bays.

Backing the winners

Elizabeth was introduced to horse racing in 1942 when she and her father visited the Wiltshire stables of Fred Darling, one of the country's top racehorse trainers. She was awe-struck by Big Game, her father's horse that had recently won the prestigious 2000 Guineas race at the historic Newmarket course in Suffolk. From that moment on, racing ran in her blood.

World War II limited Elizabeth's equine opportunities, and it was not until 1949, the year of her marriage, that she got a racehorse of her own. Astrakhan, a wedding gift from the Aga Khan, came second on its first outing. A few days later, Monaveen, the horse Elizabeth co-owned with her mother, gave the Princess her first winner at Fontwell Park races on the south coast of England.

REMEMBER

The victory at Fontwell Park was the first of more than 1,600 chalked up by the Queen over the years. The best jockeys have ridden for her, proudly wearing the royal colours first displayed by jockeys riding for the Prince Regent (the future George IV – see Chapter 2 for more about him) at the start of the nineteenth century: gold braid around a purple vest, scarlet sleeves, and a black cap with a gold fringe. Elizabeth's horses have won all the major races in England, Wales and Scotland – the *Classics* – apart from the Derby at Epsom, Surrey.

Winners have brought Elizabeth prize money running into millions of pounds sterling. Eager to maintain her form, each morning she opens a horse racing newspaper – generally the *Racing Post* – before she turns to the *The Times* or *The Telegraph* for the usual news and comment.

Of course, the Queen doesn't actually *need* the prize money. Her love of all things equestrian runs much deeper than cash: all her life she has adored the animals and been fascinated by them. Her interest even extends to her reading for pleasure, for among her favourite authors is Dick Francis. And what did Francis do before turning to storywriting? He was a jockey!

Attending Royal Ascot

The racecourse established by Queen Anne in 1711, only six miles from Windsor Castle, is the one Elizabeth visits most frequently. She cannot attend all of Ascot's

26 days of flat and steeplechase racing, but there are two meetings she tries never to miss:

» Royal Ascot in June, a centrepiece of the English social calendar. It features the Queen in a Royal Procession of carriages down the track before the racing begins, and is almost as renowned for the sartorial elegance of the visitors (see the nearby sidebar) as for the racing.

» The July meeting at which the prestigious King George VI and Queen Elizabeth Stakes is run. First held in 1951, the 'King George' is a flat race for horses three years and older over a course measuring one mile, 671 yards. The total prize money (2021) was £875,000, with £496,212 for the winner. The 'Queen Elizabeth' honoured in the race's title is Elizabeth II's mother (the Queen Mother).

TIP

WHERE SOCIETY SHOWS OFF: ASCOT

For five days each summer, British society gathers at Ascot Racecourse to show off its wealth and their style – and if they remain sober, to watch five days of top-class racing. Each day begins at 2pm with the Royal Procession when the Queen and her family drive slowly down the 'straight mile' of the course in open-top carriages known as 'landaus'. The national anthem is played and the royal standard raised.

Royal Ascot's flat races are top quality, with the Gold Cup on the third day – Ladies Day – the most prestigious. Throughout the meeting, champagne-sipping spectators gather in enclosures. The Royal Enclosure, with its strict and detailed dress code dating from the nineteenth century, is reserved for the well-connected.

The Royal Enclosure dress code is:

- **Men** – morning dress, top hat, black shoes.

- **Women** – formal daywear with skirts of 'modest length' and shoulder straps one inch or more in width.

What readers think of this flaunting of class, wealth and privilege is up to them. It's certainly glamorous. Whether the monarchy benefits from being associated with it is a matter of opinion.

Her Majesty's notable racehorse winners

The following five horses are considered among Elizabeth's most successful racers:

>> In 1957, **Carrozza** won the Oaks race for three-year-olds (first run in 1779) at Epsom, helping the Queen become the year's Champion Owner.

>> In 1958, running over approximately one mile at Newmarket, **Pall Mall** triumphed in the Newmarket 2000 Guineas at a price of 20-1.

>> In 1974, again at Newmarket, **Highclere** – named after Porchie's castle – won the 1,000 Guineas. (A 'guinea' was a coin worth one pound and one shilling – £1.05.)

>> In 1977, Elizabeth's Silver Jubilee Year, **Dunfermline** pulled off a remarkable double by winning two Classics: the Epsom Oaks and the St Leger in Doncaster, Yorkshire.

>> In 2012, to the Queen's delight, **Estimate** won the Ascot Gold Cup.

Keeping Pets and Receiving Presents

Medieval monarchs kept dogs as guards and for hunting. Around the time of the Renaissance (from the fifteenth century), smaller species were kept at court as pets, the best known being the King Charles Spaniel. Dogs were among Queen Victoria's favourite pets, and she even established a burial ground for them at Sandringham.

The corgis

Elizabeth is always associated with corgi dogs. Her attachment to the breed is probably explained because her first Welsh corgi – Dookie – was a gift from her father when she was seven years old. Since her accession, she is said to have owned more than 30 dogs of this breed. Bearing names such as Monty, Susan, Holly, Noble, and Linnet, they accompany her, in the words of Princess Diana, like a 'moving carpet'.

Monty, Willow and Holly featured in the opening ceremony of the 2012 Olympic Games, and a corgi (anonymous) was engraved on the Golden Jubilee (see Chapter 23 for more details of this event) crown coin.

The dorgis

When the girls were young, Princess Elizabeth had a Welsh corgi and her sister Margaret had a dachshund named Pipkin. As will happen in the doggy world when their owners are less than attentive, the corgi and Pipkin mated. The result was a corgi–dachshund cross – a *dorgi*.

Finding the breed rather attractive, Elizabeth bred more of them. It is said that, during her lifetime, the Queen has owned around a dozen dorgis, and still has one (Candy) at the time of writing. Despite the dorgi's seal of royal approval, dog breeders say skeletal problems make the cross unhealthy.

As made clear in several episodes of *The Crown*, the Royal Family are avid hunters (and see below), and the kennels at Sandringham and Balmoral house a variety of working dogs trained to accompany a shoot. The prominent breeds are cocker spaniels and Labrador retrievers.

Exotic animals as gifts

As Head of State, the Queen is continually showered with gifts from around the world. In the past, these were often animals, and not all of them were suitable for keeping in the corridors or on the lawns of a palace.

The more domesticated species (pigs, cows, horses, and similar) are kept on the royal estate, while the wilder ones are donated to a zoo.

TIP

Here are six of the more memorable exotic animals gifted to the Queen:

» A pair of pygmy hippopotami from the President of Liberia (1961).

» A Nile crocodile from the River Gambia, a gift for the one-year-old Prince Andrew (1961).

» Four bare-eyed cockatoos, two white Bennett's wallabies and one dwarf cassowary from Sydney, Australia (1963).

» A sloth and two black jaguars from Brazil (1968).

» An African forest elephant from Cameroon (1972).

» Six red kangaroos, two Brolga cranes and one fat-tailed dunnart from Melbourne, Australia (1977).

Supporting Bloodsports

REMEMBER

In her youth, Elizabeth went fox hunting, an essentially aristocratic pursuit. It featured huntsmen in red jackets, blaring horns, baying hounds, and riders charging across the countryside in pursuit of their bushy-tailed quarry. When caught, the fox was invariably torn to pieces by the hounds. Though she objected strongly (though never publicly) when Tony Blair's government banned hunting with dogs (see Chapter 21), Elizabeth did not become an aficionado of the pursuit herself. Her real love was breeding and racing horses.

Elizabeth's attitude towards animals has not always met with approval. She is clearly devoted to domestic species, especially horses and dogs, and shows a keen interest in all the creatures on royal farms. It is thought, too, that she cares for the bats in the rafters of Balmoral Castle. Ancient laws give her ownership, and therefore guardianship, of certain swans and large sea creatures (such as whales and dolphins) within three miles of the UK's shoreline.

Nevertheless, the Queen and her family actively support hunting. Gone are the days when the Duke of Edinburgh shot an eight-foot tiger in India (1961). Indeed, between 1981 and 1996, he was President of the World Wide Fund for Nature (WWF, known as the World Wildlife Fund until 1986). Nevertheless, the royals regularly shoot game birds and stalk deer, and both Prince William and Prince Harry are said to have hunted large wild animals like wild boar.

When Elizabeth lobbied against a ban of hunting with dogs, Prince Charles went as far as to say he would leave the country if the law passed. It did, and he didn't! The royals justify their hunting and shooting by claiming that it ensures species such as deer are properly managed. Opponents say that hunting is cruel, and that maintaining vast stretches of moorland as game habitat prevents urgently needed rewilding and tree-planting on semi-barren hillsides.

» Rejoicing at Queen Elizabeth's Diamond Jubilee in 2012

» Planning for Queen Elizabeth's Platinum Jubilee in 2022

Chapter **23**

The Golden and Diamond Jubilees

This chapter looks at the celebrations and other events held to mark the 50th (2002) and 60th (2012) anniversaries of Queen Elizabeth II's accession to the throne. It also looks forward to her 70th anniversary – her Platinum Jubilee of 2022. These are interesting occasions to compare with her Silver Jubilee of 1977, which is covered in Chapter 15.

The unique occasion of Elizabeth's Platinum Jubilee, and her unprecedented 70-year reign, was the inspiration for this book!

Celebrating 50 Years on the Throne: The Golden Jubilee

TIP

There was some trepidation in court circles about how a celebration of monarchy would go down with the public in 2002. As you can read in Chapter 21, by the twenty-first century the British were less inclined to bow and scrape and tug at their forelocks in the presence of their 'betters'. Moreover, the behaviour of some royals – especially the younger generation – had not done much for the family's image, and unquestioning support from the press and other media could not be guaranteed.

Making careful preparations

As a consequence of the uncertain reaction the Golden Jubilee celebrations would cause, precautions were taken to prepare the ground for a successful Jubilee:

>> A representative panel – including some of the monarchy's critics – was established well in advance to advise on preparations and planning.

>> Throughout 2002, the Queen was careful to avoid any impression that the Jubilee was something she was owed by her people (contradicting her remark to Prime Minister Blair that it was 'my' Jubilee – see Chapter 21). Instead, she emphasized her years of service, and thanked the people of all her realms for their loyalty and devotion. The theme was reinforced by launching the Queen's Golden Jubilee Award, later renamed the Queen's Award for Voluntary Service.

>> In April 2002, 750 members of the press were brought onside with a reception at Windsor Castle. Sympathy for the Queen was already running high after the deaths earlier in the year of Princess Margaret and the Queen Mother (see Chapter 21).

>> Criticism was further deflected by wealthy individuals and corporations, keen to support the Establishment, funding the Jubilee out of their own pockets. This obviated the need for a taxpayer contribution, other than for extra security and policing.

>> The Queen's tours around the UK were arranged to start in regions where support for the monarchy was strongest. That way, positive images of Elizabeth's reception could be presented in advance of her arrival in areas that were less enthusiastically royalist.

>> Similarly, favourable coverage of overseas visits earlier in the year and of an address to both Houses of Parliament on 30 April helped give an impression of undiluted support for the Crown.

>> The Queen's Jubilee itinerary around the UK included visits to a mosque and a Sikh temple, reinforcing an emphasis on inclusivity and unity.

>> The four-day heart of the celebrations in the UK was billed as a 'people's party', suggesting that it would be a fun time for all.

>> As well as the traditional elements of royal pageant – carriage parade, divine service at St Paul's Cathedral, lunch at London's Guildhall, and so on – the celebrations were given a distinctly modern twist with a pop concert in the

grounds of Buckingham Palace. Though not keen on the idea, Elizabeth was persuaded to attend for a short time – wearing earplugs! The Queen (oh the irony!) guitarist Brian May memorably played 'God Save the Queen' while standing on the palace roof, and Paul McCartney led a rendition of 'Hey Jude'.

Dining with five prime ministers

The day before the official celebrations began, Elizabeth and Philip had dinner at Number 10 Downing Street (the prime minister's official London residence) with all the living prime ministers whom she had appointed. The older ones had passed away long before, but the 90-year-old Jim Callaghan was there, together with Edward Heath, Margaret Thatcher, John Major, and Tony Blair, the incumbent of Number 10 at the time. Many were accompanied by their partners.

Further echoes of the past were provided by relatives of Winston Churchill, Harold Macmillan, Alec Douglas Hume, and the widows of Anthony Eden and Harold Wilson. What they all made of each other and what they said now their political rivalries were over, we will probably never know. But they were in agreement over one thing: their constitutional monarch had done her job excellently.

Proving popular at party time

REMEMBER

The cynics and sceptics were proved wrong, and the Golden Jubilee proved a great success. The Buckingham Palace concerts (there was a classical gig as well as a pop one) were attended by sell-out crowds and watched by millions all around the world. The parade on 4 June attracted a crowd of over a million. Spectators remained afterwards to cheer the 76-year-old Queen as she stood on the balcony of Buckingham Palace. Spontaneous renditions of the national anthem and the patriotic song 'Land of Hope and Glory' rose into the London air.

TIP

For most people, the enduring memory of the occasion was participating in one of the outdoor parties held in streets and on village greens up and down the land. In my own small village, a local farmer hired an enormous marquee for the occasion. Amid the flags and streamers, we ate and drank, chatted, and sang traditional songs in a spirit the elderly said they had not experienced since the days of World War II.

The jollity was probably more patriotic and community-orientated than royalist. But that didn't matter much. The Jubilee had been an excuse for a splendid party – directly or indirectly, Elizabeth had warmed the heart of the nation.

Lighting up the Empire State Building

Reflecting the growing spirit of republicanism in many of Elizabeth's overseas realms, Jubilee celebrations beyond the UK were relatively muted. However, one striking tribute sticks in the memory.

As a gesture of thanks to the Queen and the UK at the time of the 9/11 attacks, New York City marked the Golden Jubilee in its own special way. On the night of 4 June 2002, the top of the Empire State Building was flooded with the Queen's purple and gold colours.

Jaunting 40,000-miles around the world

The Queen and Prince Philip kicked off the Jubilee year in February with a brief yet quite well-received visit to Jamaica. The reception in New Zealand, whose prime minister had recently spoken of the inevitability of the country becoming a republic, was less warm. The five-day visit to Australia that followed was a relatively low-key tour too, reflecting Australians' ambivalent attitude towards the couple's monarchial status.

In contrast, the royal couple's 12-day Jubilee tour of Canada in October, though not attracting massive crowds, was generally well-received. Only in French-speaking Quebec did the Queen meet with open hostility. Elsewhere, she watched parades, attended lunches and dinners, gave tactful speeches, attended religious services and unveiled monuments with her customary unspectacular calm.

Following In the Footsteps of Victoria: The Diamond Jubilee

TIP

Perhaps taking a leaf from the book of Queen Victoria, who had celebrated her own Diamond Jubilee on 20 June 1897, Elizabeth established the conservative tone of her Jubilee on 18 May 2012 with a private dinner in Windsor Castle. Her guests? Not the poor and downtrodden, nor those whose tireless voluntary work kept society going, but a glittery galaxy of the world's hereditary heads of state.

Beside the Royal Family sat an unprecedented collection of kings and queens (some who had lost their thrones and one – the King of Yugoslavia – whose country no longer existed), crown princes, ordinary princes and princesses, emirs, sheikhs, a sultan, an emperor, and a Yang di-Pertuan Agong (from Malaysia):

- >> **European countries represented:** Belgium, Bulgaria, Denmark, Greece (Hellenes), Monaco, Liechtenstein, Luxembourg, the Netherlands, Norway, Romania, Sweden, Yugoslavia.
- >> **Middle Eastern states represented:** Abu Dhabi, Bahrain, the Hashemite Kingdom of Jordan, Kuwait, Qatar, Saudi Arabia.
- >> **Asian states represented:** Brunei, Japan, Malaysia, Thailand, Tonga.
- >> **African states represented:** Lesotho, Morocco, Swaziland.

Becoming re-dedicated to a life of service

Other features of the Diamond Jubilee mirrored those of the Golden Jubilee ten years earlier. Countless pieces of memorabilia were made, medals struck, street parties enjoyed, beacons lit, thanksgiving services and a Palace pop concert held, and the Queen made the obligatory appearance on the balcony of Buckingham Palace before an enthusiastic crowd.

REMEMBER

Unlike in 2002, the 86-year-old Queen did not tour the Commonwealth in person. It was now the turn of the younger generation. Princes Charles and Camilla (now Duchess of Cornwall) went to Australia, Canada, New Zealand, and Papua New Guinea. Prince William and the Duchess of Cambridge visited Malaysia, Singapore, and islands in the Pacific, while Prince Harry toured the Caribbean.

Perhaps the most touching moment of the entire Jubilee came at the start of the year. Recalling the speech she gave on her 21st birthday all those years ago, when she had promised to devote her 'whole life' to her people's service, on 2 February 2012 Elizabeth announced, 'In this special year . . . I dedicate myself anew to your service.'

Even her sternest critics appreciated the transparent sincerity of her words.

Falling (a little) flat

Compared with the 2002 Golden Jubilee, Elizabeth's Diamond Jubilee of 2012 was less successful. A number of factors contributed to this:

- >> Following the global banking crisis of 2007–2008, Britain's Conservative government had instigated a policy of strict economic austerity. Local and national government services had been cut back and the household budgets of many families were under strain. Against this background, in some circles the decision to fund the Diamond Jubilee with £1 million of taxpayers' money was resented.

>> The Jubilee celebrations of 2–5 June came only a few weeks before the opening of the Summer Olympic Games in London. Inevitably, mounting excitement over the forthcoming sporting extravaganza overshadowed the royal celebrations.

>> The centrepiece of the 4-day Jubilee weekend (a Diamond Jubilee Pageant on the River Thames of 1,000 boats from around the Commonwealth) failed to capture the public's imagination. Featuring the Queen being rowed along in a brand-new retro barge, the show was quaint and backward-looking – not an impression the monarchy wanted to give in the 21st century. To make matters worse, the event took place on a miserable cold day of pouring rain.

>> The hospitalization of Prince Philip with a urinary infection on 4 June put another dampener on the occasion.

>> Banksy, the popular street graffiti artist, articulated anti-Jubilee sentiment with a striking mural on the wall of a store in London's Wood Green area. Entitled 'Slave Labour', it showed a deprived child sewing together small Union Jack flags to make Jubilee bunting. The image attracted widespread attention in the UK and overseas.

Planning for the Platinum Jubilee

At the time of writing, arrangements are under way for what the British government has described as a 'once-in-a-generation' show to commemorate Elizabeth's 70th year on the throne in 2022. The description might be dismissed as over-zealous hype from a boosterish administration. In fact, it is an understatement – *no* previous generation has ever witnessed a monarch of Elizabeth's longevity.

Celebrations begin on 6 February and culminate in a four-day *bank holiday* (national public holiday) 2–5 June. Among the planned street parties, pageants, parades and so forth, two special events have caught the public imagination: a competition to bake the finest 'Platinum Pudding' and the Queen's Green Canopy scheme ('Plant a Tree for the Jubilee').

TIP

Though genetics and medical science have undoubtedly helped in enabling the Queen to keep going so long, her remarkable self-discipline has been significant. Excess in all things is unknown to her. And yet . . . before we start celebrating too early, perhaps a whispered word of caution is in order.

The health of the 95-year-old Elizabeth cannot be taken for granted. In the autumn of 2021, she went into hospital for tests and subsequently missed a number of engagements, including the important Remembrance Day service (see Chapter 25). Some commentators suggested that she looked older and frailer since the death of her husband, Prince Philip. She had also appeared in public walking with a stick.

For more than a year, lives and livelihoods beyond the Castle and Palace walls had been smitten by the COVID-19 pandemic. People's energy was low, their spirits dampened. Economic stagnation and inflation loomed in post-Brexit UK, and global tensions ran high along disputed borders.

Against this background, would the nation be ready to party?

Holding unprecedented popularity

REMEMBER

Opinion polls are fickle, but on the whole it is probably true to say that the Queen's popularity has never been higher. The great bulk of the population of the UK and the Commonwealth had never known any other Head of State. Very few have ever sung 'God Save the King'. A world without her steady, familiar presence on TV, on coins, and on postage stamps is almost unimaginable.

For millions if not billions, Elizabeth Windsor has become a comfort blanket in a turbulent world. What was there for confused citizens to hold on to when ecologists prophesied doom, religious fundamentalists threatened Armageddon, social radicals overturned long-held beliefs about personal identity, academics rejected history and tradition as the spawn of blinkered bigotry? Politicians came and went; media celebrities were revealed to have feet of clay; respected clerics and community leaders were exposed as abusers; the morning's news was stale by the afternoon.

To paraphrase Macbeth's famous adage, 'nothing was but what was not.' Except the Queen of England.

In the words of Prime Minister Cameron (see Chapter 25 for more about him) this frail yet indomitable old lady was 'a permanent anchor . . . grounding us in certainty.' Small wonder that people all over the world were prepared to honour her with a party like no other.

Unique celebrations for a unique queen

The planned Platinum Jubilee celebrations include:

>> A cornucopia of flags, medals, mugs, plates, and other memorabilia.

>> A four-day UK national holiday (2–5 June 2022).

- An extra-special, larger-than-ever Trooping the Colour (see Chapter 1 for more about this event).

- As at previous Jubilees, a chain of flaming beacons to be lit across the UK. Beacons also to be lit in Commonwealth capitals.

- A thanksgiving service at St Paul's Cathedral.

- A 'Platinum Party' at Buckingham Palace.

- A 'Big Jubilee Lunch' on Sunday 5 June in every city, town, village, and street in the UK.

- A 'Plant a Tree for the Jubilee' scheme to produce a lasting Queen's Green Canopy across the realm.

TIP

Britain does not have a national day like the USA's Thanksgiving or France's Bastille Day, but when the occasion arises it does know how to party. Let's hope Elizabeth II's Platinum Jubilee is remembered as such an occasion.

Chapter **24**

Succession Secured

This chapter focuses on the years surrounding Elizabeth's Golden and Diamond Jubilees (roughly 2003–2013). After the turbulence of the 1990s, for the Queen and her family the new millennium brought in a period of relative domestic calm and stability.

Moreover, as three of her children settled into stable marriages and she into old age, Elizabeth took heart from the arrival of great-grandchildren. This ensured that her direct Windsor descendants would be on the throne for many, many decades – so long as (I'm sure she would add) it was what the people wanted.

Entering a Brave New World

The course of history never runs smooth. For the UK, the years following the 2002 Golden Jubilee (see Chapter 23) were no exception.

Britain's decision to join the US-led invasion of Iraq in 2003 attracted massive protests in many cities around the UK. These in no way reflected sympathy for the

Islamic terrorism that had caused the death and destruction in New York on 9/11. Rather, they were based partly on opposition to war as a matter of principle, and partly on rejection of the inclusion of Saddam Hussein, Iraq's essentially secular dictator, in President Bush's 'axis of [Islamic] evil'.

Scepticism was compounded when Blair's Labour government announced that the invasion was justified because Iraq harboured 'weapons of mass destruction'. The assertion – apparently believed by most in the British government – was supported by what the press called a 'dodgy dossier' of evidence. After the invasion, no nuclear, chemical or biological weapons were found in Iraq.

REMEMBER

The war and the opposition to it put the Queen in a tricky constitutional position. She is nominal commander-in-chief of Britain's armed forces, and all senior members of her family hold military positions (check out the sidebar, "The Queen as head of the armed forces"). Charles, grandest of all, holds the ranks of admiral, general and air chief marshal. Even meek and mild Edward, the failed Royal Marine (see Chapter 20), is Commodore-in-Chief of the Royal Fleet Auxiliary.

WARNING

The invasion of Iraq took place in Elizabeth's name because the government was *her* government. We do not (yet) know what she personally thought of that move. That has not stopped speculation. The 2013 play *The Audience*, by *The Crown* author Peter Morgan, suggested (without firm evidence) that Elizabeth strongly urged Blair to reconsider the invasion. In her significant 2003 Christmas message, delivered from an army barracks in Windsor, she spoke of the military's professional teamwork rather than how it was ousting a dictator who threatened world peace. More recently, journalists have suggested (again, without evidence) that Prince Charles was even more opposed to the invasion than his mother.

THE QUEEN AS HEAD OF THE ARMED FORCES

The Queen's role as head of the armed forces goes back to the time when kings literally led their armies into battle. Today, ultimate allegiance of the army, navy and airforce to a constitutional monarch rather than to a politician is – theoretically, at least – a safeguard against the misuse of power by an overmighty subject. It also means that a non-political figure is the focus of attention on ceremonial military occasions, such as the Remembrance Sunday Parade and the awarding of military honours.

Elizabeth, whose son and grandson have seen active service, sees the military through the eyes of a mother as well as a commander. Accordingly, in 2009, she set up the Elizabeth Cross medal for families who had lost one of their number in a military operation, or as a result of terrorism, since 1948.

In 2005, British-born extremist Islamic suicide bombers struck in central London, killing 52 and injuring over 700. The Queen and other members of the Royal Family visited the injured in hospitals, and Elizabeth made a significant contribution to the London Bombings Relief Charitable Fund. Her Christmas message that year, while drawing people's attention to the remarkable acts of selflessness and charity that the attacks had inspired, was blunt in its condemnation of 'brutal terrorism'.

TIP

From one crisis to another . . . in 2008, the world was hit by a critical failure in its banking system and Britain was plunged into a serious recession. The Palace's reaction is examined below. All I will say here is that the recession drew attention to the privileged and super-rich (such as the American Warren Buffett) who were able to ride out the downturn unscathed. This (as well as foul weather!) may go some way to explaining why the Diamond Jubilee of 2012 (see Chapter 23) was not greeted as rapturously as the Golden Jubilee had been.

Becoming a Happier Family

Compared to the upheavals going on outside the Palace during the 'noughties', within those dull grey walls all was much calmer than it had been during the 1990s. The biggest change was in Elizabeth's children, three of whom developed into models of domestic stability.

Charles

REMEMBER

On 9 April 2005, Charles did what many say he should have done 35 years previously – he married Camilla Parker-Bowles. Had he done so when they first met in 1970, and she was Camilla Shand, how much pain might have been avoided? But it was not to be.

After their first marriages had broken down, Charles and Camilla re-established their relationship around 1985 (see Chapter 16). She divorced in 1995, he in 1996. The Queen publicly accepted Camilla as part of her son's life in 2002. Despite the Church of England's more relaxed attitude to divorce and remarriage, Charles thought it wise as heir to the throne not to be married in a religious ceremony (as Anne had done, outlined later in this chapter) but in Windsor's fine seventeenth-century guildhall. His mother and father did not attend.

After their marriage, Charles and Camilla attended a service of prayer and dedication in Windsor Castle's St George's Chapel conducted by the Archbishop of Canterbury. This time his parents were among the 720 high-profile guests.

Outside, a crowd of 2,000 waited to greet them. Poor Camilla! Crowds of that size materialized on a mere rumour that Princess Diana might appear on her way to the gym.

Foreign media was reluctant to forgive Camilla. They unfairly held her partly responsible for breaking their dream, depriving them of their fairy tale princess. At first, many in Britain felt the same way. But opinions gradually changed. Memories of the 'People's Princess' faded, and people became accustomed to Charles and Camilla attending royal functions together. Those who met the Duchess of Cornwall (Camilla's new title) appreciated her open, straightforward manner.

TIP

Camilla could not, of course, hope to match Diana's charm and personal magnetism, and she was sensible enough not to try. She had qualities that the 'Queen of Hearts' lacked. Strong, practical and pragmatic, she has proved a good foil to her insecure husband. Above all, she is devoted to him. As many came to see, she was the sort of partner the unconfident Charles had needed all along.

Anne

Anne, whose divorce and remarriage to Sir Timothy Laurence in 1992 (see Chapter 19) had broken the mould of royal marriages being for life, continued to earn public respect for her tireless round of royal duties.

In 2006, she and the wider family received further favourable publicity when her daughter Zara (Phillips), an equestrian star just like her mother, was voted BBC Sports Personality of the Year. Zara's marriage to the England rugby star Mike Tindall in 2011 was also well received.

Edward

As far as PR was concerned, Edward and his wife Sophie (nicknamed 'the girl next door' because of her relatively normal background) got off to a distinctly rocky start. The Prince's widely mocked 'Royal Knockout' TV show (see Chapter 20) was followed by a string of unwatchable (except in the USA, apparently) programmes produced by his loss-making TV company. Sophie had her difficulties, too, when she was duped into making indiscrete remarks about members of the Royal Family.

The next year, the royal couple – sporting the title Earl and Countess of Wessex – gave up their outside interests to concentrate on royal duties. Though Edward failed to inspire, Sophie's unpretentious and down-to-earth manner won her friends among the public and the media. Indeed, she appears to have become one of Elizabeth's most trusted family members. Furthermore, unlike Edward's three siblings, he and Sophie managed to stay married! Their two children, Lady Louise Mountbatten-Windsor and James Mountbatten-Windsor, Viscount Severn, were born in 2003 and 2007 respectively.

Opening the London Olympics

Elizabeth's role in the spectacular opening of the 2012 London Olympic Games may well come to be regarded as her finest hour. Directed by Danny Boyle, it featured a film clip in which James Bond (played by the British actor Daniel Craig) entered Buckingham Palace to rescue Her Majesty. He finds her working at her desk and waits patiently for a while before she turns to him with the now famous greeting, 'Good evening, Mr Bond'.

TIP

It is said that the Queen agreed to take part in the sketch on condition that she was given a speaking part – and she chose the line to deliver. For someone who, on her own admission, is not an actor, the timing was perfect.

The film shows the Queen and Bond boarding a helicopter and flying low over iconic London landmarks. Below them, crowds wave and cheer. Inevitably, Winston Churchill gets a look in as his statue in Parliament Square comes to life and salutes the monarch as she soars by.

Back in the Olympic stadium, a real helicopter hovered overhead and a figure wearing the same outfit as the Queen when she met Bond at the Palace, parachuted to the ground. Elizabeth herself, expressionless as ever, then entered the stadium to take her seat. Gasps of astonishment melded into rapturous applause. The memorable stunt and the Queen's participation in it changed many people's perception of her. Why couldn't she have more people like Danny Boyle on her staff, they wondered, rather than those stuffy Eton-and-Army types?

Making Ripples on the Royal Pond

Not quite everything was sweetness and light at the Palace. Most of the incidents may be passed over as the sort of slip-ups that inevitably arise when someone is under intense media scrutiny:

» In 1997, Paul Burrell, a footman at Buckingham Palace and Princess Diana's butler, had been awarded the Royal Victorian Medal, an honour given by the monarch for services to the Royal Family. Five years later, the police charged him with stealing and hoarding some of Diana's possessions. The case was dropped when Burrell revealed that he had previously told the Queen what he had done. Why had Elizabeth not made this known when Burrell was accused? Had she forgotten? Or did she want the trial halted to avoid embarrassing revelations about Diana and the Royal Family?

» The following year, *Daily Mirror* newspaper journalist Ryan Parry got a job as a *footman* (male servant) inside Buckingham Palace. When his illicit photographs and observations, which included the sort of TV programmes Elizabeth watched and Andrew's liking for stuffed toys, were splashed across his newspaper, the Palace was furious. It obtained an injunction banning further revelations and ordering all unpublished pictures to be destroyed. But the damage had been done: what if Parry had been a terrorist rather than a journalist?

» In 2003, Elizabeth literally slipped up at Sandringham, leading to a cartilage repair operation on her right knee. The procedure was repeated on her left knee the following year.

» In 2005, Harry made a fool of himself and attracted worldwide opprobrium when he was photographed at a fancy-dress party wearing a Nazi uniform, complete with swastika armband.

» Philip's tactless remarks continued to cause embarrassment. In 2002, he lived up to his reputation as 'Wince Philip' by telling a security officer in a bullet-proof vest that she looked 'like a suicide bomber'. While talking to the leader of the Scottish Conservatives in 2010, he pointed to a tartan design and asked, 'Do you have a pair of knickers made out of this?' Her response was not recorded.

Unfortunately, not all fall into this category, especially where Andrew is concerned.

Andrew's murky goings-on

With Charles, Anne and Edward in secure marriages and behaving more or less as she expected them to, the only one of Elizabeth's children left for her to worry about was Andrew. Randy Andy's lack of brains and haughty nature had always been a bit of a problem, but as the years went by there were rumours that he had added a new sin to his portfolio – avarice.

Andrew, Duke of York, is not and never has been short of money. In 2008, his mother was giving him an annuity of around £250,000. Refundable expenses are believed to have almost doubled this. Two years later, his expenses as a UK trade envoy were said to have topped £620,000. His critics attest that Andrew's extravagant expenses are the least of their concerns.

In 2001, Andrew was appointed to the unpaid position of the United Kingdom's Special Representative for International Trade and Investment. The suitability of 'Airmiles Andy' for the post seemed to come from his title rather than any innate ability or track record in business, trade or finance. Once in post, he is said to have mixed with wealthy men of dubious reputation in countries like Kazakhstan, Uzbekistan, Libya, and Tunisia, and to facilitate arms deals with regimes that had a poor record on human rights. His alleged backhanders are rumoured to run into many millions – how else, some ask, could he live the life of a jet-set oligarch?

TIP

All these stories of Andrew's misconduct may be untrue, figments of the fevered imagination of jealous republicans. But when compounded with allegations of abusive racial language and serious sexual misconduct (see Chapter 25), they cannot but harm the standing of a monarchy that Elizabeth has worked so hard to protect. We are left wondering whether, in pursuing her own course so rigorously, she paid insufficient attention to the emotional and ethical training of her children.

Weathering recession and austerity

TECHNICAL STUFF

After the banking crisis and the recession that followed (see earlier in this chapter), the British expressed no overwhelming confidence in any of the political parties standing in the 2010 general election. The result was a *hung parliament* (one in which no single party has a majority of seats). After discussion, the Conservatives (307 seats out of 650) under David Cameron formed a coalition government with the Liberal Democrats (57 seats) led by Nick Clegg. The defeated Labour Party of Prime Minister Gordon Brown had mustered 258 seats.

George Osbourne, the Chancellor of the Exchequer, instituted a programme of financial austerity in which government expenditure was trimmed by an average of 19 percent across all departments. Understandably, questions were asked about whether the Royal Family were sharing in the hardship experienced by everyone else.

WARNING

Against this background, the Civil List was replaced by the Sovereign Grant (see Chapter 17). A reduced amount of taxpayer funding received by the Royal Family was fixed for 5 years. Nevertheless, critics still felt that, at a time of austerity, the disparity in wealth between the royals and nearly everyone else was morally objectionable. One noted how wrong it was for the monarch to announce in the 2010 Queen's Speech (see Chapter 8) that the legislative programme of reduced spending would be 'based upon the principles of freedom, fairness, and responsibility.' Could a woman wearing a hat (the crown) worth £1,000,000 really talk of fairness?

Going Green: Environmental Efforts

In some ways, the Royal Family's green credentials have always been strong. Growing up during World War II, the Queen is well known for opposing waste, and Prince Charles was into environmental matters long before they were widely recognised as a major issue.

In her recorded address to the 2021 COP26 Climate Summit, Elizabeth quoted a prescient statement her husband had made way back in 1969:

If the world pollution situation is not critical at the moment, it is . . . certain . . . [to] become increasingly intolerable within a very short time . . . If we fail to cope with this challenge, all the other problems will pale into insignificance.

How have his wife and family reacted to Philip's warning? Let's take a look:

>> Charles has led the Royal Family's green challenge, expressing sympathy for the aims and frustrations of environmental campaigners. He runs his vintage Aston Martin car on E85 (85 percent bioethanol and 15 percent unleaded petrol), with much of the latter coming from surplus wine and alcohol from fermented whey. The Duchy of Cornwall (see Chapter 17) is strong on organic farming, and Charles is Patron of the Rare Breeds Survival Trust as well as running Highgrove (see Chapter 9) on a sustainable basis. He works to ensure that all timber bought by the Royal Household is sustainably sourced, and he has recently overseen the conversion of 6,000 acres of the Sandringham estate to organic farming. The estate now has ten managed areas of wetland.

>> The Royal Household has, where practicable, fitted solar panels on its buildings and improved insulation. As you may imagine, this is not easy in a palace or castle. Waste materials are recycled, energy-efficient lighting installed, and the household's partnership with Computer Aid International has led to thousands of pieces of electronic equipment going to developing countries.

>> The household has also installed numerous smart meters and encouraged further green initiatives. The installation of heat and power units at Buckingham Palace and Windsor Castle have lowered greenhouse gas emissions. Forty percent of Windsor Castle's electricity is produced by hydroelectric power generated by the nearby River Thames.

>> Measures taken in the Buckingham Palace gardens, including the introduction of colonies of bees, have made an environmentally friendly haven in the heart of London. The same spirit inspired the Queen's Green Canopy initiative for the 2022 Platinum Jubilee (see Chapter 23).

> » Princes William and Harry have expressed serious concern over environmental degradation. In 2021, William set up the £50 million, celebrity-backed Earthshot Prize Awards. Their aim is to stimulate five areas of progress towards restoring nature and limiting global warming. To mark the scheme's launch, Buckingham Palace was floodlit with green light.

WARNING

While recognising the Royal Family's environmental efforts, campaigners say its green credentials remain chequered:

> » If Charles is serious about protecting the environment, should he be flying to Switzerland for an annual skiing holiday, and maintaining three stately homes (Clarence House, Highgrove, and Birkhall on the Balmoral estate)? Apparently, he has objected to the construction of wind farms near his estates.

> » The Royal Family are prodigious travellers by air, often using private jets and helicopters (that are particularly environmentally unfriendly).

> » To facilitate deer stalking and grouse shooting, large areas of the 800,000-acre royal estate are kept devoid of all but basic vegetation. Environmentalists say the land is suitable for rewilding, fostering biodiverse natural growth, especially of trees, and locking up more carbon.

> » According to the Wild Card campaign group, the Duchy of Cornwall estate has significantly fewer trees per acre than the national average.

> » Horse-drawn carriages are fine, but does the Royal Family need all its fleet of gas-guzzling limousines?

TIP

The Queen and her family are great at making green gestures, but – given the global reach of their brand – there is more they could to take the lead over environmental issues and inspire others to build a greener, more sustainable future. Happily, there were signs of this in the autumn of 2021, when Prince William featured prominently at the Glasgow–based United Nations Climate Change Conference.

Exploring the Difficult Lives of William and Harry

Considering William and Harry's difficult early lives (see Chapter 24), one can begin to understand why Queen Elizabeth was brought up the way she was (see Chapters 4 and 6). Raised in the bubble of a royal court, she never went to school, met few children of her own age, and had very little practical understanding of the everyday lives of those beyond the Palace walls. In other words, her upbringing was anything but normal.

But that was the whole point – Elizabeth's life would never be 'normal', so why pretend that it would be? Normal people are not curtseyed to and bowed at from childhood; they are not surrounded by photographers whenever they set foot outside the front door; they do not have their every move shadowed by a detective.

This is the modern British monarchy's dilemma:

>> From Elizabeth it has inherited many of the forms and customs of the Victorian and Edwardian eras: the deference and deliberate remoteness that to some is the 'magic' of monarchy and to others the unacceptable snobbery of entitlement.

>> Princesses Anne and Diana, and Sophie Countess of Wessex (and even Prince Philip) have shown there is a less remote, more grounded way of going about its business.

Unfortunately, these approaches are largely incompatible, leaving Charles, heir to Elizabeth's throne, torn between the two. Prince William and to a lesser extent Prince Harry have the same problem. The normal and the royal – McDonalds and magic – just don't mix.

The princes at their mother's funeral

The clash of the two styles of monarchy was vividly illustrated at the funeral of Princess Diana. Her family initially wanted a low-key private funeral. Her popularity demanded something larger, grander.

And her sons? Tradition needed them walking, stony-faced and sombre-suited, behind their mother's coffin. William opposed the idea but was persuaded by his grandfather to set aside his teenage instinct for self-preservation. Harry later described the funeral walk as an 'out of body' experience. Beside the road thousands wept, but the two young boys, because of who they were, had to remain dry-eyed. It was what monarchy Elizabeth-style expected.

Don't be too hard on the Royal Family because of this one incident. For many children, parental separation is a painful and confusing process. It is almost impossible to imagine how difficult it was for William and Harry to process it under the salacious glare of the media. Charles and Diana – and to some extent Elizabeth – must take credit for the boys turning out as well as they have.

The Queen received a lot of flak for remaining in Balmoral with her grandsons when the news of Diana's death came through (see Chapters 21 and 27). With hindsight, perhaps the decision does not look as cold-hearted as some made it out to be at the time. Elizabeth, having seen the strain of merciless media attention on her children, was doing what she could to protect her grandsons from the same.

The steady one: William's education and service

The Royal Family made a wise move when they sent William and Harry to Eton for their secondary education rather than to the heartier Gordonstoun where their father had been so disconsolate (described in Chapter 14). Eton's urbane and sophisticated atmosphere, high academic standards, and wide range of top-quality facilities gave the boys a more rounded education than they would probably have received elsewhere (see Chapter 6).

TIP

That said, the choice of school had two drawbacks:

>> Eton is an all-boys school. Throughout their teenage years, neither William nor Harry had daily contact with girls. This may have made them awkward when trying to establish meaningful relationships with the opposite sex for the first time.

>> For all its excellence, Eton is a very privileged and exclusive institution. During their time there, the boys mixed with none but the wealthy from upper and upper-middle-class backgrounds. The rest of the world was socially and economically below them. This made it harder for them to understand the lives of ordinary citizens. This applied less to Harry, who was not burdened from birth with the title 'heir to the throne'.

Thanks partly to his own academic ability and partly to excellent tuition, William achieved sound A-Level results: an A grade in Geography, a B in Art, and a C in Biology. It is to his credit that he motivated himself to do as well as he did, as his future employment in no way depended on his school or university performance.

After school, when the media had agreed to let him get on with his life in peace, William took a *gap year* (12 months out between school and university). He spent it gaining military experience with the army in Belize, working on a farm, travelling in Africa, and teaching in Chile. Though somewhat tokenistic activities (like Elizabeth joining the ATS during the war – see Chapter 6), they did allow him to see a little of the outside world and learn to care for the less fortunate as his mother had taught him.

The wild one: Harry, soldier and playboy

TIP

It is thought that Prince Harry, only 12 when Princess Diana died, was more affected by his mother's death than his older brother. He would later criticize his father's stiff-upper-lip attitude at the time of Diana's fatal accident as unsympathetic, even wounding (see Chapter 25).

Just like his mother and Uncle Andrew, Prince Harry was not cut out for academic study. In fact, given the expertise of Eton's teaching, his meagre A-Levels grades (a B in Art, and a D in Geography – just enough to allow him to train as an army officer) were almost embarrassing. There are rumours that he had a bit of extra assistance to achieve even those grades. He did, however, thrive on the school's extra-curricular activities, especially sport and the military cadet force.

Harry followed William with a gap year after school. He worked on a cattle station in Australia before spending two months with orphaned children in the tiny kingdom of Lesotho. Here he became close friends with the king's youngest brother, Prince Seeiso, with whom he shared a commitment towards charity work.

REMEMBER

Harry returned to the UK in May 2005 and enrolled at the Royal Military Academy, Sandhurst, as Officer Cadet Wales. He graduated as a commissioned officer a year later and joined a regiment of the prestigious Household Cavalry. By now he was beginning to get a reputation in the tabloid press as a bit of a lad. Girls, alcohol, drugs. As he would candidly admit in 2021, there were times when he struggled to come to terms with his mother's death and the events surrounding it. The constant attention brought on by his royal position did not make things any easier (see Chapter 25).

Introducing Catherine Middleton

For the better part of the first decade of the new millennium, the relationship between Prince William – second in line to the throne – and Catherine Elizabeth Middleton (b. January 1982) was a gossip's dream. It showed the piranha-like hunger of social media, and how hard it is for the monarchy to maintain its magic at a time when deference is distinctly unfashionable.

In the end, showing strength and affection in equal measure, the relationship survived into what appears to be a highly successful marriage. They were left wary of the press, whom William blamed for hounding his mother to an early grave. But monarchy thrives on the oxygen of publicity . . . before William inherits the Crown, he and his wife will have to decide where and how to draw the line.

In the autumn of 2001, Catherine – Kate – and William enrolled at St Andrews University, near the famous golf course on the east coast of Scotland. They were in the same hall of residence and ended up taking the same Art History MA degree. They were able to strike up a relationship relatively free from media intrusion because the press – as they had during his gap year – agreed to leave William in peace during his time as an undergraduate. He also adopted the pseudonym 'Steve' to make it more difficult for stories about him to get into the hands of the media.

The couple shared houses together (with friends) from 2003 onwards, and by the time of their graduation in 2005 they were very much an item. That's when the press ended their ceasefire and the trouble began. As William did business internships before joining the army in January 2006, Kate began working in London. She was pestered night and day by journalists seeking pictures and stories. When did you last see William? Are you engaged? Would you like to marry him? Do you think you'll be queen one day?

The pursuit was reminiscent of the hounding of Diana. More than once, William and the Middleton family asked the pack to back off. Eventually, the strain on Kate and the pressure on William became too much. In 2007, when he was posted to an army camp in Wiltshire and she remained in London, they ended their relationship.

A new marriage for a new age

During their time apart, Kate and William realized how much they meant to each other. What drew them back together was more than rose-tinted romance. They had discovered their respective strengths and weaknesses, and were sufficiently mature to understand what resuming their relationship would mean. William saw that he was unlikely to find someone better able than Kate to bear the burdens of a royal marriage; she decided that, despite the loss of privacy, helping William in his inherited task was what she really wanted to do.

The couple announced their engagement on 16 November 2010. The Queen, who had got to know Kate a couple of years earlier, was delighted.

The wedding on 29 April 2011 had to be spectacular – and it was. Many of the traditional elements of a royal marriage were retained – the tiara, the horse-drawn coach, the dress to die for, glorious music, the kiss on the balcony of Buckingham Palace, cheering crowds in the street, and many millions more following the ceremony on TV. Yet, alongside all that pageantry, significant changes had been made.

This wedding ceremony, although a state occasion, was very much about the bride and groom. At their insistence, it had a green theme. The grey stone nave of Westminster Abbey was lined with 25-foot field maple trees and emblazed with 30,000 blooms from the royal estate. The guest list included the usual diplomats, foreign royals, officers of state, and the like, but the majority were the couple's personal friends and family. The brief honeymoon had to wait, too: the day after his wedding, William went back to work as an RAF Search and Rescue Pilot.

WARNING

There were complaints, of course. Were those lavish celebrations really in order at a time of painful austerity? Didn't they illustrate all too clearly the gulf between the haves and the have-nots? The Palace countered by saying that much of the cost of the wedding had been borne by Prince Charles, with the Middletons chipping in their bit. Nevertheless, the taxpayer had forked out millions for the elaborate security and an airforce flypast.

Catherine's non-royal upbringing

TECHNICAL STUFF

When Kate Middleton entered William's orbit, the media liked to describe her as a normal English girl. This was misleading. She was not an aristocrat, certainly, but her social status was very much upper-middle class. Her parents were wealthy, and their elder daughter attended expensive fee-paying schools. Marlborough College, Kate's private secondary school in Wiltshire, is regarded as one of the best in the country.

But Kate is not a Sloane Ranger (see Chapter 20). Unlike Diana, she is her partner's equal in intellect, education and talent. As a young woman, she obtained excellent A-Level grades, enjoyed all sports, and won the top award in the Duke of Edinburgh's Award Scheme for self-discipline and self-improvement. Whereas Charles had been the first man with whom the naïve Diana had a serious relationship, Kate had gone out with boys since her time at a co-educational boarding school.

The differences between the young Kate Middleton and Diana Spencer should not be overdone. They share outgoing personalities and a marked eagerness to help others through charitable work. They are blessed with good looks, too – William is said to have first noticed his future wife when she appeared (in a see-through dress!) at a charity fashion show. It was not love at first sight, however, and they did not get together for at least another year.

Changing the Rules of Succession

REMEMBER

Succession to the Crown of Great Britain and Northern Ireland, and the other countries of which Elizabeth is queen, such as Canada and Australia, was changed in 2015. A new law overturned the centuries-old custom of males taking precedence over females. The succession protocol, called *absolute primogeniture*, works like this:

>> First in the line of succession is the monarch's oldest child. If the monarch has no *legitimate* (born in wedlock) children, next in line is the monarch's oldest sibling, then their children, and so on.

>> Children of a monarch's oldest child take precedence over the monarch's other children and their offspring. Thus Prince George, Princess Charlotte and Prince Louis all come before Prince Harry and his children (see below).

>> Only children born to a married couple may succeed to the throne.

>> Roman Catholics are still excluded.

TIP

Striking developments have taken place within the make-up of the Royal Family over the past 50 years. Gone completely is the obligation of one royal to marry another royal, or even someone of aristocratic lineage. Charles's marriage to Lady Diana Spencer was the last union of this traditional kind. In modern times, it is not unusual for those of royal birth to opt out of the obligations that come with the heritage. Prince Harry is the most recent example, but back in 1973 Anne's first husband, Mark Philips, rejected a title on the occasion of his marriage. It's possible, I suppose, that one day no one will step forward to take up the heavy crown when it falls vacant. Given the immense burdens and restrictions that come with it, few would blame those who choose to step aside.

Updating the Monarchy In The New Century

While Elizabeth remains on the throne, the British style of monarchy will not change much. It may not be hugely different when Charles dons the Crown. With his fly fishing, tweedy dress, and aristocratic confidants, he is essentially a conservative man.

Should hereditary monarchy survive the reign of King Charles III, however, there are signs that William V and Queen Catherine may do things differently.

Relaxing into the role

To guess what direction the Duke and Duchess of Cambridge (the titles awarded to William and Kate at the time of their marriage) intend to take the monarchy is tricky. Yet there are signs that they would like to make the institution less remote.

TIP

Several influences are at work:

>> The 'common touch' of Princess Diana, both as a mother and as one who showed genuine concern for those she came into contact with.

>> William's work as a Search and Rescue helicopter pilot (2010–2013) and, especially, as a civilian air ambulance pilot (2015–2017) brought him into close contact with a world most other royals never saw. He was the first heir to the throne ever to take a paid non-military job, donating his salary to charity.

>> Kate's middle-class upbringing in a world without footmen, dressers or curtseys.

>> The couple's relatively normal life together as students. Since their marriage, they have attempted the keep these memories alive. Kate is in regular touch with her parents, and William still finds time to play the occasional game of football.

Welcoming George, Charlotte, and Louis to the family

The Cambridges have three children:

>> George Alexander Louis (b. 22 July 2013)

>> Charlotte Elizabeth Diana (b. 2 May 2015)

>> Louis Arthur Charles (b. 23 April 2018)

TIP

George, who may one day be called upon to wear his great-grandmother's heavy crown, is already being prepared for what lies ahead. His parents know only too well how cruel the media can be, and they do their best to shelter him from unwanted and unwarranted intrusion.

William and Kate are hands-on parents, and, to judge by their public demeanour, they have created a close, loving family unit. The amount of time the Duke spends with his family has earned him the unflattering soubriquet 'Work-shy William' in some circles. Nevertheless, royal duties mean the family can't be together all the time, and in their absence the children are looked after by their full-time nanny, Maria Teresa Turrion Borrallo.

Chapter **25**

Home Alone

This chapter looks at the events and issues of the years following Elizabeth's Golden Jubilee in 2012, and concludes with an appreciation of her long reign.

One wonders whether Elizabeth has seen the 1994 movie *Forrest Gump*. If she has, then she must have nodded in agreement when Forrest (Tom Hanks) declares, 'It must be hard being a king', adding quietly to herself 'and a queen'. And if she had thought that her job would get easier with the passing years, she was sadly mistaken. The second decade of the twenty-first century was one of the toughest of all her reign.

Not only did the Queen lose Philip, her husband and lifetime partner, but her own health began to fail at a moment when her country was wading through a swamp of political and economic difficulties. An austere economic programme, fervent Scottish nationalism, and *Brexit* (the vote for Britain to leave the European Union) sorely tested the fabric of the state. They also obliged the Queen to navigate a couple of awkward constitutional squalls.

Living Without Philip

In later life, Philip suffered from a number of infections and was hospitalised quite regularly from 2011 onwards. He had at least three surgical interventions (the Royals are never very forthcoming about such matters), including a hip replacement in early 2018. He recovered quickly enough to attend the wedding of Harry and Meghan (see later in this chapter) in May of the same year.

REMEMBER

With the advent of the COVID-19 pandemic, Philip isolated with the Queen in Windsor Castle, where they were vaccinated in January 2021. Thereafter, he went rapidly downhill before dying in bed at the castle – peacefully, we are told – on 9 April 2021. He was 99.

TIP

Towards the end of his life, Prince Philip broke a couple of records. He became:

>> the longest-serving British royal consort (April 2009)

>> the oldest-ever male British royal (February 2013)

He continued to undertake royal duties to the age of 95 (2017), though his workload had fallen away sharply in his 90s. By the time he retired to the Sandringham Estate, he had clocked up 22,219 solo engagements. He had, he said at the age of 90, 'done his bit' and would now hand over to others.

That did not mean handing over the steering wheel of his car. In January 2019, he was involved in a crash near Sandringham in which the 97-year-old was almost certainly to blame. He apologized to those injured in the other vehicle. Finally admitting to poor health, he handed in his driving license and thus avoided any further action on the part of the authorities.

The Land Rover funeral

TECHNICAL STUFF

Philip was always going to have a ceremonial rather than a state funeral. Owing to the government's COVID-19 regulations then in force, it was hardly ceremonial, either, but a private, relatively low-key affair within the grounds of Windsor Castle. To compensate for the lack of public participation, the ceremony was broadcast on TV.

The Duke had planned his own funeral in detail. The unusual, even eccentric, proceedings of 17 April 2021 included bearing his coffin on a converted Land Rover (which he had designed) rather than on a gun carriage or in a hearse. The occasion included a solemn procession, bagpipes and naval pipes, the firing of guns, and the steady boom of a curfew bell. A role was found for the Prince's favourite ponies. The national anthem rose into the damp afternoon air.

Grenadier Guards bore the coffin into St George's Chapel where a congregation of 30 mask-wearing and suitably distanced family members had assembled. The Dean of Windsor and the Archbishop of Canterbury conducted a service that included a gloomy Russian hymn – a reminder of the Duke's roots in the Greek Orthodox church. Prayers were said, and after the final 'Amen' the coffin was lowered mechanically beneath the chapel floor.

Tributes and complaints

REMEMBER

Tributes came in from members of the Royal Family and politicians in the UK and beyond. For the first eight days of the official two weeks of mourning, Parliament passed no new legislation. Yet there was no great outpouring of national grief, as there had been for Diana and the Queen Mother. The pandemic regulations played their part in dampening things down, but in truth Philip had never won the hearts of the majority of the British people.

The Duke's charitable works were appreciated and his Award Scheme (see Chapter 24) remains both popular and hugely appreciated. The tributes to him spoke of these things and almost all of them, including those of Prime Minister Johnson and Prince Charles, praised him for the support he had given to the Queen over many years. She herself is reported to have talked of a 'huge void' in her life. Few recalled Philip's warmth or kindness, however, and the Press enjoyed reflecting on his many gaffes (see Chapter 10).

WARNING

It was significant that the very extensive coverage the BBC gave to Philip's funeral, life, and times received more complaints than any other group of programmes in its entire history. At a time when thousands were dying of a lethal virus and families were turning out to applaud health workers struggling to cope, endless programmes about a privileged and sometimes tactless man – whatever his exalted status – were felt to be excessive.

And Elizabeth?

REMEMBER

After Philip, his wife . . . It will happen one day, and may be nearer than anticipated before the death of her husband. Some sources suggest that she appeared tired and had lost some of her normal steely determination to keep calm and carry on under all circumstances. 'None of us can slow the passage of time,' she reflected in an official statement.

OPERATION LONDON BRIDGE

The plan for what to do on Elizabeth's death is codenamed Operation London Bridge, with a launch code of 'London Bridge is Down'. Arrangements for Charles's accession are set out in Operation Spring Tide. They include detailed and specific anti-terrorism measures when, as expected, crowds flood into the capital from all around the country.

Guns will sound salutes, broadcasts interrupt and then reschedule, and Parliament adjourn. The country will come to a halt for a two-minute silence. For three days, the public will be able to pay tribute to their departed queen as her coffin lies in state. It is not expected that anyone will object to the extent of the coverage.

Many were taken by surprise when, in October 2021, Elizabeth was reported to be unwell. She had looked spritely for a 95-year-old, and had not been admitted to hospital since 2013. Details were scarce. However, when *The Sun* tabloid newspaper revealed that she had been hospitalised, the Palace could no longer maintain its customary silence. Critics felt the matter might have been better handled, arguing that the health of a widely respected Head of State was hardly a private issue.

Elizabeth, the world was told, had gone into hospital for tests. She had then recovered quietly at home before resuming light duties. It was all a bit vague – the Palace has long refused to give what it calls a 'running commentary' on royal illnesses. Tests for what? Alarm bells started to ring. Elizabeth pulled out of the COP26 Climate Change Conference in Glasgow, cancelled a two-day trip to Northern Ireland, and missed the Remembrance Day parade (see Chapters 8 and 19) with a 'sprained back'.

See the sidebar, "Operation London Bridge" for details of what will happen when Elizabeth passes away.

Facing Britain's Current Big Issues

Two running political sores had bedevilled British politics for much of Elizabeth's reign: the call for Scottish independence, and Britain's relationship with the European Union. The economic downturn following the 2008–2009 banking crisis added to the government's difficulties. The ministries of Conservative Prime Minister David Cameron (2010–2015 and 2015–2016) determined to tackle all three issues.

Austerity

The Government's austerity programme of cuts and wage freezes continued after the Conservatives won the 2015 general election. They were now in power on their own. Museums and libraries were closed, invoking bitter criticism especially from the arts sector. The growth of food banks to feed the needy was castigated by the political opposition as shameful.

TIP

What the Queen thought of this we don't know. At the time, she almost certainly liked Prime Minister David Cameron – he was the sort of well-mannered, upper-middle class, Eton-and-Oxford type with whom she felt comfortable. Also, like her, he was descended from George II, making him her fifth cousin twice removed.

WARNING

The angry anti-austerity protests in the media and on the streets, however, must have caused her concern. If Cameron and his chancellor of the exchequer George Osbourne were targeted as 'posh boys' whose wealth insulated them from the hardships of ordinary people, what about her? One didn't get much posher than the Queen.

Scottish independence

TECHNICAL STUFF

A referendum on the question 'Should Scotland be an independent country?' was held on 18 September 2014. The 'Yes Scotland' and 'Better Together' (against independence) campaigns were fiercely fought, and the 84.6 percent turnout was the highest recorded at any British election or referendum since 1910. In the end, Scots voted to remain part of the UK, with 2,001,926 (55.3 percent) voting 'no' to independence and 1,617,989 (44.7 percent) voting 'yes'.

As crowned head of a united kingdom, we may safely assume that Elizabeth was opposed to Scottish independence. The Scottish National Party's pledge to retain the monarchy if they won the referendum ensured that the Crown was not an issue in the campaign.

The nearest the Queen came to expressing an opinion in public on the independence issue was when she told an onlooker outside Crathie Kirk (see Chapter 19), 'I hope people will think very carefully about the future' when casting their votes. When this was widely interpreted as being anti-independence, the Palace retorted that the Queen was 'above politics'. That might have been that had not Cameron admitted in 2019 that he had asked the Queen to intervene subtly in the independence debate. The Palace was furious at this breach of confidence, and also when he let it slip that on hearing the referendum result Elizabeth had 'purred' with delight.

In the light of Cameron's revelation, Elizabeth's 'think very carefully' remark takes on a whole new significance. It looks as if, at the Prime Minister's request, she was offering a personal political opinion. In that case, when else had she influenced, or attempted to influence, a prime minister? Over Suez (see Chapter 12)? The Falklands (see Chapter 18)? Unfortunately, we'll have to wait a long time to find out. (Important government papers remain secret for at least 30 years.)

Brexit

The second boil that Cameron sought to lance was disagreement over Britain's membership of the European Union (known as the EU, see Chapters 12 and 15). In his 2015 election manifesto he had promised a referendum on the issue in order to put the matter to rest.

On 23 June 2016, the matter was indeed put to rest, but not in the manner Cameron anticipated. Here's how the population voted:

>> Remain in the EU: 16,141,241 votes (48.11 percent of the total cast)

>> Leave the EU: 17,410,742 votes (51.89 percent of the total cast)

Thus began the long and painful process of Brexit. Debate during the run-up to the vote had focused on issues such as immigration and the EU's bureaucratic wastefulness. Few had expected the Brexiteers to win, and there had been little talk of what Britain's relationship with the EU would look like if it were to leave.

The most difficult question was how to handle the border between Northern Ireland (outside the EU) and Eire (inside the EU). The Good Friday Agreement (see Chapter 21) had promised no 'hard' border between the two – but how could that be reconciled now there was no free trade between Britain and the EU? As of January 2022, the issue still rumbles on.

Cameron resigned immediately the result of the Brexit result came through. Theresa May, his successor as prime minister, struggled to find a deal acceptable to the EU and to Parliament. She won an election in 2017 before her government suffered a succession of parliamentary defeats, and she tendered her resignation to the Queen on 24 July 2019. She was replaced by Boris Johnson, a scruffy-haired populist rhetorician and arch-Brexiteer.

Approaching the deadline to leave

What happened next is extremely complicated. The details need not concern us, though the general principles – notably the extent of the royal prerogative (see Chapters 1 and 8) – are important. To set the scene, we need to remember that the Brexit issue divided the nation like no other had done for over a century. It split families, friendships and political parties, and undermined confidence in the entire political process. Tempers ran furnace-hot.

The deadline for the UK and EU to agree to the terms of Brexit was initially set for 29 March 2017. As Parliament was unable to reach agreement over a deal, the deadline was extended three times, the final one being 31 January 2020.

Johnson became prime minister during this process. When Parliament declined to support his deal with the EU, he asked Elizabeth to use her royal prerogative to *prorogue* (suspend) Parliament for over a month. This would inevitably lead to a no-deal Brexit, which many believed would be an economic and political disaster for Britain. Should Elizabeth grant the request of her prime minister and grant a prorogation, or should she abide by the wishes of the majority of MPs and reject it?

Save us, Your Majesty!

Constitutional experts were divided. Opposition MPs called on the Queen to save them from 'dictatorial' Johnson who was 'ripping up the constitution' (technically impossible as Britain's constitution is nowhere written down in a single document) by planning to bypass the people's elected representatives.

Remembering that the Queen is not above the law

Intense discussions are believed to have taken place between the Queen's private secretary (Edward Young – see Chapter 9), the cabinet secretary, and Johnson's private secretary. These resulted in a cabal of privy counsellors (see the sidebar "The Privy Council") flying to Balmoral to meet the Queen. Jeremy Corbyn, the leader of the Labour opposition, asked to see the Queen himself.

Too late.

The Queen had granted her prime minister's wish. On 10 September 2019, Parliament was prorogued for over a month. Meanwhile, the legality of proroga- tion against the wish of Parliament was being tested in the courts. On

24 September, citing a case from the year 1611, the Supreme Court of the United Kingdom ruled unanimously that the prorogation was unlawful. This meant that:

>> The sovereign had acted on incorrect advice.

>> More significantly, as the court had ruled the Crown's action unconstitutional, the sovereign was not above the law.

I told you this was complicated stuff!

The whole episode was embarrassing for the Queen. It had drawn her deep into the Brexit maelstrom, and left her looking like an enemy of Parliament. In 1649, that stance had cost Charles I his head (see Chapter 2). One day, her entry on the issue in her private diary will be unputdownable!

TIP

It is to Elizabeth's credit that her personal view on Brexit remains unknown. She was so detached, so inscrutable, that both Brexiteers and Remainers claimed her as one of their own.

TIP

BLM and culture wars

The effect of American imports into the UK can be double-sided. Fast food, for instance, is convenient and tasty but can promote obesity! The arrival from the US of the Black Lives Matter (BLM) movement, and culture wars over issues such as gender, have helped promote a healthy reassessment of Britain's social and political values. At the same time, their more militant expressions have caused pain and division.

THE PRIVY COUNCIL

Founded in 1708, the Privy Council is an advisory body of senior figures in public life, usually politicians or former politicians. Its members are appointed by the Crown, though normally on the advice of the government of the day.

The council, whose members by tradition meet standing up, is one of the UK's odder institutions. Its purposes, a mix of formal and practical, include advising the sovereign on how to use the royal prerogative (as in 2019, above), putting Acts of Parliament into effect, and approving the membership rules and qualifications of the professions.

Elizabeth has managed to remain aloof from the culture wars. However, the marriage of her grandson Harry to an American woman of colour made it impossible for her family and household to avoid engagement with the BLM concept:

>> William, Duke of Cambridge, has insisted that the Windsors are 'very much not a racist family.'

>> After discussions at the highest level, Sir Ken Olisa, the first black Lord-Lieutenant of London, assured a questioner that the Palace certainly supported BLM.

>> In 2021, when attending the ceremonies marking Barbados' shift from a monarchy to a republic (detailed later in this chapter), Prince Charles said that 'the appalling atrocity of slavery' remains a 'stain' on Britain's history.

Critics remain unconvinced. They call for the Queen and her family to:

>> Make a specific declaration of support for BLM.

>> Return royal treasures taken from other countries during the colonial era.

>> Support reparation payments for slavery.

>> Increase the diversity of Palace staff.

>> End the Queen's exemption from employment laws relating to race or ethnicity.

COVID-19

The Queen and her family were inevitably impacted by the spread of the COVID-19 pandemic in the UK and the national lockdowns imposed in 2020 and 2021. Elizabeth and Philip were among the first to be vaccinated against the virus. Engagements were cancelled, including the 75th anniversary of VE Day and the State Visit by the Emperor and Empress of Japan, and in March 2020 the Queen made a rare special broadcast to the nation.

Elizabeth had made only four previous special broadcasts:

>> 1991 The start of the invasion of Iraq

>> 1997 The death of Diana

>> 2002 Her mother's funeral

>> 2012 The Diamond Jubilee

During her Covid broadcast, the Queen thanked all key workers for their efforts, hoped everyone would look back with pride on how they 'responded to this challenge', and assured them that 'better days will return'. Most of the 25+ million who tuned in found her words comforting and reassuring.

It is hard to imagine a speech by any other public figure at the time being so well received. It was monarchy at its best.

Going It Alone: Harry and Meghan

Sporty, genial, and photogenic, Harry continued to attract a lot of media attention after his graduation from Sandhurst in 2006 (see Chapter 24). His military career was, for a modern-day royal, distinguished. He did two tours of duty in Afghanistan (2007 and 2012), the latter as a co-pilot and gunner in an Apache gunship helicopter. As a prime target for the enemy, his first deployment was kept secret until after his return.

Harry had his own office for royal business from 2009 onwards. Four years later, he took time out from the military to pay an official visit to the Caribbean. In 2013, his royal duties took him to the USA and Australia. By now, he had an extended list of charitable interests, including combatting HIV, the preservation of wildlife, and protecting the environment. The Queen appointed him Commonwealth Youth Ambassador in 2018.

Perhaps Harry's most notable work has been for servicemen and women injured in body or mind during their time in the armed forces. In 2014, this led to the establishment of the international Invictus ('Unconquered') Games for serving or veteran service personnel who were in some way sick or disabled.

Despite his notable military and charitable service, Harry still attracted controversy (see Chapter 24). In his youth he was criticized for being drunk in public and for using language deemed racist. In 2012, he appeared naked in pictures taken in a Las Vegas Hotel. The sincerity of his support for environmental issues was undermined by frequent use of private jets in 2019 and 1920.

Marrying a TV star

Harry, with his good looks and lively personality, was always going to marry an attractive woman. After serious long-term relationships with Chelsey Davy (ended 2009) and Cressida Bonas (ended 2014), in 2016 he met the American TV star Meghan Markle. Many of the ancient taboos about whom a royal should or should not marry had been overridden by the previous generation. Nevertheless, when three of them were rolled into one – Meghan was divorced, of mixed race, and not British – some sections of society and the media raised critical eyebrows. In 2016, Harry's office issued a formal rebuke against what it called 'a wave of abuse and harassment', some of a racist and sexist nature.

The majority of people in Britain and around the world liked Harry's choice of partner. Meghan was refreshingly different – a breath of fresh air blowing into an ancient institution. Her mixed-race heritage was warmly appreciated, especially in Commonwealth countries. The all-white countenances of existing royals carried overtones of former colonial status and slavery.

Harry and Meghan made their first official public appearance in September 2017 and announced their engagement the following month. The Press could not get enough of the glamorous royal couple. Kate and Meghan were seen smiling together, the Queen actually laughed with her in public, and we are told that even the royal corgis took to the new soon-to-be royal.

It all climaxed with a sumptuous wedding in St George's Chapel, Windsor on 19 May 2018. An estimated worldwide audience of almost two billion tuned in to see Megan stunning in a Givenchy dress and her husband smartly resplendent in his military uniform. UK tourism soared.

REMEMBER

Perhaps it was all too good to be true? There had always been rumours and these multiplied in the year following the wedding:

>> Meghan found court formality and etiquette painfully cramping.

>> Harry and Megan fell out with William and Kate over a number of what appeared to be quite minor issues.

>> Harry was very much under Meghan's thumb and she had not set her heart on remaining in Britain.

>> Some members of the royal entourage persisted in their disparaging, perhaps sometimes racist attitude towards Meghan; she said she was made to feel like an outsider.

>> Harry and Meghan had difficulty retaining their staff.

The media, especially the tabloid newspapers, seized on the slightest sign of tension and turned it into a story. Meghan was worn down by this continual and intrusive harassment, and Harry, with bitter memories of his mother's harassment, shared many of her feelings. Both were frustrated that the 'grin and bear it' response required of the Royal Family did not allow them to strike back.

Before the birth of their first child, Archie Harrison Mountbatten-Windsor (b. 2019), the Duke and Duchess of Sussex (as Harry and Meghan now were) moved into Frogmore Cottage on the estate of Windsor Castle. The taxpayers' Sovereign Grant had it refurbished for £2.4 million, giving the tabloids a field day. The couple later repaid a proportion of the money. At the end of the year, the Sussexes announced that they would be spending Christmas with Meghan's mother in Los Angeles, USA, rather than with the Queen and the rest of the Royal Family at Sandringham.

Things were not looking good.

Heading into American exile

The bombshell exploded on 9 January 2020: the Duke and Duchess of Sussex would be stepping down from royal duties and splitting their time between the UK and North America. They planned on becoming financially independent, too. The announcement was made without consultation with the Queen or any other member of the Royal Family.

After discussion, it was decided that the Sussexes could not be half-in, half-out of the family. The severance would be complete. They would lose their 'Royal Highness' titles, but retain those of Duke and Duchess. Their children would not be princes or princesses, and financial support from the British state would cease. What went on behind the scenes is not known. In March 2021, Harry and Meghan put their side of the story in what looked like a rehearsed interview with the US talk show host Oprah Winfrey. The Palace's response was simple, subtle and dignified: 'recollections may vary'.

Preparing For The Crown: King Charles III

Charles Duke of Cornwall, Duke of Rothesay, Duke of Edinburgh, Earl of Merioneth, Earl of Carrick, Baron Greenwich, Baron of Renfrew, Lord of the Isles, Prince and Great Steward of Scotland, has mellowed with age and became less outspoken. He has also become more conservative, more like his mother.

As advancing age caught up with Elizabeth, and especially after the death of her husband in April 2021, Charles made a conscious effort to mould himself into the role of king. He was the only family member to visit Philip during his stay in hospital a few weeks before his death, and with his father's passing Charles became patriarchal head of the family.

On Charles's shoulders now fell the task of supervising how the Royal Family presented itself. He continued to consult with the Queen, of course, and his son William was brought in on the conversation more often. Two issues were most pressing: the separation from his US-based son and daughter-in-law, and the ongoing case against his brother Andrew regarding what he had got up to during his friendship with the subsequently convicted US sex offender Jeffrey Epstein.

By the start of 2022, the Andrew story had become the Royal Family's nightmare. A much-reproduced and much-questioned photograph, supposedly taken in 2001, shows the Prince with his arm around the 17-year-old Virginia Giuffre. She subsequently accused him of sexual assault, and he failed to get the trial called off on legal grounds. The third figure in the picture, the socialite Ghislaine Maxwell, was found guilty in 2021 of sex trafficking for Jeffrey Epstein. By this time, Andrew had become toxic for the Windsor brand. In January 2022, apparently at the request of all the senior members of the family (the Queen, Charles and William), the Prince's honorary military affiliations and charitable patronages were returned to the Queen.

REMEMBER

Charles himself continued to attract unfavourable headlines. As late as 2021, he was being linked to a 'cash for honours' scandal, and his long-standing aid, Michael Fawcett, resigned as CEO of The Prince's Foundation. Fawcett had been accused of getting a knighthood and British citizenship for a Saudi billionaire who had donated to one of Charles's charitable funds.

Issues like this did the Prince's popularity no good. When surveyed by the global public opinion and data company YouGov in 2021, people gave him a less than 50 percent approval rating – well below Anne, William and Kate, and not in the same league as his mother (97 percent). Camilla, Duchess of Cornwall, scored even lower, though she might have taken some comfort at being above Meghan (28 percent) and Andrew (13 percent). None of this was particularly good news for the future of the Windsor dynasty.

TIP

Prince Charles once suggested that he hoped to see a 'slimmed-down' version of the monarchy one day. With his father no longer on the scene, his elderly mother taking on less and less, and Harry and Meghan out of the picture, it looked as if his wish would come true by default. The duties carried out by the 73-year-old Prince and his 74-year-old consort now included several that might previously have been handled by his mother. Here's a selection of the sort of things they did before and after the 2020–2021 pandemic lockdowns:

>> **20 January 2020:** Charles attended the presentation to his sister of an honorary degree from the University of Aberdeen. Camilla (Duchess of Rothesay in Scotland) also presented an award.

>> **22 January 2020:** Camilla visited Elmhurst Ballet School, Birmingham.

- **4 March 2020:** Charles and Camilla rode on a new electric double-decker bus to celebrate 20 years of Transport for London (the capital city's public transportation network).

- **18 June 2020:** They formally received Emmanuel Macron, President of the French Republic.

- **19 September 2021:** They attended a Westminster Abbey service of Thanksgiving and Rededication marking the 81st Anniversary of the Battle of Britain.

- **28 September 2021:** They attended the world premiere of the James Bond film *No Time to Die*.

- **30 November 2021:** Charles represented the Queen during ceremonies that marked Barbados becoming a republic.

- **8 December 2021:** He presented the Queen Elizabeth Prize for Engineering at St James' Palace, London, on behalf of the Queen.

What Will History Make of Her Majesty, Queen Elizabeth II?

It is too soon to reach a definitive conclusion about Elizabeth's role in the ongoing drama of Britain and its monarchy over the past 70 years. The play is not yet concluded, and we are too close to the stage and its actors to make even moderately objective evaluations. A royalist, for example, takes a very different view of things from a republican.

Nevertheless, certain facts speak for themselves. First, Elizabeth has been on the throne during a period of unprecedentedly swift and spectacular change. Second, whether for better or for worse, the Queen has preserved intact the Crown she inherited in 1952. These two salient facts are inextricably intertwined.

Her reign was not without difficulties

Elizabeth could not possibly have foreseen the difficulties that lay ahead when she came to the throne. This was not just due to her lack of education. She might have guessed at the onward march of meritocracy and the decline in Britain's global power and influence, but only science-fiction writers predicted the world of robots, the internet, and genetic engineering.

Critics say Elizabeth did not help herself by failing to adapt quickly enough to a changing world. This led them to suggest that some of her difficulties were of her own making. Examples of specific incidents can be found in Chapter 27 and earlier in this chapter. More generally, they add, she should have been more proactive in reducing formality. She certainly could have reduced the links between the Crown, the aristocracy, and conservative institutions such as the army and the public schools.

Over the years, popular support for the monarchy has followed a downward path. From an average of about 70–80 percent in the first half of her reign, it fell to 54 percent in a 2009 newspaper poll. In a 2021 YouGov poll, overall support had risen to 61 percent. Though a majority of 18–24-year-olds thought the monarchy should be abolished, such a move was low on their list of priorities.

She did her duty

In her 1953 Christmas broadcast, Elizabeth said she wanted to show her people that the Crown was not just an 'abstract symbol' but 'a personal and living bond between you and me'. That may indeed have been her wish. Many would now question the 'personal and living bond' idea. They haven't seen much sign of it.

REMEMBER

For all her good intentions, the Queen has largely remained a distant, detached figure. Paradoxically, this may have been helpful, enabling her to preserve the magic of her monarchy, 'a symbol of unity in a world of insecurity':

>> At all times, in all situations, she has done what she believes to be her duty.

>> She never acted or pretended. You always know where you were with the Queen.

>> She is unfailingly punctual, polite, tactful, and sympathetic.

>> She is prepared to adapt, but only when circumstances make it unavoidable.

Given her upbringing and her personality, could Elizabeth have done a better job? I doubt it.

6

The Part of Tens

IN THIS PART . . .

The Part of Tens enables you to do a quick catch-up on key social and political aspects of the Elizabeth story.

As Britain's a-political head of state, the sovereign is supposed to be outside – or above – politics. But she still has the right to be consulted on political affairs. This is largely done through her regular meetings with prime ministers. Her relationship with ten of them is examined in Chapter 26.

Chapter 27 looks at ten instances where the Queen's multi-faceted role has been compromised or criticized. Several of these moments have featured in the ten dramatic presentations of the Queen that are the subject of Chapter 28.

Finally, you can't have Elizabeth without the Royal Family! Her parents, sister, husband and children have been well covered in previous chapters. The last chapter, therefore, introduces you to ten of her grandchildren. Quite a mix they are, too!

Chapter **26**

Ten Prime Ministers Elizabeth has Worked With

The monarchy is sometimes referred to as the decorative or dignified side of the British constitution, meaning the side that acts as a splendid but ultimately powerless symbol of the state. This leaves the executive or 'efficient' side – messy and divisive but genuinely powerful – in the hands of an elected government.

The two parts are not completely separate. The government acts in the sovereign's name; their legislative programme is known as the 'King's/Queen's Speech', and the monarch reads it out in Parliament (see Chapter 8). Furthermore, as the sovereign meets and chats with other heads of state, many of whom wield political power, she needs to know what her own government is up to.

REMEMBER

The sovereign is briefed by a daily report from Parliament, behind-the-scenes meetings between officials, and most importantly by weekly one-to-one audiences with the prime minister of the day. It is at these top secret, highly-personal get-togethers that the sovereign may, we assume, exercise their three constitutional rights laid out in Victorian times: the right to be consulted, the right to encourage, and the right to warn.

Winston Churchill (1952–1955)

REMEMBER

Winston Churchill and Queen Elizabeth were besotted with each other. The 77-year-old premier adored his weekly heart-to-heart chats with the attractive young woman he had watched growing up. Her unashamed adulation of him appealed to his vanity. He had a romantic dream that her accession would herald Britain's new Elizabethan Age. (The first, 1558–1603, had been the time of Shakespeare, the founding of an overseas empire, and military glory, as examined in Chapter 2). We are told that the chats between Churchill and Elizabeth might go on for as long as two hours.

The Queen was in some ways fortunate to have a man like Churchill as her first prime minister. From a family with a long history of inherited titles and wealth himself, he was a firm believer in hereditary monarchy. He was happy to guide the young Queen along what he considered the right paths. Her conservatism was already deeply engrained; he shored it up considerably.

WARNING

The Crown makes a lot of the relationship, and suggests it went on after Churchill stepped down from office.

The template for Elizabeth's monarchy was formed by her father and Churchill. The relationship between these men was one reason why she regarded Churchill with such high esteem. Not only had he – as the story goes – single-handedly 'saved the free world' – but he had also flattered, supported and boosted the morale and reputation of the fairly nondescript George VI. He had made a king of him.

Churchill – Elizabeth's teacher, admirer, father figure and family friend – would remain her first prime minister in more than a chronological sense. She was distressed when he stepped down in 1955, and even more so at his funeral ten years later. She even broke customary protocol by not being the last to arrive at the great man's funeral. She left that honour to the relatives of the one person she had respected more than any other outside her own family.

Harold Macmillan (1957–1963)

In 1955, Churchill was succeeded as prime minister by his foreign secretary, Anthony Eden. In truth, the elderly and unwell Churchill had been largely a figurehead premier, with Eden, his acting deputy, the real controlling figure, especially in foreign affairs.

Eden's illness (explained in Chapter 12) and his relationship with Elizabeth is explored quite extensively – and fictionally – in *The Crown*. If she liked him at first, she had probably changed her mind by the time he resigned in 1957: he had kept Churchill's stroke a secret from her, and – far worse – had not informed her of the secret plans to attack Egypt in league with France and Israel (see Chapter 12).

The appointment of Harold Macmillan, who took over from Eden in 1957, presented Elizabeth with one of the first constitutional headaches of her reign. The Conservative (Tory) Party did not then elect their leader. Instead, he (never she) 'emerged'. Elizabeth was expected to be the midwife to this emergence. She did so after consulting with two Tory grandees: Churchill and the senior peer of the realm, the Marquis of Salisbury. It was hardly democratic, but the party accepted Macmillan, who turned out to be a successful leader.

Though twenty years younger than Churchill, at 63 Macmillan was no spring chicken. He brought with him the same manners, deference for the monarchy and dreamy-eyed admiration for the young Elizabeth as Churchill. He wrote long and detailed letters to her, informing her of every move of 'your majesty's servants' – by which he meant the government!

When his time in office ended in scandal (see Chapter 12), he apologized profusely lest the matter had added to Her Majesty's already heavy burden. And when she came to see him in his hospital bed to seek advice on his successor, he drooled in his autobiography over the 'bright shining eyes' that were her 'chief beauty'.

As detailed in Chapter 12, Elizabeth almost certainly overstepped the bounds of constitutional propriety when, at Macmillan's recommendation, she invited the Conservative Lord Home (soon to renounce his peerage and become plain Alec Douglas Home) to form a government. She could hardly be blamed for the Tory Party's byzantine manner of choosing a leader, but she should have been less taken in by Macmillan's smooth talk.

Harold Wilson (1964–1970, 1974–1976)

Commentators are often surprised at the apparently close friendship between Elizabeth and her first Labour prime minister, Harold Wilson. Socially, she was poles apart from the academic raised in a lower middle-class Yorkshire (north-east England) family. The Establishment regarded his left-wing views as sufficiently dangerous – in Cold War terms – for the secret services, allegedly, to keep a file on him.

But Wilson was no communist firebrand. Genial, softly spoken and relaxed, he reportedly put Elizabeth at her ease so successfully that after their first meeting she invited him to stay for a drink! Later, she even permitted him to smoke his pipe in her presence.

WARNING

The Crown captures the pair's unusual friendship with skill: she welcoming the chance to get to know about a side of the country that had remained hidden from her, he relieved to find a ready, non-judgmental ear as he ran through the country's myriad political, social and economic problems (see Chapters 12 and 15).

James Callaghan (1976–1979)

TIP

'Sunny Jim' Callaghan and Elizabeth got on famously well. Though a Labour politician, he was conservative in his attitude towards the country's traditional institutions, such as the House of Lords and the monarchy. He found Elizabeth easy and pleasant company, too. It is said that he felt so relaxed in her presence that he was able to complement her on her wardrobe.

For personal and political reasons, Callaghan took great pleasure from the 1977 Silver Jubilee. He genuinely felt the Queen's devotion to her duty deserved widespread recognition, and thought Britain needed a unifying pageant at a time of discord and hardship. He was rewarded with widespread popular support for the celebrations (see Chapter 15).

REMEMBER

As Elizabeth supported Callaghan in his relations with the breakaway regime in Rhodesia (see Chapter 18), so he tried to help her by getting Prince Charles more interested in affairs of state. The Prince would one day have to hold meaningful conversations with prime ministers, and Callaghan felt he should know a bit more about what was going on. By all accounts, the mission was not a great success.

Margaret Thatcher (1979–1990)

TIP

At first glance, the relationship between the Queen and Thatcher had everything going for it. They were roughly the same age, were both hardworking women in positions of immense authority, and Britain's first female Prime Minister had the deepest respect – reverence even – for the institution Elizabeth represented. There the similarities ended.

The differences began with personality. Thatcher, a townie, was a driven workaholic with little time for frivolity, sport, or humour. It's said she didn't always understand her scriptwriters' jokes, notably the line about her inflexible monetarist policies: 'The lady's not for turning.' (A parody of Christopher Fry's 1948 drama, *The Lady's Not for Burning*.) Elizabeth the country woman, while also diligent, likes a joke and insists on mixing work with relaxing at the racecourse, riding, or walking in the fresh air.

REMEMBER

Thatcher's weekly audiences were said to be 'difficult'. She would arrive early and itch to get back to her Downing Street desk as soon as possible. Elizabeth refused to be hurried. We are told she had to endure Thatcher's long diatribes about the correctness of the government's approach and policies. Behind the scenes, the Royal Family are said to have made fun of Thatcher's elaborate curtsies and faux-posh accent.

REMEMBER

On two issues, the differences between the two women were very serious.

>> Sanctions against the apartheid regime in South Africa pitted Elizabeth's devotion to the Commonwealth against Thatcher's obsession with hard-nosed economics (see Chapter 18).

>> Thatcher, determined to force through economic changes, clashed headlong with the trade unions. Reacting to the hardship suffered in some sections of society, the Palace was rumoured to criticize the Prime Minister as 'uncaring'. Some sections of the press wondered whether the Queen had breached her lifelong constitutional neutrality on political issues. Horrified at the suggestion, apparently Elizabeth phoned Thatcher with a personal apology for the way her staff had behaved (see Chapter 18).

TIP

In the end, Elizabeth generously buried the hatchet. She invited Thatcher to join her at the races as a way of expressing regret at how she had been ousted from office in a party coup in 1990. Finally, she broke with tradition in 2013 by attending Thatcher's funeral – a rare honour for a commoner.

John Major (1990–1997)

John Major, Thatcher's Conservative successor, was a prime minister in the Callaghan/Wilson mould. This made him a more welcome guest at the Palace than the 'Iron Lady', Margaret Thatcher. Though not born into the upper strata of society, he found the Queen easy to get on with. She liked him, too, especially when he was solicitous over the future of Princes William and Harry when their parents split up (see Chapter 21).

Always discreet and well-mannered, if somewhat prosaic, Major was scrupulous about keeping the Queen informed of what he and his government were doing. This involved not just the regular weekly meetings at the Palace and at Balmoral, but letters and telephone calls to the Palace whenever there was something significant to report.

REMEMBER

In his autobiography, Major acknowledged his indebtedness to the Queen for sharing the benefits of her long experience. He said how 'invaluable on many occasions' he had found her advice. Frequently, he recalled, she began their discussion of a subject by saying, 'I remember . . .', And her knowledge of Commonwealth matters was 'encyclopaedic'. Longevity, though no guarantee of usefulness, clearly brought tangible benefits.

Tony Blair (1997–2007)

WARNING

The early relationship between the Queen and Prime Minister Tony Blair is explored in the well-received 2006 movie *The Queen* (see Chapter 28). Initially, relations between the sovereign and her third Labour prime minister were uneasy. Tony's wife Cherie was a known republican, and he himself headed a party eager to cut down the power and privilege of the hereditary Establishment.

The reactions to the death of Diana in 1997 did not make things easier (see Chapters 21 and 27). Blair, the great communicator, judged the public mood perfectly. Elizabeth, shut away in Balmoral Castle and harbouring unfortunate memories of the capricious late princess, got things horribly wrong. However much it irked her, Blair's 'People's Princess' trumped 'Her Royal Highness'. Later, Blair annoyed the Queen again when he repeated in public her private remark – 'please don't be too effusive' – when they had discussed her 50th wedding anniversary.

REMEMBER

In time, things improved. Blair remained, a bit like Thatcher, a politician in the messianic mould. Unlike her, however, he enjoyed taking time out from the day-to-day business to give the Palace a ring or pop along the road from Downing Street for a gossip. He felt able, as some other premiers had, to broach almost any subject that took his fancy, knowing that his interlocutor would 'never divulge anything to anyone'. In 1999, the Queen learned about Cherie's pregnancy before it became public knowledge.

Some of Blair's reforms – such as removing most hereditary peers from the House of Lords, and establishing devolved administrations for Scotland and Wales – probably worried the hereditary head of a united kingdom. If they did, she never let it show. Nor did she make her views known to anyone but him on the wisdom of joining the US invasion of Iraq in 2003.

Gordon Brown (2007–2010)

Blair, who liked nothing better than a good natter, was followed by a mega-bright, serious-minded Scot, Gordon Brown (also Labour). The Queen was now on safer if duller ground.

Very little has emerged about their relationship, save how much she appreciated his liking for and concern for the ailing Duke of Edinburgh. The Queen responded by granting Brown an unprecedented honour: on leaving office, his wife and family were permitted to accompany him at his final audience. It meant a great deal to all of them.

David Cameron (2010–2016)

Like Blair, the Conservative Prime Minister David Cameron was a great communicator and smooth operator. He was distantly related to the Queen and from an impeccable Eton-and-Oxford Establishment background. All this should have added up to the sort of friendly relationship between sovereign and premier enjoyed by former Tories such as Harold Macmillan.

It was not to be.

REMEMBER

Cameron made two classic blunders. Both involved indiscretions about private conversations. At the time of the vote on Scottish independence, Elizabeth advised voters to 'think very carefully about the future'. Cameron later said how he had asked that the Queen 'raise an eyebrow' at the prospect of an independent Scotland, revealing that her 'think very carefully' had indeed expressed her political opinion (see Chapter 25). Cameron got into hot water again when he told an interviewer how the Queen had 'purred down the line' when he told her about the result of the referendum. Such remarks undermined the whole concept of the Head of State being above politics. Elizabeth is not, obviously – it's just that only prime ministers know what she really thinks. Most of the time.

Boris Johnson (2019 to the time of writing)

It's too soon to know what Elizabeth thinks of her boisterous, 'Get-Brexit-Done' 14th prime minister. She might appreciate his sense of humour and fervent nationalism, but it's doubtful she's attracted by his naked opportunism or cavalier attitude towards the truth. He has little in common with the premiers she clearly liked, such as Winston Churchill and Harold Wilson.

WARNING

When Johnson illegally exploited the royal prerogative to suspend Parliament in 2019 (see Chapter 25), the Queen rightly kept her own counsel. Nevertheless, it is not hard to guess what she thought of such behaviour.

Chapter **27**

Ten Tricky Moments for Elizabeth

After 70 years on the throne, it is remarkable how few *faux pas* Elizabeth has made, and how little criticism has been levelled at her personally. Nevertheless, there have been a few awkward moments, some created by others and some by the Queen herself.

TIP

In the end, none of them really mattered. I've read recently that one of the purposes of modern hereditary royalty, the very apex and epitome of celebrity, is to give the rest of the world something to gossip about!

Rumours of Prince Philip's Infidelity (1948 onwards)

REMEMBER

In a reign punctuated with spicy stories of royal philandering, one might forget that the first scandal did not concern the Queen's children or relatives but the very heart of the family. The rumour mill was whirring so fervently that in 1957 the Palace released an unprecedented statement:

'It is quite untrue that there is any rift between the Queen and the Duke.'

Why was this deemed necessary? Because journalists all over the world had put two and two together and made five. There were no confessions, no lawsuits, no pictures. And yet:

>> Philip was a renowned 'ladies' man' before his marriage.

>> His solo four-month Commonwealth tour of 1956–1957, when his wife and two children remained at home, involved a number of jolly parties and other social occasions (as tactfully depicted in *The Crown*).

>> After the Commonwealth tour, Philip's private secretary and confidant, Philip Parker, resigned. His wife was suing him for divorce on grounds of adultery. Hmm!

>> Backstairs palace gossip said that after the coronation Philip was no longer so welcome in the Queen's bed.

>> He frequently slipped out of the Palace in disguise for an evening of fun with his male friends.

>> He was romantically linked with a string of attractive young women, including actress Pat Kirkwood, novelist Daphne du Maurier, and his cousin, Princess Alexandra.

>> When asked for the key to a successful marriage, Philip replied that 'tolerance is the one essential ingredient.'

>> Unless there is a legal judgement to the contrary, no-one will learn the contents of Philip's will for 90 years. Who benefitted and why remains a mystery – very probably an innocent one.

TIP

Ultimately, of course, none of this really mattered. If anything, it only added to people's admiration for the unimpeachable Elizabeth.

The Affair Between Princess Margaret and Peter Townsend (1952–1955)

When Prince Harry married Meghan Markle in 2018, the union spawned yards of column inches in the media and thousands of glossy photographs. Bride and groom were attractive celebrities in their own right, and the marriage between a very English royal and a mixed-race American was a striking and very welcome first. The fact that Meghan was a divorcée was unremarkable.

REMEMBER

Turn back the clock 55 years, and we are in a different world. Divorce, always then a matter of someone's fault, was unusual and not recognized by the Church of England. When it became clear that Margaret, the Queen's sister (a status similar to that of Harry, whose brother was destined to be king), had fallen in love and wished to marry a divorcee, the nation divided. (See Chapter 13 for more on this story, which is also treated movingly in *The Crown*.)

Whose side would Elizabeth take? Her heart sided with her sister, to whom she was devoted. If she, Elizabeth, had married the man she loved, why shouldn't Margaret marry Group Captain Peter Townsend? There were two difficulties:

>> As Margaret was under 25, the marriage needed the monarch's consent.

>> The all-male Church of England and the bulk of the largely male Establishment opposed the marriage.

There was an answer to the first problem. After her 25th birthday, Margaret would be free to do as she wished, as long as the government agreed. It might mean a civil marriage, and ceding her right to the succession, some titles and financial support, but wasn't love more important?

WARNING

If Elizabeth had been on the throne for longer, giving her sufficient experience to develop confidence in her own judgement, she might have stood up for her sister more forcefully. However, she:

>> witnessed the turmoil caused by her uncle's decision to choose the women he loved before the throne (see Chapter 5).

>> was under the influence of the traditionalist prime minister, Winston Churchill.

>> was surrounded by deeply reactionary advisers.

But she didn't back her sister against the Establishment, and Margaret therefore did not marry her Group Captain. Elizabeth had sided with the status quo against the will of her people. Perhaps unfairly, the less deferential among them felt she might have shown a more independent spirit.

Lord Altrincham Criticizes the 'Priggish School Girl' (1957)

TIP

One of the difficulties faced by heads of state is that, surrounded by sycophants and their own kind, they can become isolated from the truth. This applies to hereditary monarchs as well, as criticism of the Crown can be seen as unpatriotic, almost traitorous. Similar accusations were levelled at John Grigg, Baron Altrincham, after he condemned the way the monarchy was being run in the August 1957 edition of *The National and English Review* (see Chapter 12 for more on this incident).

Grigg's article 'The Monarchy Today', which attracted three times as many letters of support as criticism, was effective because of who he was (an Eton-and-Oxford-educated peer, Tory ex-army officer, a monarchist, and son of a former member of Churchill's war cabinet), and because what he said was palpably true. It struck straight at the heart of the old imperial, aristocratic Establishment. Led by the Archbishop of Canterbury, they closed ranks to condemn it.

What did Grigg say? Here goes:

» The coronation, utterly unrelated to reality, was a superficial show reflected in 'hideous coloured photographs of a glamorous young woman in sparkling attire'.

» The Queen had to do more than 'go through the motions' of monarchy, and let her personality show by saying 'things which people can remember', and doing 'things on her own initiative which will make people sit up and take notice.'

» The Queen's upper-class (non) education had left her reliant on a 'tweedy aristocracy' unable to transcend race and class. She needed to establish a 'truly classless and Commonwealth Court'.

» *Debutante balls* (where young ladies were presented to the Queen and society) were 'a grotesque survival' from the past.

» In public, Elizabeth appeared as a 'synthetic creature', unable to 'string even a few sentences together without a written text.' She spoke like 'a priggish schoolgirl', too.

Elizabeth was shocked, but the truth of the criticisms gradually sank in. While admitting nothing in public, very slowly the Palace began to change. It did just enough to enable the monarchy. Debutante balls were abolished, the Queen televised her Christmas address, and attempted – with limited success – to moderate her flat tone and easily mocked accent.

WARNING

Grigg's scorn for a court linked to a tweedy, polo-playing upper class is still pertinent. For the sake of the future of the monarchy and the Commonwealth, Prince Charles might find time to read those well-meaning words from 1957.

The Unwise Appointment of Lord Home as Prime Minister (1963)

Britain's Conservative (Tory) Party is intensely pragmatic. It dislikes anything that might lessen its chances of winning elections and maintaining power. Unlike enthusiastic (and some would say unrealistic) supporters of the Labour Party, it esteems pragmatism over principle; its ultimate test of person is whether the electorate likes them, and of a policy is whether it works.

TECHNICAL STUFF

That is why the most successful political party in democratic history (in terms of elections won and years in power) for so long refused to elect its leader. Elections mean declaring differences, and that sends out the wrong message to the electorate. Far better for a leader to 'emerge' through consensus.

This was fine, except when the Tories were in power and their leader was prime minister. Theoretically, the appointment of a prime minister is the job of the sovereign. Normally, the party conducted its shenanigans in private before presenting the monarch with a single name. But in the autumn of 1963, the matter was not that simple:

>> Macmillan, the incumbent prime minister, was hospitalized with a prostate problem and unable to continue his premiership.

>> It was the season of party conferences; Parliament was not sitting.

>> The leading Tory contenders to replace Macmillan each had their own constituency of support: Butler was the choice of the cabinet, Maudling was backed by the parliamentary party, and Lord Hailsham was the darling of ordinary party members.

What should Elizabeth do? The wise choice would have been to wait until the party agreed on a single figure to send to the Palace. Instead, she visited Macmillan in hospital where he handed her a memorandum. It recommended a compromise candidate, the Queen's old friend Lord Home. She duly asked him to form an administration.

The press and many in the Tory party were gobsmacked. They cursed Macmillan for his 'gesture of sickbed levity' and muttered that the Queen should have consulted more widely. In the end, the Tories accepted Home rather than split. The amiable peer returned to the Palace, where Elizabeth appointed him prime minister. The last premier from the House of Lords and the last from the Edwardian era, he survived as prime minister for just 363 days (see Chapters 12 and 14).

Dismissal Crisis: The Governor-General Sacks Australia's Prime Minister (1975)

Although looking like a republic, Australia is still a monarchy. Queen Elizabeth II, the Head of State, has visited the country 16 times during her reign.

In her absence, the Queen's place is taken by a governor-general, a Crown appointment following recommendation from Australian ministers. The choice has generally been a wise one – but not always.

In the autumn of 1975, Australia's Labour-controlled House of Representatives and Liberal-controlled Senate were deadlocked. Governor-General Sir John Kerr, having previously discussed the matter with Prince Charles and the Queen's Private Secretary, Sir Martin Charteris (see Chapter 9), took decisive action to solve the crisis. He dismissed the controversial Labour Prime Minister Gough Whitlam and invited his opponent, the Liberal leader Malcolm Fraser, to form a government.

Fraser obliged, broke the deadlock, and called a general election which he won handsomely. The greatest constitutional crisis in Australian history had divided the country, and made Kerr a figure of hatred. It is generally agreed that he had acted peremptorily and unwisely. The Queen watched events 'with close interest and attention' but did not intervene. Nevertheless, as Kerr was her representative, Australia's status as a monarchy was inevitably called into question.

Elizabeth was not amused.

Michael Fagan Sneaks Into the Queen's Bedroom (1982)

Nor was the Queen amused when, in both June and July 1982, 33-year-old Michael Fagan entered Buckingham Palace unchallenged. The first time, he wandered about for a bit, helped himself to a bit of bread, cheese and wine, and left. On the second occasion, he found his way into Elizabeth's bedroom.

WARNING

Queen and intruder did not sit and chat, as in *The Crown*, because she had fled in search of help.

Fagan, arrested but never charged, spent three months after the incident in a psychiatric hospital. The Palace's wholly inadequate security caused considerable national and personal embarrassment.

A New Biography Reveals Criticism of Prince Charles's Upbringing (1994)

Prince Charles has always felt he has received an unfair press. In some ways he is right: in his youth, he lacked his mother's reserved dignity and his father's non-nonsense directness. Later, he found himself in an impossible marriage with someone he struggled to understand and whose magnetic presence left him struggling for recognition.

To the public, most of whom knew Charles only through the lens of a critical media, he was not what they expected of a future king. In an attempt to set the record straight, therefore, he gave the respected journalist Jonathan Dimbleby hours of his time and access to his papers in order to produce a 'warts and all' biography. It was a brave move that Charles later said he did not regret.

REMEMBER

In *The Prince of Wales, a Biography*, the public were given glimpses of the Royal Family close up. Most readers focussed on the pages dealing with the Charles–Diana–Camilla triangle (see Chapter 16). Elizabeth was not a 'natural' mother. She did her duty by her shy, insecure son – as she did by everything else – but cuddles and kisses did not come naturally to her. Open demonstrations of affection, whether in public or in private, were not on her family's hard drive.

Elizabeth greeted the children at breakfast, and played – even 'romped'– with them at bedtime. But it was all done to timetable, and only when she and her husband were at home. Between November 1953 and April 1954, when Charles was five and Anne three, mummy and daddy went on a Commonwealth tour leaving the children at home. The young Prince found his main 'comfort and support' provided by his nanny, Mabel Anderson.

The Queen was not consciously detached towards Charles and Anne, nor did Philip bully Charles deliberately. It was the way they were, and the way they had been raised. 'Stiff upper lip' and all that. As Elizabeth read about her son's struggles, did she reflect how she might have done things differently? Could she have shown him more affection? Might she have intervened to protect her timid eldest son from the cutting barbs of his father?

WARNING

The heart-rending scene in *The Crown* where the Queen scorns Charles after his investiture as Prince of Wales is exaggerated fiction. But it draws on the painful truth that, for all her sterling qualities as a queen, Elizabeth did not always appear a very good mother.

See Chapters 6 and 14 for more on Charles' upbringing.

The Palace is Slow to Capture the Public Mood on Princess Diana's death (1997)

The Palace's reaction on hearing of the death of Princess Diana in a car crash on 31 August 1997 is covered in some detail in Chapter 25. It is also the subject of the successful film *The Queen* (2006). The occasion was certainly one of Elizabeth's trickier moments, and taught her a salutary lesson.

TIP

Public opinion in the age of social media is a fickle creature. Like summer tempests, currents of powerful feeling can suddenly arise and sweep across the country with surprising ferocity. Those responsible for promoting and protecting hereditary monarchy would do well to bear this in mind.

Today, thanks to near universal admiration and respect for the elderly Queen, the Crown is riding high. But tomorrow, who knows?

Prince Charles Says he is 'Impatient' to Succeed to the Throne (2012)

'Impatient? . . . Yes of course I am,' Charles is reported to have said in 2012 when asked about becoming king. Ten years later, he is still waiting. The situation has become difficult for Elizabeth.

TIP

The Queen's refusal ever to consider abdication after the scandalous reign of her uncle Edward VIII (see Chapter 5) might be seen as cussedness. She has had to change her mind over divorce, so why not over abdication? If popes step down, why not monarchs? But the words of her Coronation Oath are imprinted on her heart (see Chapter 7). There have even been rumours that she is hanging on because she doesn't trust Charles with the Crown.

What was tricky in 2012 had become almost embarrassing by 2022. Aged and unwell, Elizabeth had all but stopped undertaking her customary round of royal duties. Charles and Camilla were getting on a bit too, placing an ever-increasing burden on the shoulders of the younger royals. Charles, we are told, has ideas for slimming down the monarchy (even, it's been said, moving out of Buckingham Palace), but he can't do anything yet. Might there be a better way of doing things?

President Trump Pats the Queen on the Back (2019)

WARNING

A great deal of nonsense is talked about the do's and don'ts concerning etiquette in the presence of the Queen. The Palace says there are no hard and fast rules. It is generally accepted, however, that it is not good form to lay hands on the Queen unbidden. (For more on protocol, see Chapter 8.)

The custom goes back centuries to the time when the monarch was a semi-sacred figure whose touch could cure certain illnesses (such as scrofula). There's also the matter of security: someone seeking to touch the sovereign might be doing so for a malicious reason. Best stay clear.

That's why the elderly and frail Margaret Thatcher, ever the most correct of royalists, asked the Queen's permission if she could take her hand to steady herself while curtseying in 2005. And why the media were swift to jump on Donald Trump – never popular in the UK – for walking ahead of the diminutive Queen and putting his hand on her back uninvited at a state dinner in 2019. Ever dignified, she batted not an eyelid.

Interestingly – as the media were quick to pick up on – during the Obamas' visit to Britain in 2009, First Lady Michelle had placed an affectionate arm around the Queen, and was much lauded for doing so. Again, Elizabeth batted not an eyelid.

» Discovering how those acting as the
Queen have found it a fascinating
challenge

Chapter **28**

Ten Royal Portrayals

Queen Elizabeth II has appeared as a character in over 100 films and TV dramas, not to mention the many thousands of comedy shows and revues featuring a formal lady with a handbag saying, in a distinctly aristocratic voice, 'My husband and I'.

This chapter looks at ten of the best-known screen portrayals of Elizabeth. It suggests why actors have found the role tested their mettle, why they have enjoyed it, and why the Queen of England has been such good box office for so long.

WARNING

Make sure that you head off and watch these films and TV shows . . . but apply your own For Dummies Warning icon to them all!

Jeanette Charles in *Austin Powers in Goldmember* (2002)

No one has played the Queen more often than the British actor Jeanette Charles (b. 1927). She came upon the role by accident in 1972, when people were struck by how a portrait of her in London's Royal Academy looked just like the Queen. Many thought the subject actually *was* Elizabeth! The actor saw her opening, and started studying Elizabeth's manner and deportment. So began a 40-year career.

Before long, Charles was in high demand as the Queen at all kinds of events. TV shows and films soon followed. She readily accepted, always insisting that her portrayal of the Head of State was never demeaning of the woman she impersonated. She would not, for example, be photographed as the Queen modelling underwear!

Charles's movies are largely spoof action comedies, requiring no in-depth psychological analysis of the role. In *Austin Powers in Goldmember*, for example, she appears in a brief cameo as Elizabeth knighting Powers for arresting the wicked Dr. Evil and his sidekick Mini-Me.

Helen Mirren in *The Queen* (2006)

Though Helen Mirren's father (Vasily Petrovich Mironoff) was descended from Russian aristocrats, her own working-class upbringing could hardly have been less top-drawer. But she had talent and intelligence, and was soon winning critical acclaim for her portrayal of queens and high-born ladies on the stage in London and with the Royal Shakespeare Company in Stratford-Upon-Avon, Warwickshire.

At the age of 61, now an actor of world-class renown, Mirren was invited to play Queen Elizabeth II in the film *The Queen* (2006). She went on to reprise the role in the stage play *The Audience* (2013). She won an Academy Award and a British Academy Film Award for her performance in the former, and a Tony Award and a Laurence Olivier Award for the latter.

How did she do it?

The key was to get inside the character, she said, not the figurehead. To this end, she watched videos of Elizabeth as a child, reflected on her wartime experiences, and carefully observed the Queen's obsession with neatness.

From this, a real person emerged at one of the most difficult junctures of her life – when news came through of the death of Princess Diana in 1997 (see Chapters 16 and 21). Not so much through the spoken word as through expression, gesture and posture, Mirren captured the Queen at a time when she was being pulled in multiple directions. Elizabeth did not especially warm to Diana, but felt deeply shocked by the tragedy of her death; she wished to care for William and Harry at Balmoral, but was persuaded by Prime Minister Blair to return to London; she did not understand the outpouring of public grief at Diana's death, or necessarily approve of it, but she knew she had to acknowledge it.

TIP

And all the while, by instinct and training, Mirren's screen Elizabeth, like the real one, had to remain outwardly calm and detached. A living totem, a survivor. In getting to grips with this unique character, Mirren said she came to see the Queen as 'like a submarine'. The periscope appeared above the surface, while the feelings, the emotions, and the long, long centuries of history remained out of sight below.

Barbara Flynn in *The Queen* docu-drama (2009)

The groundbreaking Channel 4/ATV TV docu-drama *The Queen* (2009), not to be confused with Helen Mirren's film of the same name (2006), was a forerunner of the larger and more lavish *The Crown* (2016 onwards).

The series told the story of Elizabeth's reign through five key episodes:

>> Princess Margaret's romance with Peter Townsend (see Chapter 13).

>> The attempt to kidnap Princess Anne in 1974 (see Chapter 15).

>> The 1986 Commonwealth Games and Britain's reaction to South African apartheid (see Chapter 18).

>> The *Annus Horribilis* of 1992 (see Chapter 20).

>> Prince Charles' marriage to Camilla Parker-Bowles in 2005 (see Chapter 24).

A different actor took the part of the Queen in each episode: Emilia Fox in episode 1; Samantha Bond in 2; Susan Jameson in 3; Barbara Flynn in 4; and Diana Quick in 5. It was generally recognised that Flynn, normally cast in the role of a 'feisty strong woman', had the toughest task.

Somehow, like all those who have played the Queen, Flynn said she had to discover – or at least suggest – the wife and mother behind the façade of formality. She found her subject to be 'a woman of great internal stability' but sensed that somewhere inside she harboured 'massive doubts and massive troubles'.

Flynn found it hard to imagine having your family's relationships endlessly analysed in public. The more she thought about the role, the more she found herself empathizing with Elizabeth. How dreadful to be 'forced by duty to lunch with these people she must have loathed!' By the time the filming finished, Flynn concluded that she had played 'one of the most remarkable people of our recent history'.

Freya Wilson in *The King's Speech* (2010)

Freya Wilson was only 11 when she was given the part of Princess Elizabeth in the successful film *The King's Speech* (2010). She had done a bit of acting in her school drama club and already had an agent. So when the part of Elizabeth came up, she prepared for the auditions like a professional, listening to the Princess's speeches to get the voice right.

Her homework was successful. After three auditions, she got to play in a movie that went on to win multiple awards – not bad for a beginner!

Emma Thompson in *Walking the Dogs* (2012)

WARNING

Everything touched by the great British actor Emma Thompson turns to gold – well, almost everything. Even she admitted that the 'Walking the Dogs' mini-drama in the first season of the Sky Arts Playhouse Presents series (2012) did not see her at her best. Much of the problem stemmed from the drama's scenario.

It was based on the real-life incident of July 1982, when Michael Fagan climbed into Buckingham Palace and entered the Queen's bedroom (see Chapters 18 and 27). As Peter Morgan did when writing about the incident in *The Crown*, Helen Greaves, writer of *Walking the Dogs*, felt that the queen-meets-commoner situation had too many dramatic possibilities to be dealt with in a purely factual manner.

Morgan treated Elizabeth's one-to-one with a very ordinary commoner as a sort of educational experience for her. He played with the truth, but the episode works in terms of the series because it presents a queen, painfully isolated from reality, willing to learn about the world outside her bubble. Helen Greaves goes one step further. As Elizabeth comforts the distressed intruder, she emerges as a rather normal, sympathetic human within a touching fairy tale set in never-never land.

TIP

This, I believe, is what Emma Thompson found difficult. Because of her upbringing and experiences, Elizabeth – however much one might wish it – is not just another normal human being. In attempting to portray her as one, Thompson had to create another character, another queen. In other words, she had to fit a different person into the Queen's skin. Successful dramas about Elizabeth start with her as she appears, and then try and work out who the person really is.

Sarah Gadon in *A Royal Night Out* (2015)

Elizabeth has rarely, if ever, let her hair down in public. Not in private either, if reports are to be believed. There has been a lot of speculation, therefore, about what she got up to on the night of Tuesday 8 May 1945, VE Day (see Chapter 6).

TIP

The official line is that she and her sister Margaret, escorted by a dozen young army officers, got parental permission to leave Buckingham Palace and mingle incognito with the celebrating crowds outside. There is no evidence suggesting that this isn't what happened, and the two princesses were safely back in the palace, none the worse for wear, by 1am that morning.

But what if . . ?

A Royal Night Out (2015) suggests in a tongue-in-cheek manner that what really happened on that night was rather different from the story put out by the Palace. The princesses's escorts are predatory rather than protective, and the girls, having become separated, are introduced to a seedy-romp world of nightclubs, gambling, and brothels. It's all standard romantic comedy fare and no harm is done to the naughty girls. Indeed, many viewers found the film very good fun.

Elizabeth's adventures might have borne no relation to reality, but 18-year-old Sarah Gaydon, who played the Princess, worked hard to ensure that at least her accent and deportment were correct. She watched movies and newsreels from the time and took lessons in etiquette. The transformation was so complete that, when first interviewed by director Julian Jarrold, he didn't realize she was in fact not English but Canadian.

Penelope Wilton in *The BFG* (2016)

Lovers of Roald Dahl's books for children were a little apprehensive when it was announced that Disney would be making a film of the ever-popular BFG (Big Friendly Giant). They need not have worried. Directed by Steven Spielberg and starring British classical actor Mark Rylance, it won huge critical acclaim. So too did Penelope Wilton, who played the Queen of England with glorious aplomb.

The key to the role, Wilton said, was not to play a fantasy figure in a fantasy film. Instead, she had to make the character of the Queen of the United Kingdom – Elizabeth II, of course – real and credible. As the movie's Queen has to appear with the child Sophie and the childlike BFG, Wilson studied film of Elizabeth reacting with children. She observed that Elizabeth was 'very straightforward and matter-of-fact with them' (as she is with everyone, one might add). 'She doesn't patronize them,' Wilton said, but 'talks to them as if they are grown-ups.'

WARNING

The result was a thoroughly believable Elizabeth for the BFG film. What it did for the myth of royal power, however, was quite another matter! In the film, as in the book, the Queen is an all-powerful sovereign able to command soldiers to do her bidding in an instant. No wonder children who have seen the film gaze wide-eyed and awe-struck through the bars of Buckingham Palace when they visit London.

Claire Foy in *The Crown* (2016–2017)

TECHNICAL STUFF

Claire Foy had a bit of experience of queen-playing before she came to take the role of the young Elizabeth in seasons 1 and 2 of this popular TV series. Having starred as Anne Boleyn, second wife of England's Henry VIII, in the BBC TV series *Wolf Hall* (2015), she knew all about the dignity expected of a crowned lady of the court. Even so, she very nearly didn't get the lead role in the smash-hit TV drama *The Crown*.

Peter Morgan, the writer and creator of series, apparently looked at many actors in search of the right Elizabeth. He even heard Foy four times in audition before it suddenly struck him that she was the one he had been looking for all along. She was pregnant at the time, and breastfeeding her newborn child when filming began. Halfway up a mountain, heavy with milk but with no baby to feed, she had serious doubts about whether she was doing the right thing.

She was. She may not then have been an international star, but she certainly was after the release of the first episode of *The Crown* in 2016. Critics and public alike were captivated by her performance.

What was it that made her Elizabeth so convincing?

Foy clearly enjoyed the role, relishing the royal mix of sparkling tiaras, horsey jodhpurs and muddy boots. On a more subtle level, often by nothing more than a wide-eyed look, she enabled the watcher to understand the many contradictions within Elizabeth's position as Head of State, and within her own personality:

>> Her embarrassment at her own lack of education combined with a determination not to let this undermine her authority.

>> Her love for Philip going hand in hand with irritation at his faults.

>> Her wish to move the monarchy forward and at the same time keep it rooted in the past.

> » Her wish to receive the best advice, but not be controlled by those who gave it.
>
> » Her place as a woman in a world still largely controlled by men, and her awareness of her own supreme status as sovereign.

Above all, Foy managed to convey what lesser actors struggled to do: reveal without parody or simplification the complex personality beneath the thick veneer of royalty. Thanks to her performance, many saw the human side of their queen for the first time. For this Foy won numerous glittering awards. But perhaps the ultimate accolade came from the Royal Family itself, many of whom admitted to watching and enjoying Foy's arresting performance.

Olivia Coleman in *The Crown* (2019–2020)

Olivia Coleman was both delighted and anxious when asked to take over from Claire Foy as Elizabeth II in seasons 3 and 4 of *The Crown* – delighted at the prospect of two years' work, but anxious at the size and difficulty of the task.

TIP

Coleman's eyes are the wrong colour: Elizabeth's are blue, the actor's brown. Then there was the awesome responsibility of taking over from Foy, who had performed the role so brilliantly and been showered with awards. Even trickier was playing someone who was still very much alive and known to billions all around the world. What if she offended royal fans, or, worse still, offended the Queen herself?

Coleman's fears were unfounded. Eye colour was noticed but set aside once she had made the part her own. Continuing after Foy was more difficult because the Queen of the 1950s and 1960s was already an historical figure, while the Elizabeth of Thatcher's premiership and Charles's marriage to Diana was still fresh in many memories. It was like having to interpret the psyche and behaviour of someone simultaneously remote yet in the same room.

To solve this problem, Coleman – who admitted she had 'always been a fan of the Queen' – approached the character as she would someone in a famous novel. She watched, read and studied in order to do justice to the part, then interpreted the role her way, remembering that the person she was playing was, 'as a human being . . . marvellous and amazing'.

As the series progressed through Elizabeth's mounting political and personal difficulties, so Coleman's performance became stronger and stronger. She was rewarded with the Golden Globe Award for Best Actress in a TV Series Drama, and the Primetime Emmy Award for Outstanding Lead Actress in a Drama Series.

Imelda Staunton in *The Crown* (2022)

Seasons 5 and 6 of *The Crown* takes the royal story into the twenty-first century. At the helm, stepping into the shoes previously worn by Claire Foy and Olivia Coleman, is Oscar-nominated Imelda Staunton. Though already well known for roles that include Dolores Umbridge in the *Harry Potter* films and Maud Bagshaw in the *Downton Abbey* film, the actor confessed she was a little 'frightened', as Coleman had been, at taking on such a demanding and controversial role.

She needn't have worried. *The Crown*'s track record on casting is first class, and early releases reveal that Staunton certainly looks a perfect fit in the role of the ageing Elizabeth. She also asks viewers to use their imagination and not see the TV show as history. No one could possibly know what was going through Elizabeth's mind as she watched her beloved Windsor Castle burn at the end of her *annus horribilis* (see Chapter 20). But the super-talented Staunton is certainly going to give us some credible and moving suggestions.

Chapter **29**

Ten Grandchildren and Great-Grandchildren

E lizabeth has four children, eight grandchildren and, as of 1 January 2022, twelve great-grandchildren. For the purposes of this chapter, to the eight grandchildren I've added the two great-grandchildren – George and Charlotte – closest in line to the succession (see Chapter 24).

The line of succession to the throne of Queen Elizabeth II, as of 1 January 2022, is as follows:

1. Charles, Prince of Wales (b. 1948)

2. Prince William, Duke of Cambridge (b. 1982)

3. Prince George of Cambridge (b. 2013)

4. Princess Charlotte of Cambridge (b. 2015)

5. Prince Louis of Cambridge (b. 2018)

6. Prince Harry, Duke of Sussex (b. 1984)

7. Archie Mountbatten-Windsor (b. 2019)

8. Lilibet Mountbatten-Windsor (b. 2021)

9. Prince Andrew, Duke of York (b. 1960)

10. Princess Beatrice (b. 1988)

11. Sienna Mapelli Mozzi (b. 2021)

12. Princess Eugenie (b. 1990)

13. August Brooksbank (b. 2021)

14. Prince Edward, Earl of Wessex (b. 1964)

15. James Mountbatten-Windsor, Viscount Severn (b. 2007)

16. Lady Louise Mountbatten-Windsor (b. 2003)

17. Anne, Princess Royal (b. 1950)

18. Peter Phillips (b. 1977)

19. Savannah Phillips (b. 2010)

20. Isla Phillips (b. 2012)

21. Zara Tindall (née Phillips; b. 1981)

22. Mia Tindall (b. 2014)

23. Lena Tindall (b. 2018)

24. Lucas Tindall (b. 2021)

Prince William, Duke of Cambridge

The early life of Prince William, his education, military service, and marriage to Kate Middleton are covered in Chapter 24. This section looks at where he is now, and where he and the monarchy he represents may be headed.

TECHNICAL STUFF

William, Kate (Duke and Duchess of Cambridge) and their three children – George (b. 2013), Charlotte (b. 2015) and Louis (b. 2018) – divide their time between Flat 1A Kensington Palace, London, and Anmer Hall, Norfolk, a wedding present from the Queen. The parents are both full-time royals. Here's a snippet from their engagements diary of early November 2021:

1st Together attend three engagements in Glasgow, Scotland.

2nd William attends COP26 Climate Change Conference in Glasgow. Meetings and presentations all day, including talks with the Secretary General of the United Nations.

9th William carries out investitures (awarding honours or rank) in Windsor Castle on behalf of the Queen.

11th William visits HQ of M15 Security Service, London.

13th Together attend Royal British Legion Festival of Remembrance in the Royal Albert Hall, London.

14th Together attend Remembrance Day Ceremony, London.

As the couple are frequently required to be away from home on official business, they are supported by a number of household staff. We are told that Kate, who was not brought up in a house full of servants, keeps help to a minimum as she likes to do as much as she can herself, especially where the children are concerned.

TIP

The Cambridges' style is already more informal than that of William's father, Charles, and certainly more than that of his grandmother.

If all goes according to plan, one day William will be King William V with Queen Catherine at his side. They must have already thought how the monarchy might look in the middle of the twenty-first century:

>> **Money:** Should the monarch's private wealth be made public, all taxes paid, and the anomalous status of the Duchies of Lancaster and Cornwall be clarified?

>> **Property:** Does the Royal Family need all those houses, castles, and palaces?

>> **Class:** Could the Royal Family do more to help break down Britain's still formidable class barriers? Might future royal children go to *state schools* (non-fee-paying schools), for example?

>> **Numbers:** Might the royals' titles and stipends be stripped back to just the monarch and their immediate family?

>> **Commonwealth:** To finally lay the idea of empire to rest, might the UK's Head of State rule themselves out of also being head of the multi-national, multi-faith Commonwealth?

TIP

All we can say for now is that, as long as Elizabeth II remains on the throne, further informality is likely to remain on the backburner.

Prince George of Cambridge

At what point do you tell a little boy that one day he will be king? Prince George has undoubtedly been told, though what his parents said is, of course, not known. Does the rather anxious look the lad sometimes wears suggest he is already a bit worried by what lies ahead, or is he simply serious-minded, like his great-grandmother?

REMEMBER

William and Kate have done all they can to keep their children's lives as normal as possible, doing the school runs and taking holidays with Kate's commoner sister and her family. We're told that Kate's mother, Carole Middleton, is quite often around the house, too.

But there's no getting away from the ever-present security officers, the gawping people in the street, the intrusive media commenting on everything George does and wears. Fancy the *Tatler* (a magazine of glamour, fashion, society and features) placing a five-year-old on its best dressed list! Little George has sometimes accompanied his parents on formal occasions, too. Maybe there was some merit after all in the near-splendid isolation in which Princess Elizabeth had been raised (see Chapters 4 and 6 for more about her upbringing)?

Princess Charlotte

Princess Charlotte Elizabeth Diana (her names are a history book in themselves) came into the world with a burst of traditional colour: on the announcement of her birth, Tower Bridge and other London landmarks were flooded with pink light.

TIP

The little princess, known by her parents as 'Lottie', already has three claims to fame:

>> In photographs she bears a striking likeness to her great-grandmother Elizabeth at the same age. In other snaps she resembles her beautiful grandmother, Diana.

>> With cute looks and a naturally smiling face, she always looks good in the off-the-peg dresses chosen by her mother.

>> Thanks to the 2015 law change (see Chapter 24), Charlotte is the first princess to be placed above a younger brother in the line of succession.

Prince Harry, Duke of Sussex

Henry Charles Albert David Windsor, Duke of Sussex, generally known as Prince Harry, split the country just as his great uncle Edward VIII had done (see Chapter 5). How ominous, therefore, that Harry bore the name 'David', for that was what family and close friends had always called the king who abdicated.

The story of Harry's early life, much-reported military career and marriage to Meghan Markle are covered in Chapter 25. Here I take a closer look into why, in January 2020, The Duke and Duchess of Sussex chose to quit royal duties and start a new life in California, USA.

In a famous interview with the American talk-show host Oprah Winfrey in March 2021, which some claim was rehearsed and semi-scripted, the couple laid the blame for their decision to opt out fairly and squarely at the door of the Palace and the media:

» The Palace's 'lack of support and understanding' left the couple feeling isolated and unwanted.

» Harry hinted that constant harassment by the tabloid press, which persisted despite his repeated pleas for privacy, reminded him of the fate of his mother. Some claim Princess Diana was killed while desperately fleeing intrusive paparazzi.

» Harry said he did not want to feel 'trapped' like his father and brother, who could not escape their destiny.

» Harry said his father was cold and unsympathetic, refusing to support him financially or take his phone calls after his decision to step down.

» Meghan, of mixed race, hinted at racism within the Royal Family.

Those offering the Windsor side of the story (remember the royals are not able to answer back directly) suggest the following:

» Never happy with the life of a royal, Harry had wanted out for a long time. Meghan gave him the excuse he needed.

» Meghan, despite her protests to the contrary, never committed to being a working royal. The couple get as much media attention in the US as they did in the UK.

» Like Margaret to Elizabeth and Andrew to Charles, Harry and Meghan hated playing second fiddle to William and Kate.

» The Palace found Meghan demanding and extravagant.

» The racism claim grew out of a remark that was deliberately misinterpreted to get sympathy from the American media.

No doubt the truth lies somewhere between the two positions. To parody the Palace's own words, recollections on both sides will probably always vary. Unfortunately, whichever way one looks at it, the whole unsavoury episode was another step towards the monarchy becoming what Elizabeth always despised – a glitzy soap opera with easy bucks on the side for the cast.

Princess Beatrice

Given that her mother received a lot of flak for her un-royal lifestyle, and her father even more for his choice of friends, Princess Beatrice (Mrs Edoardo Mapelli Mozzi since 2020) has led a pleasantly normal, scandal-free life. Though not a working royal and in receipt of no money from the sovereign grant, she has given generously of her time and patronage in support of a wide range of charities.

Beatrice overcame dyslexia to get a good university degree before earning her living with the civil service and in private businesses. At the same time, she engaged regularly with her charities, many for children. Her active support has led her to climb Mont Blanc and Mount Etna, and become the first royal to run a marathon (in 2010, for the charity Children in Crisis).

TIP

Perhaps as a mark of appreciation for all the voluntary work Beatrice undertakes, Elizabeth leant the Princess her own wedding dress to be remodelled for Beatrice's private wedding on 17 July 2020. Mrs Mozzi has a stepson and a daughter, Sienna, who was born on 18 September 2021.

Princess Eugenie of York

Like her sister Beatrice, Princess Eugenie has led a life remarkable for its dissimilarity from that of her parents. She was well educated and works in the art world. Diagnosed with scoliosis in her youth, she underwent major spinal surgery. At her wedding to Jack Brooksbank in October 2018, she wore a dress with an open back that exposed the scar left by her operation, a brave and much admired gesture to promote understanding of scoliosis. The couple's son, August, was born in February 2021.

Eugenie remains true to the royal tradition of service by undertaking occasional royal duties and a lot of charity work. She is particularly associated with environmental organizations and those tackling modern slavery. In 2019, she became patron of Anti-Slavery International.

James Mountbatten-Windsor, Viscount Severn

TECHNICAL STUFF

Those entitled 'Prince' or 'Princess' do not need a surname. But since 1973, royals without one of those titles use the family name Mountbatten-Windsor (Prince Philip = Mountbatten; Elizabeth = Windsor). Curiously, the decision about whether to be called a prince is one that James (b. 2007), the son of Prince Edward and the Countess of Wessex (née Sophie Rhys-Jones), will make himself on reaching the age of 18. For the time being he is a viscount. 'Severn' comes from the River Severn which rises in Wales, the land of his mother's family.

As the 2015 Succession Act applied only to those born after 2011, James takes precedence in the succession over his older sister, Louise. As neither of them is likely to wear the Crown, they do not appear troubled by the ruling and appeared to get on well when they accompanied their parents on an official visit to South Africa in 2015.

Lady Louise Mountbatten-Windsor

Thanks to a careful upbringing overseen by her mother, Sophie, Countess of Wessex, Louise (b. 2003) appears to be as happy and well balanced as any of the young royals. She is soundly educated and has inherited the family's love of riding and horses. The Duke of Edinburgh passed on to her his passion for carriage driving, and in his will left her his driving ponies and carriage.

As a teenager, Louise made a few public appearances with her mother, notably at the final of the Woman's World Hockey Cup in 2018 and the International Horse Show at Olympia, London, in December that year. It is testament to Louise's maturity and unspoilt approach to life that she was not unduly phased by the esotropia (an eye condition) with which she was born.

TIP

In 2021, the 17-year-old Louise entered the public arena with commendable poise and articulacy when taking part in a BBC documentary about her grandfather. Like her brother James, at the age of 18 she will be free to decide on her title: remain Lady Louise or move up a notch to Princess Louise.

Peter Phillips

Peter Phillips (b. 1977) is the first grandchild of a monarch to be born and raised without a title. Son of the no-nonsense Princess Anne and her first husband, Mark Phillips, Peter is perhaps the most 'normal' of all the royals. After education at Gordonstoun (see Chapter 14) and Exeter University, he has held a variety of posts connected with motor sports and promotional work.

In general, Peter avoids the limelight and does not like to wave his royal background around. An exception occurred in 2020 when he took part, as an acknowledged member of the Royal Family, in an advertisement for a Chinese company. Exploitation of royal heritage for commercial purposes is frowned upon by the Palace.

Peter and his Canadian wife Autumn, who divorced in 2021, have two children, Savannah (b. 2010) and Isla (b. 2012).

Zara Tindall

Zara, Queen Elizabeth's oldest granddaughter, was born to Princess Anne and her first husband Mark Phillips in May 1981. Like her mother, in her youth Zara was known as the wild one of the family, famed for her pierced tongue at the age of 17 and riotous times with boyfriends. By the time she married rugged England rugby star Mike Tindall in 2011, she had settled down a lot.

Alongside Zara's feisty side went superb talent as a horsewoman. Inheriting her mother's skill and determination, in 2006 she won the World Eventing Championship and was voted BBC Sports Personality of the Year. The following year, the Queen awarded her an MBE (see Chapter 12) for services to equestrianism. In 2012, when Princes Anne handed Zara the silver medal she had won at the London Olympics as a member of the Great Britain Eventing Team, it was Anne's turn to decorate her daughter.

Zara and Mike now care for their three children, Mia (b. 2014), Lena (b. 2018) and Lucas (b. 2021), and support a wide range of sporting and other charities.

Index

A

absolute monarchy, 38

absolute primogeniture, 319

Adams, Bryan, 217

Adeane, Michael, 92, 119

Adelaide of Saxe-Meiningen, 44, 255

Aethelbald, 28

Aethelbert, 28

Aethelbert of Kent, 27

Aethelbert's Laws, 29

Aethelred I, 28

Aethelred II, 28

Aethelwulf, 28

'African Queen' scandal, 236, 245

Albert, Duke of York. *See* George VI

Albert Edward. *See* Edward VII

Albert of Saxe-Coburg-Gotha, Prince Consort, 44, 46–48, 52, 58, 116, 121, 254

Alexander III (pope), 30

Alexandra, Princess, 155, 348

Alexandra, Tsarina of Russia, 44, 49

Alexandra of Denmark, 44, 48, 204, 256, 259

Alfred, Duke of Saxe-Coburg-Gotha, 49

Alfred the Great, 10, 28–29

Alice, Princess, 44, 49

Alice, Princess of Battenberg, 89

American Revolution, 42, 51

Amies, Hardy, 103

Anderson, Mabel, 354

Andrew, Duke of York, 105, 277, 281, 291, 295

  affairs, 263

  approval rating, 333

  birth and early life of, 182

  education, 182

  family tree, 8

  finances, 310

  game show, 266

  line of succession, 365

  marriage, separation, and divorce, 244, 257, 263–264, 271–272

  misconduct, 310, 333

  naval service, 182–183, 243, 263

  official duties and engagements, 143

  satire, 275

  Windsor Castle fire, 267

Andrew, Prince of Greece and Denmark, 89, 182

Anglican Church. *See* Church of England

Anglican Communion, 250

Anglo-Saxons, 11, 27–30

animals, 287–296

Anne, 15, 37, 40, 43, 288, 292

Anne, Princess Royal, 20, 92, 115, 119, 178–180, 256, 281, 314, 333

  birth and early life of, 168, 178–180, 354

  education, 180

  equestrianism, 193, 262, 266, 289, 308, 372

  family tree, 8

  finances, 227

  game show, 266

  kidnap attack, 193–194, 359

  line of succession, 366

  marriage, wedding, and divorce, 193, 196, 254, 257, 262–263, 319

  motherhood, 263, 372

  official duties, engagements, and travels, 111, 142

  remarriage, 254, 308

  Royal Family documentary, 187

  social life, 180

  title, 194

Anne Boleyn, 33, 249, 362

Anne Hyde, 59, 210

Anne of Cleves, 258, 263

Annus Horribilis (1992), 258–268, 359, 364

Anthony, Lord Snowdon. *See* Armstrong-Jones, Anthony

apartheid, 89, 123, 240–241, 343, 359

Archbishops of Canterbury, 30, 60, 70, 97–98, 156, 163, 210, 214, 216, 249, 251, 256, 323

Archie Mountbatten-Windsor, 8, 49, 256, 332, 365

Armstrong-Jones, Anthony, 173–176, 187

Arthur, Prince, 49

Arthur, Prince of Wales, 258–259

Asquith, Herbert, 80

Astor, Lord, 156

Athelstan, 11, 28

Atlee, Clement, 82

Audience, The (play), 306, 358

Augustine (saint), 27, 29, 32

austerity programme, 311, 321, 325

Austin Powers in Goldmember (film), 357–358

Australia, 127–128, 198, 272, 352

Auxiliary Territorial Service (ATS), 86, 315

B

Bagehot, Walter, 22

Baldwin, Stanley, 65, 70–73, 81

Ball, Ian, 193–194

Balmoral Castle, 20, 52, 86, 103, 105–106, 116, 134, 173, 187, 190, 211, 228, 253–254, 275–277, 283, 295–296, 314, 327, 343–344

bank holidays, 199, 302

Banksy, 302

Bashir, Martin, 219, 272

About the Author

After several years teaching at university and college level in Britain, the USA, the Middle East and Sri Lanka, **Stewart Ross** became a full-time writer some thirty-two years ago. With some 350 published titles to his credit, he is one of Britain's most popular and versatile authors. His fiction and non-fiction works include widely acclaimed and prize-winning books for adults and children, particularly on British monarchs, Scotland, Sherlock Holmes, the World Wars, and the Middle East, many of which have been translated into other languages. He has also lectured on cruise ships, at ICES (La Roche sur Yon, France), Rollins College, Florida (US), and Canterbury Christ Church University (UK). Stewart lives near Canterbury, Kent, and commutes each morning to work in a large hut in the garden.

Author's Acknowledgements

I would like to express my sincere thanks to my patient editor Daniel Mersey, and my ever-supportive and eagle-eyed wife Lucy, for their help and advice in the preparation of this book.

Publisher's Acknowledgements

Acquisitions Editor: Zoë Slaughter
Development Editor: Daniel Mersey
Managing Editor: Michelle Hacker

Production Editor: Mohammed Zafar Ali
Cover Image: © Chris Jackson/Getty Images